ELEMENTAL ECOCRITICISM

Elemental Ecocriticism

Thinking with Earth, Air, Water, and Fire

JEFFREY JEROME COHEN *and*
LOWELL DUCKERT, *Editors*

University of Minnesota Press
Minneapolis • London

The University of Minnesota Press acknowledges permission to reprint the following poetry in this book. William Carlos Williams, "A Smiling Dane," in *The Collected Poems of William Carlos Williams*, vol. 2, *1939–1962*, ed. Christopher MacGowan (New York: New Directions, 1986), 306; copyright 1962 by William Carlos Williams; reprinted by permission of New Directions Publishing Corporation. Seamus Heaney, "Viking Dublin: Trial Pieces" and "Kinship," in *Opened Ground: Selected Poems, 1966–1996* (New York: Farrar, Straus and Giroux, 1998), 178 and 196; copyright 1998 by Seamus Heaney; reprinted by permission of Farrar, Straus and Giroux LLC. Brenda Hillman, "The Elements Are Mixed in Childhood," in *Seasonal Works with Letters on Fire* (Middletown, Conn.: Wesleyan University Press, 2013), 55; reprinted by permission of the author. Wallace Stevens, "Of Mere Being," in *The Palm at the End of the Mind: Selected Poems and a Play*, ed. Holly Stevens (New York: Alfred A. Knopf, 1971), 398; copyright 1967 by Wallace Stevens and renewed 1971 by Holly Stevens; reprinted by permission of Alfred A. Knopf, an imprint of the Knopf Doubleday Publishing Group, a division of Random House LLC. All rights reserved.

Published by the University of Minnesota Press
111 Third Avenue South, Suite 290
Minneapolis, MN 55401-2520
http://www.upress.umn.edu

Library of Congress Cataloging-in-Publication Data
Elemental ecocriticism : thinking with earth, air, water, and fire / Jeffrey Jerome Cohen and Lowell Duckert, editors.
Includes bibliographical references and index.
ISBN 978-0-8166-9307-8 (hc)—ISBN 978-0-8166-9309-2 (pb)
1. Environmental ethics. 2. Four elements (Philosophy). 3. Materialism—Moral and ethical aspects.
I. Cohen, Jeffrey Jerome, editor. II. Duckert, Lowell, editor.
GE42.E44 2015
179'.1—dc23 2015008721

Printed in the United States of America on acid-free paper

The University of Minnesota is an equal-opportunity educator and employer.

21 20 19 18 17 16 15 10 9 8 7 6 5 4 3 2 1

Contents

introduction

Eleven Principles of the Elements

JEFFREY JEROME COHEN
and LOWELL DUCKERT

The elements are never easy.

A chain of helices rotates in a pond, chemical corkscrews extruded by a paper mill. Industrial aerators churn air and water through fire's force, forging vibrant rounds, poisonous beauty. Photographed from the sky, this congregation of volutes resembles a surgical cross section, neurons in an intimacy of memory-making, or jellyfish wandering a depleted sea. Meanwhile, a patch of plastic larger than Texas spins in the Pacific, swirling salt water, sea life, and the disowned detritus of human industry into choked cacophony. Over the Atlantic a vast convolution of air and water rotates, its satellite image rendering its spiral a miniature Milky Way, formed of drenching winds, not blazing stars. The hurricane arrives through the marine transport machine of the North Atlantic Gyre, a conveyer belt of currents that whirls Saharan storms against American coasts. The popular film *The Day after Tomorrow* (2004) predicted the end of the world would arrive in the eye of an erratic vortex whose cryogenic force instantly, lethally immobilizes. Yet as photographer J. Henry Fair suggests in a sumptuous book also named *The Day after Tomorrow,* catastrophe's playthings are never frozen in place.[1] Environmental violence might be slow, but it is not still.[2] We compose this introduction in the midst of what has been called the "Winter of the Polar Vortex": snowed into Washington, D.C., because of roving

FIGURE I.1. "Baton Rouge, Louisiana." Image copyright J Henry Fair, 2014. www.IndustrialScars.com.

arctic chill, brief reprieve from relentless global warming. The hairy ball theorem of algebraic topology holds that at any given moment at least one vortex spins in earth's atmosphere, even if we cannot know precisely where that spiral turns. The polar vortex—earth's most persistent cyclone, enormous in scale—is only one such presence. The day after tomorrow always seems to arrive too early, temporal and material intimacy that has been there all along. To evade Scylla, daughter of a poisoned spring, is to hazard the whirlpools of Charybdis, rocky straits of catastrophic engulfment. Lethal and alluring, toxic and lyrical, force of cohesion and strife, a vortex is elemental: ubiquitous, generative matter for a transhistorical ecopoetics, involute origin for words and worlds.

And philosophy. The cosmologist, physicist, and poet Empedocles (ca. 495–435 BCE) argued that all matter consists of four elements in shifting combination: earth, air, fire, water. Held together by chains of love *(philia),* pulled apart through endemic strife *(neikos),* these primal "roots" *(rhizomata)* are enduring and unstill.[3] Empedocles wondered why the cosmos is not some immobile sphere (the lethal triumph of love, seeking to bind and to fix), nor a chaos of the unconjoined (strife's striving, a universal itineracy), but an impure expanse of ardently connective matter, hybrid proliferations, and fecund-destructive breaks. This disharmonious simultaneity of desire and discord includes the human without centering itself around so small a figure. Elemental matter is inherently creative, motile, experimental, impure because fire, water, air, and earth are never inert.[4] In their ardor for combinatory novelty, the four rhizomata fashion ephemeral things that wander for a while, seeking embrace. A kinetic intermingling at every scale, the Empedoclean cosmos offers (in Drew Daniel's apt description) a "psychomachia of Love and Strife as rival, dynamic forces in which the world itself is a material assemblage constantly under (re)construction," a machine for the production of hybrid objects, bodies, forces.[5] Sometimes these compositions arise with no hope of futurity. Empedocles imagined arms seeking shoulders, eyes in search of foreheads, misfit burgeonings of tragic beauty and ambulatory desire. Sometimes these elemental creations engender unanticipated forms, indiscriminately crossbred things, queer ecologies of unnatural flourishing: "creatures compounded partly of male, partly of the nature of female, and fitted with shadowy parts."[6] Charles Darwin observed of nature's biological generativity that "from so simple a beginning endless forms most beautiful and most wonderful have been, and are being, evolved."[7] Empedocles went further, insisting that in the form of the elements, matter itself is ceaselessly productive, heedless of the partitionings that will in future days dismiss the inorganic to lifelessness. Elements connect or wander. Love fastens, strife divides. Through the push-pull of philia and neikos the cosmos begins to whirl, assuming in this movement its distinctive vorticular form. Unlike René Descartes, who thought all space to be occupied by vortices, interlocked but singular, for Empedocles the elements themselves are vortex-spawning, without partition, from micro- to macrocosm. Dense earth and weighty water sink, air and fire rise, and all matter spirals, a gyre of renewal and catastrophe.[8]

For millennia the Empedoclean elements offered a mode of conceptualizing materiality that conveys how difference underlays all substance, how nature covets entanglement, how entropy promises universal ruin as well as unceasing regeneration. The physician Hippocrates medicalized this quadratic schema, adding cold, wet, hot and dry to the equation and mapping elemental materiality across four bodily humors, the active thingliness of flesh, animal intimacy with the cosmological. Plato, Aristotle, Lucretius, Ovid, Boethius, Chaucer, Dante, Pico della Mirandola, Walter Raleigh, Margaret Cavendish, William Shakespeare, John Milton, Gaston Bachelard, David Macauley, and Jane Bennett (among many others) have ensured that the Empedoclean elements would be passed along in new forms, a spur to cosmology, environmental awareness, story, trope, and art.[9] Outgrown as a science, supplanted by atomism and particle physics, elemental theory has been left to that repository where superseded knowledges molder. Yet, with subatomic and cosmic scales have arrived an estrangement from materiality, the reduction into mere utility known as resourcism, and an intensifying ecological crisis rather than greater worldly intimacy, an ethic of nonhuman care, or the ability to acknowledge that the cataclysms that assail us are largely of our own making. In returning to earth, air, fire, and water as apprehensible environmental agents, we are not arguing for the uncritical embrace of outmoded epistemologies. *Elemental Ecocriticism* is not a project of nostalgia, not a wistful retreat from present-day concerns into supposedly simpler cosmogenies. The contributors to this volume find in the literature of the past a storehouse of provocations for present environmentality.[10] The multitemporal elements we offer are not all that true to their origins in Greek philosophy. They do not yield a theology of love, strife, air, water, fire, or earth in immortal perseverance. Like medieval, early modern, and contemporary writers, we think with and adapt these six partners in material vitality. We accept their invitation to build carefully and compose creatively. Our collaborations stage inventive reencounters with historical frames that powerfully foreground worldly activity and material agency, the limits of anthropocentricity, and the intimacy of narrative-making to ethics. We seek an elemental ecocriticism that discovers in imaginative and critical texts a lush archive for thinking ecology anew. We believe that attending to matter and writing against the reduction of world to commodity (resource, energy) is a powerful aid to activism. Supposedly outdated articulations of elemental activity and the fraught human-nonhuman collaborations they convey can propel care, grasp, and justice.[11] The less human the collective, the more humane it may become—and by "less human" we do not mean *The World Without Us,* but a disanthropocentric reenvisioning of the complicated biomes and cosmopolities within which we dwell. Empedocles might not have had a periodic table full of elements, a serene sequence of atomic numbers that begins with hydrogen and terminates (for the time being) at scarce ununoctium, but in his quadripartite sorting of quotidian substance he realized the same rebuke to human-centered cosmologies.

How did we forget that matter is a precarious system and dynamic entity, not a reservoir of tractable commodities? How did we cease to know that earth, air, fire, and water move, rebel, ally, crush, and desire? We cannot see the trees for the deforestation. Environmental historians have well documented the human toll upon ecologies, so that oaks and pine become compliant timber, fire becomes extractable coal, air is transformed into a carbon offset, rivers are converted into potable water expressed as a mathematical quantity. At its most extreme, this relentless objectification transforms even humans into expendable resources: miners who can be discarded once they develop black lung, or minority communities that can be tallied, televised, and toured after a hurricane obliterates homes. To the discourse of cultural materialism we would add an *ecomaterialism* that conjoins thinking the limits of the human with thinking elemental activity and environmental justice. There is no "out-" to which things are sourced, but always a wherein, with whom, wherefore. As essential as traditional environmental history has been for understanding anthropogenic planetary change, especially when it comes to despoliation of raw materials and global warming, the only room such models typically leave for the agency of forests, streams, weather, and mountains is a pressing back in the form of cataclysm. To think that the world is ours to ruin or to save are two expressions of the same hubris. When did economy become a story of vendible commodities, bounded identities, and reduction into market exchange rather than an open ecology irreducible into small settlement? No space exists within this polarized, innately gendered model (*mater* to matter) for the apprehension of the cross-ontological alliances by which ecosystems thrive, change, commingle, create.

Through active and recurring forgetting, the apprehension of material vibrancy evident in elemental theory has been obscured by mechanistic models that serve commodity capitalism well but license environmental devastation.[12] To counteract the flattening force of this collective amnesia, we need more and better models of inhuman challenge, an environmental agentism. Call it *re-activism,* where the "re-" is not a simple repetition of a previous form but a renewal of non/human ethical enmeshment, a transhistorical call to attention, in which lessons from the past are reactivated for better futures. History offers a storehouse of imaginings in which nature is understood as active force, unlooked-for partner, an etymological as well as material archive of irremediable precarities, a dynamic source for what David Macauley calls the "re-story-ation" of the elements.[13] The past is never really past. As an inheritance from philosophies we no longer study we continue to speak of the elements, but now as that against which we protect ourselves: from their harshness, especially in an uncertain climate, from their capriciousness, from their peril. *Storm and tempest.* But what if the elements are more than a threat? In the wake of tsunamis, earthquakes, and superstorms, we know all too well elemental discord, battle, and strife (the work of neikos). In the face of ruin, what invitations do the elements extend? What of Empedoclean philia: binding, love? Can materialities long surpassed precipitate new modes of ecological engagement? Can the four elements assist in imagining a world that is postsustainable, intracatastrophic, and yet a place for hope?[14] Rather than centers that do not hold and pitiless revelation, might the elements in their widening gyre open portals to spaces that pulse with inhuman life? Can they restore vivacity to substances (mud, water, earth, air), chemical processes (fire), and natural phenomena (earthquakes, floods, landslides) over which we have imposed an imagined ecological sovereignty?[15] Is there potential in the impossible, in the purely imaginary, in the abandoned and the unreal (ether, phlogiston, the sea above the clouds)? Can the elements invite contemporary thinkers not to some lost Eden or Golden Age (no simpler time has ever existed, no age without its complex convolutions, spirals of possibility and time) but to a reinvigorated, future-laden mode of ecomaterial inquiry?

Elemental Ecocriticism embraces the challenges, paradoxes, and productive anachronism inherent to thinking in elemental and thereby nonreductive terms, to thinking within the spirals of entanglement that the elements in motion form. The collaborative project of this book is to elaborate a truly material ecocriticism that is at once estranging, disanthropocentric, *and* apprehensible, hospitable to new companionships. Because they are smaller than gods and larger than atoms—not theological or metaphysical, not only the unseen stuff of physics' elegant equations—earth, air, fire, and water, alone and in their promiscuous combinations, function within a humanly knowable scale while extending an irresistible invitation to inhuman realms. The structure of this introduction is therefore errant, winding, to trace elemental paths. Plato believed that each of the primordial substances possessed a distinctive shape: tetrahedron, icosahedron, octahedron, cube. What happens, though, when still geometric forms tumble into activity, when we companion their whirl?

We offer eleven interlocking and provisional principles to guide inquiry when this invitation is accepted, some rules of thumb for hitching a ride with this restless foursome, partners in world-making.

1. The Elements Are Never Easy

That which is elementary is quietly foundational, natural, and ultimately self-evident—even if such child's play requires a Sherlock Holmes to reveal. Of course the Red-Headed League was not a club for men of a certain complexion to copy out pages of the *Encyclopedia Britannica* but a ruse to mask the subterranean robbing of a bank. Of course the dog not barking in the night was the clear signal of an ecology insufficiently perturbed. "It's elementary" strips convolutions of matter and inquiry to substratum but masks in the process the exertions behind stories of mystery solved, replacing composition with revelation.[16] Yet the work of divulging elemental foundation is never so effortless. An austere practice of deduction is still a carpentry, a making: creative even in its subtractions, an intricate narrative of unnoticed agencies, of first principles at work.[17]

Elementary school starts with ABCs and 123s, the blocks from which are constructed words, equations, and worlds. Any child can tell you that there is nothing undemanding about rudiments. Secure beginnings obscure other possible initiations. Taxonomies that seem self-evident to teachers at comfortable desks are, from the back of the room rigid, forced, and insufficiently connective. When labor trumps play and discipline diminishes epistemological possibility, antimonies of love and strife surface. In German the word for element is *Urstoff,* "primordial substance," and in Aristotle's

Greek *stoikheion,* a beginning or step. *Elementum,* the Latin translation of *stoikheion* from which our English words *element* and *elementary* derive, denominates a first principle or an alphabet. The elements are matter's kinetic syllabary. *A* is for air (let the breath this word requires animate those lesson-inscribed paper landscapes, let eraser fragments gust). *E* stands for earth (are your hands sufficiently clean? Does dirt cling, and unwanted life? Are you contagious or contained, soiled or ethereal?). *F* initiates fire (pull that alarm and the building empties, red annunciation that the world is limned by catastrophe. Exit in silent single file, as if in ordered solitude safety might arrive). *W* is that fountain in the hallway, the one that confirms that the elements have been domesticated to push-button commands.[18] Yet *F* remains wild, *W* full of flood. The earth shifts. Tempests do not cease to howl.

The elements gather the slow and swift, the durable and ephemeral, the flowing and the deceptively still. Even stone undulates within its native duration. They promise that few things easily divide. Impurity insists. Chaos and binding spur emergent, spiraled orders. "It's elementary" speaks a separation, a reduction into clarity, but underneath elements enmesh. Empedocles named his primordial components *rhizomata,* tangling roots. Readers of Gilles Deleuze and Félix Guattari will recognize in that Greek word proliferative rhizomes, the radicles that course subterranean connection and surface intricate surprise.[19] Linking agents and multiplicity machines, the elements are straightforward but not simple. Irreducible and initiatory, they are lively as language, a storied tumble of relation, sudden rupture, and material burgeoning.

2. *The Elements Are Never Still*

The foundations of knowledge as well as things, the elements (like all sturdy foundations) must remain grounded. Be close to the earth, the old adage goes, for the earth is a good place to be. Desires for emplacement run deep. The Copernican Revolution in Enlightenment science, at least according to Bruno Latour, has fixed the elements' trajectories.[20] The "eco-cosmopolitanism" of Ursula Heise—a truly radical (from the Latin *radix,* "root") concept of placement that necessitates critical leaps from the local to global—gets buried under our fears of deracination.[21] But, just as earth turns around a fiery sun, the Modern Constitution maintains that scientific objects and their objective truths orbit around the human mind. The elements squarely fall into place. Knowledge, but not the elements themselves, is on the move. To argue against this code means you can always expect the Modernist Inquisition. Build your house *(oikos)* here, on the immobile rock. Only a fool builds a house on the sand. For when the rain falls, the flood rises, and the wind blows, only the house founded on the fundamental (earth) science remains. Find your element. Get to know it. Stay put. You know what to do. Earth—you are grounded!

Eppur si muove! ("And yet it moves!").[22] Like good inheritors of Galileo, we cannot truly believe the charges or else we condemn the elements to a no-wake zone, where little trace of their mobility remains and their inroads are left untaken ("wake" comes from Old Norse *vǫk, vaka,* "hole or opening in ice"). Yet the elements did not stop moving with the Copernican Revolution, Latour says under his breath. This counter-Copernican revolutionary motto reads, "And yet the elements have never been still." Our elemental houses of knowledge have always been built on unstable ground. Seismic shifts are difficult to tell from epistemological ones. When John Muir felt an earthquake in Yosemite Valley in the spring of 1872, he ran outside, "both glad and frightened . . . feeling sure I was going to learn something."[23] Less than a hundred years later, in the fall of 1989, and near the same location, Michel Serres "tasted joy" during an earthquake while everyone else was terrified: "the spasmodic earth comes to unite . . . with my shaky body. The world finally comes to me, resembles me, all in distress." We "liv[e] in a permanent earthquake."[24] Like them, we reside in a "bewildering order," the first word purposefully verbal and adjectival at once, a phrase the elemental philosopher David Macauley uses to highlight how the elements "wild" orders and methods of ordering.[25] This is what we have learned. What a fool believes is that the rock will actually ground you. Elements-as-fundamentals trigger beginnings, catalyze arrangements that resist totality, open never-ending archives, labyrinthine libraries of the not-quite-read. Ether is the fifth element. How many more to add? Can you count them all?

3. *The Periodic Table Has No Period*

Diagram as you will. Compose the chart of four divisions, but ether and phlogiston will deprive your earth, air, fire, and water of quadricameral sovereignty. Suppose the elements are that which rage outdoors, that against which you take shelter, but the house is drafty and the roof leaks and your home is made of wood and stone anyway. Table your chemicals into eighteen columns and seven rows, but you will require a double tier below and supplementary denotation for isotopes. A taxonomy of atomic weights and shared properties is one possible arrangement among many, imposing some separations where overlaps and entanglements flourish. The table hung upon the school wall is a work of aesthetics and formatting practicalities as much as chemical affinities. Some of its elements are natural, some primordial, some synthetic. Many possess a lifespan of eons, while others are so ephemeral as to remain unconfirmed. Even the noble gases, solitary and inert, swell quickly into metaphor and particles of biography.[26]

The elements resist enduring partition, spatial or historical. Intimates of monsters, they rise from any table upon which they have been pinioned or etherized, keen for activity. Even the table (chart, writing desk, or place for community) shifts and reorganizes.[27] Elements are finite: bounded and, in their conjoined state, quite mortal. But finitude does not entail compliance, does not mean that they do not yearn for extension (the force of love) or the breaking of confines in the hope of ardent fragments (strife). Like fire leaping or water that seeps and drenches, air that rises or earth that clings and pulls, the elements press insistently against boundary, spark couplings and fertile schisms, a push-pull to trigger slow or rapid spin. The table of the elements is an alphabet without zed, a liquid lexicon of spiraled connection. Elemental words are therefore a stormy cultural and material intermixing, their etymologies an open-ended archive of ecological and linguistic enmeshment: tornado (Latin *thunder* plus Spanish *twisting*), monsoon (Portuguese by way of Arabic, for the season's change), hurricane (from the language of the Taino, designating the Arawak storm god), derecho (Spanish for destruction's *straight line*), tsunami (Japanese, a *harbor-wave*), typhoon (Portuguese, Arabic, and dialectical Chinese swirled into whirlwind). These words of wind, whorl, and water yearn to be metaphors, linguistic conveyance devices. The elements might be described as metaphor magnets, but their ability to bond materiality and narrative is deeper than mere impress or gravitational trajectory. Through their action metaphor becomes *matterphor,* a tropic-material coil, word and substance together transported: of language but not reducible to linguistic terms, agentic and thick. The elemental table offers a helical interface of world and words, the vibrant twining of love and strife, a motor for perceptual gyre. Unsatisfied with stabilities like spheres or solitudes like withdrawn shards, the elements whirl in unremitting itineracy, *etceteracy,* an invitation to lyrical drift and continuous conjoining.

4. You Are Never Out of Your Element

The elements, writes Jane Bennett, *"will do you in."* Hapless adventurers exposed to wind, rain, stone, and cold air will find they possess a temporal and spatial endurance no organism can hold: "the untiring shining of the sun, the inexorable movement of the tides, the pitiless impartiality of ground temperature."[28] Ensnaring quicksand, numbing ice, parching desert, relentless watery flow will overwhelm because they do not cease in their attempts to submerge, immobilize, desiccate, drown. Close your doors against gale and flood, safeguard your kin, mind the roof as lightning flickers, but know that weathering will someday leave you nothing but stones where a hearth once warmed. The elements are hostile: nature as adversary, a force to subdue and survive, not to live with.

Except, of course, the house is composed of domesticated earth, air, fire, water: house-breaking yet housebroken; companions, for a while, and the very substance of shelter. The hearth around which the house is arranged is where flame crackles, tamed by stone. Warmth rises in slate-sheltered currents while water, wine, and beer are passed. This expanse is "storied matter," a space for the narrative of the elements, a space where these four substances inscribe themselves, material traces of discord and bond.[29] But that is not all. The human bodies that serve as temporary hosts for itinerant tales are themselves elemental, every mind, soul, eye, or book a recording device to give local habitation as story proliferates, mutates, moves along. Our knowing the world is matter-mediated (enabled, impressed), an intimacy of substance, force, flesh, trope, plot, and weather. Through strategic anthropomorphisms—speaking of the elements as if we could know the

"Strategic anthropomorphisms"
L ties to Env. Rhet

elements, allying with air, water, fire, and earth to comprehend what exceeds us in scale—real entities that too often vanish into abstraction become tangible, urgent.[30] Climate may be difficult to grasp, but storm and swelter are unmistakable. Ecologies become intimate, even as they retain a wildness dangerous and alluring.

The elements offer temporal and spatial magnitudes neither too miniscule nor too vast, not so slow that they cannot be seen nor so swift that they defy envisioning. They arrive within a mundane and relentlessly material poesis (from *poiein,* a "making" but also a lyrical exceeding) rather than through an abstract theological, metaphysical, or mathematical discourse in need of translation, concepts or formulae seeking priests or professional interpreters. Ian Bogost writes that an object-oriented ontology must examine inhuman things at every scale of being, from the tiniest particles to cosmological extension.[31] *Elemental Ecocriticism* acknowledges this necessity: the world is not adequately discerned when it must be miniaturized, enlarged, slowed, or speeded to a merely human point of view that obscures inherent challenge.[32] Yet to comprehend objects, materiality, and ecosystems within their native flourishings is no easy task. If at every level of magnitude and within every timeline the world escapes us (too small, too immense, tectonic or glacial to the point of imperceptibility, so rapid as to remain unseen), the elements shift perspective yet inhibit retreat back into the self-satisfied mastery of reduction into quantities, formulae, and inert resources. This prospect is as essential to imagine as it is difficult to inhabit long.

Empedocles believed human bodies to be microcosms: composed of all four "roots," with love and strife as roiled soul. Yet earth, air, water, and fire do not exist in order to become *anthropos.* Human form is simply one composition among many, not the measure of the world. Material affinity unites the elemental cosmos and the little universe that is the human, an intimacy rather than an invitation to dominance, an ingress for human knowing of world that would otherwise exceed. Strategic anthropomorphism is allied with the elements, and its goal is to decenter the human from its accustomed universal midpoint. To plumb the relations of hydrogen to oxygen or organic life to sidereal bodies is essential, of course, but these intangible connections are difficult to deploy as a means of intensifying environmental consciousness. We therefore focus upon the four classical elements and their interstices because their scale is roughly familiar, nearly human in duration and extension. No telescopes, microscopes, computer imaging, or time lapse are necessary to perceive their agency, follow their vectors, collaborate with their force. Smaller than Nature, larger than quarks and leptons, the elements are the perceivable foundations of which worlds are composed, the animated materialities with and through which life thrives. They therefore constitute the most promising of inhumans with which to ally, especially because they offer conveyance beyond familiar frames. The elements are the threshold beyond which the posthuman awaits. They are the outside that is already within, the very stuff of cosmos, home, body, and story.

5. *You Are Always Exposed to the Elements*

Are you afraid of the elements? You should be. Exposure kills: ask Robert Falcon Scott (found frozen in Antarctica, currently the coldest place in the world) or '49er Richard Culverwell (found desiccated in Death Valley, currently the hottest). Common deaths by exposure include hypothermia and dehydration, too little or too much fire. Yet the Latin *expositus,* "put or set out," betrays the indistinction between inside and outside, the indivisibility of body and environment, that elemental encounters demonstrate. As Stacy Alaimo argues, transcorporeality "is a site not for affirmation," for these interactions are usually recognized through toxicology narratives of both "slow" and fast violence: black lung disease (fleshy organs hardening into earth), the additives in last night's dinner, and MCS (multiple chemical sensitivity).[33] The rhetoric of pollution fails when "purity" itself is put under pressure. Exposure is mediation: 60 percent of the human body is water, 96 percent of it is made up of four chemical elements—oxygen, carbon, hydrogen, and nitrogen—and all mix into an elemental cocktail that fluctuates, secretes, absorbs. Galenic humoralism got it right: earth (black bile), fire (yellow bile), water (phlegm), and air (blood) are not outside of us, not "out there," but are the shared ecomateriality that is both us and world.[34] Erect walls against the elements, but they are always-already inside—and they did not even require a Sinonical betrayal! Your body is a wilderness, an in/organic tempest that the elements are and convey.

But *expositus* as "put someone out" (as annoyance) rings true here, as well as its corollary to "put something out": to *put out* the light (the metaphorical soul) is to *put out* the light (the material fire). A tornado puts organisms out on the road; a hurricane snuffs an electrical grid; a forest fire overwhelms the flames of nerve endings and incinerates arboreal synapses. Elemental exposure requires narratives of survival and shared vulnerability. To counteract exposure to the cold we must build a fire—just as Jack London's unnamed man tries (yet fails) to do in the short story of the same name—expose ourselves to the flame, draw nearer, and become intimate with those who gather round the light.[35] We must invent, improvise, and take pleasure in our shared elementality not despite its precariousness but because of its desirability. There are more poses to make and take besides instant recoil. So strike a pose. Or a match. Fire is but one co-corporeal. Are you still afraid of the elements? You should be. But you are much more than that.

6. Elements Are Steps, Not Stairs

Step six in becoming a pre-Socratic philosopher: if you wish to follow in Empedocles's tracks, consider how far you are willing to travel. It is said that the philosopher hurled himself into the lava of Mount Etna in Sicily. The next morning his brass sandals were found on the crater's rim, jettisoned from the white-hot abyss. Although Empedocles's detractors might ridicule the manner (and matter) of his suicide, believing in elemental non/human enmeshment requires not just an imaginative leap of faith but also a desire to take a physical plunge into the stuff of which we are composed, to immerse oneself in a potentially lethal elementality, "to wash" *(lavare)* away. Yet narrativity is born of the volcano as well, from the steps Empedocles left for following. His sandals do not signify merely the absence of a human body—Empedocles versus the volcano would make for an unimaginative story of anthropocentricity— they invite us to realize what combustion does: a contact zone, liquid earth, swirling concoctions that eventually solidify into embodied narratives. (You are holding one right now: are your hands getting warmer?)

But back to the philosopher's feet, step two, those footprints in the sulfur leading . . . where was it again? Follow Plato and Aristotle's term for "element," *stoikheion*, to arrive at "step, component part." This etymological shift is not an example of elementary logic, however, as if the world could be so simple (repeat principle 1). Advertisements that authoritatively announce how many steps you can take to accomplish any number of things are gaining popularity in our era of do-it-yourself "greening" but fall for the same teleological trick as those who see Empedocles's sandals as a slightly scorched, but still functional, pair of stair climbers. The Greek word *stoikheion* does not designate a series of steps to a perceivable goal or end for which the elements supply an illusion of equilibrium—a stairway to harmonious sustainability at your feet. The Latin translation of *stoikheion* into *elementum* ("principle, component part") took that dead-end path, fixated on the volcano's rim, satisfying a sandal fetish gone wrong. *Elementa* make poor guides—so why follow?

Despite the elements' arrangement in most premodern cosmologies into vertical forms, the elements have no destination in particular, regardless of our attempts to order them into goal-driven ascent. Instead, the elements are steps that lead to more steps, even to missteps, to errancy. Nature's ladder proves slippery; it does not convey but trips you up (and down) from one rung to the next. The chain of being goes from vertical to vortical. Yet we must acknowledge that some elemental actants inescapably take us where we fear to tread, or wish not to. The number of environmental refugees is on the rise, predicted to reach fifty million by 2020.[36] Thus the elements are situated encounters that allow us to reimagine, and critique, the steps that shape our bodies, texts, and desires in the urgency of *now*,[37] our current environmental crises and injustices—not just to ask what steps we *should* take to avoid or prevent disasters but to ask where we, as collectives, are going; what assemblages are being made; what futures are yet to be made in the twenty-first century—for whatever happens, we know the elements will be there, lava-like, every step of some way.

7. The Elements Make Love and War

According to the cosmological matchmaker Empedocles, the elements are held together by love and disordered by strife. While some desiring bodies tangle into in/human trysts, others unravel into rough patches of discord, and yet others suffer the traumatic violence of divorce. There is hope for those looking for companionship, however. At all times, there are at least four ways to meet a lover: in the woods, on the beach, above the clouds, under the sun. Whereas unidirectional affection from humans to elements can be damaging—the land knows rape too well[38]—true wanderlust is multidirectional, interpenetrative: clean-cut hierarchies enmuck; the senses in-, per-, and ex/s/pire. Sticky, slippery, smoldering, steamy. Like good lovers, the elements make hungry where most they satisfy, when most they nourish. *Elementum* feels like *alimentum* at these moments. Ecosexuals, for instance, host weddings to snow, rocks, and the sea.[39] Is there any reason to object to these queer couplings? Speak *now* or hold your peace.

But the elements speak up precisely because peace, as another lover of the elements, Serres, reminds us, is fleeting: "Every existence thus shows something stable in divergence from stability."[40] Peace does not stand a chance in the flux of Empedoclean love-strife. All is encounter, but not all is love (even if it is all we need). And yet this world is nevertheless the one we try to know, we love, we wish to live within. *With,* a stance that demands a reorientation of intimacy even toward beings we consider ugly, mundane, antagonistic. As Serres considers the cold, he uncovers himself, presents his skin to the chill: "How can we live without or against the four elements, without thinking like them, without turning toward them, into them, through them, for them, with them?"[41] The commonplace rhetoric of "battling the elements"—an outright *against*—demonstrates how prepositions shape our physical relationships. For better and for worse: we must continually take (new) positions *with,* and occasionally renew our vows to, the elements that make love and war, that engender both joy and misfortune. What do you pre/pro/pose? And to whom?[42]

8. The Elements Rise and Fall

Empedocles was a poet as well as philosopher and physicist—or, better, he composed at a time when those callings had yet to find their segregation. His verse staggers: whirling, elegant, oblique. He annoyed Aristotle through lyrical ambiguity. Empedocles described the sea as "the sweat of the earth," and Aristotle declared that such irresolute metaphor obscures unambivalent science.[43] Yet Empedocles knew that elemental impress is seldom a thing of keen and parsimonious language, arriving through intensities of poetic transport as well as blunt equation. "Sweat of the earth" reveals the elements as substance and energy, the working or movement of earth and water. *As earth and water sink, air and fire rise.* Matter and metaphor coil: gravity, weight, the ponderousness of the world, upward lift of the imaginative, the passionate, the ecstatic. These vectors converge, struggle, and in their shifting trigger shared gyre. The elements circulate, spark dense and light effusion, turbulent narrative, a vorticular and disanthropocentric perspective of force as much as matter. In that spiraled intimacy abides the revolutionary power of the aleatory, entropy's loosenings, desire's clasp.

The etymologist Isidore of Seville believed words and things to be materially coextensive, discerning in the derivation of words storied matter. Isidore wrote that the term for universe *(mundus)* originates from its ceaseless motion, "for no rest is given to its elements."[44] Such tumbling of the seas and stars, the lands and the heavens, conveys them out of celestial abstraction, so that even for a devout interpreter like Isidore the elements bear tales of mundane inhabitance and inhuman forces. Thus a marginal illustration on a copy of Macrobius's commentary on Cicero's *Dream of Scipio* includes the four elements represented as a kind of multipart Möbius strip that invites the eye to glide its contours.[45] This ceaseless motion is inbuilt, moreover, into the very word *element,* which condenses a linguistic multiplicity and restless etymological archive that ensures the term will not stabilize into a monolith. Isidore turned to etymology not because derivation fixes word or world but because storied matter ensures their ceaseless and productive motion. The elements extend an invitation to stumbling, stuttering, to getting stuck in the past or not getting things precisely right. The temporality they convey is an enfolded one, polychronic, an invitation to play with knots. The structure they form is a tempest of both storm and time, matter and history: *tempest* comes from a noun for time *(tempus)* that is also a weather word *(temps).* History-laden and yet not reducible to discrete origin, the elements connect epochs through time-storm.

9. *To Live with the Elements Is to Dwell within Catastrophe*

It was bound to happen: like the *virer* ("to turn, veer") lingering in the word *environment,* we turn now to the catastrophes that have come and are yet to arrive (*kata-*, "down," and *strophē,* "turning"). Like the untimeliness of the tempest, catastrophes are transhistorical in their impact. But some accounts have survived: Herodotus writes that when a storm destroyed the bridge Xerxes built over the Hellespont in order to invade Greece in 480 BCE, the Persian ruler flogged the water. King Cnut commanded the tide to stay still as it slowly crept up to his knees. When Hurricane Sandy barraged the shores of the eastern Unites States in 2012, worried citizens turned to President Barack Obama, wondering how he would respond to the disaster a week before elections. Hubristic political ecologies like these laud leaders who will whip harder, linger longer, build the bigger seawall to prevent the next elemental comedown. In sovereign-engineered sustainability we trust. *Misplaced trust.* "We take care of our own."[46] *Myopic care.*

In a world imagined sustainable, catastrophes prove dramatic in more than one sense: as a kind of denouement—a theatrical term for the moment in classical tragedy when disparate threads of action come together, reach their climax, and are (potentially) resolved—the agentic elements band into their Gordian four-folded knots only to be severed by the sword of the sovereign (human).[47] Crisis averted. Here is the moment you have been waiting for. But—oh, sorry!—you must have taken a wrong turn back there. In reality, time and tide wait for no human. Just as sustainability is too small in ambition, so is sovereignty too anthropocentric in opinion, too "antipolitical and antiecological" in principle.[48] Living within catastrophe rather than ridding the world of its turbulence means instead to embrace the elemental *now* (in all its urgency); to explore the dis-anthropocene rather than relinquish the human's anthropocentric title that it never had; to dive deeper into our elemental embeddedness. Catastrophe is a type of "forward thinking" in search of more capacious futures, a drama of unidentifiable genre, a tragicomedy that picks up where the "comedy of survival" left off.[49]

Still waiting for that deus ex machina to set the elemental world straight? Take another turn: the denouement of catastrophe has been onstage all along, just not in its typical explanatory guise; to "unknot" is to proliferate instead of to solve, to unleash a series of even more knots, even more threads. Some might glimpse in these downturns of unpredictable enmeshment and precarity a discourse of postsustainability. Steve Mentz, for example, argues for a "swimmer poetics" to capture the "twinned joy and danger of a disorderly, threatening, world."[50] A poetics of the elements includes stories about how we have always been catastrophic. Yet re-storying the elements in disequilibrial ways does not imply restoring harmony by *tending* to disasters and becoming cautious ecological stewards. This is the sovereign's promise: that we will be better prepared *next* time. Elemental poetics instead ask us to *attend* to the elements better, to stretch our imaginations and interdependent senses (from *attendere,* "to stretch"), to listen to the calls of intracatastrophic things. How postsustainable are we? The human's perspective and prospects are but few among many. To everything, turn—and to turn, everything: an ethics of gyre.

10. The Elements Oblige

Elemental obligation arrives in a doubled sense. The elements companion and assist; they also materially and ethically bind. The mixed trajectory of their activity amounts to an environing: an encircling (they limit) as well as a veering (they convey, and that process can better or imperil). Elemental agency engenders perspective tumble, an unstable shift between familiar, domestic frames (the elements are the substance of the inhabited world) and the disorientations of a wildness that may be distant or within (the elements are climatic as well as corporeal and diegetic forces). The apprehensibility for which we have praised earth, air, fire, and water is also an allurement toward betrayal. Once invited to think ecologically in their good company, the elements reveal that their narratives are not undemanding, that their material poesis requires unremitting labor. We cannot be onlookers, but makers, companions in whirl. Elemental alliances are sure transport to uneasy realms. Earth becomes water, air becomes sea, foundation is no longer secure. Ethics is difficult matter.

We are left nowhere definite. No environment is wide enough for every thriving, not even this inhuman expanse. Cary Wolfe writes of the pragmatics that must subtend capacious welcome.[51] Not every thing can enter the home, and each choice we make for inclusion is in the end a failure of embrace . . . and yet we must delimit and decide. Whenever we attempt to imagine some universal space for effective and united political action, we deny from the beginning what Bruno Latour describes throughout his work as the collective or parliament of humans and nonhumans necessary to begin to think beyond bifurcations of nature and culture. Stacy Alaimo observes that "the lively, agential world of diverse creatures" too often becomes through this process of boundary a silent void within reductively anthropocentric space, so that "the problem of how to include the claims, needs, and agencies of other living creatures, habitats and ecosystems remains."[52] The elements oblige, but they do not solve.

Yet we cannot give up. Turn nature's ladder sideways, seek something more democratic than metaphysical hierarchies, and you get a prison of objects, a sequence of uncommunicating cells. A space of private immurement, this horizontal scheme offers objects impossibly withdrawn. But twist the ladder into a spiral, force its oubliettes to touch, and you might get a chain wreck, the vortex that is elemental enmeshment, some principles of muddled relations to knot, ooze, and interpenetrate, a place for clouds, eddies, and tempests. No well-ordered macrocosm here. The binding of the elements is love. Without strife, though, they and their makings could never be free. We are, irremediably, within a swirled mess of obligation. The earth, air, fire, water, love, strife, interstices, and impossible hybridities with which we are coextensive are strange strangers, intimate aliens.[53] Even more difficult, they are at once compulsions to lyric and story, unremitting *tropes,* material and language that turns (from the Greek *trepein*). The combinatory world they compose is *universe,* a cosmos that is quite literally a spinning thing (from the Latin *vertere*). Where does that leave us?

11. The Shape of the Elements Is a Vortex

FIGURE I.2. Photograph courtesy of NASA.

Notes

1. J. Henry Fair, with essays by James Hansen et al., *The Day after Tomorrow: Images of Our Earth in Crisis* (Brooklyn, N.Y.: PowerHouse Books, 2010).

2. "Slow violence" is Rob Nixon's term for "a violence that occurs gradually and out of sight, a violence of delayed destruction that is dispersed across time and space, an attritional violence that is typically not viewed as violence at all." His work importantly shows the links between ecological degradation and socioeconomic marginalization. Rob Nixon, *Slow Violence and the Environmentalism of the Poor* (Cambridge, Mass.: Harvard University Press, 2011), 2.

3. For the surviving corpus of Empedocles's writing and its intellectual context, see M. R. Wright, *Empedocles: The Extant Fragments* (New Haven, Conn.: Yale University Press, 1981); and Brad Inwood, *The Poem of Empedocles: A Text and Translation with an Introduction,* rev. ed. (Toronto: University of Toronto Press, 2001). The scholarship on Empedoclean philosophy is extensive in scope and diverse in interpretation of his work—and this diversity existed among Empedocles's Greek inheritors as well. For excellent overviews, see Richard Parry, "Empedocles," in *The Stanford Encyclopedia of Philosophy* (Fall 2012 edition), ed. Edward N. Zalta, http://plato.stanford.edu/archives/fall2012/entries/empedocles/; and John E. Sisko, "Anaxagoras and Empedocles in the Shadow of Elea," in *The Routledge Companion to Ancient Philosophy,* ed. James Warren and Frisbee Sheffield (New York: Routledge, 2014), 48–64.

4. Although Aristotle tended to describe the elements as "inert material causes," Empedocles discerns in them inherent motion, independent of external forces. See especially Inwood, *The Poem of Empedocles,* 29.

5. Drew Daniel, *The Melancholy Assemblage: Affect and Epistemology in the English Renaissance* (New York: Fordham University Press, 2013), 15–16. This love, strife, and hybridity engender a "consistent incoherence or generative indeterminacy" that ensures the longevity of elemental theory. Daniel succinctly describes Empedocles's "quadratic elemental metaphysics" as "an ontology of mixture and assemblage" (17, 19). See also Daniel's excellent essay "The Empedoclean Renaissance," in *The Return of Theory in Early Modern English Studies,* vol. 2, eds. Paul Cefalu, Gary Kuchar, and Bryan Reynolds (Basingstoke: Palgrave Macmillan, 2014), 277–301.

6. Fragment B 61, quoted in Parry, "Empedocles." On the concept of queer ecologies, see Catriona Mortimer-Sandilands and Bruce Erickson, eds., *Queer Ecologies: Sex, Nature, Politics, Desire* (Bloomington: Indiana University Press, 2010); and Timothy Morton, "Queer Ecology," *PMLA* 125, no. 2 (2010): 273–82.

7. This is the last line of *The Origin of Species.* See *Darwin: Texts, Commentary,* 3rd ed., ed. Philip Appleman (New York: W. W. Norton, 2001), 174.

8. Empedocles describes this vorticular process in *On Nature,* B 35. Parry ("Empedocles") gives a good account of the passage's interpretive difficulties.

9. On the survival and transformation of Empedocles from the classical to the early modern period, see Sacvan Bercovitch, "Empedocles in the English Renaissance," *Studies in Philology* 65, no. 1 (1967): 67–80. On the elemental linkages uniting Gaston Bachelard (whose dream-like, phenomenological investigations of the four elements have inspired this collection), see James L. Smith, "New Bachelards? Reveries, Elements and Twenty-First Century Materialisms," *Altre modernità* (October 16, 2012): 156–67.

10. In connecting past to present ecologically we build upon a flourishing scholarship within medieval and early modern studies, even as our not-very-green ecomaterialism departs from some of this work in significant ways. Among this essential scholarship: Todd A. Borlik, *Ecocriticism and Early Modern English Literature: Green Pastures* (New York: Routledge, 2011); Dan Brayton, *Shakespeare's Ocean: An Ecocritical Exploration* (Charlottesville: University of Virginia, 2012); Lynne Bruckner and Dan Brayton, eds., *Ecocritical Shakespeare* (Farnham: Ashgate, 2011); Jeffrey Jerome Cohen, ed., *Animal, Vegetable, Mineral: Ethics and Objects* (Washington, D.C.: Oliphaunt Books, 2011); Gabriel Egan, *Green Shakespeare: From Ecopolitics to Ecocriticism* (London: Routledge, 2006); Simon C. Estok, *Ecocriticism and Shakespeare: Reading Ecophobia* (New York: Palgrave Macmillan, 2011); Jean Feerick and Vin Nardizzi, eds., *The Indistinct Human in Renaissance Literature* (New York: Palgrave Macmillan, 2011); Thomas Hallock, Ivo Kamps, and Karen L. Raber, eds., *Early Modern Ecostudies: From the Florentine Codex to Shakespeare* (New York: Palgrave Macmillan, 2008); Barbara A. Hanawalt and Lisa J. Kiser, eds., *Engaging with Nature: Essays on the Natural World in Medieval and Early Modern Europe* (Notre Dame, Ind.: University of Notre Dame Press, 2008); Steve Mentz, *At the Bottom of Shakespeare's Ocean* (London: Continuum, 2009); Jennifer Munroe and Rebecca Laroche, eds., *Ecofeminist Approaches to Early Modern Literature* (New York: Palgrave Macmillan, 2011); Vin Nardizzi, *Wooden Os: Shakespeare's Theatres and England's Trees;* Gillian Rudd, *Greenery: Ecocritical Readings of Late Medieval English Literature* (Manchester: Manchester University Press, 2007); Alfred K. Siewers, *Strange Beauty: Ecocritical Approaches to Early Medieval Landscape* (New York: Palgrave Macmillan, 2009); Robert N. Watson, *Back to Nature: The Green and the Real in the Late Renaissance* (Philadelphia: University of Pennsylvania Press, 2007); Mary-Floyd Wilson and Garrett A. Sullivan Jr., eds., *Environment and Embodiment in Early Modern England* (New York: Palgrave Macmillan, 2007); Julian Yates and Garrett Sullivan, introduction to forum "Shakespeare and Ecology," *Shakespeare Studies* 39 (2011).

11. In this linking of the critical rethinking of materiality to environmental justice, we are inspired by the work of Stacy Alaimo, especially *Bodily Natures: Science, Environment, and the Material Self* (Bloomington: Indiana University Press, 2009). Also indispensable is her book *Undomesticated Ground: Recasting Nature as Feminist Space* (Ithaca, N.Y.: Cornell University Press, 2000) and her edited collection (with Susan Hekman) *Material Feminisms* (Bloomington: Indiana University Press, 2008).

12. Our project has benefited profoundly from the work and example of Jane Bennett, whose scholarship centers around forgotten alternatives to disenchanted modernity. See especially Jane Bennett, *The Enchantment of Modern Life: Attachments, Crossings, and Ethics* (Princeton, N.J.: Princeton University Press, 2001) and *Vibrant Matter: A Political Ecology of Things* (Durham, N.C.: Duke University Press, 2010).

13. David Macauley, *Elemental Philosophy: Earth, Air, Fire, and Water as Elemental Ideas* (Albany: State University of New York Press, 2010), 5. Macauley writes that "with some patience, fortune, and persistence, we might be able to rediscover and recover a deeper and more lasting connection with the elemental world and in the process find our place—reside in our own element or elements, with the bewildered and bewildering beauty everywhere around us" (355).

14. See the "Sustainability" cluster of *PMLA* 127, no. 3 (2013), especially Stacy Alaimo, "Sustainable This, Sustainable That: New Materialisms, Posthumanism, and Unknown Futures" (558–64); Stephanie LeMenager and Stephanie Foote, "The Sustainable Humanities" (572–78); and Steve Mentz, "After Sustainability" (586–92).

15. Mick Smith, *Against Ecological Sovereignty: Ethics, Politics, and Saving the Natural World* (Minneapolis: University of Minnesota Press, 2011).

16. Despite its attribution to him, Sherlock Holmes never precisely declares "It's elementary, my dear Watson" in Arthur Conan Doyle's writings. He does describe his method of deductive reasoning as "elementary" in the story "The Crooked Man." See Randall Stock, "Sherlock Holmes Quotes," http://www.bestofsherlock.com/top-10-sherlock-quotes.htm.

17. On carpentry and its active relation to objects and ontology, see Ian Bogost, *Alien Phenomenology, or What It's Like to Be a Thing* (Minneapolis: University of Minnesota Press, 2012), 85–112.

18. On the domestication of the elements (and the ways in which, even when tamed by plumbing, they remain wild), see Macauley, *Elemental Philosophy,* 255–82. Macauley also writes extensively about the relations between Empedoclean roots and deleuzoguattarian rhizomes.

19. Gilles Deleuze and Félix Guattari, *A Thousand Plateaus: Capitalism and Schizophrenia,* trans. Brian Massumi (Minneapolis: University of Minnesota Press, 1987). For a vivid ecological reading of Deleuze and Guattari's work, see Bernd Herzogenrath, *Deleuze/Guattari & Ecology* (New York: Palgrave Macmillan, 2009).

20. Latour critiques Kant's "science-fiction nightmare" of the Copernican Revolution: "instead of moving around the objects, scientists make the objects move around them." Bruno Latour, *Pandora's Hope: Essays on the Reality of Science Studies* (Cambridge, Mass.: Harvard University Press, 1999), 16, 101. For more on his call for "a Copernican counter-revolution," see Bruno Latour, *We Have Never Been Modern,* trans. Catherine Porter (Cambridge, Mass.: Harvard University Press, 1993), 76–79.

21. See Ursula K. Heise, *Sense of Place and Sense of Planet: The Environmental Imagination of the Global* (Oxford: Oxford University Press, 2008).

22. This is Galileo's famous quote, supposedly mumbled as the Inquisition forbade him to teach terrestrial motion. The sentence is a rich spur to thinking for Michel Serres in *The Natural Contract,* trans. Elizabeth Macarthur and William Paulson (Ann Arbor: University of Michigan Press, 1995); and Bruno Latour, "Agency at the Time of the Anthropocene," *New Literary History* 45, no. 1 (2014): 1–18.

23. John Muir, *Our National Parks* (San Francisco: Sierra Club Books, 1991), 196.

24. Serres, *The Natural Contract,* 124.

25. Macauley, *Elemental Philosophy,* 352–55.

26. On the chemical-biographical interface, see, for example, Primo Levi, *The Periodic Table,* trans. Raymond Rosenthal (New York: Schocken Books, 1984).

27. On the *table* (as writing desk and place for community) as a provocative philosophical and phenomenological expanse for rethinking community, materiality, history, and identity, see Sarah Ahmed, *Queer Phenomenology: Orientations, Objects, Others* (Durham, N.C.: Duke University Press, 2006), 42–45, 157–79.

28. Jane Bennett, response essay, "The Elements," *postmedieval* 4, no. 1 (Spring 2013): 105, 111. Bennett writes in conclusion, "'The Elements readily become metaphors for something besides themselves: the elements as the Big Other or Nature or What Lies beyond Human Knowing, or as a quaint term for what is really a science of meteorology. Yeah—the Elements are metaphorical. But they can also kill you, or inspire you, or help to organize you" (111).

29. Serenella Iovino and Serpil Oppermann describe "storied matter" as "matter's 'narrative' power of creating configurations of meanings and substances, which enter with human lives into a field of co-emerging interactions. . . . Matter itself becomes a text where dynamics of 'diffuse' agency and non-linear causality are inscribed and produced." Serenella Iovino and Serpil Oppermann, "Material Ecocriticism: Materiality, Agency, and Models of Narrativity," *Ecozon@* 3, no. 1 (2012): 79–80.

30. Our term "strategic anthropomorphism" is inspired by Jane Bennett's notion of "a touch of anthropomorphism" in *Vibrant Matter* (98–99). We are also hoping to evoke Gayatri Chakravorty Spivak's cogent formulation of a postcolonial "strategic essentialism" as a politically effective zone for temporary collective inhabitance. For an excellent overview of the phrase and Spivak's later qualifications of its use, see her interview with Sara Danius and Stefan Jonsson in *Boundary 2* 20, no. 2 (1993): 24–50.

31. See the definition Bogost offers in "What Is Object-Oriented Ontology?," http://www.bogost.com/blog/what_is_objectoriented_ontolog/.

32. Lemenager and Foote ("The Sustainable Humanities," 574–78) argue that because of their grounding in narrative, the humanities are especially well suited to exploring the problems of scale that ecological crisis demands (576). In the same issue of *PMLA,* Lynn Keller ("Beyond Imagining, Imagining Beyond," 579–85) looks to the "representations of scale shifting" necessary to the apprehension of "geologic time and of intergalactic space" (583) as well as deathless hyperobjects like Styrofoam (584).

33. Alaimo, *Bodily Natures,* 144. On Rob Nixon's "slow violence," see note 2.

34. Gail Kern Paster and Suzanne Conklin Akbari have eloquently detailed the intimacy of the humoral body environment, mapping a "geohumoralism" that resonates profoundly with the material turn in posthuman ecotheory. See especially Gail Kern Paster, *The Body Embarrassed: Drama and the Disciplines of Shame in Early Modern England* (Ithaca, N.Y.: Cornell University Press, 1993); *Humoring the Body: Emotions and the Shakespearean Stage* (Chicago: University of Chicago Press, 2004); "Becoming Landscape: The Ecology of the Passions in the Legend of Temperance," in *Environment and Embodiment in Early Modern England,* ed. Mary Floyd-Wilson and Garrett A. Sullivan (New York: Palgrave Macmillan, 2007), 153–70; "The Tragic Subject and Its Passions," in *The Cambridge Companion to Shakespearean Tragedy,* ed. Claire McEachern (Cambridge: Cambridge University Press, 2013), 152–70; and Suzanne Conklin Akbari, "From Due East to True North: Orientalism and Orientation," in *The Postcolonial Middle Ages,* ed. Jeffrey Jerome Cohen (New York: St Martin's, 2000), 19–34; *Idols in the East: European Representations of Islam and the Orient, 1100–1450* (Ithaca, N.Y.: Cornell University Press, 2009); "Becoming Human," postmedieval 1 (2010): 272–89.

35. Jack London, "To Build a Fire," in *Jack London: Novels and Stories* (New York: Literary Classics of America, 1982).

36. Joanna Zelman, "50 Million Environmental Refugees by 2020, Experts Predict," *Huffington Post,* February 22, 2011, http://www.huffingtonpost.com/2011/02/22/environmental-refugees-50_n_826488.html.

37. Like the editors of *Shakespeare and the Urgency of Now: Criticism and Theory in the Twenty-First Century* (New York: Palgrave Macmillan, 2012), Cary DiPietro and Hugh Grady, we believe that thinking elementally "involves a negotiation and constant renegotiation between horizons of interpretation and an ever-shifting present" (2).

38. The classic example is Annette Kolodny's *The Lay of the Land: Metaphor as Experience and History in American Life and Letters* (Chapel Hill: University of North Carolina Press, 1975).

39. For starters, see Elizabeth Stephens and Annie Sprinkle's SexEcology project, http://sexecology.org/.

40. Michel Serres, *Biogea,* trans. Randolph Burks (Minneapolis: Univocal, 2012), 178.

41. Ibid., 176.

42. While necessary, choice is admittedly difficult. "The trouble with love," Timothy Morton points out, "is that it has a tinge of 'evil' about it." Timothy Morton, *The Ecological Thought* (Cambridge, Mass.: Harvard University Press, 2010), 96.

43. Aristotle makes this statement in his *Meteorology* 357a24; see Ralph McInerny, *A History of Western Philosophy,* vol. 1 (Notre Dame, Ind.: University of Notre Dame Press, 1963), 65.

44. Isidore, *Etymologiae* 3.29, quoted and translated by Robert Bartlett in an excellent overview of the relation of motion to medieval natural science and theories of the universe. See Robert Bartlett, *The Natural and the Supernatural in the Middle Ages* (Cambridge: Cambridge University Press, 2008), 35–70 (quote at 38).

45. Macrobius, *Commentarii in Somnium Scipionis* (ca. 1150), Copenhagen, Det Kongelige Bibliotek, ms. NKS 218 4° 3 recto. Available online at http://base.kb.dk/manus_pub/cv/manus/ManusPage.xsql?nnoc=manus_pub&p_ManusId=33&p_PageNo=3%20recto&p_Lang=alt.

46. The unofficial song of Barack Obama's 2012 presidential campaign was "We Take Care of Our Own," written by Bruce Springsteen.

47. The reference is, of course, to Alexander the Great's famous solution. Latour asks to retie the knot of non/human complexity that the Moderns have sliced: "on the left, they have put knowledge of things; on the right, power and politics" (*We Have Never Been Modern*, 3).

48. M. Smith, *Against Ecological Sovereignty*, xx.

49. "Forward thinking" is the subject of Morton's third chapter in *The Ecological Thought*: "The ecological thought must transcend the language of apocalypse" (19). The phrase "comedy of survival" refers to one of the first ecocritical studies of literature, Joseph W. Meeker's *The Comedy of Survival: Literary Ecology and a Play Ethic*, 3rd ed. (Tucson: University of Arizona Press, 1997). "Comedy is a contributor to survival, and a habit that promotes health" (11).

50. Mentz, "After Sustainability," 589.

51. Cary Wolfe, *Before the Law: Humans and Other Animals in a Biopolitical Frame* (Chicago: University of Chicago Press, 2013), 102–5.

52. Alaimo, "Sustainable This, Sustainable That," 563.

53. On the "strange stranger," see Morton, *The Ecological Thought*, 47.

one

Pyromena

Fire's Doing

ANNE HARRIS

There is no fire in Eden. There is Air, the wind of God hurtling through this new creation from the start. There is Earth, seized up from the formless void, made fertile on the third day. And there is Water, churned by the wind of God, lapping up at earth already and filling with sea monsters by the fifth day. But no Fire: no sputter of spark, no lick of flame, no fright of flash, no spread of blaze, no glow of ember. The cycle and spread of fire is still far off, its quality of light promised by God's "Fiat lux!" but yet to be materialized and manipulated. Nor is there rain. Water swells up from the ground and slakes the earth, tracing out the four rivers of Paradise. No rain means no storms, no flashes of lightning, no tree limbs left burning for Adam and Eve to find, no discovery of ways to disrupt the dark with fierce light. God forbid the Tree of Knowledge should burn down.

Fire is the late-comer element, the supplement, that which complicates things. The authors of Genesis reveal an inability to imagine fire at the start. Presenting the scientific framework for imagining fire, Stephen J. Pyne points out that "the primordial earth did not have fire: it acquired it over long aeons."[1] Fire comes in the Devonian Age, 420 million years ago, in the midst of the Paleozoic Era, the *fourth* great era of Earth's formation. It comes a good 100 million years after the first forms of life appear; it comes, basically, when there starts to be enough oxygen in the air for things to ignite. With these aerations, fire performs its first *arias,* building, through its cycles of combustion, to its *opera,* its works, its multiple effects. The "Cycle of Fire" that Pyne is composing is operatic, focused on the movements of the element, on how it acts.[2] The idea of arias within an operatic cycle shapes my own approach. It does so in terms of structuring my chapter upon specific acts of fire, moments of ignition that fired the human imagination and make manifest fire's own artistry. And it does so in expressing the tension between metaphor and materiality within elemental ecocriticism. Language will seek to shift the element from its material form: beyond the descriptive level, it can quickly subsume materiality into metaphor, and thus we speak of fevered minds and we burn with love and our gazes smolder and our words are fervent. But the material presence of fire is immediate and consequential: it can warm or it can burn, it is flame or conflagration—no matter its form, its materiality must be tended to. "Fire is a vast, violent element of Nature," Pliny writes of this struggle, "and it is a moot point as to whether its essence is more productive or creative."[3] I have chosen instances in which the materiality of fire is insistent and the articulation of its metaphor far-reaching; instances in which fire and humanity meet, and their ontologies and histories intertwine in simultaneous immediacy and sublimation.

This chapter will pursue fire, look after what fire *tends to,* where it appears and what it disappears into, what it alters and shapes, what new or unfinished realities it leaves behind—first in marvelous things, then in fevered minds. It will claim that an elemental ecocriticism of fire can pursue fire as a living thing (with movement and aspirations) into the forms it has transformed, following the manifold directionality of a spreading fire. It is this nonlinear ontology that David Macauley emphasizes in calling attention to Empedocles's term *rhizomata* for the elements.[4] Fire is one of the four "rhizomes" as much because of the inability to fix its starting and ending points (fire's enduring past, present, and future) as because of its ability to spread and permeate (fire's endless potential). To paraphrase Macauley, it is perpetual, uncreated, and perpetually creative. And it creates by moving and changing: the permutations of rhizomes are famously explored by Gilles Deleuze and Félix Guattari,[5] but it is the *movement* of the rhizome that I wish to emphasize. Its crooked paths and fusings, its lack of origin and finality, are the characteristics of fire that shape this chapter. Like Deleuze and Guattari's "principle of asignifying rupture," the rhizomata that is fire catches up "movements of deterritorialization and processes of reterritorialization."[6] Fire is constantly interrupted yet consistently rekindled.

The aria from spark to flame is taken up again and again in fire's aspiration to burn. In his book *The Psychoanalysis of Fire* (and its later companions *The Flame of the Candle* and the unfinished *A Poetics of Fire*), Gaston Bachelard asks after what fire desires, what it wants, where it goes, and what it creates. It is Bachelard who suggests that we examine the *pyromena* of fire, its products and phenomena. He begins with the reverie in front of the fire: the mind of inquiry adrift, tempered by neither science nor fiction, not quite conscious or unconscious, but led by fire beyond fire: "this hypnotized form of observation that is involved in gazing into a fire."[7] From that reverie comes invention and imagination. What follows is devoted to pyromena—to fire's doings, to those things whose existence is predicated on fire.

The Bricks of Babel and the Pillar of Seth

The first biblical sighting of fire is on that awful threshold, East of Eden, where God "placed the cherubim, and a sword flaming and turning to guard the way to the tree of life" (Genesis 3:24). Fire is not made, it is wielded; it appears fully formed and active. No one *discovers* fire in Genesis: it appears in moments of transformative action; it is always active, always *doing* something, moving the story along. After the flood, Noah builds an altar and burns sacrificial animals upon it and "when the Lord smelled the pleasing odor, the Lord said in his heart: 'I will never again curse the ground because of humankind . . . nor will I ever again destroy every living creature as I have done'" (Genesis 8:21). Fire changes the mind of God. It makes God make promises, covenants even, the next one to Abraham when, in the presence of the "smoking fire pot and flaming torch," God grants the Holy Land to Abraham and his descendants. Fire has an afterglow: its presence and promise are felt long after it can no longer be seen.

The first things that are *made* with fire are the bricks of the Tower of Babel. Until now, fire has *appeared:* it has marked the expulsion, danced upon the altar of Noah, and charged the air between Abraham and God.

But the first things that it *makes*, that are *infused* with it, and that bear it aloft in new form are the bricks of Babel. Now we start to see how fire moves through metamorphosis, how it is strategic in the diffusion of its energy. Its elemental intention is to shift, and humans take up the calling. "'Come,'" say the immigrants to the plains of Shinar in Genesis 11:3, "'let us make bricks and burn them thoroughly.' And they had bricks for stone, and bitumen for mortar." Tubalcain and his ability to forge tools of bronze and iron are listed in the generations of Cain and Enoch, but it is not until Babel that a tale is told in which fire is used to make something: bricks and sticky bitumen—millions of bricks, all of a sudden. To mark the foundation of the Tower of Babylon, Nabopolassar (r. 650–625 BCE) writes: "I had them shape mud bricks without number, and mold baked bricks like countless raindrops."[8] Bricks are modular and multiple: they quickly and easily systematize fire's doing; they are primal pyromena. Fire suffuses earth to make brick. It concentrates its energy and overwhelms earth so as to transform it.[9] No longer out in the open, occasional and waning, it is now inside, systematic and sustained. Bricks are fire transfigured, fire moving into permanence.

And so the first thing that is built with fire is a tower designed to reach Heaven. Here is fire bypassing Eden again, mediating itself through brick upon brick, reaching higher and higher, intent upon a perfect place, but denied entry again by God, who destroys the pyromenon of Babel by confusing the language of its makers.[10] "They left off building the city," continues Genesis, conjuring up the abandoned bricks of Babel, fire fused into form with no function: the ones freshly mortared in, the ones still of soft clay, those left to burn. This great, first ruin of making left unmade, a first fusing that fails to join heaven and earth: fire's attempt to reach the heavens through humanity's desire.

Pieter Brueghel's (ca. 1525–69) Vienna *Tower of Babel* from 1563 is a meditation on fire in its modular form (Figure 1.1).[11] His conceptualization of the Tower of Babel as a multilayered structure comprised of living rock, brick, and stone is brilliantly described by Edward Snow as "an exfoliating presence, an opening in nature where transformative energies (catalyzed by human industry) are erupting."[12] It is macaronic architecture, polyglot construction,[13] in which the bricks are the sinewy, pulsing life element.

FIGURE 1.1. Pieter Brueghel, The Tower of Babel, 1563. Oil on oakwood, 115 x 155 cm. Reprinted with permission of the Kunsthistorisches Museum, Vienna.

They seem to bleed out of the body of Babel, raw wounds in a building that may already be collapsing in on itself. Fire burned in bricks both becomes and forces that opening, and the structure of the Tower makes it appear as though the bricks are bursting forth from the earth, and only later (and only maybe) are tamed by the stone casing being quarried and sculpted around it.

The bricks are everywhere and insistently gathering: hundreds are shipped in on boats and rafts, hundreds more wait to be transported inside the tower to build it up further, hundreds are loaded onto carts that pass beneath a brick arch, while workers quarry the living rock and stone blocks tumble. In contrast to the orderly and measured architectural progress presented in contemporaneous depictions,[14] Brueghel's tower displays an edifice in fervent disarray, arguably of construction and deconstruction both. Do the workers already not understand each other anymore? Do the bricklayers and the masons and stonecutters already not speak the same language?

How to explain that the bricks are being walled up by stone? Detritus starts to overtake design: wooden scaffolding supporting stone arch waits to be fitted with interlocking stones, stairs start to appear out of the living rock, piles of rubble await, and, here the only one thus far but more will follow, an unorganized pile of bricks, some being moved in, but others already abandoned.

Brueghel's Vienna *Tower of Babel* prizes materiality: the multitude and array (and disarray) of bricks call forth their own representation, a prime example of what Bachelard calls "the fundamental influence on the life of the mind of certain meditations aroused by objects."[15] Fire makes things, and its possibilities as maker, its many ignitions, fuel the imagination. The eternal return to the Tower of Babel as object is consistently accompanied by a fascination with its materials and modes of construction. To paint or to write of Babel is to rebuild it, to meditate on methodical fire multiplied and formulated in bricks. Herodotus writes of digging moats, and cutting bricks, and baking in kilns, and growing numbers, of reeds and bitumen for sealing and stability, and royal cubits, and shifts in intervals.[16] His fascination brings him to the smallest unit operation of the edifice.[17] Flavius Josephus (37–ca. 100 CE), in the *Jewish Antiquities,* also provides method to the madness, citing bricks and mortar and bitumen and the "multitude of hands" that raised the tower faster than anyone expected (*Jewish Antiquities* I.4.3).[18] Once the fire in the kilns has been lit, production does not cease, and the tower rises with great speed.

The multiplicity of the bricks of Babel fascinates. They are both object and meditation, what Bachelard might identify as "the *contact* of the metaphor and the reality."[19] They are the things to which both archaeologists and artists hold themselves accountable. Archaeological work on the architectural structures of ancient Babylon has identified a mud brick core with a baked-brick mantle and stone reinforcements, and measured and extrapolated and estimated that between thirty-two and thirty-six million bricks were used in the main ziggurat of the city.[20] Infused in the building materials of the tower, fire remains present not only in defiance of the divine in its reach upward but also as defense to safeguard against divine wrath. The builders of Babel wished to keep from being "scattered abroad upon the face of the whole earth" (Genesis 11:4), as their Deluvian ancestors had been.

Josephus cites Nemrod, the grandson of Noah's son Ham, as the mastermind who has the tower built, not trusting God to not flood the world again. The fired bricks can be assembled ever higher but need to be assured by the tar-like sealant, bitumen, "that [the tower] might not be liable to admit water" (*Jewish Antiquities* I.4.3.).[21] Noah's progeny had reason to worry. Jeremiah prophesizes an elemental maelstrom for the end of Babel: fire and water both will overtake the city and its tower that God promises to make into "burned out mountain" (Jeremiah 51:35), covered by the roaring waves of the sea (42), to "sink to rise no more because of the disaster that I will bring on her" (64). Fire is the element that can strategize.

By the sixteenth century, the pursuits of Freemasons, Alchemists, and Humanists will have made of Babel a lost treasure-house of knowledge, whose recovery could lead humanity closer to the ultimate building project: a Jerusalem both allegorical and possible.[22] In these discourses, the bricks of Babel have a predecessor in one of the pillars of Seth, an earlier instance of bricking up knowledge reported by Josephus in the *Jewish Antiquities.* In Josephus's version of events, Adam warns his son about the world's future destruction, and Seth and his descendants seek to preserve not just their knowledge of how to work the earth but also how to reach the heavens.

> And that their inventions might not be lost before they were sufficiently known, upon Adam's prediction that the world was to be destroyed at one time by the force of fire, and at another time by the violence and quantity of water, they made two pillars, the one of brick, the other of stone; they inscribed their discoveries on them both, that in case the pillar of brick should be destroyed by the flood, the pillar of stone might remain and exhibit those discoveries to mankind, and also inform them that there was another pillar of brick erected by them. Now this remains in the land of Siriad to this day. (*Jewish Antiquities* I.3.69–70)

The brick pillar perishes in the Flood and, with the Tower of Babel, initiates what Myriam Jacquemier has called "an eternal return to the quest for human knowledge."[23] Bricks are a manufactured solidity; they make a fragile vitreous sound when they break.[24] The immigrants of Shinar and the descendants of Seth used bricks to embrace the lightness of being in the face of a ponderous God at times bent on their destruction.[25]

It is not so much their success or failure that should interest us, though the triumph and poignancy of both are palpable, but rather their *intention*. They are humanity's attempt to ward off destruction with fire before and after the flood. They were joined, in Gervase of Tilbury's (ca. 1150–ca. 1228) account, by Tubal, who wished to save his art of music and, prompted by the same fear of Adam's prophecy, also made a column of marble and one of brick.[26] It is a risky proposition, bringing inscription to fire, and using the materiality of the element to preserve the metaphors of knowledge. Fire's relationship to writing is problematic, as the singed edges of the Beowulf manuscript remind us. Bricks and pillars are the ultimately fragile remnants of the pyromena of knowledge.

As we turn to leave the Tower of Babel, we might join those who do the same within Brueghel's painting, those workers at the upper right edge of the tower who have stopped working and are looking out to sea, hypnotized no longer by fire but by a water reverie instead, leaving open the brickwork that waits to interlock with a future wall. Fire remains forever immanent in the abandoned bricks of Babel, in the kinetic energy of the structure that could always come together.

Prince Rupert's Drops

Glass is made within the "pyrotechnic paradigm" identified by Stephen J. Pyne that begins with a cooking fire and domesticates fire to human use.[27] But fire's domestication simultaneously tamed the human species: it made us tenders of flames and pyro-technicians; it made us marvel more closely at the element.[28] The paradox of the pyrotechnic paradigm is that under human sway, fire's operations became both more useful and more mysterious. Emilie du Châtelet marveled at the ability of rocks, "bodies that have the coldest appearance," to produce hot, violent fire when struck together.[29] The cooking fire can both nourish and burn, that in the foundry can produce or explode. In his treatise *Pirotechnia* (1540), the Sienese metallurgist and metalsmith Vannoccio Biringuccio (1480–ca. 1539) identifies glass as "one of the effects and peculiar fruits of the art of fire," a mystifying result of fire's fecundity. Glass is fire beyond human perception: to make glass, fire must rouse itself to around 2,700 degrees Fahrenheit (1,482 Celsius). It must melt sand into glass and provoke a manifest metamorphosis. Glass's identification as an "amorphous solid" indicates its paradox as "fusible material that is almost made mineral by art and by the power and virtue of fire."[30] Men have dreamed of unbreakable glass. One claimed to be able to make it, but emperor Tiberius had him killed because, writes Biringuccio in telling us Petronius's tale from the *Satyricon,* if glass were unbreakable, "it would be a thing to esteem . . . more than any metal, even gold."[31] In the age of alchemy, fire and human obsession would once again vie to make glass unbreakable.

Prince Rupert's Drops are tear-shaped glass drops that are unbreakable at the head, but will shatter explosively if even lightly touched at the tail (Figure 1.2). They are one of the first scientific puzzles the British Royal Society tried to solve.[32] Prince Rupert's Drops are fire extracted from usefulness and thrown into play. They are fire's playthings, fire's paradox: they are fire *as* paradox, and fire's paradox becomes that of its pyromena. This paradox of strength and fragility began in the 1550s, when glassmakers let dollops of molten glass fall into buckets of cold water and pulled out the tear-drop shapes. These were called *lacrymae Batavicae,* Holland tears, before the German-English Prince Rupert made them famous by giving them to his cousin King Charles II for the examination of the new Royal Society in 1661.[33] The thrill was in being able to touch what had just been engulfed in flames and cooled by water. The elemental mystery is in what fire and water can make. The scientific puzzle lay in the fate of the glass drop to human touch. How can the same substance simultaneously create an impenetrable solid and a volatile shattering?

Treasured objects of experimental philosophy, Prince Rupert's Drops became an obsession at the Royal Society and among science enthusiasts in general.[34] They displayed the wonder of the pyromena of glass and marked some of the earliest inquiries into the phenomenon of fire. Margaret Cavendish (1623–73) and Christian Huygens (1629–95) began a correspondence in 1657 about a few Prince Rupert's Drops that he had sent her.[35] Her examination led her to conclude that a "Licquer" ("a fluid, sulphurous substance")[36] emerged in the glass's transition from fire to water (what we have now identified as air bubbles within the glass). The paradox of Prince

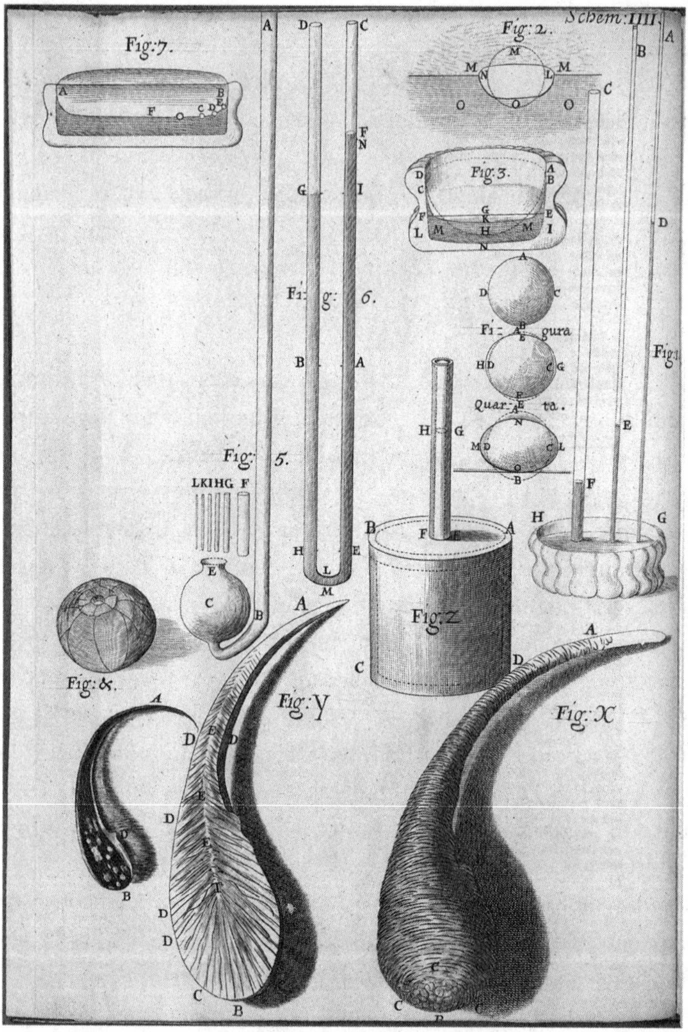

FIGURE 1.2. Robert Hooke, Scheme IIII [IV], third plate, Micrographia: Or Some Physiological Descriptions of Minute Bodies Made by Magnifying Glasses. With Observations and Inquiries thereupon (London: printed by Jo. Martyn and Ja. Allestry, printers to the Royal Society, 1665). Engraving. 29.8 × 20.5 cm. The Fine Arts Museums of San Francisco, museum purchase, The Herman Michels Collection, bequest of Vera Michels, 1993.1.3. Reprinted with permission of the Fine Arts Museums of San Francisco.

Rupert's Drops was so insistent as to make fire itself a liquid. Fire's unpredictability, its constant reminder that its domestication is predicated upon human vigilance but might still escape human understanding, is also manifest in the drops. Cavendish, Huygens, and other students of the drops remark upon the shock of the glass explosion, the violence of the paradox.

The paradox has since been resolved: it is a matter of competition between solid, molten, and cooling glass—fire in three different stages of immanence. The drops explode because of a combination of surface compression and core tension. The molten glass inside the drop is locked in by the solid and cooling glass on its outside, as this forms on impact with water. The cooling glass pulls in against itself, causing it to be in extremely high compressive tension pressing in from the outside; the molten glass at the center of the drop, meanwhile, is still expanding, causing intense tensile stress as it expands from the inside.[37] At its thickest part the compressive and tensile tensions work together in opposition—this is often likened to the oppositional forces that come together for the strength of an arch.[38] At its thinnest part, the tail, the tension still exists but could now be broken much more easily. Because the tensions are so high throughout, even one break in the link would cause the disintegration of all links. One touch at the tail, and the Prince Rupert's Drop instantaneously explodes *and* disintegrates into powder: the glass flies apart on its own energy.

This is fire resisting containment: kinetic energy unleashed, traded objects of desire between emerging natural philosophers, and fueling obsession. Prince Rupert himself set up a forge at Windsor Castle so that he could make drop upon drop, revisiting the volatility and paradox of fire within his reach.[39] Samuel Butler (1613–80) satirized the obsession for Prince Rupert's Drops in teasing lines from his massive poem *Hubridas* of 1663–78:

> Honour is like that glassy bubble
> That finds philosophers such trouble
> Whose least part crack'd, the whole does fly
> And wits are cracked, to find out why.[40]

Fire contained can addle the brain. And so, on to fevered minds.

Flash Point: Charles VI, the Bal des Ardents, and the Glass Delusion

As Jane Bennett has identified hoarders as "differently-abled bodies that might have special sensory access to the call of things,"[41] I would like to consider medieval pyromaniacs, or pyrophiliacs, whose passions resulted in their *embodying* it within themselves, as having "special access" to the transfigurations of fire. Their fires burn within. They are, in Bachelard's words, "the problem [that] lies in the *contact* of the metaphor and the reality."[42] Pyrophiliacs collapse the metaphors and realities of fire into their own tormented minds and bodies, and perceive the transformative, purgative power of fire most acutely. In them, fire is revelatory, fusing perceptions of self and element. In them, and in us for that matter, materiality and metaphor collapse to create what Lowell Duckert has termed "matterphor."[43] Our very thoughts are matterphors, the material reality of *firing* synapses sublimating into metaphors of thought and language. "If fire, which, after all, is quite an exceptional and rare phenomenon, was taken to be a constituent element of the Universe," asks Bachelard, "is it not because it is an element of human thought?"[44] Our passions are matterphors, ignited by music or poetry or others, pumping our blood and warming our faces, our necks tingling with fervent realizations. In the perceptual shift enacted in Cary Wolfe's "Learning from Temple Grandin,"[45] I propose that we learn from Charles VI (1368–1422) that we strive to understand the extreme end of the spectrum of matterphor that he inhabited. He exists, in both history and the imagination, as a provocative hybrid of person and object: a man who believed he was made entirely of glass. In this chapter, he bears the task of bridging those pyromena we dub things and those we dub humans.

Fire came upon the French king Charles VI throughout his life. A first violent, panicked attack came upon him on a day in August 1392 as he and his retinue were making their way to Brittany under a sun that was "dazzlingly bright, blazing down in full strength," reports Froissart. "Its beams shone with such force that they penetrated everything."[46] To bring the young king out of his ensuing melancholy, his physicians recommended amusements and distractions. A night of revelry and masquerade on January 28, 1393, saw the king and five companions dressed as Wild Men, their linen vestments lined with bitumen pitch to hold strands of flax that flapped crazily about.[47] It was the flax that caught fire first, either from a dropped torch or from Duke Louis d'Anjou's curiosity to know the real identity of the Wild Men by flashing a flame near their masked faces. The poetry and lyric form assigned to the tragedy has named the evening the Bal des Ardents but four of the men died while the Duchess of Berry put out the fire on Charles VI with her gowns, and the other remaining companion dived into a wine barrel.[48] The king's "melancholy" increased after that night, his manic and catatonic states distancing him from his rule. And then he started to believe that he was made of glass.

The glass delusion is one of the most historically precise of perceptual disorders, identified from the fourteenth century, with Charles VI's case, onward to the late eighteenth century, never crossing over into the modern age, always remaining a pre-Industrial psychosis.[49] Charles could not let anyone touch him when he perceived himself as glass. His entire body was glass, fused and brittle, fired into a whole that could shatter everywhere. Some "Glass Men," as they were called, perceived only a limb or a part of their body as being made of glass, protecting it, wrapping it in blankets. Was it their knowledge of their own made-ness, of their easily destroyed manufacture, that terrified them? A pristine realization of self as object, flesh and bone fused into excruciating crystal clarity? Doing away with the illusion of an organic and emerging self and acknowledging that humans are fire's made things?

Constantijn Huygens (1596–1687), father of the scientist Christian Huygens, who corresponded with Margaret Cavendish about shattering Prince Rupert's Drops, gave several lines of his satirical poem "Costly Folly" of 1622, targeting decadence, to sufferers of the glass delusion. The beauty of glass, its resplendence, its shimmering, and its fragility, mark it as decadent, and blame those who see themselves as glass as debauched and excessive objects.

> Here's one fears everything that moves in his vicinity.
> What's wrong? Well everywhere he's touched is made of glass, you see;
> The chairs will be the death of him, he trembles at the bed
> Fearful the one will break his bum, the other smash his head
> Now it's a kiss appalls him, now a flicked finger shocks.
> Just as a ship that's gone off course sails fearful of the rocks.[50]

Moving between their reality and others' metaphors, the Glass Men of medieval and early modern Europe lived in impossible bodies fused by fire, perceived as decadence. Their embodiment of fire in its manufacture of beautiful things reveals Bachelard's claim that "like any form of wealth, fire is dreamed of in its concentrated form."[51]

Richard Rolle

Are the imaginary effects of fire as much a part of the ontology of the element as its real actions? Can we come to know fire's being through its manifestations in metaphor as well as matter? Might we keep looking for the collapse of the two, for further matterphors? It may be that "fires within" reveal as much about the element as exposed fire. Bachelard elaborates a "theory of fire immanent in matter" that pertains to those inner fires that burn outside of physical reality but deep enough within the imagination to feel real. The fire that fused the limbs of Charles VI into brittle breakage was physically impossible but psychically real to him. A kindred spirit, the hermit Richard Rolle (1290/1300–1349), would be adamant about the heat of the fire that burned divine love into him. These are strange fires, caught between reality and representation, but Bachelard creates an interpretive space for them:

> The theory of this fire, immanent in matter, leads to a special form of materialism for which a word would have to be created, for it represents an important refinement of philosophical opinion, indeterminate between materialism and animism. This *calorism* corresponds to the materialization of a soul or the animation of matter; it is a transition between matter and life.[52]

For Richard Rolle, the human soul framed by the sensations of the human body will be that matter. Once felt by the body, fire quickens the transition between a dormant soul and one lit by divine love. Calorism is then fire's ability to warm and transform; it is a state in fire's fluctuating ontology that calls for attention to the transformative capacity of the element, one that permeates *materia* and *anima.* Fire radiates throughout Rolle's body, fusing with it and fusing his soul to God. As he writes about the real presence of fire to awaken it in his readers,[53] he articulates what Stacy Alaimo has called "the self of the material memoir."[54] Alaimo's analysis of the material memoir occurs within the contemporary discourses of science and environmental justice and addresses biographical writings whose personal accounts project scientific findings into vivid relief. Rolle's *Incendium Amoris (The Fire of Love)* as material memoir shifts the conversation into the discourse of mysticism but maintains the critical edge that Alaimo discusses.[55] The hermit is impatient with the world, its arid busyness, its lack of obligation to the time and pace of fire, and to the spirituality of material transformation that, for him, fire sets alight. His material memoir gathers insistently around the materiality of fire: his fusing with fire, and fire's fusing with him, create "a self that is coextensive with the environment, trans-corporeal, and posthumanist."[56] Rolle's connection with fire begins with its operations in the lived environment. These permeate his body in real and immediate sensations, and result in a soul "purged by sacred fire," a self no longer singularly operative in the world but loosened from the binds of individuality in a sought-after "perfect union with God."[57]

The Fire of Love blends a series of words for the calorism Rolle experiences: fire *(igne, incendium),* warmth *(calor),* burning *(fervor).* Fire slips through many words and forms in Rolle's mystic progression and can never be isolated: from the first line of the treatise, fire is incorporated.[58]

> I cannot tell you how surprised I was the first time I felt my heart begin to warm. It was real warmth, too, not imaginary, and it felt as if it were actually on fire. I was astonished at the way the heat surged up, and how this new sensation brought great and unexpected comfort.[59]

His insistence on the reality of his fire prioritizes what Nicholas Watson has called "the authority of experience."[60] Rolle's spiritual knowledge is gleaned from the events of his lived experience as well as from his deep study of scripture. His sensation of the fire drives his wonder and curiosity: he feels the fire in his heart, and holds fast to its realism, its real presence; he reassures himself that there is no external cause, touching his chest, assuring his readers the fire is both real *and* divine. The fire is instantly beautiful to him: delight and longing follow rapidly, and Rolle is sure he is in the presence of the divine.

The elements gain an aesthetic dimension through human sensation. Mary Carruthers has recently argued that "medieval aesthetic experience is bound in human sensation" and "human knowledge is sense-derived, the agents of which are all corporeal."[61] Throughout his text, Rolle describes the fire as beautiful, bountiful, and even sweet. The realism of the fire begins to get bound up in its aesthetics. Deep into his treatise, he recounts the tale of the fire's ignition once again: "It was just over nine months before a conscious and incredibly sweet warmth kindled me."[62] His bodily experience makes the fire vivid and immediate and physically possible, and simultaneously begins to reshape it within an aesthetics of beauty and sweetness.

The spreading warmth of the fire is additionally modeled on the connection between fire and love in Song of Songs 8:6: "for love burns like blazing fire, like a mighty flame."[63] Rolle's insistence on the fire's realism renders intertextuality a transcorporeality. The fire he feels is the fire of love of the Song of Songs, transmuted through devotional reading and desire.[64] The originary moment of this fire becomes more ambiguous. Did the fire start in Rolle's heart, or was Rolle's heart kindled by a spark from the never-quite-extinguished fire of love of the Song of Songs? Among the words and sensations of the erotic-spiritual poetry of the Song of Songs and the metaphoric-material manifestations of fire, Rolle's writings create a "contact zone," in Alaimo's words, "between human corporeality and more-than-human nature."[65] The Song of Song's rich material imagery conjures up lush pomegranates, leaping gazelles, strapping cedars, dripping myrrh, and dancing fire. Rolle uses it to expand the contact zone between his body and fire to allow for the transformation of both.

Fire embodies a metamorphic multiplicity: its manifestations are flame, ember, coal, ash, smoke; its states of being include ignition, conflagration, smoldering, and dying; its effects are light, warmth, and pleasure.[66] For Rolle, fire's ability to be multiple things in transformative succession leads to the spiritual progression of *fervor—canor—dulcor:* warmth and song and sweetness.[67] Like fire, song is both actual and mystical: "I knew the infusion and understanding of heavenly, spiritual sounds, sounds which pertain to the song of eternal praise."[68] Are song and sweetness fire's transcendence? Do they sublimate fire into its divine form? Rolle will conflate (and conflagrate?) the agency of metamorphosis: at times, fire and song will lead to sweetness, at others fire and sweetness become song.[69] "Sweet warmth," "sweet harmony," and "ardent sweetness" are all merged. Carruthers signals the ability of sweetness, as both goal and agent of transformation, to unite disparate elements.[70] Its sensation is itself a combination of desire and taste. For Rolle, it will characterize mortal man's yearning "to breathe his soul out . . . in this honeyed flame" of the fire of love.[71] This is fire as sensual substance, as materialization of the spiritual, as real presence, with a longing for release from a fallen world—for fire to carry the spirit to a perfect place in an ecstatic apocalypse.

Empedocles

Fire oscillates between concept and event with Empedocles (ca. 495–435 BCE). The poetic fragments of his philosophy were reassembled into collections in the late Middle Ages and lent inspiration to emerging theories of origins and evolutions.[72] Simultaneously, the legend of his death, willed by leaping into the mouth of the volcano on Mount Etna, was graphically represented in multiple manuscripts of the *Roman de la Rose:* two fires, then, that burn hotly.[73] I will attempt neither to reconcile them nor to keep them in distinct spheres of metaphor and reality. The brutality of the death of Empedocles quickens his philosophy and forces a realization of the all-consuming, all-explaining character of the idea of just four elements. The poetic fragments that make up *On Nature* and *The Purifications* formulate a crucial moment in the history of elemental ecocriticism: they isolate and prize these four elements of fire, water, earth, and air that Western culture will come to see as constitutive of every thing for hundreds of years. It did not have to be this way, it did not have to be these four: Chinese cosmology, for example, announces five elements—water, fire, wood, metal, and earth—as fundamental and formative elements.[74] Powerful and long-lasting material and humoral realities were established in the West with the elevation of the four elements: they have intermixed into endless combinations, entertained then eventually dismissed possible fifth elements, and held creation firm until the atomic age.

As the author of the poetic cosmology of Love and Strife, Empedocles activated the four elements of water, air, earth, and fire to exist between the powerful pulls of coalescence (Love) and separation (Strife).[75] Being (and reality) are not assured but in constant wondrous flux. In this cosmology, fire is granted a formative role in all existence. It gathers fiercely only to collapse into a singular, brutal event with the philosopher's death at Mount Etna. The challenge is not to let that very real and present fire recede into allegory, but to keep fire's realism active within its cosmological operations. In the words of the poet Horace Gregory, it is to be, like Empedocles, unable to "unkindle fire."[76]

All creatures are born from and borne by fire, sings Empedocles. In Fragment 67/62 from *On Nature,* fire is the shaper of life. Through its intensity and its intention to surge upward, it forms life and projects it into the world.

> First there came up from the earth whole-natured outlines,
> Having a share of both water and heat;
> Fire sent them up, wanting to reach its like,
> And they did not yet show any lovely frame of limbs,
> Nor voice nor again the limb specific to men.[77]

Fire generates humanity before it can regenerate itself. This is no Genesis story of a world neatly divided into spheres and of bodies fully formed by divine will. Rather, it is an amalgam of desire, of bodies coming-into-being *amid yearning.* Bodies are made of a fire that strives ever upward. Before they are shape, before they are will, before they can assure their own existence, bodies rush and heave with the movement of fire. They are caught up in fire's desire to gather itself until itself. Or rather, fire's desire to engulf and perpetuate births their own. The will of fire burns brightly here: it is a creative force with no boundary or limitation save its own reach. The fire of Empedocles is willful; it has *phronesis* (intent) and *noma* (thought).[78] It seeks its own in the heavens, girding this world and imbuing it with dynamic energy. It has direction and volition, an elemental will to gather and surge.

Empedocles assembled the four elements as perpetually formative of all energy, denying the linearity of life and death, and seeing a world of "mingling only" (Fragment 21/8), a great and eternal coalescence quickened by fire. There is "only mixture and interchange of what is mixed."[79] In the perpetual struggle between Love and Strife that Empedocles names as the tension of existence,[80] fire is the force that assembles and joins. In the elemental assemblage of Love, all is "only mixture and interchange of what is mixed."[81] The perpetuity of mixture and interchange is what Bachelard isolates as unnerving about both Empedocles and his cosmology. We can reconcile ourselves to his cosmology by seeing it in terms of the dynamic between Love and Strife, but the philosopher's death blends and mixes reality and representation to the point of confusion. What is real fire, and what is metaphorical fire in the leap from Mount Etna?

Bachelard works out his thoughts on Empedocles in his unfinished book *Fragments of a Poetics of Fire.*[82] The ancient philosopher's elemental cosmology, as carefully articulated and dynamic a system as it was, falls short of explaining both the ferocity of fire's destruction and the wild gesture of the leap into the volcano. The confrontation between human and element leaves Bachelard asking: "Is the Act of Supreme Will on the Summit of the Mountain of Fire human circumstance or cosmic event?"[83] It pushes him to ask, "What does the volcano want?" and to pursue fire's desire. Bachelard turns the agency from the human to the element: "The Volcano has in mind more than just a victim, more than simply any human sacrifice whatever. The Volcano wants Empedocles."[84] The reach and unpredictability, and I would add the brutality, of that desire unsettles the modern scholars who have tried to represent and understand the death of Empedocles. Friedrich Hölderin (1770–1843) wrote three versions of *The Death of Empedocles,*[85] and Matthew Arnold (1822–88) wished for the destruction of his *Empedocles on Etna* after only fifty copies had been sold.[86] The death of Empedocles in the volcano defies the logic of the human in direct confrontation with the elemental. Perhaps we cannot bear to be in the full presence of any element.

The death of Empedocles in the volcano has never been easy. Diogenes Laertius struggles through several death narratives in his third-century biography of the philosopher,[87] but it is the leap into the fire that will prevail: "He set out on his way to Etna; then, when he had reached it, he plunged into the fiery craters and disappeared."[88] His motivation is multiple and ambiguous: to confirm for himself that he had become a god, or to prove to an assembly that he was a god. They simultaneously demand and defy explanation. The philosopher's death irks Nature in the *Roman de la Rose,* and she cites him in her confession and complaint to Genius.

> Empedocles took poor care of himself. He looked in his books so long and loved philosophy so much, full, perhaps, of melancholy, that he never feared death but threw himself alive into the fire. With feet joined he jumped into Etna in order to show that those who want to fear death are indeed of weak mind. Therefore he wanted to throw himself in voluntarily. He valued neither honey nor sugar but chose his own sepulcher there among the boiling sulfur. (ll. 17,039–51)[89]

The philosopher's death is intimately tied to his philosophy:[90] the compiler of elements "drank fire from immortal bowls."[91] He meets his end in direct and absolute confrontation with the element that engulfs, with the element that can overtake and with which he can fuse perfectly. As a reality, it angers Nature; as an image of troubled authorial agency, it moves Bachelard; as a metaphor or allegory of death, it is rendered insistently symbolic.[92]

Medieval images of Empedocles in the *Roman de la Rose* manuscripts dispense with the volcano altogether, and reveal Empedocles framed by flames or about to leap into fire itself. They concentrate the scene on its human and elemental confrontation, creating an almost meditative framework: Empedocles stands still in the fire, the fire arranging itself around his body. Both rely on mimetic representation, the philosopher clad in robes, the fire curving upward in tongues of red. But this scene is abstracted, absurd, some extreme distant version of Bachelard's reverie into the fire. It can't be a man standing in fire; it has to be something else. Empedocles's death pushes fire from the real to the metaphorical: from flame to inspiration, from ember to allegory. It's as though the element becomes more restless, unable to stay in the realm of the real for too long, or perhaps it becomes impatient with our desire to separate metaphor and materiality, and fuses the two.

Michel Serres strives for a simultaneity of the real and the revelatory, of "science and sapience." His meditation on "Three Volcanoes" from *Biogea* traces the forms of fire through the young Italian physicist Ettore Majorna's disappearance in 1938 (the dangers of possible [nuclear] fire);

the third-century BCE mathematician Archimedes and his invention of the parabolic mirror (fire at a distance); and Empedocles (fire up close).[93] By the end, he is walking with Empedocles over the rough terrain of Mount Etna; by the end, "I want to speak like him, at the global dimensions of the world in which we live and think like guests."[94] The inhospitable and shifting ground of the volcano becomes a place to realize the expanse of fire, one so vast as to encompass any contradictions of Love and Strife, warmth and danger, and to render human rationalizations out of place. Finally, Empedocles listens and the immediacy and volatility of the volcano's fire leaves Serres asking:

> How to speak in this voice? How to speak in several voices, that of things, that of knowledge, of emotions, of each and everyone, that of humanity?[95]

Conclusion

Fire, where we find it, never really stands still—it skirts the edges of Eden, makes bricks, glides into glass, fevers minds, sparks philosophy. Fire, when we find it, is always after origins—in being a post-Edenic, post-Creation, mid-Paleozoic element it can be sought and found in what has changed, in what has been wrought, in what will be made through it. I would argue that it is fire that has made humanity. We are its creatures, the only species to use it, and when we do, we mediate its desires for heat and calorism, transformation and change. Fire's restlessness emerges from its having no fixed place: no seat in Eden, no primordial presence. Of that stretch of time in fire's existence between the Devonian Age and the first time *homo erectus* made fire, around four hundred million years later, Pyne writes, "What life [and here he means nonhuman life] could not supply . . . was ignition."[96] Humanity is a more reliable source of ignition than lightning is, and we might think that we control fire in igniting it, but it is fire that allowed *homo erectus* to sleep safely at night on the ground; it is fire that cooked the food that nourished and developed our outrageous brains; and it is fire that made us human. In our intertwined ontologies we collapse materiality and metaphor: we are fiery, and fires die. We can understand these fusions and confusions when we see the bricks of Babel remain as relics of the architecture of a common language; when we see glass mediate impossible truths of immanent matter; and when we grant that pyrophiliacs feel the objecthood and artistry of being made by fire. We can realize it: we are pyromena—we are fire's doing.

Notes

1. Stephen J. Pyne, *Fire: Nature and Culture* (London: Reaktion Books, 2012), 15.

2. An overview of "The Cycle's Suite," as he calls it, can be found on Pyne's website at http://www.stephenpyne.com/cycle_of_fire___and_more_92910.htm.

3. Pliny the Elder, *Natural History: A Selection,* trans. John F. Healy (New York: Penguin Books, 1991), 363.

4. David Macauley, *Elemental Philosophy: Earth, Air, Fire, and Water as Environmental Ideas* (Albany, N.Y.: State University of New York Press, 2010), 108.

5. Gilles Deleuze and Félix Guattari, *A Thousand Plateaus,* trans. Brian Massumi (Minneapolis: University of Minnesota Press, 1987), 3–25. The operations of rhizomes are exploited by Macauley to use Empedocles to move "from a form of philosophical essentialism and toward a pragmatic environmentalism." David Macauley, "The Flowering of Environmental Roots and the Four Elements in Presocratic Philosophy: From Empedocles to Deleuze and Guattari," *Worldviews* 9, no. 3 (2005): 306.

6. Deleuze and Guattari, *A Thousand Plateaus,* 10.

7. Gaston Bachelard, *The Psychoanalysis of Fire,* trans. Alan C. M. Ross (Boston: Beacon Press, 1963), 3.

8. A. R. George, "The Tower of Babel: Archaeology, History and Cuneiform Texts," *Archiv für Orientforschung* 51 (2005/6): 83, provides a modern translation of the full royal inscription.

9. James W. P. Campbell, *Brick: A World History* (London: Thames and Hudson, 2003), 14–16, and "The Fired Brick in Mesopotamia," 30–35.

10. Babel's antithesis, as Lowell Duckert has provoked me to think in private communication, can be found in the flaming tongues of Pentecost, where language is made clear. Pentecostal fire is ecstatic, experienced by the most fervent religious bodies; it is a material metaphor—invisible to material investigation but an immediate means of communicating religious experience. Babel's fire, by contrast, or better yet, as antithesis, is strategic, put into action by the most ambitious of political bodies.

11. Brueghel painted three versions of the Tower of Babel: that in Vienna in 1563, an unsigned and undated version now in the Museums Boymans-van Beuningen in Rotterdam, and a lost version on ivory panel.

12. Edward Snow, "The Language of Contradiction in Bruegel's 'Tower of Babel,'" *RES: Anthropology and Aesthetics* 5 (Spring 1983): 40.

13. S. A. Mansbach, "Pieter Brueghel's Towers of Babel," *Zeitschrift für Kunstgeschichte* 45, no. 1 (1982): 43–56, argues that Brueghel was responding to the humanist

Plantin's polyglot Bible made up of Hebrew, Aramaic, Syriac, Greek, and Latin texts, denounced to the Spanish Inquisition to which all of Flanders, and Antwerp humanists especially, were accountable under the reign of Philip II, king of Spain.

14. The Grimany Breviary (Cod. Marc. Lat. I, 99, fol. 206r., Biblioteca Nazionale Marciana, Venice), for example, depicts the Tower of Babel as a steadily tapering structure girded by a ramp along which workers bring supplies in measured progression. For further contemporaneous comparisons and a discussion of the simultaneity of quarrying and construction, see Margaret D. Carroll, "The Conceits of Empire," in *Painting and Politics in Northern Europe* (University Park: Pennsylvania University Press, 2008), 64–87.

15. Bachelard, *The Psychoanalysis of Fire,* 102.

16. Herodotus, *Histories,* trans. Aubrey de Sélincourt, rev. John Marincola (New York: Penguin, 2003), 78–79 (Book 1, chaps. 178–79).

17. John MacGinnis, "Herodotus' Description of Babylon," *Bulletin of the Institute of Classical Studies of the University of London* 33, no. 1 (1986): 67–86, catalogues all of the physical details that Herodotus describes, including a meticulous account of brick-making. McGinnis concludes that the level of detail and accuracy of Herodotus's descriptions indicates his presence in Babylon, but the matter remains a subject of debate.

18. Josephus, *Jewish Antiquities,* in *The Complete Works,* trans. William Whiston (Nashville: Thomas Nelson, 1998), 40.

19. Bachelard, *The Psychoanalysis of Fire,* 102.

20. George, "The Tower of Babel," 83.

21. George A. Barton, "On Binding-Reeds, Bitumen, and Other Commodities in Ancient Babylonia," *Journal of the American Oriental Society* 46 (1926): 297–302, cites multiple water-proofing uses of bitumen. Nabopolassar boasts of having "the River Arahtu bear asphalt and bitumen like a mighty flood." George, "The Tower of Babel," 84.

22. Myriam Jacquemier, "Le mythe de Babel et la Kabbale chrétienne au XVIe siècle," *Nouvelle Revue du XVIe Siècle* 10 (1992): 51–67.

23. Myriam Jacquemier, "Babel dans la tradition scientifique," *Nouvelle Revue du XVIe Siècle* 14, no. 1 (1996): 75.

24. The etymology of the word *brick* itself is related to the verb *to break.*

25. Nemrod is a pivotal figure between these two populations, worthy of further exploration: both a descendant of Seth and an immigrant to Shinar, he is at once the mastermind of the Tower of Babel, and reputed to be an astronomer. Charles Haskins, "Nemrod the Astronomer," *Romanic Review* 5, no. 3 (1914): 203–12, traces this characterization of the ancient king in the twelfth-century Anglo-Norman text *Li cumpoz* by Philippe de Thaon.

26. Gervase of Tilbury, *Otia Imperialia,* trans. S. E. Banks and J. W. Binns (Oxford: Oxford University Press, 2002), 106–7 (1.20).

27. Stephen J. Pyne, *Vestal Fire: An Environmental History* (Seattle: University of Washington Press, 1997), 42–43.

28. Richard Wangrahm, *How Cooking Made Us Human* (New York: Basic Books, 2009), 185.

29. Bachelard, *The Psychoanalysis of Fire,* 27.

30. Vannoccio Biringuccio, *Pirotechnia,* trans. Cyril Stanley Smith and Martha Tech Gnudi (Cambridge, Mass.: MIT Press, 1966), 126. With many thanks to Professor David Harvey for introducing me to this text.

31. Ibid., 127.

32. Laurel Brodsley, Charles Frank, and John W. Steeds, "Prince Rupert's Drops," *Notes and Records of the Royal Society of London* 41, no. 1 (October 1986): 1–26.

33. For a recent biography of Prince Rupert, see Charles Spencer, *Prince Rupert: The Last Cavalier* (London: Widenfeld and Nicolson, 2007).

34. Brodsley, Frank, and Steeds, "Prince Rupert's Drops," cite multiple "drop-breaking" experiments in domestic laboratories and at dinner parties. A late seventeenth-century ballad describes a drop's explosion at the slightest touch of its tail: "How this was donne by soe small Force / Did cost the Colledg a Month's discourse" (13).

35. Nadinne Akkerman, "Mad Science beyond Flattery: The Correspondence of Margaret Cavendish and Constantijn Huygens," *Early Modern Literary Studies* 14 (May 2004): 1–21.

36. Ibid., 9.

37. These are the terms used to explain the phenomenon of Prince Rupert's Drops in both of the following videos, available online from the blog *Smarter Every Day* at http://www.youtube.com/watch?v=xe-f4gokRBs and the website of the Corning Museum of Glass, http://www.cmog.org/video/prince-ruperts-drop.

38. Brodsley, Frank, and Steeds, "Prince Rupert's Drops." Hooke, one of the earliest to record the phenomenon of Prince Rupert's Drops in his *Micrographia* of 1665, made the comparison.

39. Kenneth Dewhurst, "Prince Rupert as Scientist," *The British Journal for the History of Science* 1, no. 4 (December 1963): 367.

40. Brodsley, Frank, and Steeds, "Prince Rupert's Drops," 4.

41. Jane Bennett, "Power of the Hoard: Further Notes on Material Agency," in *Animal, Mineral, Vegetable: Ethics and Objects,* ed. Jeffrey Jerome Cohen (Washington, D.C.: Oliphaunt Books, 2012), 244.

42. Bachelard, *The Psychoanalysis of Fire,* 102.

43. The marvelous term "matterphor" was brought forth by Lowell Duckert during discussion at the Elemental Ecocriticism Symposium at the University of Alabama in April 2013. See section 3 in the introduction to this volume for a brief explanation of the term.

44. Bachelard, *The Psychoanalysis of Fire,* 18.

45. Cary Wolfe, "Learning from Temple Grandin," in *What Is Posthumanism?* (Minneapolis: University of Minnesota Press, 2010), 127–42. In his critique of liberal humanism's dependence on normative subjectivity, Wolfe seeks "new lines of

empathy, affinity, and respect between different forms of life, both human and nonhuman" (127).

46. Jean Froissart, *Chronicles,* trans. Geoffroy Brereton (New York: Penguin, 1978), 393.

47. Pierre Gascar, *Charles VI: Le Bal des Ardents* (Paris: Gallimard, 1977), provides the fullest account of the Bal des Ardents and its consequences in the French court.

48. A vivid modern retelling of the event is "Hop-Frog" by Edgar Allan Poe, in *Edgar Allan Poe's Tales of Mystery and Imagination* (London: J. M. Dent and Sons, 1912).

49. Gill Speak, "An Odd Kind of Melancholy: Reflections on the Glass Delusion in Europe (1440–1680)," *History of Psychiatry* 1, no. 2 (1990): 191–206.

50. Constantijn Huygens, "Costly Folly," quoted in Gill Speak, "'El licenciado Vidriera' and the Glass Men of Early Modern Europe," *The Modern Language Review* 85, no. 4 (October 1990): 850.

51. Bachelard, *The Psychoanalysis of Fire,* 49.

52. Ibid., 75.

53. Lisa Manter, "Rolle Playing: 'And the Word Became Flesh,'" in *The Vernacular Spirit: Essays on Medieval Religious Literature,* ed. Renate Blumenfeld-Kosinski (New York: Palgrave, 2002), 1–14. Within the context of Rolle's meditations, Manter argues that his reader "will find herself meditating on Rolle's own mystical path" (27).

54. Stacy Alaimo, *Bodily Natures: Science, Environment, and the Material Self* (Bloomington: Indiana University Press, 2010), 89.

55. *The Incendium Amoris of Richard Rolle of Hampole,* ed. Margeret Deanesly (Manchester: Manchester University Press, 1915).

56. Alaimo, *Bodily Natures,* 89.

57. Richard Rolle, *The Fire of Love,* trans. Clifton Wolters (New York: Penguin Books, 1972), 184. Rolle will repeat this posthumanist hope of the dissolved and absolved self throughout the treatise: "when the fire of the Holy Spirit really gets hold of the heart it sets it wholly on fire, and . . . turns it into flame, leading it into that state in which it is most like God" (101).

58. For discussions of Rolle's embodiment of fire, see John C. Hirsh, "The Liberation of Mysticism: A Reflection on Richard Rolle," in *The Boundaries of Faith: The Development and Transmission of Medieval Spirituality* (Leiden: Brill, 1996), 111–23; Karen Armstrong, "Richard Rolle of Hampole, *The Fire of Love,*" in *Visions of God: Four Medieval Mystics and their Writings* (New York: Bantam Books, 1994), 2–9; and Robert Boenig, "Contemplations of the Dread and Love of God, Richard Rolle, and Alered of Rievaulx," *Mystics Quarterly* 16, no. 1 (March 1990): 27–33, which traces the amplification of Rolle's *Incendium Amoris* in *Fervor Amoris* (as the "Contemplations" treatise was sometimes known).

59. Rolle, *The Fire of Love,* 45.

60. Nicholas Watson, "Translation and Self-Canonization in Richard Rolle's *Melos Amoris*," in *The Medieval Translator: The Theory and Practice of Translation in the Middle Ages*, ed. Roger Ellis (Cambridge: Brewer, 1989), 168.

61. Mary Carruthers, *The Experience of Beauty in the Middle Ages* (Oxford: Oxford University Press, 2013), 8.

62. Rolle, *The Fire of Love*, 93.

63. Annie Sutherland, "Biblical Text and Spiritual Experience in the English Epistles of Richard Rolle," *The Review of English Studies* 56, no. 227 (November 2005): 702.

64. Rosamund S. Allen, "Tactile and Kinasthetic Imagery in Richard Rolle's Works," *Mystics Quarterly* 13, no. 1 (March 1987): 12–18. For Allen, devotional reading involves Rolle in the movements and texture of the Song of Songs and infuses his writings with imagery of "the sitter, the runner, the lover, or the pilgrim" (17). In contrast to Allen's kinesthetic argument, Christopher Roman, "Opening the Inner Doors: Richard Rolle and the Space of the Soul," *Mystics Quarterly* 32, nos. 3/4 (September/December 2006): 19–45, argues for stillness as the necessary element for Richard's mysticism.

65. Alaimo, *Bodily Natures*, 2.

66. Stephen J. Pyne, "Fire Studied and Fire Made," in *Fire: Nature and Culture*, especially 101–9.

67. Rolle, *The Fire of Love*, 88–89. See *Incendium Amoris*, chapter 14: "inueni et cognui quidem quod summus amor Christi in tribus consistit: in *fervore*, in *canore*, et in *dulcore*."

68. Rolle, *The Fire of Love*, 93.

69. Roman, "Opening the Inner Doors," 34, quotes William F. Pollard, "Richard Rolle and the 'Eye of the Heart,'" in *Mysticism and Spirituality in Medieval England*, ed. William F. Pollard and Robert Boenig (Cambridge: Brewer, 1997), 90: "(perhaps somewhat in exasperation), 'the elements of the triad frequently overlap.'" Roman concludes, "Even more than simply overlapping them, Rolle enfolds the three" (34).

70. Mary Carruthers, "Taking the Bitter with the Sweet," in *The Experience of Beauty*, 80–107. Carruthers studies sweetness as a prized term of aesthetic pleasure, often caught in "sensory paradox" (90). See also Mary Carruthers, "Sweetness," *Speculum* 81, no. 4 (October 2006): 999–1013.

71. Rolle, *The Fire of Love*, 45. See *Incendium Amoris*, Prologus: "mellite incendio animam exalans."

72. According to Sacvan Bercovitch, "Empedocles in the English Renaissance," *Studies in Philology* 65, no. 1 (January 1986): 67–80, specifically "between 1493 and 1629" (73). Continuing the supposition put forth by Evelyn May Albright in 1929 ("Spenser's Cosmic Philosophy and His Religion," *PMLA* 44, no. 3 [1929]: 715–59), Bercovitch provides further evidence that Spenser had access to the ideas of Empedocles.

73. It is because of his death, and because of the prevalence of his ideas in the medieval and early modern period, that I focus on Empedocles in favor of Heraclitus, the pre-Socratic philosopher who isolated fire as the elemental element. Empedocles united the four elements into a self-perpetuating cosmological whole supplanting mythology, adding earth to Thales's water, Anaximenes's air, and Heraclitus's fire.

74. Macauley, *Elemental Philosophy,* 74–76.

75. F. Solmsen, "Love and Strife in Empedocles' Cosmology," *Phronesis* 10, no. 2 (1965): 109–48.

76. Horace Gregory, "Death & Empedocles 444 B.C.," *Modern Poetry* 122, no. 2 (May 1973): 64.

77. Brad Inwood, *The Poem of Empedocles: A Text and Translation with an Introduction* (Toronto: University of Toronto Press, 1992), 237.

78. Macauley, *Elemental Philosophy,* 115.

79. Inwood, *The Poem of Empedocles,* 213.

80. Ibid., 219: "And in wrath all are distinct in form and separate, and they come together in love and are desired by each other" (Fragment 26/21).

81. Ibid., 213, Fragment 21/8.

82. Gaston Bachelard, *Fragments of a Poetics of Fire,* ed. Suzanne Bachelard, trans. Kenneth Haltman (Dallas, Tex.: Dallas Institute Publications, 1990), 91–119.

83. Ibid., 92.

84. Ibid., 93.

85. Friedrich Hölderin, *The Death of Empedocles: A Mourning-Play,* trans. David Farrell Krell (Ithaca, N.Y.: State University of New York Press, 2008). All three versions of the play are edited, translated, and annotated.

86. Bachelard, *Fragments,* 104.

87. Diogenes Laertius, *Lives of Eminent Philosophers,* vol. 2, trans. R. D. Hicks (Cambridge, Mass.: Harvard University Press, 1965), 381–90: "As to his death different accounts are given." The "other deaths" of Empedocles are the result of a broken hip or a suicide by hanging.

88. Ibid., 383.

89. Guillaume de Lorris and Jean de Meun, *The Romance of the Rose,* trans. Charles Dahlberg (Princeton, N.J.: Princeton University Press, 1971), 286; Guillaume de Lorris and Jean de Meun, *Le Roman de la Rose,* ed. Daniel Poirion (Pairs: Garnier-Flammarion, 1974), 423.

90. Ava Chitwood, "The Death of Empedocles," *American Journal of Philology* 107, no. 2 (Summer 1986): 175–91, traces the biographical uses of the philosophy of Empedocles.

91. Diogenes, *Lives of Eminent Philosophers,* 389. Diogenes himself identifies the epigram from which this line is taken as "satirical." Ava Chitwood interprets this satire as a critique of Empedocles's boast that he could control the elements. Ava Chitwood, "Empedocles," in *Death by Philosophy: The Biographical Tradition in the*

Life and Death of the Archaic Philosophers Empedocles, Heraclitus, and Democritus (Ann Arbor: University of Michigan Press, 2004), 53–54.

92. Peter Kingsley, *Ancient Philosophy, Mystery and Magic: Empedocles and Pythagorean Tradition* (Oxford: Clarendon Press, 1995). In this work, Kingsley presents one insistent example of this approach and argues for the confrontation of Empedocles with fire as an initiation into complex rituals of death. See especially "Death on Etna" and "Sandals of Bronze and Thighs of Gold," 278–316.

93. Michel Serres, *Biogea,* trans. Randolph Burks (Minneapolis: Univocal, 2012), 53–80.

94. Ibid., 75.

95. Ibid., 79.

96. Pyne, *Fire,* 15.

two

Phloginston

STEVE MENTZ

> Let us destroy the fire of our life with a superfire, by a superhuman superfire without flame or ashes, which will bring extinction to the very heart of the being. When the fire devours itself, when the power turns against itself, it seems as if the whole being is made complete at the instant of its final ruin and that the intensity of the destruction is the supreme proof, the clearest proof, of its existence. This contradiction, at the very root of the intuition of being, favors endless transformations of value.
>
> —GASTON BACHELARD, *The Psychoanalysis of Fire*

We all crave ignition. Sparks lead to fire, blazes that spring up, alive and crackling, giving life to inert things. Combustion makes visible once-hidden power, consumes matter, generates heat and light. What we think of as fire, however, is not simply an isolated element, one of Empedocles's four primary substances. In order to burn, fire must engage a semi-substantial companion element, air. Burning requires multiple substances to come together, fire plus air plus heat. What modern chemistry and fire safety manuals call the "fire tetrahedron" combines heat, fuel, and air into a chain reaction that produces more heat and light.[1] Even exotic forms of combustion, from the nuclear cauldron inside the sun to the subcellular energy generated within mitochondria, produce energy through rapid combinations of substances that resemble the elements of fire and air. After Antoine Lavoisier, the "father of chemistry," discovered and named the elements oxygen and hydrogen in the late eighteenth century, enlightenment science came to recognize burning as rapid oxygenation, a heat-producing combination of fuel with a particularly flammable part of the air. The shift into modern chemical terminology identified a number of physical substances that paralleled and subsequently displaced the classical Empedoclean quartet of elements. Before the ascendency of Lavoisier's model, however, combustion remained mysterious. The relationship of burning to air, and the precise nature of flame itself, remained difficult to quantify.

Into this theoretical vacuum rushed an imaginary substance, phlogiston. Its imagined unity figures the fire-air combination as both substance and process. Exploring phlogiston's fiery essence reveals the human desire to isolate and name substances while exposing the elusive and combinatory nature of physical processes. Phlogiston, itself an error, emphasizes the errant nature of all physical interactions. Phlogistication mixes matter and the imagination. Fire and air, substance and fiction, material and metaphor, phlogiston captures the vexed unity and multiplicity of elemental mixtures. This imaginary substance offers a potent structure for ecomaterialist thinking across the boundary of matter and metaphor.

This fictional material, variously characterized as invisible fluid or mobile earth, provided early chemists with a possible answer to the question of why and when some things would burn when heated and others would not. Phlogiston represented an invisible but material "principle of inflammability" whose presence indicated whether a substance would burn, which process would then consume its hidden stores of undetectable phlogiston. Phlogiston's fundamental mystery, both to its theoretical champions and even more to we who accept modern chemical theories, insists that burning is both tangible and fictional. Like the object-oriented ontologist (OOO) Graham Harman's exploration of "the relationship between fire and cotton," an imaginative return to phlogiston emphasizes the essentially fictional nature of relations between physical objects.[2] Under phlogiston's light, modern trends in materialist philosophy resemble fictions of errancy, all the more valuable for their fictional trajectory. The substance is famous today, if at all, as a scientific error, though a few bloggers and policy intellectuals including Matt Yglesias and Paul Krugman have recently employed the term "phlogiston economics," by which they means systems for describing fiscal policy that are not just wrong but intricate and silly.[3] In his book *The Psychoanalysis of Fire,* the French philosopher Gaston Bachelard subtitles his chapter on phlogiston "History of a False Problem."[4]

This unreal substance traces conceptual paths about ignition and burning that remain valuable even after the supposed displacement of error by accuracy.[5] By isolating and consolidating the explosive mixing of fire and air, phlogiston burns with poetic ecological meaning. The substance shines a light on the mixing of fire and air, the two least physically substantial of the four elements. Interrogating this imaginary substance reveals a paradoxical entanglement of separation and combination that is itself characteristic of elemental relations. Both process and substance, story and matter, phlogiston models an ambivalence crucial to ecomaterialist thinking.

The concept of phlogiston emerged in the late seventeenth century in the work of the German alchemist Johann Becher. Becher's model attempted to simplify and purify the four classical elements by removing insubstantial fire and air from the group and replacing their chemical functions with three different kinds of earth. Beecher seems to have recognized that the lighter elements were the hardest to describe and represent, so he attempted to build a material system without them. Oily and sulfurous earth, which Becher called *terra pinguis,* eventually morphed into invisible phlogiston, with that Greek-derived word arriving in the works of the German chemist Georg Ernst Stahl in 1718.[6] The poster boy for phlogiston, however, was the eighteenth-century Enlightenment scientist Joseph Priestley, who clung to the theory even as nearly every respectable chemist had come to follow Lavoisier's new system. In an open letter of 1796 published in Philadelphia, Priestley outlined a "short defense of the concept of *phlogiston.*"[7] In places the rhetoric of Priestley's letter may sound familiar to academic readers, as when he writes, "I cannot help thinking that what I have observed in several of my publications has not been duly attended to, or well understood" (*Considerations,* 3). Priestley's attachment to phlogiston, however, was not simply a matter of clinging to a theory he had previously advanced in print. Retaining this invisible, odorless substance as concept and as the material basis of all inflammable substances followed his basic commitments to moral and physical symmetry, as well as his faith in his own experimental practice. "In all other cases of the calcination of metals in air, which I have called the *phlogistication* of the air," he writes, "it is not only evident that [the metals] gain something, which adds to their weight, but that they likewise part with something" (4). That something-lost, for Priestley, is phlogiston. In my analysis, phlogiston represents a double loss:

it is consumed in the process of burning, and, after the triumph of modern chemical theory, this substance itself has vanished almost entirely from intellectual history. Taking Priestley's essay as tinder for my blaze, this chapter traces the speculative value of a nonexistent substance through its connections to early literary depictions of combustion. Phlogiston shows why things catch fire and why conflagration makes us feel certain ways. In spanning the divide between matter and metaphor, it speaks to human needs, if not chemical processes.

The intellectual and conceptual benefits of what I call, following Priestley, "phlogisticated thinking" include three major claims. These premodern semiscientific principles reveal how an imaginary substance can inform twenty-first-century ecocritical analysis. All three claims point toward the larger subject of my investigation, the vexed interplay between the physical and the imaginary. Phlogiston's entangled insistence that there is no combustion without invisible consumption generates a possible building block for an environmental ethics that preserves space for errancy and fiction. This nonexistent substance whispers in our ears: phlogisticate the world! You have nothing to lose but bare matter.

1. *Isolating Ignition:* The key insight that emerges from phlogiston is the desire to treat ignition as its own system. Accepting that combustion requires fire and air together leads to a system that might keep these two elements separate, but phlogiston thrusts them together. This notional, invisible substance embodies and represents the explosive meeting of fire and air. Priestley's obsession with gain and loss implies a vision of burning as a unified process. Burning cannot simply be, according to Priestley, nothing more than air (oxygen) and fuel coming together rapidly and exothermically; it must be its own entity and dynamic process. Looking in premodern literature for the fiery seeds of this kind of thinking shows that the attribution of life to fire is both an ancient spiritual belief and a versatile poetic trope. For the sixteenth-century alchemist and physician Paracelsus, "fire is life" (Bachelard, *The Psychoanalysis of Fire,* 73), as it was also for the pre-Socratic philosopher Heraclitus. The most explosive engagements come when human bodies encounter fiery ignitions, as my literary examples will show.

2. *Negative Weight:* Once scientists began isolating the burning process and weighing the resultant gaseous and solid residues, they discovered that lighting things on fire makes them slightly heavier. Eventually Lavoisier showed that burning requires oxidation, and the addition of oxygen increases the weight of the substance burned, including the weight of any smoke or gases that escape during burning. But the stop-gap possibility that phlogiston had negative weight, such that losing it through burning could cause an object to gain mass, remains deeply attractive. Negative weight destabilizes physical systems, as if something could exist and not exist at the same time. This very poetical idea speaks to Bachelard's claims for a more-than-human "psychoanalysis" of the material elements, in which these substances embody human as well as physical principles. "In this way, then," Bachelard writes, "our scientific and philosophic reverie work[s]: it accentuates all forces; it seeks the absolute in life as in death" (*The Psychoanalysis of Fire,* 79). Following James Smith's recent call for a rereading of Bachelard that encompasses ecocriticism and new materialism, I find in *The Psychoanalysis of Fire* suggestive traces of phlogisticated thinking.[8] Bachelard never really escapes his "false problem."
3. *Physical Properties in/and/as Moral:* Though it gets discarded along the way, phlogiston speaks to us today through what we might call the "light" in Enlightenment, the visionary moral quality at the heart of early science. Seeing ignition as both physical and moral, early scientists such as Priestley imagined deeply interpenetrated human and nonhuman world-systems. As ecomaterialist criticism attempts to recross boundaries between objects and ideas, including Jane Bennett's new work on Walt Whitman, among other examples,[9] the speculative thinking of phlogiston chemists compellingly supplements more familiar discourses in intellectual history, including linear conceptions of progress in experimental science and discursive developments in the histories of poetry and narrative. Phlogiston turns out to be an ecologically and philosophically compelling non-element. The fictional substance entangles things with ideas.

These three concepts—ignition, negative weight, and moral burning—underlie my analysis of phlogiston. Employing literary works from before the brief "age of phlogiston," I treat premodern depictions of combustion as a physical and symbolic process in terms of their fiery anticipations of phlogisticated thinking. I hope thereby to suggest that losing phlogiston has entailed losing a valuable way of narrating combustion and a sympathetic fantasy about the relationship between matter and thought. These encounters with burning advance the efforts of literary ecocriticism to reanimate stories about physical elements, to make them glow with renewed meaning. For this critical project, phlogiston's scientific falsehood is a feature, not a bug. Its error makes it pure story, while its fiery heat recalls the physical process it was invented to explain. Reading phlogiston insists upon repeated crossings of the divide between metaphor and materiality. The largest intellectual benefit of this analysis, in fact, may be revealing that divide itself, the intangible but noticeable shift that occurs between abstract and physical meanings. Phlogisticating ecomaterialist thinking can make us less resistant to metaphor while also being more attentive to the tangled history of physical processes. A fictional source of real flames, phlogiston sheds light on how the dynamic and unstable elements of fire and air combine.

A Literary Prehistory

What did early modern writers see in flames? A theatrical Muse, famously in Shakespeare's *Henry V* but also burning histories and a poetics of fire, as well as ecological traces of dependence and terror.[10] Symbolic plurality makes burning a mysterious thing. Bachelard helps diagnose combustion's divided nature by emphasizing its dual promises of destruction and purity. This symbolic split, fire's forked tongue, makes it hard to represent, especially in the flammable world of mostly wooden early modern cities and theaters.[11] Understanding early modern ideas of combustion and the prehistory of phlogiston requires attending to multiple allegories, being willing to employ many different keys to understand light or heat or smoke or the ashes left behind. Air and fire together produce a dangerous dynamism, a process of mutual consumption in which nothing lasts. On a physical level, early modern ideas about combustion bridge ancient alchemical fantasies and impending changes in how physical processes were imagined and investigated.[12] For poets and dramatists, burning registers a limit-case, something that cannot be held or captured. Representing fiery change requires constructing a system in which this unruly spirit can roam, burn, and amaze. Thinking with flames outlines a twinned ecology of consuming and remaking. The fire ecologies in this chapter grapple with the insubstantial at the center of the relationship between human bodies and the nonhuman environment. Living with inflammability risks conflagration but promises perfection, even if its story often ends with piles of smoldering ash.

My analysis of the literary prehistory of phlogiston builds on this split at combustion's symbolic core. Drawing on alchemical traditions that see fire as a principle of agency and change makes sense of both the need for and fear of flames. This dynamism also combines the two principles Priestley values in phlogiston, agency and analogy, physical force and moral meaning. The logic of phlogistication may in fact transform all analogies into forms of agency. Burning liberates the agency of radical individualism and also binds together kingdoms and households with moral knots. Exploring fire knowledge in premodern culture suggests that this element marks a disorderly and dangerous boundary between human experience and the nonhuman world.[13] The mixing of air and fire creates and also destabilizes order.

The structuring conceit of the five middle sections of this chapter is a series of names that straddle the human-phlogiston divide. The literary model for these names comes from my first example, Shakespeare's Roman anti-hero Coriolanus, who wants to burn himself a new name by firing Rome. The connection his play reveals between flames and identity underlines the conflicted intimacy between humans and burning. We need combustion but cannot touch it comfortably, and we fear we will not be able to control it. Grasping a fire name entails harnessing this destructive element for human purposes, filling mortal vacancies with blazing energy. The desire to imprint fire and make it receptive of, if not quite subservient to, human desires marks a refrain in early modern literature, and arguably in human culture since before the dawn of history. Burning is companion, tool, handmaiden, scourge. As Stephen J. Pyne has observed about the Americas and Australia before European contact, the supposedly untouched landscapes of these continents were sculpted and shaped by human hands and intentional burning.[14] The controversial thesis of the ecologist William

Ruddiman, who argues that humans have been modifying the earth's climate since the dawn of agriculture ten thousand years ago, relies on evidence of carbon in the atmosphere caused by large-scale burning to clear cropland, a process that began before recorded history.[15] Recent scientific research suggests that fire has shaped global ecosystems both with and without human influence over the long course of environmental history.[16] Current evidence argues for placing fire, the phenomenon that phlogiston was invented to explain, at the center of ecological history.[17]

My core literary examples find phlogisticated thinking in Shakespeare, Robert Greene, Edmund Spenser, and the writings of early modern alchemists. This chapter's five fire names—Coriolanus, Pyrochles, Roger Bacon, Pistol, and Cleopatra—sketch a variety of ways early modern humans imagined and interacted with combustion. My hope is less to arrive at complete understanding—flames do not do well when boxed in—than to trace the physical and symbolic pressure that active burning puts on the way humans represent themselves within nonhuman environments. Each fire name does what the name *phlogiston* also does: gestures toward fractured intimacy. We huddle as close to flames as we can. Sometimes we get a little too close. Across that blazing border phlogiston builds its unstable house.

Fire Name 1: Coriolanus

Fire burns inside and out. Burning Rome and forging an unshakeable heroic identity require the same blazing energy. Shakespeare's Coriolanus craves fiery identity:

> He was a kind of nothing, titleless
> Till he had forged himself a name o' the fire
> Of burning Rome. (5.1.13–15)

The first fire name exposes the element's rage against plurality, its desire to transform many differences into one glowing thing. Just imagine it in your city or your home: phlogiston, everywhere. It's invisible, like radon, and equally hard to avoid.

Shakespeare's warrior-hero is a creature of many names, earning a new surname early in the play by his solitary assault on an alien city (1.4–9).

"Coriolanus," the name he gets after conquering the Volscian city of Corioles, names his Roman identity and also his play. The "name o' the fire" that may follow, however, represents something else. While his geographic name fixes the hero, locating spirit and body in the city where he ultimately dies, the apparently unspeakable fire name—perhaps it might turn out to be that strange faux-Greek word, *phlogiston?*—unlooses him into radical singularity. This name redeems him from the "titleless" identity he assumes in exile. With "his eye / Red as 'twould burn Rome" (5.1.63–64), Coriolanus reapproaches the eternal city as living conflagration. Burning would eliminate all differences and remake the city as unified flames. In this phlogisticated state, he refuses to acknowledge "wife, mother, child" (5.2.82) because he sees bodies and material objects only as fuel. He will not spare the city to save his family because he does not care about a few stray objects: "He said 'twas folly, / For one poor grain or two, to leave unburnt" (5.1.26–27) the whole. Fire naming transforms Roman superman into raging force, sweeping across Italy. He burns as uncontrolled velocity. The play's language emphasizes his inhumanity and opacity:

> He is their god; he leads them like a thing
> Made by some other deity than Nature,
> That shapes men better; and they follow him
> Against us brats with no less confidence
> Than boys pursuing summer butterflies,
> Or butchers killing flies. (4.6.90–95)

The god Coriolanus requires a new name; this passage emphasizes its own inability to describe the hero. The approaching Coriolanus is never precisely seen, always not quite legible: "like a thing," "some other deity," "shapes . . . better," "no less confidence." Like fire itself, like phlogiston in both its material function and historical narrative, the god-man flashes, frightens, and is gone.

This collection of images is not Coriolanus's only connection to an ecology of combustion. Accepting exile, the hero likens himself to a firedrake to explain his removal from human contact: "Like to a lonely dragon, that his fen / Makes fear'd and talk'd of more than seen" (4.1.30–31). The hero as dragon, inhuman and alone, craves a name of the fire to transform Roman warrior into alien monster. As his friend Meninius says, "This [Coriolanus] is grown from man to dragon: he has wings, he's a more than creeping thing" (5.4.13–14). Like Cleopatra, Coriolanus is fire and air; he escapes sublunary human connections and ascends to inhuman spaces. Is it blood in his veins, or phlogiston?

Fire Name 2: Pyrochles

The second hero has no need of a new fire name: he burns from the start. The pyromaniac knight Pyrochles challenges the Knight of Temperance in Book II of Spenser's *Faerie Queene* in an allegorical contest between "raging yre" (2.5.8.5) and "wary wise" (2.5.9.6):

> One in bright arms embattled full strong,
> That as the Sunny beames doe glaunce and glide
> Upon the trembling waue, so shined bright,
> And round him threw forth sparkling fire,
> That seemed him to enflame on euery side:
> His steed was bloody red, and fomed yre,
> When with the maistring spur he did him roughly stire. (2.5.2.3–9)[18]

Pyrochles appears less as static symbol than as burning contaminant; as these lines show, he literally and metaphorically transforms "Sunny beames" into "sparkling fire." Phlogisticated selfhood disrupts and resists the Knight of Temperance's moralizing; Pyrochles is instructed to "fly the dreadful warre, / That in thy selfe thy lesser partes doe moue" (2.5.16.1–2), but his fire will not go out. While Coriolanus threatens to engulf the collective, Pyrochles's smaller fires dot the allegorical landscape of Faerie Land. These are not all-consuming blazes but brushfires of human temptation.

Pyrochles's presence underlines the destructive and pluralizing side of phlogiston, as opposed to its destructive but unifying qualities, which Coriolanus displays. With his assortment of chaos-producing companions, the fire-knight blazes through Spenser's epic allegory. Pyrochles represents phlogiston's self-consuming nature when he laments being caught between fiery body and inner flames: "I burne, I burne, I burne, then lowd he cried / O how I burne with implacable fyre" (2.6.44.1–2). Consumed by a conflagration of fire and air, he seeks wetness as an elemental countercharm: "Yet nought can quench mine inly flaming syde, / Nor sea of licour cold, nor lake of myre, / Nothing but death can doe me to respyre" (2.6.44.3–5). The "flood" into which Pyrochles finally plunges turns out not to be cleansing water but a combination of the two heavier elements, water and earth: "The waues theeof so slow and sluggish were, / Engrost with mud" (2.6.46.6–7). Pyrochles's encounter with the physical world represents the mutual quenching of light things by heavy ones, fire and air by water and earth. The overall effect resembles a "natural" balance or temperance, but this outcome rescues, rather than moderates, the burning knight. In an act of violence that anticipates the subsequent destruction of the Bower of Bliss, Prince Arthur first offers Pyrochles his life but finally cuts off his head when Sir Phlogiston predictably rejects mercy.[19] Allegorically, Spenser implies, the burning self cannot be reformed, only destroyed.

Fire Name 3: Roger Bacon

At the heart of combustion lurks mystery and secret knowledge. The third name retreats from the destructive powers of Coriolanus and Pyrochles to begin, through magic, to redeem flames. Roger Bacon would become a watchword for medieval alchemy in sixteenth-century England. When Robert Greene first introduces the famous medieval alchemist Roger Bacon in his Elizabethan play *Friar Bacon and Friar Bungay* (1589?), the wizard gets described as "read in magic's mystery; / In pyromancy, to divine by flames" (1.2).[20] Bacon also knows "hydromantic" and "aeromancy," but burning comes first. The thirteenth-century doctor had become by the Elizabethan period a familiar figure for alchemical mysteries.[21] Before Bacon arrives in the play to humiliate the rival German scholar Vandermast, however, a revealing exchange shows Vandermast and the English scholar Friar Bungay debating the relative powers of fire and earth, pyromancy and geomancy. Vandermast, the foreigner, makes the case for fire: "If, then, as Hermes says, fire be the greatest, / Purest, and only giveth shape to spirits, / Then must these daemones that haunt that place / Be every way superior than the rest" (3.2). Bungay's rebuttal insists that "the fiery spirits are but transparent shades / ... But earthly fiends, clos'd in the lowest deep, / Dissever mountains, if they be but charg'd, / Being more gross and massy in their power" (3.2). As in Spenser's narrative of burning and healing, heavy and light elements struggle against one another. Vandermast's narration of the fall of Lucifer claims that the archfiend's imprisonment in "the centre of the earth" (3.2) gives only evil power to that underground realm, though he also recognizes the power of "mighty, swift, and . . . far-reaching" fire spirits (3.2). These doctors achieve a kind of elemental stalemate like Spenser's, but Bacon himself, who arrives triumphantly at this juncture, banishes Vandermast through the force of his "necromantic charms" (4.1). Bacon's magic was first introduced by fire, but he rejects Vandermast's attempt to exalt fire above other elements. Fire for Bacon appears mysterious but controllable, at least by English doctors.[22] Perhaps he knows the recipe for phlogiston?

Greene's play was one of many Elizabethan works that used Bacon to represent occult chemical knowledge. In *The Mirror of Alchemy,* one of two translations of Bacon's Latin treatise into English in this period, Bacon claims that "heat perfecteth all things."[23] Fire, of all the elements in Bacon's alchemical system, most explicitly resembles humanity, though here it might be important to distinguish between a slow, nurturing "Infant" fire and a raging, phlogiston-fueled adult blaze:

> This worke is verlie like to the creation of man: for as the Infant in the beginning is nourhsed with light meates, but the bones being strengthened with stronger: so this masterie also, first it must haue an easie fire. . . . And though we always speake of a gentle fire, yet in truth, we think that in gouerning the worke, the fire must always by little and little bee increased and augmented unto the end. (10)

It is not fire in isolation so much as burning, or what later alchemists would name *phlogiston,* that provides the force that generates perfection. To grow beyond a "gentle fire" in order to encourage greater growth requires that the burning process be carefully cultivated, or, to use Bacon's term, "gouerned." In *The Secrets of Alchimy,* bound with the 1597 *Mirror,* the narrator emphasizes that "the benefit or less of this thing, proceedeth from the benefit of the fire" (43). For these alchemical thinkers and their early modern heirs,

Air	Fire
Material	Metaphor
Reading (narrative)	Analysis (argument)
Homogenocene	Anthropocene

FIGURE 2.1. The phlogiston box.

burning represents the mystery at the heart of things and the primary tool through which alchemical magic may be manufactured. Phlogiston burns and destroys but also remakes.

Interlude: Metaphoric Materialism

The benefits of this chapter's analysis of phlogiston structure the concept-box (Figure 2.1) that I have named for my imaginary element. The two columns represent things distinguishable from each other but mutually dependent. They must be combined to assume full potency but cannot be simply amalgamated. Just as no burning occurs without fire and air, so no metaphor functions without materiality, no narrative without argument, and no phlogiston without all these things together. (The Homogenocene and Anthropocene are slightly trickier cases, as I will explain shortly.) The intentional, frequent, and self-aware crossing between the two columns comprises my own rough definition of a critical method for ecomaterialists. I remain very aware that full separation between material and metaphor is not tenable, and I do not claim that we really know what "metaphor" is on the level of substance.[24] Like phlogiston, metaphor remains elusive; perhaps the concept is not substantial at all, though it functions through its entanglement with matter. As fire-air defines its shared materiality through mutual exchange and consumption, the metaphor-materiality dyad seems not really to be a question of separation or what the box represents as the vertical line separating distinct terms. The division between the columns signals a necessary oversimplification, a temporary structure that must always be broken and remade.[25] I cherish this act of crossing. Sudden shifts of perspective, of subject matter, even of rhetorical mode, create intellectual combustion. What humanities scholars do best is perform that jump, the turn from the minutely textual to the wildly general, from tensions inside a single word ("phlogiston," in this case) to the endlessly flickering dance of the organic within and entangled with the inorganic. Phlogiston spans divides without obviating division as such. Crossing is more meaningful when there are boundaries to leap over.

This provisional scheme and the micro-close readings it generates produce a compelling image of variety and multiple opportunities for analytic engagement. Into this utopian vision of free play and difference, however, the specter of the Homogenocene lurks in the lower left. This term names an era in which all material objects on earth spread themselves evenly across the globe, a kind of heat-death of maximum exchange.[26] An earth subject to total mixing becomes a space of terrifying material sameness. Alongside the better-known Anthropocene, which refers to the era during which humans have become drivers and disruptors of the global climate, the Homogenocene represents our unstable present. As depictions of global exchange and catastrophe, both terms present difficulties, and including them in this box argues that they, too, are best read as a fraught binary. My own critical methods seek variety and push against the Homogenocene, though I have also come to suspect the hubristic *anthropos* in the Anthropocene.[27] To rephrase this problem of separation and entanglement in slightly different terms, Jeffrey Jerome Cohen suggested after the Elemental Ecologies Symposium that my analysis of phlogiston aims "to move beyond the metaphor / materiality impasses native to speaking about the elements."[28] I value these comments for doing that great thing that commentary can sometimes do: exposing what the original wanted but did not fully articulate. But I also feel compelled to own my own attachment to metaphor/materiality as impasse and necessary boundary, to the lines inside and around my phlogiston box as well as the combinations the structure produces. Thinking about elemental relations generates multiple difficulties and textures. I do not want (or expect) to escape error. Phlogisticating emphasizes a return to a nearly forgotten error, which can be followed toward new entanglements.

Back now to the last two fire-names: two more chances to straddle the elemental and the human.

Fire Name 4: Pistol

The mock-chivalric spat between bar-buddies Pistol and Nym, fighting over the Hostess, who has married Pistol and jilted Nym in Shakespeare's *Henry V*, shifts fire symbolism down the social and intellectual ladders. This fourth name humanizes and socializes burning, while also returning to its disruptive nature. As Pistol describes himself, "Pistol's cock is up, / And flashing fire will follow" (*Henry V*, 2.1.52–53). With language that recalls the demon-speak of Friar Bacon—Nym at one point counters Pistol's rage with "I am not Barbason, you cannot conjure me" (2.1.54–55)—this exchange miniaturizes Spenser's epic treatment of burning. Pistol names Nym "Iceland dog" (2.1.42), possibly for his unruly hair, but the epithet also enlarges their brawling enmity into a faux-Spenserian conflict between fire and ice. Bardolph's and Mistress Quickly's successful efforts to pacify the pair thus solder together the elemental opposites that Spenser's landscape repeatedly fails to unify. The flashing fire of Pistol's pistol never goes off, at least not in the tavern. Pistol's mock-heroic language rages against Nym's purported treachery; he calls his antagonist "O hound of Crete" (2.1.73) and offers to "let floods o'erswell, and fiends for food howl on!" (2.1.92–93). The alliteration contributes to the sense that Pistol, like Pyrochles but more humorously, blazes beyond control.

In the socialized rather than allegorized world of Shakespeare's history play, Pistol's burning smothers in the mud of France. Another tavern character, the unnamed Boy, provides a shrewd analysis of what will happen when these drinkers go to war. Pistol, the Boy predicts, will drop bombast and reveal cowardice: "For Pistol, he hath a killing tongue and a quiet sword; by the means whereof a' breaks words and keeps whole weapons" (3.2.34–36). The drinking buddies Nym and Bardolf become "sworn brothers in filching," and their object of theft occasions a fiery pun: "in Callice they stole a fire-shovel, and I knew that by that piece of service the men would carry coals" (3.2.44–46). The fire-shovel, a tool used to place coals safely on a fire, anticipates the neutralizing of Pistol as well, who fails to preserve Bardolph from hanging (3.6), extorts two hundred crowns from a French prisoner whose speech he cannot understand (4.4), and finally must eat raw leeks at Fluellen's command after Agincourt (5.1). All this humiliation, however, sends the burning rogue back home blazing with violence: "Well, bawd I'll turn, / And something lean to cutpurse of quick hand. / To England will I steal, and there I'll steal" (5.1.85–87). Taking his place among Elizabethan war veterans turned criminals, Pistol encapsulates a social slow burn, festering within.[29] Combustion lives uneasily within human, social, and legal constraints.

Fire Name 5: Cleopatra

When fire and air burn, smoke rises, and this physical movement toward the heavens fuels many allegorical interpretations. Like the action of an alchemical experiment, Shakespeare's Cleopatra ascends into fire and air, consumed by her own heat and the amalgamation of forces she ignites around her: "I am fire and air; my other elements / I give to baser life" (*Antony and Cleopatra,* 5.2.288–89). In the final coup de théâtre of her spectacle-rich play, Cleopatra combines Egyptian liquidity and erotic spark to perform suicide in "the high Roman fashion" (4.15.91). Reimagining Caesar's "time of universal peace" (4.6.5) as the "paltry" (5.2.2) rule of a "universal landlord" (3.13.76), the Queen of the elements uses all four substances to perform her eventual purification. Her final scene employs water from the Nile, earth from a "ditch in Egypt" (5.2.56), fire, and air. She, more than any other of my fire names, epitomizes negative weight. As Bachelard shows, this antigravity principle was attributed by phlogisticators to fire: "Fire is then the perpetual antagonist of gravity. . . . To insist that fire has weight is to destroy nature" (*The Psychoanalysis of Fire,* 81). Even Caesar praises Cleopatra's vertical escape, intoning over the body, "she looks like sleep, / As she would catch another Antony / In her strong toil of grace" (5.2.345–7). (Caesar, ruler of wooden cities, fears no more fire from her corpse.) In Bachelard's terms, this figure for paradox embodies "endless transformations of value." She also emphasizes an element of ignition that I have not yet discussed: sexual excitement.

As she death-suckles "the pretty worm of Nilus there / That kills and pains not" (5.2.242), Cleopatra adds sexual meaning to phlogiston's physical and moral combinations. Like all burning flames, Cleopatra's allure forks, and her bivalence, like her play, is specifically erotic, killing and loving at once. In one of the most enigmatic footnotes in modern Shakespeare studies, Janet Adelman notes in her 1973 book *The Common Liar* that the back-and-forth rhythm of scene and mood changes in *Antony and Cleopatra* imitates the rhythm of sexual intercourse.[30] (That is the sort of footnote that makes you sit up when you read it alone in a dusty library.) In a final extension of the drama's cornucopia of polymorphic sexuality, Cleopatra's hot embrace transforms a phallic death-snake into a suckling child. "Peace, peace," she coos while nuzzling the poisonous asp, "Dost thou not see my baby at my breast / That sucks the nurse asleep?" (5.2). The dying Queen embodies deadly warmth; "Have I the aspic on my lips?" (5.2.292), she asks when Iras falls after receiving her kiss. Cleopatra's almost-final lines connect her to emptiness, "as soft as air, as gentle" (5.2.310), but fiery determination fuels her death-driven performance. Her last curtain-call—"What should I stay?" (5.2.311), she asks—follows her up like a wisp of smoke. Transforming the "dungy earth" (1.1.36) through which Antony celebrated their love in the play's opening scene, this final performance completes Cleopatra's explosive dissolution. As fire and air leave the stage, we are left desiring.

Reading Cleopatra as a figure of paradox and innuendo will be familiar to most Shakespeareans and theatergoers. By connecting her sexy theatricality more precisely to phlogiston's invisible principle of inflammability, I hope to add hot sauce to everyone's favorite Queen of the Nile. For alchemical thinkers from Becher to Stahl to Priestley, phlogiston was the hidden necessity, the invisible hand on the invisible button that, when pressed, released energy. Cleopatra, in the dramatic ecology of Shakespeare's Globe Theatre, represents comparable force and attraction. Her presence ignites human and nonhuman flames. Her first entrance into the world of the play in fact recalls one of the most famous experiments in early modern science: the use of fire to create a vacuum. Before he sees her, Mark Antony, sitting "enthron'd i' the market-place" (2.2.247) as Cleopatra's barge processes downriver, whistles alone while everyone flocks to her presence. Like a burning blaze, Cleopatra sucks all the air out of the room: even "the air," Shakespeare writes, "but for vacancy, / Had gone to gaze on Cleopatra too / And made a gap in nature" (2.2.249–51). This description of the moving air mimics the use of fire in early experiments designed to produce a vacuum, performed after Shakespeare's lifetime by scientists including Galileo, Torricelli, Boyle, and Hooke. Cleopatra on her barge consumes air as does a flame, leaving Antony temporarily alone inside nature's "gap." The scene even operates through absence; Enobarbus's words conjure up absent Cleopatra across empty space and time. Displaying openness and errancy that recall the permeable boundary between metaphor and materiality, the "gap" in Shakespeare's Cleopatra represents an emptiness that attracts.[31] In following her, the Roman hero, like the play's audience, seeks the symbolic and physical force of phlogiston. Burning attracts as well as heating, and it works on our inner desires as well as our skin.

Smoldering Conclusions

I have been arguing throughout this chapter that the enduring meaning of now-forgotten phlogiston occupies an unstable mediating space across metaphoric and material realms. To some extent that instability is a welcome hazard and challenge of ecomaterialist inquiry. In this particular case I am also following the trail of earlier phlogisticated thinkers. Priestley, the last of the true believers, values phlogiston as much as metaphor as material; we recall that his pamphlet defends "the *concept* of phlogiston" (emphasis mine). My practice of shifting between material and metaphor in my discussion has been intentional, as well as unavoidable. I am happy to celebrate the productive slippage between metaphoric and substantive meanings, and I also refuse to police that boundary too rigorously. As I noted earlier, this chapter proffers my own rough definition of literary ecomaterialist critical practice as a practice that intentionally breaches the barrier between material and metaphor. It is crossing that line, repeatedly and deliberately, while at the same time never forgetting that the boundary exists, that lights my critical fire. Like Cleopatra's barge to the air around Antony, phlogiston allures. It pulls our imaginations into rich entanglements of physical, symbolic, allegorical, and moral conflagrations. Like Harman's "vicarious causation," this substance lures us between physical and conceptual realities, though perhaps even more than Harman's OOO, phlogisitcation wears its errors on its sleeve.

This imaginary, fraudulent substance cannot provide too much stability. By way of conclusion I offer up two pairs of terms that gesture toward possible futures for phlogisticated ecocriticism. These fragments are not finished thoughts so much as hot embers pointing in future directions, though I will emphasize that the first two are, at least initially, material, and the second two primarily metaphoric.

The material binary is about the physical properties of combustion and how these properties operate in space and time. Phlogiston's instability in both dimensions suggests a basic dynamism within physical processes. This incessant movement generates metaphoric fires from material sparks.

1. *Flames:* Phlogiston forks in space

   Every time you reach out to touch it, it splits. What is a singular flame? We want burning to be one thing, one process, one underlying substrate, which was once called phlogiston. But every fire-causing fluid multiples. Oxygen would be Lavoisier's answer, but he also discovered and named hydrogen.

2. *Ash:* Phlogiston burns out in time

   There's always something left behind, some bodies or fragments, warm but insubstantial to the touch. These gray remnants make good fertilizer. Despite fire's violent ascents and turnings, not everything vanishes.

Next, the metaphorical pair thinks about burning and intimacy. Humans need and fear flames. Attraction and destruction reach into our bodies and our homes.

1. *Heat:* Phlogiston warms

   The happiest part of burning comprises its social nature, making and shaping human communities. Flames gather together Cleopatra and her ladies, Bacon and his pupils, Pistol and his drinking buddies, and even the smoldering gang that follows Pyrochles around Faerie Land. Phlogiston is the fuel humans need, the engine that forges solidarities.

2. *Cooking:* Phlogiston nourishes

   Burning's role in prehistoric agriculture and climate change remains controversial, but not its essential function in rendering vegetable and animal products into digestible food. Nothing else can do this for us. Phlogiston: it is what makes dinner.

Can we tell them apart, I wonder, the material things from the metaphorical processes? Perhaps not. Perhaps the movement of phlogistication blurs these categories too thoroughly. But these strains of phlogisticated eco-thinking, materiality and metaphor, add instability and motion to static visions of sustainable ecosystems.[32] By spanning warmth and conflagration, these ideas about burning open up our engagement with this dynamic process and the massive human, cultural, and psychological trails of meaning it leaves in its wake. Like yesterday's smoke, phlogiston has nearly disappeared, but if we look carefully, we can see it going.

Notes

1. See, for example, Fire Safety Advice Centre, "Information about the Fire Triangle/Tetrahedron and Combustion," http://www.firesafe.org.uk/information-about-the-fire-triangletetrahedron-and-combustion/.

2. Graham Harman, "On Vicarious Causation," in *Collapse,* vol. 2, *Speculative Realism,* ed. Robin Mackay (London: Urbanomic, 2007), 187–221. As Harman puts it, "we have no idea how physical relations (or any other kind) are possible in the first place" (189). For Harman, this mutual withdrawal leads to an ornate post-Heideggerian metaphysics. My analysis instead emphasizes the imaginative act of material entanglement, of which invisible, fictional phlogiston serves as potent symbol. Accepting Harman's argument about the limits of our real knowledge of material encounters, I suggest that substances like phlogiston serve as imaginative prosthetics, standing in for the mysterious processes about which Harmon and other object-oriented ontologists theorize.

3. Matt Yglesias's first development of this term appears to have been in May 2011 in a blog post titled "Phlogiston Economics," http://thinkprogress.org/yglesias/2011/05/12/200954/phlogiston-economics/. Paul Krugman mentioned phlogiston a bit earlier but not in quite the same context. See Paul Krugman, "The Hangover Theory," *Slate,* December 4, 1998, http://www.slate.com/articles/business/the_dismal_science/1998/12/the_hangover_theory.html.

4. Gaston Bachelard, *The Psychoanalysis of Fire,* trans. Alan Ross (Boston: Beacon Press, 1964). Further citations appear parenthetically in the text.

5. On error and mistakes in an early modern context, see Julian Yates, *Error, Misuse, Failure: Object Lessons from the English Renaissance* (Minneapolis: University of Minnesota Press, 2002).

6. On Becher, see Pamela Smith, *The Business of Alchemy: Science and Culture in the Holy Roman Empire* (Princeton, N.J.: Princeton University Press, 1994).

7. Joseph Priestley, *Considerations on the Doctrine of Phlogiston and the Decomposition of Water* (Philadelphia: Thomas Dobson, 1796). Further citations appear parenthetically in the text.

8. James Smith, "New Bachelards? Reveries, Elements, and Twenty-First Century Materialisms," *Alter Modernità* (October 16, 2012): 156–67.

9. Jane Bennett has been previewing this material in recent talks, including a keynote at the BABEL conference in Boston in September 2012, though I am not aware of anything currently in print.

10. Famously: "O, for a Muse of fire . . ." (*Henry V*, 1Pr.1), in *The Riverside Shakespeare*, 2nd ed., ed. G. Blakemore Evans and J. J. M. Tobin (Boston: Houghton Mifflin, 1997). All citations of Shakespeare are to this edition and give act, scene, and line numbers.

11. For a compelling recent evocation of the wood ecology of Shakespeare's theater, see Vin Nardizzi, *Wooden Os: Shakespeare's Theater and England's Trees* (Toronto: University of Toronto Press, 2013). Another powerful exploration of fire and the early modern stage is Ellen MacKay, *Persecution, Plague, and Fire: Fugitive Histories of the Stage in Early Modern England* (Chicago: University of Chicago Press, 2011).

12. On the meteorological distinction between subterranean and atmospheric fire, see Craig Martin, *Renaissance Meteorology: Pomponazzi to Descartes* (Baltimore: Johns Hopkins University Press, 2011), 90–98.

13. My fire thinking owes a particular debt to Jeffrey Cohen and Stephanie Trigg, "Fire," *postmedieval* 4, no. 1 (2013): 80–92.

14. Stephen J. Pyne, *Burning Bush: A Fire History of Australia* (New York: Henry Holt, 1991). Pyne has also written fire histories of America, Canada, and the world; see http://www.stephenpyne.com for details. For engaging summations of recent research, see Charles W. Mann's two books, *1491: New Revelations of the Americas before Columbus* (New York: Vintage, 2006) and *1493: Uncovering the New World Columbus Created* (New York: Knopf, 2011).

15. William Ruddiman, *Plagues, Plows, and Petroleum: How Humans Took Control of Climate* (Princeton, N.J.: Princeton University Press, 2005).

16. See W. J. Bond, F. I. Woodward, and G. F. Midgley, "The Global Distribution of Ecosystems in a World without Fire," *New Phytologist* 165 (2005): 525–38. The data-crunching in this article is formidable, but the claims speak to humanist ears: "several of the world's major biomes owe their distribution and ecological properties to the fire regime" (525); "fire may be a primary factor in determining biome distributions, promoting flammable ecosystems where the climate can support forests" (526); "although anthropogenic fires have undoubtedly extended areas of flammable vegetation, there is now abundant evidence that natural fires occurred long before humans" (533).

17. Mann, *1493*, 39–43.

18. Edmund Spenser, *The Faerie Queene*, ed. A. C. Hamilton (London: Pearson, 2001). Citations appear parenthetically in the text and give book, canto, stanza, and line numbers.

19. Prince Arthur described it as a "windy tempest" (2.8.48.1); Guyon's "tempest of his wrathfulnesse" (2.12.83.4) in the Bower echoes this phrase.

20. Robert Greene, *Friar Bacon and Friar Bungay,* in *Robert Greene,* ed. Thomas H. Dickinson (New York: Charles Scribner's Sons, 1909). Further citations appear parenthetically in the text and give act and scene; this edition is not lineated.

21. On Renaissance astrology, see Anthony Grafton, *Cardano's Cosmos: The Worlds and Works of a Renaissance Astrologer* (Cambridge, Mass.: Harvard University Press, 2001); and Tara Numendal, *Alchemy and Authority in the Holy Roman Empire* (Chicago: University of Chicago Press, 2007).

22. On Greene's Bacon as an allegorical mixture of academic charisma and theatrical power, see Bryan Reynolds and Henry Turner, "From Homo Academicus to Poeta Publicus: Celebrity and Transversal Knowledge in Robert Greene's *Friar Bacon and Friar Bungay* (c. 1589)," in *Writing Robert Greene: Essays on England's First Notorious Professional Writer,* eds. Kirk Melinkoff and Edward Gieskes (Aldershot: Ashgate, 2008), 73–94.

23. Roger Bacon, *The Mirror of Alchemy* (London, 1597), 9. Further citations appear parenthetically in the text. A later English translation of Bacon, *Friar Bacon: His Discovery of the Miracles of Art, Nature, and Magick* (London, 1659), claims to rely on John Dee's edition of the work (ESTC R10803). Greene's main narrative source, *The Famous History of Friar Bacon,* appeared in multiple editions after 1627; Greene presumably relied on manuscript sources, the earliest of which appears in the mid-sixteenth century, or a lost printed edition.

24. I thank Julian Yates and Eileen Joy for emphasizing these points.

25. I am inspired here by Michel Serres's comments on metaphor as transport. See Michel Serres and Bruno Latour, *Conversations on Science, Culture, and Time* (Ann Arbor: University of Michigan Press, 1997).

26. For a summary of the Homogenocene and the ecological contours of globalization after Columbus, see Mann, *1493.*

27. For more speculations about these and other terms for the modern era, see my new book *Shipwreck Modernity: Ecologies of Globalization, 1550–1719* (Minneapolis: University of Minnesota Press, 2015).

28. J. J. Cohen, "Elemental in Tuscaloosa," April 29, 2013, http://www.inthemedievalmiddle.com/2013/04/elemental-in-tuscaloosa.html.

29. See Linda Solomon, "Vagabond Veterans: The Roguish Company of Martin Guerre and *Henry V,*" in *Rogues and Early Modern English Culture,* ed. Craig Dionne and Steve Mentz (Ann Arbor: University of Michigan Press, 2004), 261–93.

30. Janet Adelman, *The Common Liar: An Essay on Antony and Cleopatra* (New Haven, Conn.: Yale University Press, 1973).

31. This "gap" also suggestively parallels the hidden or withdrawn nature of substance in Harman's philosophy.

32. For my watery turn against stasis, see Steve Mentz, "After Sustainability," *PMLA* 127, no. 3 (May 2012): 586–92.

three

Airy Something

VALERIE ALLEN

In the beginning, says Plato, God made triangles and out of them he made the elements and then out of the elements he made everything else.[1] Triangles are the building blocks of earth's matter, by which numbers inhabit space and all that is air turns out to be solid. Two disparate identities become connected through a third—that is what triangles do. They give air its many faces. We start with the airy nothing of thought at its most abstract, thence to the belief or disbelief such mystery provokes, for breath and meditation have long been companionate. The story of the elements is the story of genesis and the shape of belief. We proceed to the saturated air of haloes and auras, and then, air gets moving, a current through space and time to become wind and whirlwind. As we will see, motionless and moving air require each other, for in weather systems, depression and turbulence collaborate.

This discussion of air as holy presence, empty space, and roaring wind represents an assay to place medieval theology in touch with modern science—a fumbling attempt for sure because their discourses live on different planes. The motive is to argue that where modern geometries can deepen understanding of the medieval fascination with the body of Christ crucified and resurrected, the theological problem of a risen Jesus brings to the fore the limits of the secular as a category within which to consider the elemental, the usefulness of ignorant questions, the task of materializing abstract thoughts, and the need for a genealogy or material history of scientific ideas—for a science that forgets to tell its own story thus is bound to repeat it.[2]

The paradigm-shifting theories of contemporary science (such as quantum mechanics, general relativity, string theory) can seem undecidedly situated between being airy somethings and airy nothings, for on the one hand they describe essentials of matter, space, and time, yet on the other their ideas are abstruse, counterintuitive. Modern mathematics cannot precisely articulate its content except in symbolic form, and thus any effort to express its most powerful ideas in ordinary language is set up to fail. Even in ordinary language, the abstraction is difficult to apprehend. In her book *Physics on the Fringe,* the science writer Margaret Wertheim notes that, at the time of writing, the legitimate variants of string theory numbered at about 10^{500}. Appreciating that 1,000,000,000,000,000,000,000,000,000,000,000,000,000,000 has more rhetorical impact than 10^{40} (even though the latter is the larger number), Wertheim writes the 500 zeros out in full, aligning one "O without a figure" (to quote Lear's Fool) after another in hopes that the sheer length of the line will dwarf our intuitive sense of capacity. "None of us," observes Wertheim, "will ever *see* the four-dimensional spacetime of general relativity or *touch* the eleven-dimensional manifold of string theory."[3] She identifies a problem that the apostle Thomas would appreciate.

Poetic language perhaps gets closest to articulating this mathematical sublime. In Flann O'Brien's surreal novel *The Third Policeman,* MacCruiskeen's miniature chests, which fit inside each other as exact replicas, intuit the destruction of scale that Benoît Mandelbrot uncovered in fractal geometry. Mandelbrot's landmark essay and O'Brien's novel appeared in the same year (1967), although the novel had been written almost thirty years prior.[4] The similarities are marked: where Mandelbrot demonstrates Britain's coastline to be self-similar at any level of scale, the novel's dust jacket displays a man holding a chest that discloses an identical image of another man holding a chest, and so on in infinite series. MacCruiskeen's chests become at some point invisible and when he admits that the last one he made took him a year to believe he had even made it, the narrator feels not wonder but nausea.[5] O'Brien takes nano-aesthetics beyond the sublime, where the elements appear both terrible and wonderful, to a darker place where ordinary language goes into referential shock. The question of aesthetics cedes its place to that of belief.

Since Plato at least, mathematical reality has always been at odds with common sense, but it took its own quantum leap into abstraction in the nineteenth century, when, for example, George Boole made something out of nothing by creating the empty set: "we may term Nothing a class."[6] Arguably, the twentieth century's "linguistic turn" has its roots in the logical turn of nineteenth-century mathematics, in which its language becomes self-referential, no longer necessarily being "*about* anything, other than itself."[7] This rule of logical validity loosens the hitherto indissoluble connection between truth and empirical experiment, for centuries the guarantor of the real.

The rarefied atmosphere of modern mathematics can leave an earth-bound humanities scholar short on oxygen. The sheer difficulty of the subject places him or her in the position of being asked to take on faith what can neither be seen nor understood. In this way, air constitutes the element of belief and space measures the distance between an outsider and enigma. Offered here is a famous figure of Christian history, especially important for the Middle Ages, as an objective correlative to this disciplinary perplexity: Doubting Thomas, who insisted on a reality he could make visible and palpable. His role as reluctant believer has been underrated in a medieval era that, at least till recently, has been too often represented as an age of homogeneous faith puckered by occasional bouts of heresy.[8] Beyond mere analogy between a skeptical apostle and a scientific outsider, however, his stipulation that he must "put his finger into the space of the nails," as the Gospel account phrases it, discloses a desire that seems impossible, like flying without wings, or drawing one figure in different geometries.

Within Thomas's insistence on deforming mystery into terms he can comprehend lies a big, bold question that Wertheim poses in her own terms: "*Who* gets to feel 'at home in the universe' contemporary science describes?"[9] At the same time crude and unanswerable yet essential, this question resonates with a humanities scholar of a medieval past. In his wish to put his finger into a hole, Thomas—outsider believer, insider skeptic—demonstrates the epistemic value of incredulity, naivety, curiosity, stubbornness, slow-wittedness, even ignorance.

It would be understandable for a reader to resist the parallel made here between mathematical rarefication and theological mystery, smacking as it does of some Pythagorean brotherhood, yet the philosopher of science Paul K. Feyerabend also argues for their kinship. He makes a characteristically provocative claim that what the Inquisition was to Galileo, modern science is to its outsiders: "Any criticism of the rigidity of the Roman Church applies also to its modern scientific and science-connected successors."[10] Much earlier than Galileo, and operating from within the very heart of that Catholic institution, our leery apostle provokes the same question Wertheim poses. With a view to blurring the line between devotion and blasphemy, the next section anatomizes Thomas's incredulity; thence to a consideration of sacred holes and their miraculous shapes. If that expatiation seems to delay unbearably a consideration of air, forbearance is asked. It takes a while for a medievalist (this one anyway) to get an argument about air as current off the ground. The shape of sacred holes turns out to be the shapes that air likes to knot itself into, for Christ's body and air alike constitute the invisible made visible. To register the sacramental presence of Corpus Christi (the body of Christ) as primordial, unformed matter, late Latin refers to his flesh and blood as the elements *(elementa)*.[11] The conventional form of Corpus Christi undergoes a series of continuous squeezings and stretchings that gradually reforms it into an airy funnel. That is the shape this "assay" takes.

Doubting Thomas

Painted right as Galileo developed his astronomical theories, Caravaggio's famous *Incredulity of Saint Thomas* (1603) constitutes a remarkable achievement of reverence and profanity.[12] Thomas, in the foreground, dominates the scene, while an abject Jesus—head hanging—looks more like a patient having his wound palpated than the risen Christ. To emphasize his corporeality, Caravaggio omits a halo. Champion of empirical knowledge, Thomas interrogates revelation in a way that borders on blasphemy. Later in the century, Mattia Preti's *Ungläubiger Thomas* makes the suggestion of blasphemy more obvious.[13] Christ splays his arms as Thomas pokes, an intimation of a second crucifixion, for blasphemy traditionally was thought to crucify Christ all over again. To question resurrection thus is to subject God to the ordeal—that is what the Jews do in the *Croxton Play of the Sacrament*, where they make the host bleed as if newly crucified.[14] Caravaggio's Thomas is having a good dig in that wound, lifting up the skin to get into the hole. Middle English has just the word for the deed: *gropen*, used in a number of contemporary texts to refer to his touch.[15] Other uses show that groping is what blind people do, where the reliance on touch is total; the word refers to sweaty pawing of women's bodies; Chaucer uses it in the *Summoner's Tale* to refer to the friar's grasping around Thomas's bottom for a gift of money;[16] related to "grab," it means grasping hold of something; it means medical palpation, referring (frequently) to the searching of wounds; it means to "think" or "consider" in the sense of self-examination; priests "grope" penitents when hearing confession. Groping ranges semantically from the most penetrating inquiry into hidden mystery to the most debased questioning. All of those implied meanings come across in Caravaggio's painting.

The Gospel account in St. John, however, makes no reference to Thomas actually touching Christ's wounds. In fact, there are good arguments for thinking Thomas deliberately did *not* touch Christ's wounds.[17]

> Now Thomas, one of the twelve, who is called Didymus, was not with them when Jesus came. The other disciples therefore said to him: We have seen the Lord. But he said to them: Except I shall see in his hands the print of the nails, and put my finger into the place of the nails, and put my hand into his side, I will not believe.
>
> And after eight days again his disciples were within, and Thomas with them. Jesus came, the doors being shut, and stood in their midst, and said: Peace be to you.
>
> Then he says to Thomas: Put in your finger hither, and see my hands; and bring hither your hand, and put it into my side; and be not faithless, but believing.
>
> Thomas answered, and said to him: My Lord and my God.
>
> Jesus said to him: Because you have seen me, Thomas, you have believed: blessed are they who have not seen, and have believed.[18]

The millennium-plus tradition that Thomas did touch Christ seems to have come about to counter second-century Docetist heresy, which claimed the risen Jesus to be an airy phantasm. So a doubting Thomas who actually touched Christ's body would helpfully authenticate it.[19] By the Middle Ages, however, Docetism, Gnosticism, and other such denials of the full materiality of the risen Christ are old hat, so Thomas's incredulity gets conscripted for a more timely controversy, namely, the doctrine of the Real Presence, which asserted that Christ's body was really and not metaphorically present in the elements of bread and wine. From the thirteenth century onward, both Thomas and the Eucharist enjoy coincident rising fortunes.[20]

Variously interpreted by different theologians, Thomas's incredulity can be plotted anywhere along a continuum of belief that at the positive end associates with a restless epistemic idealism and at the negative end with blasphemy. His incredulity, that is, while problematical to belief, is richly nuanced in its own right. As objective correlative to modern perplexity in the face of mathematical mystery, his ambivalence is productive, incapable of fixing to one epistemic position. In elaboration of that fruitful doubt, here are six different ways of interpreting it, from the most positive to the most negative: six stations of unbelief, six ways not to get sucked in.

First, and most positively, his incredulity presents as an extraordinary idealism that sets conditions upon belief to a degree higher than the common believer. Bernard of Clairvaux describes Thomas and Moses as "restless men, eager to penetrate the deeper mysteries, to grasp sublimer truths." Because of his "greatness of soul," his lack of faith resulted in an exclusive and privileged encounter with Christ.[21]

Second, Thomas's unbelief demonstrates healthy skepticism. The Incredulity was a theme widely associated with justice in fifteenth-century Tuscany, with images of him depicted in courtrooms and assembly halls. Christ shows clemency and Thomas the desire for evidence—any good judge needs both.[22] He was the patron saint of "the Florentine guild of Judges and Notaries."[23] For Albertus Magnus, Thomas's doubt represented simple observance of due process. By being slower to believe, he believes all the more firmly when he does commit.[24] Thomas's incredulity is then a reasonable counterbalance to overcredulity. A sermon by the Augustinian canon John Mirk refers to Thomas's recidivist doubt over the Assumption of the Virgin Mary as bringing about "*probaciones*" of the miracle.[25] The *MED* offers various meanings of *probacioun,* including that of legal proof or evidence, and it is in this neutral sense Mirk seems to use it. Taken together, these interpretations of Thomas's groping present him as simply a good critical thinker.

Third, enter Thomas the slowpoke, the plodding literalist. Evidence of this dull-wittedness comes in an earlier incident in John's gospel, when he asks Christ how they can follow him when they do not know where he is going.[26] He is the sort to hang back until he has all his questions answered, a characterization yielding a word often associated with Thomas, namely, "tarrying." Mirk speaks of *þe tarying of Thomas leue.*[27] Aquinas speaks of his tardiness *(tarditas)* to believe, a word that can also mean stupidity, and in English, of course, retard.[28] The Auchinleck manuscript notes how Thomas was always showing up late to everything, including the Virgin's funeral: "Wo was him, he was bihinde" and "He was to longe bihinde."[29] Thomas's incredulity reveals itself as being slow off the mark, a kind of hesitation, and Latin *hesitare* is indeed one of a number of verbs used to denote doubt. *Hesitare* derives from "sticking fast," implying delay in belief.[30] The arrested motion of his body through space and time corporealizes a mental stillness that foreshadows the torpid air of a storm.

Fourth, descending into the pejorative, Thomas's unbelief appears crass. Chrysostom told his Constantinople audience that Thomas was "grosser and more materialistic" *(crassior)* than the other apostles because he demanded evidence of the crudest kind, that is, touch.[31] Having acknowledged Thomas as free of overcredulity, Aquinas still thinks the disciple went too far, revealing "his stubborn doubt" *(obstinata eius dubitatio).*[32] Commonly considered the lowest of the five wits, and at the opposite end to sight (the aristocrat of the senses), touch is how rough folk understand the world and how outsiders grope their way around specialized knowledge.

Fifth, Thomas demonstrates a fatal wavering, a dangerous doublemindedness. The name "Thomas," says Aquinas, means both "twin" and "abyss," twin by dint of biology, abyss by way of the depth and darkness of his unbelief.[33] For Herric of Auxerre, *Didymus* means "doubtful" rather than "twin."[34] Not alone among languages, Latin offers an underlying linguistic affinity between doubt and doubleness. *Anceps* (literally, "two-headed") means "uncertain," and is a synonym in medieval Latin of "doubtful."[35] To be called twin suggests that you are the second born, the one who "cannot easily be distinguished from the first one."[36] In birth as in life, Thomas arrives late on the scene. Doubt behaves like a twin: uncanny in appearing similar to yet different from belief, its sibling; its proximity to belief suggesting that identity is systemically double.[37]

Sixth and at the bottom of the heap, Thomas's incredulous groping blasphemes. Peter Chrysologus, preaching in fifth-century Ravenna, says that Thomas's unbelief was cruel because by putting his fingers into Christ's side he renewed Christ's pain and made the wounds bleed again.[38] Withdrawing his hand from Christ's side, Thomas of the *Towneley Plays* gasps, "my hande is blody," as if unbelief had reopened the wound.[39] His action is motivated by active error that borders on heresy.

> It was a goost before you stod,
> Lyke hym in blood betraced;
> His cors that dyed on rood
> Foreuer hath deth enbraced.[40]

The diversity of reaction to Thomas's gropings indicates the ambiguity of his unbelief throughout this long medieval era of ecclesiastical hegemony. His desire to make the invisible visible is summed up in his insistence on the curious evidence of a hole. A risen Christ with immaculate flesh would not have satisfied the dubious apostle. He will only be convinced by a cut or tear, thereby exhibiting the desire for an added dimension to experience, for no one can cut into the two-space of a plane surface *(epiphaneia),* which, as Euclid reminds us in his *Elements,* has length and breadth but no depth. A plane surface cannot have holes.[41]

Thomas finds himself hard up against a problem of measurement: that of one dimension of experience in the quantitative system of another. For the mathematician Paul Lockhart, the measurement questions *(quot? quanto?)* are akin to poking something with a stick.[42] An entire tradition existed in the Middle Ages of poking Christ's wounds thus with a stick. His drops of blood were counted; his wounds were measured, the length of the nails calculated: a strange conjunction of religious devotion and mathematical desire. In Thomas's case, the probative touching of the wound is itself a kind of measuring. In one image from a fourteenth-century Book of Hours, the following words begirdle Christ's wound: "ci est la mesure de la plaie du costre nostre seigneur qui pour nous souffrist mort en la crois" (This is the measure of the lateral wound of our lord, who suffered death on the cross for us).[43] The numbers might be recited, as a spell or prayer (differentiating the two is not always easy), or worn wordlessly as an amulet, as if the dimensions of the wound stretched like a girdle to protect the devout wearer. In counting blood drops, the *guttae* are more than simple units of calculation. They are the solution to a mystery and exceed the class of natural numbers inasmuch as one single drop contains redemption without end.[44] Huge numbers and mysticism have a long history of association together. The devout spiritually hyperventilate as they boggle their mind with the biggest numbers they can conceptualize. In a culture that had not yet learned to measure the air (the barometer not being invented until the seventeenth century), the mensuration of Christ's miraculous cavity occurs in no everyday dimension. Less a way of controlling matter with statistics, these measurements offer a way for a southpaw to fumble around the mystery of the elements.

Sacred Holes

In the same ways that air forms both twisting storm and its calm eye, so Corpus Christi forms both the sacramental body and its ruptures. Saint Bernard, in his sermons on the Song of Songs, elevates apertures to the encounter with divinity. Clefts in the rock and crannies in the wall turn into Christ's wounds. "Why," he asks, "should I not gaze through the cleft?"[45] For the mystic Richard Rolle, Christ's body is like a net, a dovecot, or a honeycomb all because of these miraculously elastic wounds that stretch to accommodate countless hosts of souls who take shelter in the cavities.[46] The fissure is itself the shape of salvation, the form that redemption takes. This configuration does not separate into the expected dyads of frame and interior, chaff and wheat, because the interior is empty space. In Corpus Christi, the "frame" of skin that surrounds the wound is as precious and essential as the hole it surrounds. This tear in the already real resists any distinction, Kantwise, between *parergon* and *ergon*.[47]

Knots of air occurring within other knots of air, the stigmata further resist the ergon/parergon distinction by being self-similar, like Mandelbrot's fractals or MacCruiskeen's chests. In religious art of both west and east, sacred figures regularly appear within an aureola, a cloud or bubble of air made visible. Thought of variously as halo, cloud, aura, and mandorla, the aureola can manifest itself around a head or an entire body. Within the space of the aureola, the air is glorified, time and space are sacralized. In Latin these auras will often be depicted as clouds, "nimbus" or *nūbēs,* for darkness becomes the way to depict intense radiance. Air both veils sacredness and announces its presence. However lacking in scientific barometry, the medieval era was well tuned to air's different moods. Construing into English from the Latin sentence "Ego sum somnolentus quia aura est somnefera," a fifteenth-century school book records, "Y am sclepy for þe weder ys sleepy."[48] Fudging the Latin's more precise distinction between sleepy *(somnolentus)* and sleep-inducing *(somnefera),* the English depicts air as a live thing, drowsy like an animal, making heavy weather for everyone of staying awake.

The very origin of haloes lies in rituals of work and sacralization of the seasons. Their circular shape affirms their etymology: Latin *hālos* derives from Greek *halōs,* a disc-shaped threshing-floor, where actors assumed the aura of Dionysian divinity by dance, incantation, and the wearing of masks.[49] Christian iconography routinely embeds one aura, one sacred hole within another. Western representations of Christ in Judgment, for example, depict a haloed Christ within an aureola, and display the holes of his wounds, the passage through which judgment extends mercy.[50] The nesting series subtly riffs on the concentricities of rose windows, which also take the Last Judgment as their theme, their formation resonantly cosmological. The distinctive shape that Christ's lateral wound can assume echoes that of the mandorla, so named from its almond shape (Latin *amandola*) (Figure 3.1).

Sometimes the mandorla surrounds not the wound but the entire figure of Christ.[51] Sometimes it is a whole world that the mandorla encompasses.[52] Stigmata, bodies, and worlds within a mandorla and haloes within auras suggest formations that fold in upon themselves in self-similar pattern, turning frame into center and center into frame. In search of a geometry that eliminates the distractions of ergon and parergon, I turn to a topological form that better describes this recursive formation, to wit, the torus, fortuitously anticipated by the medieval glazier who made the stained glass Thomas window in Bad St. Leonard, Austria (Figure 3.2).

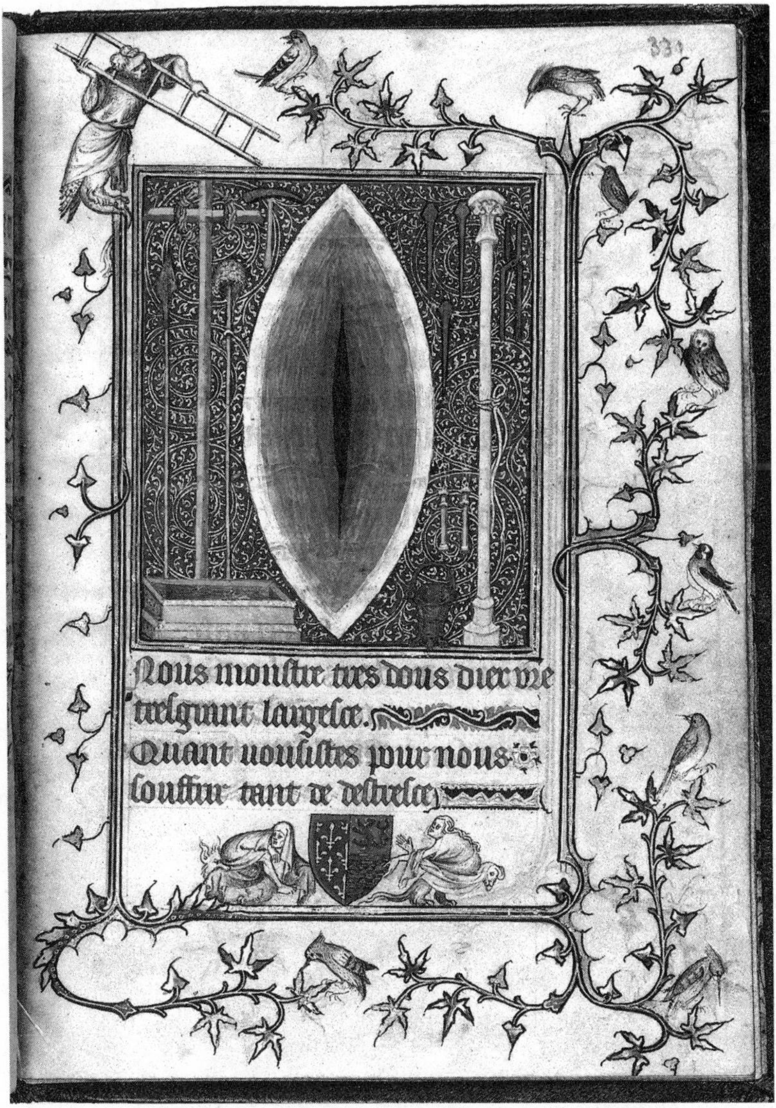

FIGURE 3.1. The Holy Wound of Christ flanked by the "arma Cristi." From the Psalter and Hours of Bonne of Luxembourg (before 1349). Courtesy The Metropolitan Museum of Art, The Cloisters Collection, 1969 (69.86), fol. 331r. Image copyright The Metropolitan Museum of Art.

FIGURE 3.2. Stained glass Thomas window. From Carinthia, Austria (1340–50). Courtesy The Metropolitan Museum of Art, The Cloisters Collection, 1968 (68.224.3). Image copyright The Metropolitan Museum of Art.

Between the exigencies of the glass medium and his desire to accentuate what Thomas is touching, the glazier makes the lateral wound stand out in relief, a circle, a halo, a donut, a torus.

Thomas desires to put his finger into a hole. Note the Latin case change from (locative merged with) ablative to accusative between his wish to see the mark of the nails *in* Christ's hands *(in manibus)* and his wish to put his finger *into* the space of the nails *(in locum clavorum).* The accusative implies the accessing of depth as well as a tangible line of connection between himself and Christ. He wants to penetrate a solid body and will not believe until the ordinarily resistant surface of skin is torn. His desire is better expressed in terms of topology than of Euclidean geometry. By incrementally transforming Corpus Christi into the abstract strangeness of topological shapes, Thomas's incredulity morphs into an outsider's perplexity before the counterintuitive "realities" of mathematical mystery. The intention is not to do math in Christ's wound, but neither is it to generate metaphors for decoration, making topology the fanciful if ultimately dispensable vehicle for the tenor of Christian mystery. Topology is not a figurative crutch that one can toss aside once the concept has been grasped. A reconceptualization of concept is called for instead. The Latin verb *concipere* yields not only the English word "concept" but also "conceit," which demonstrates better than metaphor how the heterogeneous ideas of medieval resurrection theology and algebraic topology, yoked by violence together, deform each other sufficiently to produce an argument that cannot be stated outside of the mannered analogy. Like that endless ribbon, the Möbius strip, which, having only one side and zero thickness, cannot be accurately represented in three-space, the conceit is a single concept, without obverse and reverse, tenor and vehicle.[53]

Consider then Corpus Christi as a topological formation. It is an imaginative leap, not a geometrical assertion. No disrespect meant, but the risen Jesus assumes the same topological shape as a four-fold torus (conventionally drawn as two pretzels, laid end to end). In order for two figures to be topologically equivalent either must be able to be deformed (stretched and/or contracted) in a continuous series of transformations until it assumes the other's shape.[54] Take each of the four donut-holes as the *loci clavorum* on Christ's hands and feet. To visualize this, shrink the arms and legs into the body's trunk until only hands and feet emerge, like how the Ebstorf map expands Christ's body into rotundity; contract the head entirely into the torso, like the semimythical Blemmyae of natural histories;[55] thicken the flesh surrounding each hole left by the nails until each extremity is donut-shaped but still a single mass; this is a four-fold torus, which can be further manipulated until the four rings lie conjoined in a row. One can just as easily reverse this process to turn a four-fold torus into the figure of the risen Christ.

Pulling and deforming Christ's body in this way represents a kind of poking with a stick, a groping born of curiosity and ignorance, even a buffeting born of blasphemy, for the soldiers crucifying Christ traditionally tugged his limbs in order to stretch them the length of the transverse beam.[56] It is none too clear whether such poking signals devotion or blasphemy, play or death.

These deformations of Christ's body bring to mind lines from a hymn by the eighteenth-century Wesley brothers: "Our God contracted to a span / Incomprehensibly made Man." They demonstrate a believer's perplexity at how a being of infinite dimension could squeeze himself into three.[57] Their theological musing had been foreshadowed shortly before by Leonhard Euler, who reduced a map of the city of Königsberg into a crypto-donut formation in order to demonstrate that it was impossible to cross all seven bridges of Königsberg without traversing any more than once. In a proof that enabled a new geometry called *analysis situs,* Euler ignored the city's unique landscape and scaled its contours into a graph with vertices (the city's landmass) and edges (the bridges).[58] He shrank winding streets and contracted the island into points and stretched the bridges into lines. The graph was not plotted on the Cartesian plane for this formation had no need of unique coordinates relative to external space. All Euler needed was a way of measuring the graph's internal paths of connection. Topology might be said to start here.

Precisely because topological formations take their mathematical being from their internal connectivity and not from reference to external space, it is important not to confuse the shape of the topological "object" (Christ's body as a four-fold torus) with the space that surrounds it.[59] A torus is a donut-shaped surface, thought of as hollow. Even though topology freely deforms shapes until they are equivalent, there is no way that a torus can ever be stretched or contracted into a sphere for it will always be stopped by that hole, which is definitive even though not "part" of the torus itself: "The hole is something in the surrounding space not in the surface."[60] Not constituting any part of the torus, the hole cannot be said to be the topological property that distinguishes it from the sphere. The wound is defined by its hole yet the hole is not a "part" of Corpus Christi in any properly mereological sense of the term; just as we had to jettison concepts such as ergon and parergon so "part" proves inadequate to the job of this new dimension of experience. Euler knew he was dealing with a different experience of space.

How then are these donuts measured? By covering its surface area with triangles, as if to return matter to its Platonic elemental shape.[61] Then, count all the vertices of the triangles *(V)*, all the edges or shared lines *(E)*, and all the faces (viz., surfaces surrounded by three edges) *(F)*. $V\text{-}E+F$ will give the measurement, and in any torus, $V\text{-}E+F = 0$ while in any sphere $V\text{-}E+F = 2$. For a double torus $V\text{-}E+F = -2$; for a treble, -4; for Corpus Christi, a quadruple or four-fold torus, $V\text{-}E+F = -6$.

The license of the conceit allows me to count only the violent cuts on Christ's body, to ignore skin pores as piercings of the body's surface, and to interpret bodily orifices as indentations rather than as cuts through the surface. (Were naturally occurring orifices to be considered, the human body appears already toroid in configuration, the mouth and anus marking the lips of a funnel-shaped structure.) But one indentation in this conceit of Corpus Christi as a four-fold torus cannot be ignored: his lateral wound. It cannot be defined as a piece of the surface that has been removed because that would mean that the figure's surface is no longer continuously connected and thus no longer a torus. It could perhaps be dismissed as trivial, as a cavity in the way a bodily orifice is a cavity, which can be continuously pressed and shrunk into smoothness; but that would mean that Christ only had four wounds, which, in any measurement system, is bad counting. Rather, that lateral wound might be thought of as a closed loop, continuous and non-self-intersecting, drawn in the surface of the torus.[62] Because it does not perforate Christ's body, it is only a loop drawn in the surface, not an edge. Situated where it is on the body, it can be shrunk to a point through a process of continuously performed contractions.[63] Yet even shrunk to a point, this lateral wound, the "continuous non-self-intersecting closed curve," divides the body of Christ into two distinct regions. It matters.[64]

That continuous, non-self-intersecting loop can be thought of as the simplest kind of mathematical knot, called an unknot. Knot topology can only occur in three-space because a knot is impossible to draw on a (two-space) plane, which, having no depth, cannot allow crossed strings, and impossible in any dimension above three-space because there would be so much "room" that any knot would instantly unravel.[65] That is, knots belong to this dimensioned world of elemental solids. Another name for the unknot is the torus. The closed loop of the wound on the torus that is Jesus can be thought of as another torus, embedded in the surface of another. The nesting of tori or unknots suggests, in line with the concentricities of circular rose windows, that the toroidal figure of Corpus Christi is not static but dynamic; that it is recursive, feeding upon its own feedback, generating itself, just as the sacramental body of Christ is theologically perpetual. In this recursive movement, the traditional bodily hierarchy of crown and foot gives way not to simple inversion of superior and inferior but to fluid and continuous transformations of shape.

Literary knots are narrative tropes. Classical knots denote plot complication, which leads in turn to the idea of dénouement, unraveling or unknotting—hence analysis.[66] Medieval knots, in contrast, denote plot climax, the site where everything converges into a point of intensity that makes linear time and three-space fold in on themselves. This kind of knot represents a special moment of epiphany, a new dimension. It marks the moment when Thomas sticks his finger into the wound.

Toroidal Vortices

We move our focus now from the sacred hole to the toroidal shape that surrounds it. Such shapes occur naturally, and are even commonplace. Smokers will have created their own, whether through design or accident, by quick exhalation and inhalation, using their cheeks as bellows. Halfway between intentioned signals and involuntary effects, smoke rings are a special language. They blow their way through Poe's "Purloined Letter," which, by his own claim, is perhaps the best of his tales of ratiocination and certainly the most cerebral. Save for two necessary visits by Dupin to the Minister's apartment, one faked street distraction, and a dab of forgery, the entire mystery is solved from Dupin's armchair, by analysis. Small wonder the psychoanalyst Jacques Lacan was so taken with it.[67] The story opens with Dupin and the unnamed narrator sitting silently in the dark, making "curling eddies of smoke." More telling than words, these "perfect whirlwind[s] of smoke" spiral their way through conversations with the prosaic Prefect, the air pregnant with Dupin's smoke signals. Coupled with other stories such as "A Descent into the Maelstrom," "The Purloined Letter" shows Poe's fascination with the vortex as the shape of thought, creation, destruction, of meaning itself. In the science of fluid dynamics, emerging even as Poe wrote his stories, and where the behaviors of liquid and gas are identical, smoke ring and whirlpool alike obey the same laws of physics.

Poe expresses in fiction what others were exploring in science. Within a few years of Dupin's curling eddies, in 1858, the German physicist Hermann von Helmholtz had analyzed the physics of smoke rings.[68] It was, for that matter, the same cluster of years in which George Boole declared that "we may term Nothing a class," as if in those middle decades of the nineteenth century airy knots had formed at the failing boundary between Aristotelian and symbolic logic, between referential and self-referential language. From different domains of thought, imaginations created an epoch by contemplating the vortex as the key to understanding the structure of matter itself.

Like Dupin solving mysteries from the depths of his armchair, Helmholtz, in his "most beautiful investigation," predicted without experiment the behavior of vortex rings from equations alone, which—just like any good detective story—yield results that come from left field, taking the reader by surprise.[69] Tait and Thomson's business was to put these equations to the test by means of the "homely arrangement" of a smoke machine.[70]

In an ideal (rather than actual) fluid a vortex ring will last forever once it has formed because it is self-generating. Once begun, it must either "return ring-shaped into itself" or terminate at the boundaries of the fluid.[71] In Tait's words: "All vortex-rings—and therefore . . . all atoms of matter—must necessarily be endless, that is to say, must have their ends finally united together after any number of convolutions or knottings."[72]

With reference to the behavior of two coaxial rings (A, B) traveling in the same direction, Helmholtz predicts that the one in front (A) will widen and decelerate while B will contract and accelerate until B passes through A. "Then the same game goes on in the opposite order, so that the rings pass through each other alternately."[73] Once more, empirical results confirmed the mathematical calculations. Later, James Clerk Maxwell predicted the same behavior for three coaxial smoke rings: C jumps through B, B through A, A through C, and so on.[74] Certainly one can describe this "game" as one ring swimming through another, but it is just as fair to say that the ring in front vacuums up the one behind and spits it out on the other side. Such is the movement of Poe's maelstrom and of Homer's Charybdis, which sucks down water and spews it out three times a day (*Odyssey* XII, line 130).

The B-through-A-through-B-through-A air-swimming of the tori enacts with two coaxial rings what the single vortex is doing all the time, namely, coiling and roiling indefinitely on its own axis. This is the principle of recursivity writ large, where the self-energizing vortex loops around to feed and perpetuate itself, even as friction with the surrounding air sends it tractoring forward. This is the basic motion of toroidal vortices, exhibiting remarkable integrity under conditions of turbulence, "as if they are imbued with internal knowledge of what their form *must* be."[75]

In what is probably their most delightful form, toroidal vortices appear when dolphins blow air rings and play hoop and stick with them with their noses, passing on the skill to their young.[76] Tensile and elastic, the torus freely deforms and tangles only to resume its natural circular shape as an unknot. Radically unlike the rigid transformations of conventional geometry, the fluid elegance of the toroidal vortex enacts the continuous transformations that topology performs. Whether human smoke rings or dolphins' gyrations, these bouncing toroidal vortices signal playtime.

In rather more destructive form, these vortices appear as waterspouts, hurricanes, and tornadoes.[77] Where differences collide, between faith and doubt, human and nature, thought systems, cold and warm air, turbulence creates these lovely shapes that are as deadly as they are fun. Tornadogenesis, the process by which tornadoes form, occurs at the boundary line between a warm, moist air system and a cooler air system.[78] It starts with an updraft, for example, when air rises from a sun-baked ground. The horizontal winds apply torque or twisting force to the column of rising air, causing it to rotate and creating what is called a mesocyclone. Tornadogenesis continues with a rear flank downdraft caused by the cooler, denser air above that has been displaced by the rising warm air, which wraps around the rising warm air, pulling the mesocyclone downward toward the ground. The collision between the warm and the cooler air systems creates the cloud of condensed moisture that makes the tornado visible and gives it its characteristic appearance. At the base of the funnel, where the storm cloud vacuums air upward, the colliding systems rotate most rapidly, the radius of the funnel at its tightest: nature's aureola, a halo made of condensation, dust, and debris. Like Dante's apocalyptic landscape of sins against nature, where fire descends in contrary motion, the natural motion of a tornado behaves contrary to all intuition about falling objects. Where tornadoes rage, pigs fly.

Algebraic topology explains not only the shape of these recursive toroidal formations but also their very existence through a proof called the hairy ball theorem.[79] By way of introduction, consider how the direction of a dog's fur always changes at some point on its body, usually in a parting down the back and another along the stomach. By performing a similar series of continuous transformations as those done on Christ's body, retracting head and limbs until the hound has assumed perfect roundness, one can pose the theorem's question: is it possible to dispose the hairs on this canine sphere in such a way that they lie smooth and continuous, and never in a cow-lick? No. Impossible. The theorem states that the spherical dog (or any spherical object) must always have a point where convergent hairs stand upward, as they do on a coconut. Taking the direction of each hair as a vector field on the surface of the earth's thick rotundity, and each hair as a wind current, the theorem states that somewhere, at all times on the surface of the earth, there is a point where the vector is equivalent to zero. Somewhere, at all times on the surface of the earth, the air is perfectly still, "dead becalmed," as Poe puts it in "A Descent into the Maelstrom." Around this motionless eye of the storm, winds cow-lick furiously. Somewhere, at all times on the surface of the earth, there is a cyclone, permanent denizen of the planet. Air naturally possesses a violent side, its turbulence a mathematical necessity. This fact flies in the face of what Aristotle says of the element of air (indeed of all moving bodies), namely, that it locomotes in order to be motionless. The hairy ball theorem comes closer to implying that air is at rest in order that it may be turbulent, even and with Heraclitus in mind, that through this strife within the air between stillness and agitation all things come into being. In the vortex, destruction and creation get complicated with each other in ways that disclose no obvious kind of ethical imperative for action. It is the turbulence that restores stability—at least for a while.

Out of the Corner of the Eye

The recursive motion of a toroidal vortex demonstrates a principle in physics called precession, whereby the donut ring coils in a direction perpendicular to its own plane. Imagine the inside of the cyclone as a horizontal plane. The vectors of the air's up/down motion run orthogonal to that plane. A gyroscope exhibits the same principle: when torque or twisting force is applied to the gyroscope, it causes the perpendicular axis of whatever was twisted to rotate. The force applied and the force generated are at a 90-degree angle of association to each other. Humans, machines, and moving objects avail of orthogonal precession all the time. It is why runners give themselves a bit of oomph by twisting their trunk and tucked arms slightly to the right and left. It is the reason why the baseball, as it leaves the pitcher's hand, moves in a straight line, tangent to the arc drawn by the arm (spin, gravity, and air or fluid resistance notwithstanding). It is the reason why a stone, dropping into a body of water, sends ripples out at right angles to the axis of the stone's movement.

For the systems theorist Buckminster Fuller, precession is the critical element in how complexity works, where the behavior of the system in toto cannot be predicted by simply summing "the separate behaviors of any of its parts."[80] Precession demonstrates neatly why Aristotelian teleology will not explain the complexity of systems such as a cyclone. For example, when the bee makes its "beeline" to a flower, it has the 180-degree intention to gather pollen, yet in the doing it becomes the vector for cross-pollination, which makes the flowers bloom, which makes the bees gather pollen, which makes the flowers bloom. The mutualism of insect and plant sustains the ecosystem. Honey production is the bee's telos, cross-pollination its side effect, as intention and execution occur in orthogonal relation. In complex systems, angular effects generate more angular effects in a recursive loop.

> When the stone drops in the water, ... everything is set in motion, and immediately there is a resultant at 90 degrees. The resultant is the wave; the 90 degreeness begets another 90 degreeness, this 90 degreeness begets another 90 degreeness, and so on.[81]

This manifold of perpetual angular motion has no congruence with the Aristotelian paradigm of natural and violent motion of bodies.[82] Classical natural motion follows an up/down axis depending on the heaviness of the element in question (this is the doctrine of natural place—fire and air up, earth and water down), while violent motion is any force that interferes with or prevents natural motion. What is more, the motion is finite: air moves up until it finds its element and then stays put. But the perpendicularity of tornadogenesis creates a system that sustains itself in motion. Vectors that fly off at right angles mess around with the up-and-downness of pre-Newtonian physics such that the distinctions between natural and violent or natural and unnatural (the concept-pairs are related if not identical) lose their explanatory power in complexly interacting systems. Tornadogenesis occurs under many conditions, but one of the classic ones is as the side effect of larger turbulent events such as a hurricane. Call such vortices violently natural or naturally violent, if one wishes to keep these Aristotelian predicates in play, but maybe it is better to think of them as coming from left field, taking one by surprise even when seen coming. Explicable but unpredictable, deterministic but chaotic, they blindside us by emerging into the picture from out of the corner of the eye.

Precession explains gravity itself, and in Isaac Newton, Fuller sees an early theorist of complexity. First, notes Fuller, Newton calculated the line tangent to the moon's orbit. That tangent was the line "along which the Moon would move / If it were not attracted by the Earth." Then Newton measured the rate at which the moon "fell away from that line / In toward the Earth."[83] Note his phrasing: the moon falls "in," not down. In a thoroughly un-Aristotelian manner, Fuller calls up and down illusionary orientations, even to the point of referring to upstairs and downstairs as "outstairs" and "instairs."[84] Newton also struggled with conventional idiom in describing the new concepts that were emerging from his equations. In his *Principia,* he writes the following about gravity:

> Finally if it is universally established . . . that all bodies on or near the earth gravitate [*lit.* are heavy] *[gravem esse in Terram]* toward the earth, and do so in proportion to the quantity of matter in each body, . . . and that our sea in turn gravitates [is heavy] *[grave esse in Lunam]* toward the moon, . . . it will have to be concluded . . . that all bodies gravitate *[gravitant]* toward one another.[85]

The Latin literally means "the sea is heavy toward the moon." This invisible attraction Newton visualizes, so radically different from Aristotle's up/down axis of natural motion, is nonetheless phrased by him in terms that an Aristotelian might well use to speak of the elements of air or fire, as bodies that weigh upward. We now describe gravity as one body being passively pulled by another massier body, but Newton gives gravitating bodies greater agency than that, giving the sea wings so that it may rise toward the moon, as if it were still motivated by the elemental desire he was in the process of dismantling. At the collision boundary of two cosmological systems, Ptolomaic and Copernican, lies the essential mystery of flight.

In the *House of Fame,* the dream vision gave Geoffrey Chaucer what the surreal novel gave Flann O'Brien, a narrative space for indulging in some queer physics: rings of water and air that ripple indefinitely wider, never definitively coming to rest; a house sixty miles wide that spirals without anything to ground it; the terror of aerial ascent, especially for the gravitationally challenged narrator.[86] Although no mathematician, Chaucer found in his spinning wicker structure the logic of the vortex, where up is down and down is up, for Latin *vertex* and *vortex* both mean whirlpool and crown of the head. Nesting his house of twigs inside a conventional scientific exposition of elemental natural motion, Chaucer took human speech, materialized it into elemental puffs of air, made them "heavy toward the moon," and set them spinning so fast that he surprised himself to find stability on the inside of the vortex, like the area of low pressure inside a revolving torus of air. Such imaginings could not find expression in the formal academic logic of his day, yet he made turbulence meaningful. At the collision boundary of different languages, geometries, and realities, we find a vector of zero, a moment of stability in the middle of turbulence that allows one to doubt and speculate. Only by groping like Thomas groped can we maintain ourselves in meaning at this place. It is where an outsider might feel at home in the universe.

Notes

I would like to thank the editors and other readers (especially my colleague Toy Tung, but also my reading group of Jen Brown, Glenn Burger, Steve Kruger, Michael Sargent, and Sylva Tomasch) for valuable feedback.

1. Plato, *Timaeus,* trans. R. G. Bury (Cambridge, Mass.: Harvard University Press, 1929), 126–37 (53C–56C).

2. Here I am riffing on two quotes, first one by Alfred North Whitehead, who said that "a science that hesitates to forget its founders is lost" (quoted in Thomas S. Kuhn, *The Structure of Scientific Revolutions,* 4th ed. [Chicago: University of Chicago Press, 2012], 138); and second, the famous quote that "those who cannot remember the past are condemned to repeat it" (George Santayana with Daniel Cory, *The Life of Reason* [New York: Charles Scribner's Sons, 1953], 82).

3. Margaret Wertheim, *Physics on the Fringe: Smoke Rings, Circlons, and Alternative Theories of Everything* (New York: Walker & Company, 2013), loc. 3400 of 4154, loc. 3290 of 4154.

4. Benoit Mandelbrot, "How Long Is the Coast of Britain? Statistical Self-Similarity and Fractional Dimension," *Science,* n.s. 156, no. 3775 (May 5, 1967): 636–38.

5. Flann O'Brien, *The Third Policeman* (1967; rpr. London: Harper, 2007), 75–77.

6. George Boole, *An Investigation of the Laws of Thought* (1854; rpr. New York: Dover, 1958), 47.

7. Wertheim, *Physics on the Fringe,* loc. 1205 of 4154.

8. For nuanced mappings of medieval unbelief, see John H. Arnold, "The Materiality of Unbelief in Late Medieval England," in *The Unorthodox Imagination in Late Medieval Britain,* ed. Sophie Page (Manchester: Manchester University Press, 2010), 65–91; Carl Watkins, "Providence, Experience, and Doubt in Medieval England," in *Fictions of Knowledge: Fact, Evidence, Doubt,* ed. Yota Batsaki, Subha Mukherji, and Jan-Melissa Schramm (New York: Palgrave Macmillan, 2011), 40–60.

9. Wertheim, *Physics on the Fringe,* loc. 171 of 4154.

10. Paul K. Feyerabend, *Against Method,* 3rd ed. (London: Verso, 1993), 130.

11. *Oxford English Dictionary,* s.v. "element" (n.3), etymological note: "The word *elementa* is used in late Latin in the sense of 'articles of food and drink, the solid

and liquid portions of a meal' (see Du Cange); but in the ecclesiastical use there is probably a reference to the philosophical sense of mere 'matter' as apart from 'form'; the 'form,' by virtue of which the 'elements' became Christ's body and blood, being believed to be imparted by the act of consecration."

12. Jonathan Sawday, "Self and Selfhood in the Seventeenth Century," in *Rewriting the Self: Histories from the Renaissance to the Present,* ed. Roy Porter (London: Routledge, 1997), 29–48 (esp. 34).

13. *Ungläubiger Thomas* is located at the Kunsthistorisches Museum in Vienna. See http://bilddatenbank.khm.at/viewArtefact?id=1482.

14. *Croxton Play of the Sacrament,* ed. John T. Sebastian (Kalamazoo, Mich.: Medieval Institute Publications, 2012), ll. 449–84.

15. See quotations in the *Middle English Dictionary,* s.v. "gropen" (v.).

16. Roy Peter Clark, "Doubting Thomas in Chaucer's *Summoner's Tale,*" *Chaucer Review* 11, no. 2 (1976): 164–78.

17. Glenn W. Most, *Doubting Thomas* (Cambridge, Mass.: Harvard University Press, 2005), 57–59.

18. John 20:24–29, quoted in Douay Rheims and (Clementine) Latin Vulgate, DRBO.ORG 2001–2014, http://drbo.org/index.htm. Original text: "Thomas autem unus ex duodecim, qui dicitur Didymus, non erat cum eis, quando venit Jesus. / Dixerunt ergo ei alii discipuli: Vidimus Dominum. Ille autem dixit eis: Nisi videro in manibus ejus fixuram clavorum, et mittam digitum meum in locum clavorum, et mittam manum meam in latus ejus, non credam. / Et post dies octo, iterum erant discipuli ejus intus, et Thomas cum eis. Venit Jesus januis clausis, et stetit in medio, et dixit: Pax vobis. / Deinde dicit Thomae: Infer digitum tuum huc, et vide manus meas, et affer manum tuam, et mitte in latus meum: et noli esse incredulus sed fidelis. / Respondit Thomas, et dixit ei: Dominus meus et Deus meus. / Dixit ei Jesus: Quia vidisti me, Thoma, credidisti: beati qui non viderunt, et crediderunt."

19. Most, *Doubting Thomas,* 131, quoting Tertullian: "But it [Christ's body] was trustworthy . . . when he was touched by believing Thomas."

20. Alexander Murray, *Doubting Thomas in Medieval Exegesis and Art* (Rome: Unione internazionale degli istituti di archeologia storia e storia dell'arte in Roma, 2006), 50–51. There are many iconographic connections between Thomas and the Eucharist, as in the French, thirteenth-century Tabernacle of Cherves at New York's Metropolitan Museum of Art, which depicts Thomas's Incredulity on one of its wings, directly above the Last Supper. See also Mary Hayes, "Privy Speech: Sacred Silence, Dirty Secrets in the *Summoner's Tale,*" *Chaucer Review* 40, no. 3 (2006): 263–88 (esp. 272, 286n29).

21. Bernard of Clairvaux, *On the Song of Songs,* 4 vols., trans. Kilian Walsh (Kalamazoo, Mich.: Cistercian Publications, 1971–80), 2:140–41.

22. Andrew Butterfield, "The Christ and St. Thomas of Andrea del Verrocchio," in *Verrocchio's Christ and St. Thomas: A Masterpiece of Sculpture from Renaissance Florence,* ed. Loretta Dolcini (New York: Metropolitan Museum of Art, 1992), 52–79.

See also Lisa M. Rafanelli, "Seeking Truth and Bearing Witness: The 'Noli Me Tangere' and Incredulity of Thomas on Tino di Camaino's Petroni Tomb (1315–1317)," *Comitatus* 37 (2006): 32–65 (esp. 57–58).

23. Murray, *Doubting Thomas,* 31.

24. Ibid., 31, citing Albertus's *Enarrationes in Joannem,* in *Opera omnia,* vol. 24, ed. A. Borgnet (Paris: Vivès, 1899), 689: "Sicut enim dicit Chrysostomus: 'Laudabile est rem non probatam non cito credere.' Quia, sicut dicit Salomon, Eccli. xix.4: 'Qui cito credit, levis corde est'" (For as Chrysostom says, "It is praiseworthy not to jump to believe something unproven." Because, as Solomon says in Ecclesiasticus, 19.4: "Whoever is quick to believe is a lightweight"). Aquinas quotes the same verse in his *Commentaria super Ioannem,* caput 20, lectio 5. Text available in Corpus Thomisticum (Fundación Tomás de Aquino, 2000–2013), http://www.corpusthomisticum.org/.

25. John Mirk, *John Mirk's Festial,* vol. 2, ed. Susan Powell, Early English Text Society o.s. 335 (Oxford: Oxford University Press, 2011), 203, l. 142; *MED,* s.v. "probacioun" (n.).

26. Murray, *Doubting Thomas,* 24.

27. John Mirk, *John Mirk's Festial,* vol. 1, ed. Susan Powell, Early English Text Society o.s. 334 (Oxford: Oxford University Press, 2009), 20, ll. 21–22.

28. Aquinas, *Commentaria super Ioannem,* caput 20, lectio 6.

29. *The Assumption of the Blessed Virgin,* ll. 191, 570, in *The Auchinleck Manuscript,* ed. David Burnley and Alison Wiggins, National Library of Scotland, http://auchinleck.nls.uk/mss/assumpt.html.

30. S. Flanagan, "Lexicographic and Syntactic Explorations of Doubt in Twelfth-Century Latin Texts," *Journal of Medieval History* 27 (2001): 227.

31. Murray, *Doubting Thomas,* 20.

32. Aquinas, *Commentaria super Ioannem,* caput 20, lectio 5: "Sed multum investigare, praesertim ubi de secretis Dei agitur, grossities mentis est" (But to overdo one's search, especially about the secrets of God, shows a coarseness of mind).

33. Ibid., caput 20, lectio 5.

34. Flanagan, "Lexicographic and Syntactic Explorations," 222–23.

35. Ibid., 230.

36. Most, *Doubting Thomas,* 80.

37. Sigmund Freud, "The Uncanny," in *The Standard Edition of the Complete Psychological Works of Sigmund Freud,* 24 vols., trans. James Strachey (London: Hogarth Press, 1953–74), 17:217–56.

38. Murray, *Doubting Thomas,* 20.

39. "Thomas of India," l. 570, in Martin Stevens and A. C. Cawley, eds., *The Towneley Plays,* vol. 1, Early English Text Society s.s. 13 (New York: Oxford University Press, 1994), 384.

40. Ibid., ll. 405–8, 379.

41. *Greek Mathematical Works: Thales to Euclid,* vol. 1, ed. and trans. Ivor Thomas (1939; rpr. Cambridge, Mass.: Harvard University Press, 2006), 438–39.

42. Paul Lockhart, *Measurement* (Cambridge, Mass.: Belknap Press, 2012), 5.

43. Pierpoint Morgan MS. 90, f. 130. Thanks to Anne Harris for sharing this reference. See discussions and/or reproductions in Curt F. Bühler, "Prayers and Charms in Certain Middle English Scrolls," *Speculum* 39, no. 2 (1964): 270–78 (esp. 276–77). For a richly suggestive analysis of these images of the side wound measured and of the cosmological resonance of its mandorla shape, see David S. Areford, "The Passion Measured: A Late-Medieval Diagram of the Body of Christ," in *The Broken Body: Passion Devotion in Late-Medieval Culture,* ed. A. A. MacDonald, H. N. B. Ridderbos, and R. M. Schlusemann (Groningen: Egbert Forsten, 1998), 211–38.

44. Caroline Bynum Walker, *Wonderful Blood: Theology and Practice in Late Medieval Northern Germany* (Philadelphia: University of Pennsylvania Press, 2007), esp. 175–78.

45. Bernard, *On the Song of Songs,* 3:141–42.

46. Richard Rolle, "Meditations on the Passion," in *English Writings of Richard Rolle, Hermit of Hampole,* ed. Hope Emily Allen (Oxford: Clarendon Press, 1931), 35.

47. Kant uses the terms *parergon* and *ergon* in his *Critique of Judgment* to distinguish between the oeuvre and its frame, which announces that what lies within its border belongs to a different, aesthetic order of reality. Jacques Derrida problematizes the distinction in *The Truth in Painting,* trans. Geoff Bennington and Ian McLeod (Chicago: University of Chicago Press, 1987), 37–82.

48. Nicholas Orme, *Education and Society in Medieval and Renaissance England* (London: Hambledon, 1989), 101, §17, cited in Valerie Allen, *On Farting: Language and Laughter in the Middle Ages* (New York: Palgrave Macmillan, 2010), 39.

49. Allen, *On Farting,* 40–41.

50. Instances are almost too numerous to mention: take, for example, Fra Angelico's fresco of Christ in Judgment in Florence's Museo di San Marco (ca. 1436); or Giotto's Last Judgment fresco in Padua's Scrovegni Chapel.

51. See the Incredulity of Thomas in the tenth-century Benedictional of St. Æthelwold, British Library, Add. MS 49598, fols. 56v–57, http://imagesonline.bl.uk/index.php?service=search&action=do_quick_search&language=en&q=%237154.

52. See Ranulf Higden's mandorla-shaped *mappa mundi* in J. B. Harley and David Woodward, eds., *History of Cartography,* vol. 1, *Cartography in Prehistoric, Ancient, and Medieval Europe and the Mediterranean* (Chicago: University of Chicago Press, 1987), 353. For the connection between mandorla, side-wound, and cartography, see Areford, "The Passion Measured," 223–35.

53. Ian Stewart, *Concepts of Modern Mathematics,* 3rd ed. (New York: Dover, 1995), 148–51.

54. Keith Devlin, *Mathematics: The New Golden Age,* 3rd ed. (New York: Columbia University Press, 1999), 230–32.

55. Harley and Woodward, *History of Cartography,* 310 (for the Ebstorf map), 331, and plate 21 (for Blemmyae in the Walsperger map).

56. See the York Pinners' "Crucifixion," ll. 105–20, in *The York Plays,* ed. Richard Beadle (London: Edward Arnold, 1982), 318.

57. John and Charles Wesley, *Hymns for the Nativity of our Lord* (London, 1744?), 7, Hymn V, "Let Earth and Heaven Combine."

58. Leonard Euler, "Solutio problematis ad geometriam situs pertinentis," in *Commentarii academiae scientiarum Petropolitanae* 8 (1741): 128–40 (index number E53). See the Euler Archive, http://eulerarchive.maa.org. A scan of the original publication is made available by the University of Dartmouth's math department at http://www.math.dartmouth.edu/~euler/docs/originals/E053.pdf.

59. Stewart, *Concepts of Modern Mathematics,* 144–45.

60. Devlin, *Mathematics,* 226.

61. The measurement of this topological shape is known as the Euler characteristic. Ibid., 172–85, 232; see also Stewart, *Concepts of Modern Mathematics,* 197–209.

62. H. Graham Flegg, *From Geometry to Topology* (1974; rpr. New York: Dover, 2001), chap. 4, loc. 365–543 of 3674.

63. Ibid., loc. 400 of 3674. Were the closed loop to encircle one of the "limbs" of the torus, going through the hole the way a nose ring circles through a piercing, it could not shrink to a point.

64. Ibid., loc. 448 of 3674. The number of possible closed loops drawn on a surface that do *not* separate the surface into distinct regions determines its topological genus. The genus of a sphere is 0, because no such loop can be drawn; of a one-fold torus 1; of a two-fold torus 2; of a four-fold torus 4.

65. Devlin, *Mathematics,* 233.

66. Alcuin Blamires, "Philosophical Sleaze? The 'strok of thought' in the *Miller's Tale* and Chaucerian Fabliau," *Modern Language Review* 102, no. 3 (2007): 621–40 (633–35).

67. For Poe's story and Lacan's seminar, see *The Purloined Poe: Lacan, Derrida, and Psychoanalytic Reading,* ed. John P. Muller and William J. Richardson (Baltimore: Johns Hopkins University Press, 1988).

68. H. Helmholtz, "On Integrals of the Hydrodynamical Equations, which Express Vortex-Motion," trans. P. G. Tait, *Philosophical Magazine and Journal of Science,* supplement to vol. 33, 4th ser. (1867): 485–512. The most accessible account of vortex behavior occurs in P. G. Tait, *Lectures on Some Recent Advances in Physical Science with a Special Lecture on Force,* 3rd ed. (London: Macmillan and Co., 1885), 287–316. See also Lord Kelvin (Sir William Thomson), "On Vortex Atoms," *Philosophical Magazine and Journal of Science* 34 (1867): 15–24. For full discussion of Helmholtz's, Kelvin's, and Tait's work, see Wertheim, *Physics on the Fringe,* loc. 2415–651 of 4154.

69. Tait, *Lectures,* 294.

70. Ibid., 295.

71. Helmholtz, "On Integrals," 494.

72. Tait, *Lectures,* 301.

73. Helmholtz, "On Integrals," 510.

74. Wertheim, *Physics on the Fringe,* loc. 2541 of 4154.

75. Ibid., loc. 2482 of 4154.

76. Ibid., loc. 2140 of 4154. Typing in "dolphins" and "bubble rings" to YouTube or Google will yield many video clips of these mammals at play.

77. On the etymology of *tornado* (n.), see the *OED*'s note: "But the early sense makes it probable that *ternado* was a bad adaptation (perhaps originally a blundered spelling) of Spanish *tronada* 'thunderstorm' (< *tronar* to thunder), and that *tornado* was an attempt to improve it by treating it as a derivative of Spanish *tornar* to turn, return; compare *tornado* participle, returned. It is notable that this spelling is identified with explanations in which, not the thunder, but the turning, shifting, or whirling winds are the main feature."

78. The following is taken from National Oceanic and Atmospheric Administration, "The Basics about Tornadoes," http://www.spc.noaa.gov/faq/tornado/#The%20Basics; and from exhibits such as the Vortex Machine at the Yale Peabody Museum of Natural History (July 2013).

79. Stewart, *Concepts of Modern Mathematics,* 155–57. For a more detailed account, see David S. Richeson, *Euler's Gem: The Polyhedron Formula and the Birth of Topology* (Princeton, N.J.: Princeton University Press, 2008), loc. 3295–545 of 5741.

80. R. Buckminster Fuller, *Intuition* (Garden City, N.Y.: Doubleday, 1972), 27.

81. R. Buckminster Fuller, *Synergetics: Explorations in the Geometry of Thinking* (New York: Macmillan, 1975), 287 (533.04).

82. See Aristotle, *Physics,* trans. and ed. Philip H. Wicksteed and Francis M. Cornford, 2 vols (1929; rev. Cambridge, Mass.: Harvard University Press, 1957) 1:385–9.

83. Fuller, *Intuition,* 25.

84. Ibid., 103 (101 for illusionary orientation).

85. Isaac Newton, *The Principia: Mathematical Principles of Natural Philosophy,* trans. I. Bernard Cohen and Anne Whitman (Berkeley: University of California Press, 1999), 796. I have inserted the Latin from Cambridge University's digitized facsimile of Newton's handwritten additions, http://cudl.lib.cam.ac.uk/view/PR-ADV-B-00039-00001/781.

86. *The House of Fame,* in *The Riverside Chaucer,* 3rd. ed., ed. Larry D. Benson (Boston: Houghton Mifflin, 1987), 347–73.

four

The Sea Above

JEFFREY JEROME COHEN

Scaling Nature

Nature loves a ladder.[1]

Classical, medieval, and early modern imaginings of the cosmos describe a Great Chain of Being arrayed of links, steps, or rungs.[2] At the bottom of this *scala naturae* (nature's "ladder" or "staircase") reside inert things like stones, matter that merely exists. A natural hierarchy rises through plants, animals, and humans to culminate in supernatural and divine entities, an ascent from simple being to the complexities of life beyond the organic. From this culminating perspective the scale is articulated, a god's-eye view of universal sequence. Nature's ladder is, however, built from slippery steps. Though humans are middle dwellers, the chain's order inevitably arranges itself around them. In the sixth century Pope Gregory I delineated a scale of being in which humans are nexus and microcosm, since they share essential qualities with rungs below and above: "In that he has existence *[esse]* in common with stones, with trees life *[vivere]*, with animals sensation *[sentire]*, with angels rationality *[intelligere]*, man is rightly represented by the title of the 'universe,' in whom after some sort the 'universe' itself is contained."[3] This upwardly moving arrangement intermixes as it transcends.[4] J. Allan Mitchell emphasizes that this interweaving of cosmos and human microcosm is not necessarily anthropocentric, since "creatures of all kinds are deeply enmeshed."[5] So are all kinds of materialities. Such commingling across category is paralleled by the world's elemental materiality, laddered

FIGURE 4.1. Above Apollo Bay. Great Ocean Road, Victoria, Australia.

in theory but admixed in motion. Earth provides secure foundation, and its surface is the proper domain of humans: all else is alien space. Across this heavy base flow deep seas, pristine lakes, and refreshing springs. Next rises volatile air, an invisible and nearly intangible substance that soars swiftly from mortal realms. In loftiest expanses dwells fire, stuff of celestial spheres. Each of the four elements finds a natural location according to its weight. None, however, resides exclusively within indigenous space. For matter to be created the elements must combine. An emerald, for example, is earth and water locked in durable union, while a human is earth and water (in the form of clay) plus breath and fiery soul. Despite such generative union, however, the vertical arrangement of the Great Chain of Being continually self-asserts, with material as well as moral consequence. The cosmos rises from dark underworld through oceans and air to blazing stars. Each offers a unique ecology. Even if clouds require water to burgeon, their moisture will eventually return to its proper biome, a world for coral, fish, and whales. Humans flourish at the boundary where earth, water, and air meet. To attempt to inhabit the sea is to drown; earth is a grave; air offers no skyward passage; fire incinerates fleshly forms.

Yet the elements are as restless as the human imagination, seldom content to remain in their allotted place. They ceaselessly embrace to compose new things and in that process disclose surprising worlds, challenging narratives, the tangling of nature's chain. The ocean divulges merfolk, people who dwell beneath the waves in watery kingdoms or subaqueous monasteries.[6] Subterranean realms intrude wondrously into the everyday: an unremarkable hillock one evening reveals a doorway beyond which revelers feast, inviting companionship; up from the ground rise a boy and a girl with green skin who when taught to speak their words in English describe a distant land where the sun never rises and bread is unknown; a child follows a small man into an underground country where objects are fashioned from gold, and through long acquaintance learns their Greek-like tongue.[7] Elemental ecologies are fecund spaces, rich in sustenance and story. Even the unreachable clouds sometimes reveal themselves populated not by theological angels but by mortal strangers.

This chapter explores the invitation to elemental ecologies extended by medieval stories that spin the rungs of the scala naturae and behold in the sky a navigated sea. Nature does not love a ladder, nor any of the tidy forms humans build to arrange their cosmologies. The Chain of Being is full of kinks. Instead of ordered steps that emplace humans as medial creatures awaiting postmortem flight to a heavenly realm, instead of yielding to upward vectors that urge contempt for the world and desire only for the life to come, the ladder twists into doubled helices, spirals that in their torsion yield unexpected contiguities, queer embracement. Stories of ships in the sky underscore environmental entanglement, being that is neither enchained nor great, an invitation to wonder at the work of the divine, surely, but also at the fleeting and the secular.[8] Through air that thickens into ocean, tumultuous material activity manifests, treacherous as a rogue wave, lively as a thunderhead. When the sky is traveled by sailors to whom the earthbound are unknown, worldly relations knot, become perilous, open to ethical query. Chains, ladders, scales, steps, and other placidly transcendent schematics yield to life lived within the thick of the world, life in a vortex of shared precariousness and unchosen proximities.

The Sky as Sea

Toward the end of the eleventh century, Bishop Patrick of Dublin catalogued in formal Latin verse the twenty-seven wonders of Ireland. These native *mirabilia* range from a stone that triggers tempestuous rains and an island where the unburied dead never decay to a fountain that turns hair white, a tomb that causes women to fart, men who transmigrate their souls into wolves, and a rock that oozes blood. The marvels joyfully violate the presumptions that quietly structure everyday life. Climate is no longer indifferent to human activity, death is not organic oblivion, the grave fails as a terminus of agency, humans may love the animal for its inhumanity, and the lithic becomes creaturely. As quotidian certainties dissolve, ecologies of the possible wondrously flare. Listed as Patrick's nineteenth marvel is *"De naui que uisa est in aere"* (Of a ship glimpsed in the air). The bishop writes:

> A king of the Irish once attended an assembly
> With quite a crowd, a thousand in beautiful order.
> They see a sudden ship sail the sky,
> And someone who casts a spear after fish:
> It struck the ground, and swimming he retrieved it.
> Who can hear of this without praising the Lord of the skies?[9]

An unexpected vessel glides the clouds, celestial intrusion on a day otherwise given to earthbound affairs. An astonished crowd discovers the air they breathe is sea, that fish, spears, and sky-dwelling swimmers course its elemental materiality. What had seemed a distant expanse for placing angels, fiery spheres, and other incorporealities becomes inhabited, substantial, perturbingly intimate with life lived upon the ground. The thin substance through which human bodies move unthinking firms into a support for flying fish and suspended navigators, an ocean turbulent with perspective change.

This aerial ship is predictably cited across the Internet as evidence that UFOs once visited medieval Ireland. Yet Bishop Patrick quietly stresses not the futurity the vessel might herald but its arrival from the culturally complicated past. He provides his Latin lines with a patina of antiquity through deliberate archaism. The Irish are the Scoti, the name the Romans bestowed upon these people when they raided ancient Britain. Though I translate the phrase as "Lord of the skies," Patrick actually describes the Christian God as "the Thunderer," an epithet stolen from the sovereign of Olympus (Jupiter Tonans, god of thunderbolts). The bishop's story of sailors over Ireland and the blue sky become the deep sea possesses venerable textual precedent. In the Irish annals, cloud-sailing craft are recorded for the years 743, 744, and 748, depending on the source.[10] The *Annals of Ulster,* for example, state laconically that "ships with their crews were seen in the air."[11] Patrick may have obtained his story of airborne vessels from such an archive, or he might (as John Carey has argued) have truncated the narrative from an analogue to the account that appears in the Book of Ballymote, which likewise describes an aerial ship. Congalach was a tenth-century high king of Ireland. During a political gathering he spots a vessel in the clouds. Conversing briefly with one of its sailors spurs him to realize the dangers of the ordinary world, and offers a chance for Congalach to extend humane affect across what might have been an unbreachable divide:

> Congalach son of Mael Mithig was at the assembly of Tailtiu one day when he saw a ship moving through the air. Then one of them [the ship's crew] cast a spear at a salmon, so that it came down in front of the assembly. A man from the ship came after it. When he seized one end of it from above, a man seized it from below. "You are drowning me!" said the man aloft. "Let him go," said Congalach. Then he is released, and swims upward away from them.[12]

One of twelve monarchs who were supposed to have held the entirety of the island under their dominion, Congalach reveals a wisdom lacking in the man who triggers a near drowning. He comprehends that danger inheres even in transparent atmosphere, an expanse dense in intense attachments.

Bishop Patrick of Dublin writes at a nexus in the transmission of the tale, as it mutates into further versions. For on the ground, historical reasons the episode will eventually be relocated to Clonmacnoise, a monastery by the river Shannon that built for itself a reputation for wonders. Once tethered to this new foundation, the narrative comes to feature an anchor stuck in the floor of its chapel and a swimmer who descends from the boat to free the embedded object. Seized by the curious monks, the sailor pleads for his life: "'For God's sake let me go!' said he, 'for you are drowning me!'"[13] Once released he swims upward to his ship with the retrieved anchor. The fixity of stilled enchainment is death: the ship stuck, the sailor suffocated. The sky as transport mechanism, thick with conveyance, fosters vitality and triggers art. Seamus Heaney culminates this long Hibernian tradition when he celebrates the Clonmacnoise version of the wonder in a sequence embedded in his meditative poem "Lightenings."[14] According to the annals, the poem declares, while the monks were praying at Clonmacnoise, a ship appeared in the sky: "The anchor dragged along behind so deep / It hooked itself into the altar rails" and the vessel came to sudden standstill. A sailor "shimmied" down the rope but despite his struggles could not loosen the device. The abbot realized the man could not abide their air and urged the monks to help before he drowned. His ship freed, the sailor then climbed "out of the marvellous as he had known it." With sonorous assertiveness Heaney accomplishes fully the perspective shift inherent within medieval tales of navigated ether, plumbing depths without asserting a natural, vertical hierarchy, without sounding (*sub* + *unda,* "beneath the waves") a secure bottom. *Out of the marvellous as he had known it:* when the sky becomes roiled waters for unknown mariners, when firm ground is rendered ocean floor, when unexpected fish, aquatic javelins, and wayward anchors turn air to brine and altars to reefs, prospect shifts. Impalpable air thickens to tempestuous surf, creating a denser version of what Julian Yates calls "the mutual or medial impressions left by the confluence of cloud and human person—the imagination become weather report."[15] Ecological enmeshment materializes, and habitual modes of dwelling are upended. Familiar terrain becomes unheimlich, for (to quote the poet William Carlos Williams), "the sea is *not* our home. . . . / I say to you, Put wax in your ears rather against the hungry sea / it is not our home!"[16]

How much more so when that sea is sky. Displaced from our practices of quotidian habitation—from the assemblies we attend with throngs, from the hushed regularity of the cloister—we might enact a theological impulse and declare that the stone upon which we raise our houses and the wind against which we secure the door are not ours to own. We might turn our attention to divinity and cry that mundane life is brief sojourn, that the eternal home is elsewhere, that a Paradise after death awaits. Yet *paradeisos* means "enclosed park": can we really desire to reside forever behind walls?[17] In the Middle English poem "Pearl," for example, the narrator twice chooses a life among sorrows over the stillness that holds the gem-hewn dwellings of heaven.[18] His earthly inclination is at once a religious failing and a powerfully comprehensible human choice to mourn the daughter he has lost and to love the green world in which he dwells. Like that anchor lodged in a world-not-to-be-endured, like that sailor who swims deep air and risks drowning for discovery, we could linger for a while in this dangerous space, this sky become sea, this world that is the world in which we dwell, elementally reconfigured. Upon hearing or reading such a story, we might even cast our eyes cloudward in the hope of glimpsing some vessel glide, unmoored for a few moments from the terrestrial tethering of our lives. If *mundane* expands to become more fully *sublunary,* if the "under moon" of which that adjective is composed stretches upward to embrace a heaving vastness between landed lives and closed, incorporeal heaven, then for a

FIGURE 4.2. Atop Old Rag. Shenandoah National Park, Virginia, United States.

moment we might be loosened from our earthly boundedness, unfastened from what Dan Brayton calls the "terrestrial bias" of our ecological frames.[19] Not unattached but entangled, enmeshed, refusing transcendence: the sky become sea is the drowning of our landedness, the trading of flat perspectives for vortices of water and air.

Ardent Transport

The desire that the atmosphere be peopled, oceanic, and traversed by ships is not just medieval. Our contemporary vocabulary contains the nouns *spacecraft, starship,* and *astronaut* ("star sailor"), and our dominant myths include *Star Wars, Star Trek, Babylon 5,* and *Battlestar Galactica.* Any story narrated about the sea above will be heavy with transhistorical undertow. Bishop Patrick looked back centuries to describe the contemporary Irish wonder of aerial waters. Air and water are, like fire and earth, at once the indivisible building blocks of materiality and compounded from epochal histories. Because they are fundamental as well as enduring, the elements and the narratives they engender are not easily contained within the small historicisms of place-bound exigency or contextual determinations. Through his praise of the island as an integrated geography, Bishop Patrick may have been quietly asserting the supremacy of Ireland within a Viking Dublin, but his stories arrive from a thick past and travel forward into multiple futures, including translation into Norse (the thirteenth-century *Konungs Skuggsjá*).[20] Just as lunar pull triggers tidal rush, ocean and sky invite an upsurge of human reflection, likely to carry in its story-laden swell a long accumulation of philosophy, replete with unexpected continuity and disconcerting difference. Like the nearer ocean, the sea above is not timeless, not without particular history, but its tangible intensity connects sailors with spears in pursuit of atmospheric fish with spacemen toting ray guns seeking celestial prey. Steve Mentz has argued that, unlike the history-laden ocean, air acts within a constantly evaporating temporality: "Air may be history's opposite, sheer unintegrated force . . . a palpable and present image of constant change" as well as an emblem for the otherness within "a post-sustainability ecology."[21] Yet the air as sea erodes distinction between these sibling elements, suggesting at once that the air is history filled and the ocean at times more restless, more invisible in its effects than that for which human chronicle can account. We underwater creatures live in a swirl of currents both material and temporal—or, as the elemental theory propounded by the Greek philosopher Empedocles insisted, entropy's prods to restless movement tumble ceaselessly with desire's urgings of embrace.[22] Empedoclean elemental theory entered the Middle Ages through numerous gates: Latin translations of Aristotle from Arabic sources, Ovid's *Metamorphoses,* the *Natural History* of Pliny, the encyclopedic *Etymologies* of Isidore of Seville, and the philosophy of Boethius, among many others. In the fourteenth century, Geoffrey Chaucer incorporated into *The Knight's Tale* a meditation derived from Boethius on the "faire cheyne of love" that ensures the elements remain within their divinely allotted boundaries.[23] These four substructural substances ("the fyr, the eyr, the water, and the lond," 2992) stay in place ("may nat flee") so that the world will remain, at least for a brief duration, stable. When the time arrives to escape their bonds, political and material turmoil erupts.

Traversed by shared currents, water and air are elemental intimates, residing between extremes, the density of earth and the astral levity of fire. Humans carry some of each within them, but are at home only at that edge where land meets sea and sky. The nebulous conjoining of water with air has long offered a lasting space for cosmic dreaming, a place of yearning. "Head in the clouds" and "at sea" both mean to be lost to the grounding only ponderous earth provides. At the elemental interstices of air and water desire beckons, a cognitive as well as affective lure. Think, for example, of how the pejorative vectors of the noun *porn* become recoded when applied to what froths above. On the one hand, earthbound "ruin porn" is an unsavory love of urban decay, a reverence for dilapidation's fragments obscuring the tawdry forgetting of the lives that unfolded in now-empty buildings, of the future denied vanished dwellers. Native to an expanse that never possessed a human history, "cloud porn," on the other hand, is a frequently employed hashtag (#cloudporn) on social media to share images that revel promiscuously in atmospheric phenomena. These images offer cascades of blue, white, gray, billowy eruptions that dance with light and shadow, ephemeral and kinetic. Cloud porn evinces a desire for elemental intensities so vibrant that the sky is soaked with eroticism. No accident, perhaps, that among other "good" porn is book porn, a designation that enables us to admit, quietly, that our love of the objects with which we fashion our transportive alliances is sometimes smutty. Desire for books, like yearning for atmospheric intensities, is sensuously cerebral. Both are deeply aesthetic and social modes of encountering the world that foreground libidinal impulsions. Both demand interpretation as much as enjoyment, abandoning the supposed inertness of inhuman things for encounters with what Serenella Iovino and Serpil Oppermann describe as "storied matter."[24] Though the images of nebulae and books that constitute acceptable object porn cannot, as an unspoken rule, feature people, they are always framed as if encountered by a human viewer—and what is a camera but a mechanical eye? These images are shared across social networks that embed the weather within anthropocentric plots. Likewise the tales that arrive from this narrative-laden materiality more broadly will feature humans; it is not surprising that we center our narratives around ourselves, despite the arrogance of believing the world exists for us. Yet such stories are also animated with an elemental restiveness that propels the merely human across strange skylines, into Odysseus-like journeys of adventure, discovery, and danger. Devoured by monsters, transformed into pigs, swallowed by the sea: think of how many companions were lost in the wandering toward Ithaca. The Greek hero returned home not only alone but unrecognizable, out of place. Yet whereas Odysseus suffers at that unbearable horizon where the sea of human misery meets the capriciousness of the celestial, the sky become sea instantiates a world where that elemental antagonism resolves into adventure, invention, invitation.

Even when our elemental stories are mired in anthropocentrism, their animating vectors are capable of inhuman transport, capable of provoking a vision of the world that does not simply reaffirm human primacy but conveys toward an elemental elsewhere. Thought in its extensivity, the sublunary triggers vertiginous perspective shift. When we imagine life anchored only to earth, affixed to stable foundation and lived within solidities like forests, fields, and buildings, then fluctuating air becomes immaterial, inconsequential, empty. Yet inhabitance is capacious entanglement. When earth and sky cease to be "mutually exclusive domains of habitation," so both are dwelling place for "a variety beings, including the sun and the moon, the winds, thunder," then they become "inextricably linked within one indivisible field."[25] The expanses above the earth cease to be intangible, unreal, the dominion of theology and metaphysics, sudden blue stretches of participation and astonishment. An ecological awareness burgeons in which humans are enmeshed with ethereal and climatic flux, a tangle of lives and forces binding air, land, dwelling, living. "In the very midst of clouds," writes the philosopher of the elements David Macauley, "on a high altitude hike or caught in rainfall or a snowstorm, we find ourselves ensconced and enveloped in an ambient theater of activity in which the sky drops down and becomes more palpable, textural, and even tactile."[26] Our medieval texts go further. When earth and air are so dynamically entwined, they invite into their elemental midst a sibling materiality, water. The space within which the elements bind and unbind in stormy perturbation is another name for the sky thickened into restless sea, the landscape swirled into pelagic sand, imagined borders dissolving as the ocean above curves round and roils with vast waters beside and beneath. The sky become sea is the materialization of air's elemental presence, the manifesting of its relentless

FIGURE 4.3. Near Tulum, Yucatán Peninsula, Mexico.

agency, its becoming humanly apprehensible as "never empty," "a moving fluid that stretches from the heavens to the earth," "restless shaper of the world."[27] In the words of Steve Mentz, when "air pushes back" then "the invisible becomes momentarily tangible."[28] The ladder of nature jumbles its rungs, rescaling itself: life lived on the ground becomes life within the depths of someone else's ocean floor.

For Those in Peril in the Air

Bernard of Cluny, the twelfth-century Benedictine monk, inveighed against the short-lived pleasures offered by wine, sexual indulgence, and the accumulation of wealth, enjoyments derived from secular attachment. This transient earth is a place of exile, limned by catastrophe, brief but sorrowful transit for deserving Christians into the bliss of an eternity to come.[29] With its emphasis upon the misery of the human condition and the ephemerality of mortal life, the tradition of *contemptus mundi* (disdain for the world) urges mortification of the body and retreat into thoughts of heaven. Yet stark self-distancing was one possibility among many for framing medieval earthly inhabitance. Alternative modes were constantly realizable. I turn now to a thirteenth-century narrative of the sea above that offers a glimpse of deep environmental enmeshment, of the secular saturation that the air become sea makes evident, even as it might turn away from the rich implications of such material involvement. Fuller than the Irish versions, this Latin vignette of cloud-borne navigation was likely inspired by the tradition of aerial visions that culminates in Seamus Heaney's poetic sequence. Related in lucid prose by Gervase of Tilbury (ca. 1150–1222), the story likely passed through mouths speaking Irish and English, transported aboard a vessel tracing an interisland trade route. The tale's port of debarkation may even have been Bristol, since within that city Gervase narrates a second tale confirming the truth of the skyward sea.

Gervase of Tilbury's *Otia Imperialia: Recreation for an Emperor* is a sprawling work of long gestation that appeared in the second decade of the thirteenth century.[30] Born in Britain (Tilbury is in Essex), Gervase was a polyglot member of the cosmopolitan Anglo-Norman elite who ruled England after the Conquest. His wanderings included time spent studying canon law in Bologna; an affiliation with the literary-minded court of

England's Henry II (connected to the poets Wace, Marie de France, and perhaps Chrétien de Troyes); service to the king of Sicily and the archbishop of Arles; and close association with Otto, a Plantagenet relation as well as sometime king of Germany.[31] Though much of the material gathered in its three long books likely preexisted its dedication, the *Otia Imperialia* was sent by Gervase to Otto for his royal reading pleasure. The tripartite work is divided into a substantial explication of earth's creation and early history; a comprehensive description of the world's regions, peoples, and successive ages; and a final book that gathers diverse marvels. Wonders are, however, to be found throughout the text.

Book I commences with the creation narrative from the Latin Vulgate Book of Genesis. Combining a collector's zeal and a redactor's concision, Gervase interweaves classical philosophy, poetry, science, and patristic exegesis to flesh out biblical sparseness. In a wide-angle account of cosmological structure, Ovid snuggles with Isidore, Honorius, Peter Comestor, Gregory the Great, the Psalms, and Revelation. Gervase follows ancient precedent by describing the world as "round like a ball" and composed of concentric layers like an egg.[32] Generative earth is the yolk, a solid core encircled by dense air, then pure ether, and finally shell-like heaven (1.1). The potential fixity of such a model and the external point of view necessary to apprehend its pristine ovality are quickly abandoned, however, for messier descriptions narrated from the midst of things. Gervase writes that *mundus* (world) is derived from the word *motus* (motion)—for "the universe is always in motion because no rest is given to its elements."[33] Earth, air, fire, and water are ceaselessly dynamic, together composing a restless *machina mundi* or "machine of the world."[34] Repeating Gregory, Gervase writes that humans are an intermixed microcosm, carrying with them overlapping forms of being: "existence in common with stones, life in common with trees, sensation in common with animals, and intelligence in common with angels."[35] Following Ovid (*Metamorphoses*, 1.28–31), Gervase describes a primal sorting of the elements by weight in which fire disperses to the "heaven of stars," air to the atmosphere, earth to the heavy center, and water to encircle and confine land through aqueous clasp (1.4). These four primordial substances, he adds, perpetually transform, "connected to one another as if by linked arms" *(hec uelut innodatis brachiis sibi connectuntur)*, a poetic as well as physicalizing rendition of the binding force of love. Even if their enduring stability is questionable, each element offers a distinct ecology: earth for creatures that walk and crawl, water for swimmers, air for that which flies, and fire for "everything that shines" (that is, spiritual beings).

Having gathered an array of philosophical, literary, and theological texts to describe the shape and material composition of the world, Gervase turns back to Genesis and lingers over some difficult passages. The creation story describes how God divides primal waters into portions above and below the sky:

> And God said: Let there be a firmament made amidst the waters: and let it divide the waters from the waters *[in medio aquarum et dividat aquas ab aquis]*. And God made a firmament, and divided the waters that were under the firmament, from those that were above the firmament, and it was so. . . . God also said: Let the waters that are under the heaven, be gathered together into one place: and let the dry land appear. And it was so done. And God called the dry land, Earth *[terra]*; and the gathering together of the waters, he called Seas *[maria]*.[36]

Gervase explains that the structure God has imposed upon the emergent world is a complicated layering in which the earth is "surrounded and enclosed by sea" (*Otia Imperialia*, 1.13). The heavenly waters are held aloft by divine force, and it would presumably be this empyrean ocean that God releases from his floodgates *(cataractae caeli)* to join what surges from the deep *(fontes abyssi)* when he drowns the earth at Noah's Flood (Genesis 8:2). Gervase conceptualizes the celestial sea as an encasing sphere. He reasons that ocean water from underneath the earth seeps up through the ground and, with the earth acting as a natural desalination mechanism, fresh springs bubble forth. Water, water, everywhere: beside, below, above.

The oceans upon which we sail and the streams that we behold flowing from subterranean depths need no proof, but a sea among the clouds is a different body of water altogether. Gervase supports the existence of a "*maris superioris supereminentiam*" (upper sea overhead) through vividly narrated anecdotes. The first story he tells relocates the Irish wonder of a celestial ship to Great Britain and features a familiar sailor, but his fate is sadly different when he swims to unfasten the wedged anchor. The episode unfolds on a feast day as congregants straggle from church:

> The day was very overcast and quite dark on account of the thick clouds. To the people's amazement, a ship's anchor was seen caught in a tombstone within the churchyard wall, with its rope stretching up and hanging in the air.... After a time they saw the rope move as if it were being worked to pull up the anchor. Since, being caught fast, it would not give way, a sound was heard in the humid air as of sailors struggling to recover the anchor they had cast down. Soon, when their efforts proved in vain, the sailors sent one of their number down; using the same technique as our sailors here below, he gripped the anchor-rope and climbed down it, swinging one hand over the other. He had already pulled the anchor free when he was seized by the bystanders. He then expired in the hands of his captors, suffocated by the humidity of our dense air as if he were drowning in the sea [*quasi in mari naufragium,* literally "as if shipwrecked at sea"]. The sailors up above waited an hour, but then, concluding their companion had drowned, they cut the rope and sailed away, leaving the anchor behind. And so in memory of this event it was fittingly decided that that anchor should be used to make iron-work for the church door, and it is still there for all to see. (1.13)

Gervase offers this "strange event" as if it were an everyday counterbalance to the conceptually complicated cosmological vision that precedes, that elemental configuration derived from Genesis in which seas swell above the earth, rage beneath subterranean depths, billow at its middle, and limn the far edges. On a feast day so ordinary it is not named, in a parish church so unremarkable it is not named, in a village so commonplace it is not named, churchgoers listen to Mass and dawdle at departure, exchanging gossip perhaps, in no hurry to traverse this landscape without particulars. The environmental setting is typical to the point of dullness. This is Britain, after all, where warmth and sunshine constitute a miracle and a day "very overcast and quite dark on account of the thick clouds" describes not the weather but the island's unchanging climate. Yet on this prosaic day alien intrusion renders a gray world vibrant. An anchor is stuck within a place of corpses and dead stone ("on a tombstone within the church wall"). Though caught in a morbid expanse, its taut rope thrums with the promise of unseen life. Sounds descend from the clouds to confirm that material intimation. A mariner enters the startled world from these mists, strenuously pulling himself into the "marvellous" as he knows it. Everything changes at this point—or, at least, everything should. The stranger frees the anchor from its fixity but is then bound to the perilous earth by the churchgoers. They hold him as he drowns. His shipmates wait, and wait, finally cutting the rope that tethered them for a dangerous hour to the terrestrial ordinary. When the abandoned anchor is melted into an adornment for the church's door, the remarkable story is assimilated into the structures of everyday life, and a portal for conveyance slams shut. What happens to the corpse of the sailor lost at earth we are not told. The story is as full of wonder as mistakes, violence, and a failing of that ethical regard that ought to arrive in wonder's wake.

The sailor who drowns in the heavy British air confirms for Gervase the truth of Genesis, proving that the earth is "surrounded and enclosed" by a sea that expansively encircles, separated above by a layer of air. When we look up, we behold vast waters and substantial sky, the blue of a lofty ocean. Gervase offers further proof through an additional story, this time precisely located in the seaport of Bristol. A native of the city once departed on a long maritime journey, crossing remote expanses. Having finished a meal one morning with his fellow sailors, he washes his knife at the ship's rail and accidentally drops the blade into the water. At that very moment a knife tumbles through the skylight of his Bristol home and "stuck fast in a table which stood beneath it" (1.13). His astonished wife recognizes the object immediately. When her spouse returns from his wandering, they discover that the day the knife pierced the family's wooden table was the same as when it slipped his fingers at the ship's railings. "Who then will doubt," Gervase asks rhetorically, "that there is a sea situated above the world we live in, in the air or above the air *[mare super nostra habitationem in aere uel super aerem]?*" (1.13).

The knife that plunges through oceanic depths, sky, and roof to lodge itself in a familiar surface is martialed as evidence for the truth of an aerial sea. Yet the story proves this point by making Gervase's model of the marine-enclosed earth all the more difficult to apprehend. The anchor and the drowned sailor do not pose the same conceptual challenge because we are not invited to speculate how the ship came to plow the clouds. The ethereal sailor who drowns in the "humidity of our dense air as if he were drowning in the sea" is a visitor from another world, like the fish-knights supposed to dwell beneath the ordinary ocean or the Green Children who emerged from the ground near Woolpit in the twelfth century and narrated their origin in a land where the sun never quite managed to rise. His body, like his home, is not of this world. The sailor from Bristol, however, passes above his own house. He navigates the earth to learn that to voyage ever forward is to cross your own point of departure, not realizing that beneath alien waters awaits home. The sea becomes a Möbius strip, an infinite loop rather than a sphere's reassuring embrace. That this knowledge should be conveyed by the falling of a knife into a cherished domestic space stresses multiplicity, danger, and stories untold. What tale of life-making would the sailor's wife narrate, left in Bristol during his long voyaging, left to cope with the difficulties absence brings? What if the blade had not landed upon the table, but injured family in their home? What if the sea above becoming the sea below becoming the sea across which sailors journey estranges voyagers from themselves, sends knives toppling unintentionally into intimate dwellings, into *nostra habitationem* (our inhabited world)? What if at the bottom of this ocean of *remotis partibus,* distant expanses, is everything left behind, fraught in its connectedness, forgotten at great peril? What if the sea above is not a lesson in timeless theology so much as a demonstration of shared, elemental vulnerability? What if the closures offered by theological truth and sorting of ontological status matter less here than the invitation wonder offers to a more open world?[37] What if we take seriously the possibility that through a far journey forward the sailor from Bristol has become the cloud navigator who might have drowned in an element alien to his lungs yet intimate to his home?

As the ocean cascading from heaven's vault makes cataclysmically clear at Noah's Flood, the sea holds perpetual danger no matter its location. Peril limns these stories of the becoming water of air and the sailing of the sky. "The sea is not our home" means surge, swell, and brine are inimical to human life, and so might be the expanses that find themselves at ocean's bottom. The Dublin in which Bishop Patrick wrote was a Norse city, carved from the island and settled by Vikings who at their arrival raided, murdered, destroyed. Those who lived in the city in the eleventh century did so under a Norse chieftain (during Patrick's tenure, Gothricus) and were routinely described in the Irish annals as "the Foreigners of Dublin."[38] Bishop Patrick himself perished by drowning, lost at sea with his companions while crossing between Dublin and Britain. The ocean he sailed was the same liquid road that enabled the conquests bloodily connecting one stolen patch of earth to another. The monastery of Clonmacnoise, site of the ships spotted in the air in the eighth century and Seamus Heaney's poem in the twentieth, was frequently attacked by the Vikings, their descendants the Anglo-Normans, and assorted Irish chieftains and warbands. Bristol, the port where the knife-cleaning sailor and his family dwelt, bound Ireland to England. Some ships that sailed between were full of merchants. Others held armies. The story that Gervase places at Bristol emphasizes the ocean as an interface that generates and conveys story (likely both the

FIGURE 4.4. Ogunquit, Maine.

stories of the sea above that Gervase tells), but also the sea as lethal expanse: the sailor, gone for a long while from his wife and children, uncertain perhaps of return, drops into their midst a keen and cherished blade, violence intruding through his hand upon his home. Even Gervase's bland setting of the tale of the airship and anchor in "Great Britain" *(in maiore Britannia)* is a descriptor that obscures the relentless conquest necessary to bring that united island into being. No such collectivity existed when Gervase was writing. He probably means England by the term, since only those who dwelled in the southwest corner of the island confused that kingdom for the whole of the island. Meanwhile the inhabitants of the regions destined to become Wales and Scotland, as well as many in northern England, were actively resisting assimilation. Every space the sea above touches is soaked not just in brine but in blood—and blood is as salty as the sea.

Submerged Ethics

Margrit Shildrick argues that simplification is a form of violence. The task of the critic-activist is to make situations more complicated, to make action more difficult because visibly enmeshed in consequence.[39] "The question of what comes next" must be deliberately left unnavigated to foster "the capacity to move beyond existing categories of knowledge."[40] Ethics demands an identity-shattering openness and a radical (if—as Cary Wolfe stresses—necessarily partial, conditional) welcome of the unknown.[41] An ethics rooted in environmentality requires going further, extending this open welcome to the inhuman, to what Timothy Morton describes as the "strange stranger," beings and forces that make difficult demands of us, unknown and unanswerable in advance.[42] As Stacy Alaimo shows, humans are coextensive with a material world that exceeds them, and this transcorporeality has forceful implications.[43] To acknowledge how the elements work, matter, and thrive, to realize our utter embroilment within a world of plants, animals, winds, seas, sky, stone, is to realize that environmental activism mandates ecological agentism. Not the anthropomorphic granting of rights, not the promulgation of dangerous myths of sustainability (the aim is to change the world, not to believe it livable forever in its current form), not endless and solitary continuance, but the envisioning of a future so complicated, so demanding, so necessary that we come to apprehend that we are already inhabited by ocean, that we dwell as "strange strangers" at the turbulent bottom of someone else's sea.

Medieval theologians, encyclopedists, and historians strove to imagine how the chaos and heterogeneity of this turbulent earth would array itself into order if viewed from a divine viewpoint. Geoffrey Chaucer provides a literary version of this endeavor when he concludes his narrative poem *Troilus and Criseyde* with the death of its male protagonist. Troilus is a Trojan warrior who, filled with despair at his beloved's betrayal, perishes in battle. His soul ascends through the celestial spheres, "letinge [leaving] every element" (V.1810). Having glimpsed the wandering stars, his ears filled with planetary melody, he turns back toward the abandoned earth, toward all that he has until this point known, and contemplates the small boundedness of his former home:

> And doun from thennes faste he gan avyse
> This litel spot of erthe, that with the see
> Embraced is, and fully gan despyse
> This wrecched world, and held al vanitee. (V.1814–17)

It is a strangely ambivalent moment, utterly beautiful ("this little spot of earth, that is with the sea embraced") yet triggering vigorous repudiation (he "began to despise this wretched world, and held everything to be vanity"). Troilus adopts a proper *contemptus mundi,* and yet through the exertion of lyrical friction the sea-clasped earth is never quite abandoned. Those lines of elemental embrace resound more lastingly than the "hevenish melodye" that is supposed to be the scene's soundtrack.

God and heaven-bound souls aside, can the world really be glimpsed from its exterior, or will its Möbius strip effects move us to deeper entanglements just when we think we can see a world arrayed from above? Gervase of Tilbury begins his *Otia Imperialia* with an assertive vision of the structure of the cosmos, nature's ladder rising to heavenly completion. He carefully interweaves classical, patristic, and biblical sources to narrate a vision of the universe no mortal eye could witness. Yet no sooner has that system been articulated than an anchor drops from clouds and a sailor from Bristol glides the sky over his home, episodes that taken together challenge the stability of nature's ladder. Invitations to worlds that do not fold back into neat cosmology appear throughout Gervase's text. The second book of the *Otia,* for example, provides an overview of the earth's epochs, geography, and peoples, surveying lands from Ethiopia to the Orkneys. On the one hand, realms and races align into climatologically arranged collection. On the other, these expanses are so replete with story that secure perspective is fleeting. Sicily, we are told, is the primal island of the Cyclopes. Furnace-like Etna belches sulfurous fumes here, and Gervase relates that the mountain is called Mondjibel by the locals and hides a subterranean passage through which another world may be accessed: across a radiant plain and among "delights of every kind," King Arthur dwells in a splendid palace. He is happy to entertain unexpected visitors while the wounds inflicted by Mordred heal.[44] Why Mondjibel, the Arabic word for Etna (and the very volcano into which some biographies of Empedocles say he hurled himself), should render the mountain a portal to Avalon is not unexplained. Wandering south to the Mediterranean yields an invitation to early British history, revealing in distant stone and fire conveyance to histories at the heart of home.

The final section of the *Otia Imperialia* abandons fixed perspective almost entirely, collating wonder upon wonder, some of them experienced by Gervase personally. Catalogued rather than allegorized, these marvels are challenging, interruptive, alluring: magnetic and fiery stones (3.1, 3.3); petrified timber that springs back to life upon earthly contact (3.4); a bean that can induce laughter or vomiting, depending on the alliance it forms with its harvester (3.14); the Gates of Hell accessed through an ordinary lake (3.18); medieval energy drinks (3.38); a mountain crag in which a window sometimes opens to reveal ladies laughing at a private joke (3.43); silk as an enmeshment of leaves, worms, and human labor (3.56); demons and fairies who help and hinder (3.61, 3.62); dolphins whose intimacy to the sea enable the flourishing of a cross-species friendship with sailors (3.63).[45] Gervase narrates a story about these dolphins that rewrites his earlier tale of the sailor from the sky, a swimmer who struggled against churchgoers, his body making evident what words in earlier versions expressed. Held to the sea bottom by those to whom his peril was obvious and yet who chose not to relent, Gervase's mariner from the clouds drowned. In this later story from the same text, an ordinary sailor yields to rash and "youthful exuberance" and hurls an unprovoked javelin at a dolphin, frolicking with its companions near the ship. He gravely wounds the creature. A terrible storm erupts, and the dolphin king appears in human form to demand that the young man accompany him to his realm. The sailor is there asked to remove his javelin from the injured dolphin's body. Through this remedial act the sailor establishes a lasting bond between mariners and dolphins, who thenceforth warn their human friends of approaching tempests. The young sailor learns a shared precariousness, a dignity that crosses category, uniting his life to that of a creature nearly slaughtered. Every navigator is an intimate of sea currents and air currents, a member of an enmeshed and volatile collective. The dolphin assists when these currents become vortices, when elemental commingling breaks as storm.

The last book of the *Otia Imperialia* possesses 130 heterogeneous chapters that in their proliferation bring together magic grapes, werewolves, sirens, birds that grow from trees, the horns of Moses, and fiery serpents. Within this rhizomatic expansiveness the cloud sailors of Irish legend would find a welcoming home. That they should appear earlier in Gervase's work emphasizes the intimacy of wonder to his project from the start. The fastening of the celestial sailor to this earth by churchgoers who refused to perceive the vulnerability he shares with them becomes a story of perilous entanglement.[46] It is difficult to separate the aerial sailor who perished in Great Britain retrieving an anchor from the mariner from Bristol who dropped his knife, unexpected navigator of the sea above. His blade pierced his home. Should he have swum deep into the ocean below him, would he have been held fast as alien, a strange stranger? By being bound to an element perhaps no longer his own, might he have drowned at the hands of his own intimates? Or would reparation and alliance have flourished after initial ethical breach, as in the story of dolphin amity?

The world is too vast to be encompassed by a total system. We who dwell at sea's edge and sea's bottom cannot attain any prospect but that of a vexed middle, too tangled in environmental knots to possess the confidence of secure separations, to practice anything more than an ethics of mundane precarity. As Cary Wolfe has argued, every valuation we make is likely to prove, in retrospect, not ethical enough:

> We *must* choose, and by definition we *cannot* choose everyone and everything at once. But this is precisely what ensures that, *in* the future, we *will*

have been wrong. Our "determinate" act of justice now will have been shown to be *too* determinate, to have left someone or something out.[47]

Acknowledging that the Great Chain of Being is actually an irremediable enmeshment yields a perspective from within the thick of things, from a density of air-water that, should attachment turn to transfixion, floods the lungs. Perceiving that life is shared and strange helps free us from terrestrial boundedness, urging hesitation before dividing or stilling the mixed, motion-filled elements. Earth, air, fire, and water yield not stabilities so much as catastrophes, lyrical transport as well as lethal conveyance, *philia* with *neikos.* Entropic in its unities, the universe is etymologically a "turning toward."[48] Nature does not love a ladder—nor anchors, tethers, or any device for thwarting entanglement. Nature loves perspective shift and motion. Nature loves to twist the chains and scales that would constrain its arrangement. Nature loves to spiral ladders.

Nature loves a vortex.

FIGURE 4.5. Above Arthur's Seat. Edinburgh, Scotland.

Notes

Many thanks to my elemental comrades for essential conversation, and to Lizz Angello, Karl Steel, and David Wallace for bibliographic help. Lowell Duckert and Steve Mentz provided vital suggestions for reshaping this essay, and it is much the better for their generous attention.

1. I am playing here on the famous assertion of Heraclitus, "*phusis kruptesthai philei*" (nature loves to hide). For the complexities inherent within that statement and the perils of its translation, see Pierre Hadot, *The Veil of Isis: An Essay on the History of the Idea of Nature,* trans. Michael Chase (Cambridge, Mass.: Harvard University Press, 2006).

2. "Great Chain of Being" is a modern designation for a classical trope: a progressive, vertical order thought to be inherent in nature, articulated through varied metaphors. See Arthur O. Lovejoy's influential *The Great Chain of Being: A Study in the History of an Idea* (Cambridge, Mass.: Harvard University Press, 1976), which stresses the continuity among gradations as well as plenitude. Chaucer calls this structure the "faire cheyne of love" (see below) while the *Roman de la Rose* describes "la bele chaeine doree / Qui les quarter elemenz enlace" (the beautiful golden chain that entwines the four elements); see Guillaume de Lorris and Jean de Meun, *Le Roman de la Rose,* vol. 4, ed. Ernest Langlois (Paris: Librairie de Firmin-Didiot, 1922), ll. 16707–81. That a return to the chain of being might offer a renewal of ecological possibility in the present is well argued by Gabriel Egan, *Green Shakespeare: From Ecopolotics to Ecocritism* (London: Routledge, 2006).

3. *Moralia in Job* 6.16, a commentary on Job 5:10; *PL* 76.1214. Gregory's formulation was frequently repeated in the Middle Ages. John Gower's fourteenth-century poetic version describes man as a "lasse world" (small world) since he has a "soule reasonable" like an angel, "fielinge" like a beast, "growinge" like trees, and "the stones ben and so is he" (stones exist and so does he). See *Confessio Amantis,* vol. 1, ed. Russell A. Peck (Kalamazoo, Mich.: Medieval Institute Publications, 2006), ll. 945–53.

4. Of the combination and commingling inherent to the scala naturae, Kellie Robertson writes, "in a physical world where the rock and the human differ more by degree than by kind, where the divide between the material and the immaterial was not yet so indelible, the reciprocity of moral lessons was underwritten by an ontological connection manifest in the *scala naturae.*" Kellie Robertson, "Exemplary Rocks," in *Animal, Vegetable, Mineral: Ethics and Objects,* ed. Jeffrey Jerome Cohen (Washington, D.C.: Oliphaunt, 2011), 99.

5. J. Allan Mitchell, *Becoming Human: The Matter of the Medieval Child* (Minneapolis: University of Minnesota Press, 2014), 42; or, as he puts it in the conclusion to his book, "complicated ecologies underpin even the tidiest of cosmologies" (175).

6. On fish-knights and other land creatures below the sea, see Karl Steel and Peggy McCracken, "The Animal Turn: Into the Sea with the Fish-Knights of *Perceforest,*"

postmedieval 2, no. 1 (Spring 2011): 88–100; and for submarine monasteries, see John Carey, "Aerial Ships and Underwater Monasteries: The Evolution of a Monastic Marvel," *Proceedings of the Harvard Celtic Colloquium* 12 (1992): 16–28. Alf Siewers considers Irish and Welsh "antediluvian" underwater Otherworlds in *Strange Beauty: Ecocritical Approaches to Early Medieval Landscape* (New York: Palgrave Macmillan, 2009), 20–21.

7. The story of the tumulus in Yorkshire with an unexpected door to a feast and the narrative of the Green Children of Woolpit are both told by William of Newburgh in his *History of English Affairs,* Book 1, ed. and trans. P. G. Walsh and M. J. Kennedy (Wilthsire: Aris and Phillips, 1988). I have treated these episodes previously in "The Future of the Jews of York," in *Christians and Jews in Medieval England: Narratives and Contexts for the York 1190 Massacre,* ed. Sarah Rees Jones and Sethina Watson (Suffolk: Boydell and Brewer, 2013), 278–93, and "Green Children from Another World, or The Archipelago in England," in *Cultural Diversity in the British Middle Ages: Archipelago, Island, England,* ed. Jeffrey Jerome Cohen (New York: Palgrave Macmillan, 2008), 75–94. The underground realm of gold is described by Gerald of Wales in the eighth chapter of his *Journey Through Wales and the Description of Wales.* For an excellent contextualization, see Monika Otter, *Inventiones: Fiction and Referentiality in Twelfth-Century English Historical Writing* (Chapel Hill: University of North Carolina Press, 1996), 151; and Matthew Boyd Goldie, *The Idea of the Antipodes: Place, People, and Voices* (New York: Routledge, 2010), 64–66.

8. I am inspired here by what Stacy Alaimo calls "trans-corporeality at sea," the revelation that what seems an alien and distanced world is ecologically and even corporeally intimate: "The recognition of these limits, as a suspension of humanist presumptions, may be an epistemological–ethical moment that debars us from humanist privilege and keeps us 'fixed or lost as in wonder or contemplation.'" Stacy Alaimo, "States of Suspension: Trans-corporeality at Sea," *Interdisciplinary Studies in Literature and Environment* 19, no. 3 (2012): 477.

9. Quoted from Bishop Patrick's poem *De mirabilibus Hibernie (On the Wonders of Ireland).* The Latin is from *The Writings of Bishop Patrick, 1074–1084,* ed. Aubrey Gwynn (Dublin: Dublin Institute of Advanced Studies, 1955), 64–65; the translation, somewhat loose, is my own. Patrick was bishop of Dublin from 1074 to 1084.

10. Carey, "Aerial Ships," 16. The references to aerial ships are in the Annals of Ulster, Tigernach, Clonmacnoise, and the Four Masters, as well as some manuscripts of *Lebar Gábala.*

11. Entry for 749, but annals are one year ahead at this point. See the *Annals of Ulster* in the CELT (Corpus of Electronic Texts), http://www.ucc.ie/celt/published/T100001A/index.html.

12. Quoted and translated in Carey, "Aerial Ships," 17.

13. See Carey, "Aerial Ships," 18–20, for the story and the likely historical background to its transfer to Clonmacnoise.

14. The Clonmacnoise portion of "Lightenings" may be found online at "Seamus Heaney—Poetry: Lightenings viii," Nobel Media AB 2014, http://www.nobelprize.org/nobel_prizes/literature/laureates/1995/heaney-poems-3-e.html.

15. Julian Yates, "Cloud/land—An Onto-Story," *postmedieval* 4 (2013): 43. Yates continues with some lines I will echo but amplify later in this chapter: "However, scan the skies, however you may, I defy you to discern a finite agency, the 'hand' of this or that divinity, of Providence, a final cause, human or otherwise, even as you place one there. The weather remains an open system—that by your gazing you reduce to a dwelling" (43).

16. William Carlos William, *Paterson* (New York: New Directions, 1992), 200. Cf. Steve Mentz, *At the Bottom of Shakespeare's Ocean* (London: Continuum, 2009): "If the sea is around us, it is also always outside us; it is the place on earth that remains inimical to human life. . . . The most fundamental feature of the ocean, for poets, scientists, fishermen, and swimmers alike, is neither its immutable form nor its vastness but its inhospitality" (5). On the hostile sea in medieval literature, see Sebastian I. Sobecki, *The Sea and Medieval English Literature* (Cambridge: D. S. Brewer, 2008), especially 4–12. Sobecki examines well the complexity of medieval oceanic imaginings.

17. Cf. Tim Ingold: "It is perhaps because we are so used to thinking and writing indoors that we find it so difficult to imagine the inhabited environment as anything other than enclosed, interior space." Tim Ingold, *Being Alive: Essays on Movement, Knowledge and Description* (London: Routledge, 2011), 119. Though the authors of these medieval stories undoubtedly spent more time outdoors than most readers of this chapter, the conditions under which inscription of their texts occurred would have been within enclosed habitation.

18. See "Pearl," in *The Poems of the Pearl Manuscript: Pearl, Cleanness, Patience, Sir Gawain and the Green Knight,* 5th ed., ed. Malcolm Andrew and Ronald Waldron (Exeter: University of Exeter Press, 2008).

19. Dan Brayton, *Shakespeare's Ocean: An Ecocritical Exploration* (Charlottesville: University of Virginia Press, 2012). Steve Mentz formulates a swimmer's poetics that beautifully moves beyond this landed bias in *At the Bottom of Shakespeare's Ocean,* where he writes of "abandoning certain happy fictions and replacing them with less comfortable narratives. Fewer gardens, and more shipwrecks. . . . We need sailors and swimmers to supplement our oversupply of warriors and emperors" (98).

20. Kuno Meyer gives a full account of the relation of the Norse text to Irish materials in "The Irish Mirabilia in the Norse 'Speculum Regale,'" *Folklore* 5, no. 4 (1894): 299–316 (esp. 312–13). This Icelandic text describes the Clonmacnoise version of the wonder, complete with the anchor, church, and drowning sailor.

21. Steve Mentz, "A Poetics of Nothing: Air in the Early Modern Imagination," *postmedieval* 4, no. 1 (Spring 2013): 32.

22. On these twin forces in Empedocles, see Friedrich Solmsen, "Love and Strife in Empedocles' Cosmology," *Phronesis* 10 (1965): 123–45, rpr. in David J. Furley and

R. E. Allen, eds., *Studies in Presocratic Philosophy,* vol. 2, *The Eleatics and Pluralists* (London: Routledge and Kegan Paul, 1975), 221–64.

23. Geoffrey Chaucer, *The Knight's Tale,* in *The Riverside Chaucer,* 3rd ed., ed. Larry D. Benson (New York: Houghton Mifflin, 1987). All citations of Chaucer are to this edition and give line numbers. Chaucer had previously translated the inspiration for Theseus's speech in *Boece,* 2m8.

24. Iovino and Oppermann write of "matter's 'narrative' power of creating configurations of meanings and substances, which enter with human lives into a field of co-emerging interactions." See Serenella Iovino and Serpil Oppermann, "Material Ecocriticism: Materiality, Agency, and Models of Narrativity," *Ecozon@* 3, no. 1 (2012): 79–80.

25. Ingold, *Being Alive,* 74.

26. David Macauley, "Head in the Clouds: On the Beauty of the Aerial World," *Environment, Space, Place* 2, no. 1 (2010): 153. See also David Macauley, *Elemental Philosophy: Earth, Air, Fire, and Water as Environmental Ideas* (Albany: State University of New York Press, 2010), which makes a cogent argument that when the elements "enter into our everyday worlds" they "make their presence felt as both an ecological necessity and a robust cultural resource" (14).

27. William Bryant Logan, *Air: The Restless Shaper of the World* (New York: W. W. Norton, 2012), 7, 20. See also the collection *The Life of Air: Dwelling, Communicating, Manipulating,* ed. Monika Bakke, http://www.livingbooksaboutlife.org/books/The_Life_of_Air. Bakke's introduction ("The Multispecies Use of Air") is especially good at foregrounding the disanthropcentricism inherent in thinking about air as animated matter.

28. Mentz, "A Poetics of Nothing," 31. Carla Mazzio likewise explores the forceful unknowability of air in "The History of Air: *Hamlet* and the Trouble with Instruments," *South Central Review* 26, nos. 1–2 (2009): 153–96.

29. See *Scorn for the World: Bernard of Cluny's "De Contemptu Mundi": The Latin Text with English Translation and an Introduction,* ed. Ronald Pepin (East Lansing, Mich.: Colleagues Press, 1991).

30. Gervase of Tilbury, *Otia Imperialia: Recreation for an Emperor,* ed. and trans. S. E. Banks and J. W. Binns (Oxford: Clarendon Press, 2002). Citations are to book and chapter.

31. This bare outline of Gervase's life hints at some of the limitations of the model of oceanic connectivity propounded by Peregrine Horden and Nicholas Purcell in *The Corrupting Sea: A Study of Mediterranean History* (Oxford: Blackwell, 2000). On the one hand, the Mediterranean was intimate to Gervase's life, as it was to the Norman Empire more generally. On the other hand, his movements and the multilateral cultural exchanges they make clear demonstrate the network formed by multiple seas (including the Irish, Atlantic, and North) as well as far-flung lands that sometimes (as we will see) possess connective oceans above and beneath.

32. On the generative complexity of the cosmic egg, see Mitchell's excellent discussion in *Becoming Human,* 45–52.

33. Gervase, *Otia Imperialia,* 1.1. Gervase is quoting Isidore, *Etymologies,* 3.29 (*Isidori Hispalensis Episcopi Etymologiarum sive Originum Libri XX,* ed. William Lindsay [Oxford: Oxford University Press, 1989]); see the introduction to this volume for more on the etymology.

34. Robert Bartlett, *The Natural and the Supernatural in the Middle Ages* (Cambridge: Cambridge University Press, 2008), 38.

35. "In summa, homo mundus appellatur quia in se tocius mundi representat ymaginem, habens esse cum lapidibus, uiuere cum arboribus, sentire cum animalibus, et dicernere cum angelis" (1.1).

36. Genesis 1:6–10, quotation from http://www.latinvulgate.com. Contemporary creationists and fundamentalist Christian readers of the Bible have made use of this idea of waters above the earth and their release at the Deluge to explain the geological record and its fossils. See David R. Montgomery, *The Rocks Don't Lie: A Geologist Investigates Noah's Flood* (New York: W. W. Norton, 2012), esp. 227–29.

37. I am thinking here of Cary Wolfe's very unmedieval observation that "there is no god's eye view': there are *only* 'limited points of view.' But the fact that any norm *is* unavoidably perspectival doesn't dictate relativism, solipsism, or autoimmunitary closure." See Cary Wolfe, *Before the Law: Humans and Other Animals in a Biopolitical Frame* (Chicago: University of Chicago Press, 2013), 86. In the medieval materials (such as Gervase), a divine point of view is of course possible, even inevitable, but stories of the skyward sea also complicate its imagining in ways that open other possibilities on the ground, including ethical hesitancy and a call to an extended notion of hospitality toward that which is unknown.

38. See Aubrey Gwynn's introduction to *The Writings of Bishop Patrick,* 1.

39. Margrit Shildrick, *Dangerous Discourses of Disability, Subjectivity and Sexuality* (Basingstoke: Palgrave Macmillan, 2012). See especially 171–72, where she positions herself against the "emancipatory discourse" of traditional political activism.

40. Ibid., 171–72. Like Wolfe, Shildrick is making an argument based on Jacques Derrida's notion of radical hospitality.

41. See especially Wolfe, *Before the Law,* 86, 102–5.

42. Morton articulates well the relation of the strange stranger (an entity irreducible in its otherness and integrity) to ecological enmeshment when he writes, "Interconnection implies separateness and difference. There would be no mesh if there were not strange strangers. The mesh isn't a background against which the strange stranger appears. It is the entanglement of all strangers." See Timothy Morton, *The Ecological Thought* (Cambridge, Mass.: Harvard University Press, 2010), 47.

43. Stacy Alaimo describes this entanglement as "trans-corporeality" and inspirationally draws a mode of environmental justice from it. See Stacy Alaimo, *Bodily Natures: Science, Environment, and the Material Self* (Bloomington: Indiana University Press, 2010). Cf. the eloquent closing of her article "States of Suspension":

"Both new materialisms and blue-green environmentalisms suggest that there is no solid ground, no foundation, no safe place to stand. Like our hermaphroditic, aquatic evolutionary ancestor, we dwell within and as part of a dynamic, intra-active, watery world" (490).

44. Gervase, *Otia Imperialia,* 2.12. Gervase continues that Arthurian knights have also been encountered either at noon or during a full moon wandering forests in Great Britain and Brittany.

45. On the "deep historical roots" of imagining dolphin-human proximity, see Steve Mentz, "'Half-Fish, Half-Flesh': Dolphins, the Ocean, and Early Modern Humans," in *The Indistinct Human in Renaissance Literature,* ed. Jean E. Feerick and Vin Nardizzi (New York: Palgrave Macmillan, 2012), 29–46. Feerick and Nardizzi's work on human "indistinction" has been widely helpful for framing this project.

46. For an inspirational articulation of an ethics of shared vulnerability within medieval texts, see Karl Steel, "A Fourteenth-Century Ecology: 'The Former Age' with Dindimus," in *Rethinking Chaucerian Beasts,* ed. Carolynne van Dyke (Palgrave Macmillan, 2012), 185–99.

47. Wolfe, *Before the Law,* 103.

48. Cf. Michel Serres, *Biogea,* trans. Randolph Burks (Minneapolis: Univocal, 2012), 178: "Universe, a word that signifies *verto:* that it turns; *vers* [toward]: that it goes; *uni:* that it shows stable enough unities." I am deeply grateful to Lowell Duckert for advice on the final turn of this chapter.

five

Muddy Thinking

SHARON O'DAIR

Will this description satisfy him?

—SHAKESPEARE, *Antony and Cleopatra*

The institutionalization of ecocriticism has allowed the academy to create social change in the classroom. . . . Consciousness has been raised. . . . Meanwhile [environmental] problems get worse.

—CHERYLL GLOTFELTY, interview in *PMLA*

Caesar Does Not Approve

On a galley anchored off Misenum, so Shakespeare sets the scene, a banquet celebrating the triple pillars of the world ripens toward an Alexandrian feast. Fierce and powerful men, softened by wine, dance the Egyptian Bacchanals and sing a tribute to the "monarch of the vine, / Plumpy Bacchus with the pink eyne!" "Come," they sing, "Bacchus come." Come and "cup us till the world go round . . . till the world go round!"[1]

But ripen it does not. A dozen wild boars roasted whole do not await revelers who will wake, some hours hence, badly hungover. For throughout, the banquet has been at sea, forced, strained, dangerous even. And Caesar is there, disapproving. "What would you more?" he asks the revelers, their worlds spinning 'round. "What would you more?" Not waiting for an answer, Caesar punctuates the revels by stopping them, because "our graver business / Frowns at this levity." Explaining that "we have burnt our cheeks . . . And mine own tongue / Splits what it speaks," Caesar affirms that he is one of those of whom the servants say, "the least wind i' the world will blow them down" (2.7.119, 120–21, 122–23, 2–3). But I don't believe him, do you?

I do hope you'll believe this: like other chapters in this collection, this one does not flow linearly; like Valerie Allen's spinning torus (see chapter 3), it cups a (muddy) metaphor in order to spin it out, playfully, toward a logical resting place. It is not the only one, of course, this resting place. But it is one consistent, I hope, with the allusive spiraling of its five sections. To begin, I read 2.7 of *Antony and Cleopatra* to ground Caesar, the figure I use to symbolize certain realities of academic career-making, mainly sober ambition and fear of professional disappointment, that I address in part two, principally through a discussion of not-so-academic mudslinging. In part three, I imagine the abandonment of mudslinging to offer a different remedy for professional disappointment, of being bogged down in the academy, by reading Yorick's skull as the remains of a bog body, overkilled. The reading, the remedy, is hermeneutic overkill, as indeed bog bodies were overkilled thousands of years ago, before being buried in bogs. And yet while it pleases, a personal remedy is not sufficient to understanding the muddy and boggy conditions of contemporary intellectual life or the mudslinging of much professorial disputation, so I turn in part four to Sianne Ngai's work on aesthetics to tease out the powerlessness that confronts us in late capitalist society. Throughout, danger has lurked—the temptation to recuperate mud and the mire through the usual trick, privileging that which is demonized, bringing the margin to the center. And it is true, mud is generative, fecund, and so is muddy thinking; this I do not deny. But rather than insist we admire the mired, I suggest in part five that we remember mud sticks to those who sling, even those who sling successfully; all of us are mired, muddy, even the admired, perhaps especially the admired. In this muddy recognition, I suggest, we might generate ways to sustain intellectual life that differ from those proposed by purveyors of technology and the managed university, of productivity and mere personal ambition. Edward J. Geisweidt argues that *Antony and Cleopatra* "questions humans' ability to . . . attain a nobleness of life that sets them above the animals," including other humans, and in nice formulation, he suggests that "in the Nile's watershed earth is a mother who has no favorite among her children."[2] Yet the Nile also makes our mother muddy.

In 2.7, danger lurks in upright, uptight Caesar, but the immediate threat aboard the galley is the host, Pompey, or rather his friend and confidant, Menas, who offers Pompey what Lady Macbeth offers her husband, "solely sovereign sway and masterdom."[3] Pulling Pompey aside, away from the carousing lords, Menas whispers in his ear, "I am the man / Will give thee all the world" (*Antony and Cleopatra,* 2.7.65–66). Befuddled, Pompey wonders if he is drunk, but Menas cuts straight to the chase, insisting the contrary and reminding Pompey that "these three world-sharers, the *competitors,* / Are in thy vessel." All Menas need do is "cut the cable, / And when we are put off, fall to their throats." And then, then, "all there is thine" (71–74, emphasis mine). Pompey declines. "Thou must know," he tells Menas,

> 'Tis not my profit that does lead mine honour;
> Mine honour it. Repent that e'er thy tongue
> Hath so betray'd thine act. Being unknown,
> I should have found it afterwards well done,
> But must condemn it now. Desist, and drink. (76–81)

Being led by honor rather than profit leads soon enough to Pompey's death—Menas hesitates not to register Pompey's folly—and to the extent that Pompey's fall foreshadows Antony's, one might suggest that in this play, as in so many others, Shakespeare revels in demonstrating for his audiences the compromised status of honor in this, or his, society. Some might protest that unlike Pompey, whose honor leads his judgment, Antony's love (or lust, or hedonism; call it what you will) leads his, leading to actions of "such shame" that "ne'er before / Did . . . Experience, manhood, honour . . . violate so itself" (3.10.22–24). One warrior dies because he acts according to the demands of honor, the other because he does not. So, how can I bring the two together, link Pompey's fall to Antony's, suggest that Pompey's fall foreshadows Antony's?

Because the real prize here isn't Pompey or Antony but honor itself. I like to think about honor and tragedy, and how bizarre Shakespearean tragedy seems in societies like our own, societies in which, as Susan Sontag put it fifty years ago, no one believes in "honor, status, personal courage—the values of an aristocratic military class."[4] Or, as Terry Eagleton put it more recently and more tartly, no one believes in "all that high-pitched talk of rank, evil, mystery, honour, and cosmic fatality."[5] Tragedy is anachronistic, just as its heroes are. Out of time. Unhistorical. It is disapproving Caesar's world, not Pompey's or Antony's or deeply inebriated Lepidus's.

Will this description satisfy you? I wager it would satisfy Caesar. Antony satisfies Caesar when he explains that

> . . . they take the flow o' the Nile
> By certain scales i' the pyramid; they know,
> By the height, the lowness or the mean, if dearth
> Or foison follow. The higher Nilus swells,
> The more it promises: as it ebbs, the seedsman
> Upon the slime and ooze scatters his grain,
> And shortly comes to harvest. (2.7.17–23)

What does not satisfy Caesar is what satisfies Lepidus, who wanders into this conversation to wonder: "Y'have strange serpents there," in Egypt (l. 24)? Serpents "bred now of your mud by the operation of your sun" (ll. 26–27)? And crocodiles, too? Curious Lepidus's drunken questions inspire Antony to reply tautologically. The crocodile is what it is:

> It is shap'd sir, like itself, and it is as broad
> as it hath breadth: it is just so high as it is, and
> moves with its own organs. It lives by that which
> nourisheth it, and the elements once out of it,
> it transmigrates. (42–46)

The crocodile, so Antony assures Lepidus, is of its "own colour too" (l. 48). And surprise of surprises, "the tears of it are wet" (l. 50)! At this, unable any longer to observe in silence, disapproving Caesar asks Antony, "Will this description satisfy him?" (l. 50). And Antony affirms that it will, "with the health that Pompey gives him" (l. 52). Here's mud in your eye, Lepidus!

Slinging Mud

"The underlying coherence of all this may not be self-evident." Would I be slinging mud to say that in this, their third sentence of *Practicing New Historicism,* Catherine Gallagher and Stephen Greenblatt are as clear as mud? That the rationale for their book is as clear as mud? I do not think I would be. I think I would be translating. It is as clear as mud why a book should have "two authors, . . . two chapters on anecdotes, and four on bread, potatoes, and the dead." It is clear as mud why Gallagher and Greenblatt should have authored a text about *practicing* new historicism two decades after its birth, and nearly a decade after the prime of its influence. They say they began the work of this book "by wanting to explain how new historicism had changed the field of literary history."[6] This assertion itself is muddy, because it conditions the reader to think change is afoot: we began by wanting *X* and then we changed our minds, wanted something else, wanted *Y*. Why, what they wanted was to do new historicism, to practice it again! Hence, bread, potatoes, and the dead. Not explanation of a practice's effects on the field but more examples of the practice!

Perhaps I would be slinging mud if I said that new historicism is as clear as mud, exemplifies muddy thinking, but happily for me, I do not say that. I do not have to, since colleagues have done so already, colleagues who attacked "The Cultural Turn" or promoted "The New Boredom" in literary study.[7] One cannot help but wonder, in fact, whether one motive, unstated, for Gallagher and Greenblatt in writing *Practicing New Historicism* was not defensive? Did the book begin as riposte aimed toward colleagues like Kastan, who were advancing a different practice of literary history, one against theory and more like that performed by historians, a historicism that embraces method and does not eschew it? For of this Gallagher and Greenblatt are clear, certain: "New historicism is not a repeatable methodology."[8] In the air were accusations perhaps needing reply, and two years later, Douglas Bruster went so far as to cast Greenblatt as "'an extraordinarily talented creative writer'" who undermined "traditional modes" of serious if "mechanical" scholarship by initiating a way of writing "more entertaining" than that of traditional scholarship, "more elegant and playful." Greenblatt, Bruster claims, aims to tell "a good story." And Bruster laments what is lost in this bargain—the paying of one's scholarly dues and a firm sense of what all the fancy, fun writing adds up to: "the research problem that one is addressing and the research conclusions that others have made," in addition to, of course, how one's own conclusions differ from the ones others have made. For Bruster, as for many other colleagues critical of new historicism, the storyteller is "willing to participate in critical discourse, but mainly as someone who wishes solely to be heard."[9]

If I were writing about "fire" now, like my colleagues Anne Harris or Steve Mentz, I could be hip, colloquial, and say, "Burn!" And I could note my disappointment that literary criticism periodically seems to require rhetorical moves that aim to purify, burn, elicit a response of "Burn!" Instead, failing to be hip, stuck in the mud, mired in dullness, all I can say is that literary criticism periodically seems to require the slinging of mud in the name of purity. Or method. Or of pure method. Of who is in and who is out and the borders and walls that separate. A lot of mud has flown recently: in 2012 in *ISLE,* the official journal of the Association of Literature and the Environment, Greg Garrard wanted to know "when . . . did ecocriticism come to focus so much on criticizing environmentalism?" And he slung at a lot of people, but especially Catriona Mortimer-Sandilands, queer ecocritic and a Canada Research Chair in Sustainability and Culture, suggesting that Mortimer-Sandilands's brand of ecocritique puts her, surprisingly, in agreement with "Steve Milloy, climate skeptic, Fox News pundit and scion of the antienvironmentalist 'think tank' the Cato Institute." Both "promote 'citizen science' in the face of cultures of expertise, both reject 'Malthusian' analyses of population growth, and both reject what they call 'pollution hysteria' (Milloy)—albeit for radically different reasons."[10]

Also that year, in *Critical Inquiry,* Susan Fraiman threw mud at those who remade the backwater subfield of animal studies into a "newly legitimate, high-profile area of humanities research." But this makeover, she argues, required these scholars to abandon the subfield's activism and its deep feminist roots and to find authorization, instead, in a newly nominated "forefather" of the newly high-profile subfield—a "one-off talk" by Jacques Derrida. To gain power—the "burgeoning numbers of special issues, conferences, and publications at top presses"—animal studies had to reject the "women's studies model," the activist model, the model that leads, so it is thought, to "ghettoization," a muddy place that sullies one's reputation. What this makeover implies, Fraiman insists, is that, almost a half century after women began entering the profession in significant numbers, "academic protocols [still] devalue scholarship marked as feminine."[11] Of course, as Judith Butler and any number of sociologists might point out, social or institutional roles change slowly, but Fraiman, at least, is one female scholar furious to think she must know—more than four hundred years later—what Shakespeare's Kate comes to know, that

> A woman mov'd is like a fountain troubled,
> Muddy, ill-seeming, thick, bereft of beauty
> And while it is so, none so dry or thirsty
> Will deign to sip or touch one drop of it.[12]

In queer early modern studies mud has flown, too, though obviously not in such a gendered way. Letting fly in the January 2013 issue of *PMLA* is Valerie Traub. The target is the new unhistoricism in queer studies, a not quite critical movement initiated around 2005 that argues against "a historicism that proposes to know the definitive difference between the past and the present." According to the unhistoricists, such a historicism, the hegemonic sort of historicism Traub practices, is unsuited, indeed "inadequate," to "housing the project of queering."[13] According to Traub, in addition to indulging anachronism, analogy, and associational logic, not to mention a suspicion of the empirical and a polemical style, all of which threaten method, these self-styled homohistoricists indulge in a collusive behavior Traub implies is unprofessional, unscholarly, or at least inappropriate. These are "high profile scholars," she observes, writing "high octane . . . polemics," high profile scholars who "compos[e] . . . what increasingly seems a united front," sharing "a common line of argumentation [and] regularly and approvingly cit[ing] one another's views." And these are views that "elevat[e] . . . (sexy) theory over (dour) history."[14] No wonder, then, that this position has been "embraced enthusiastically by many other scholars, inside and outside early modern literary studies, who aim 'to free queer scholarship from the tyranny of historicism.'"[15]

The new boredom. Dour history. Sexy theory. Fun, fancy writing. Unpacking the anxieties demonstrated here could take all my time; suffice to say that only by intimate contrast with the dour and the boring can theory be sexy and Greenblatt's writing fun. One might be tempted to tell everyone to take it down a notch. Instead, I will hypothesize that Traub protests too much, because what she accuses Carla Freccero, Madhavi Menon, and

Jonathan Goldberg of doing—colluding, or presenting a united front—she surely has done herself in the promotion and development of her own work; in just this article, she thanks twenty-two scholars "for their thoughtful engagements with this argument."[16] Collusion of this sort is how ideas gain power to be diffused in any era, now or in the past; and, like collusion, mudslinging is a legitimate, or, shall we say, since we are talkin' queer here, *normative* tactic in the diffusion of ideas and the building of careers: through the application of mud, one builds turf. More cynically, or as a hypothesis, collusion and mudslinging is how careers are built in the contemporary academy, which increasingly offers few careers at all. In desperate times, one might hypothesize, more mud needs to be slung. If so, if we labor under such conditions, one might congratulate Traub for her restraint, which exceeds that of her targets or certainly Jack Halberstam, who, shortly after Traub's essay appeared in print, sneered in blogged reply, "The House of Michigan can hold onto History with a capital H; it can have disciplinarity, chronology and sequence; it can misspell the names of its postcolonial critics (footnote #12) and still make a claim on accuracy ... but it cannot police what lies beyond the walls and scuttles around the edges of the House of MLA—the creatures outside the walls are the real specters haunting the field and what is dead can never die."[17]

Still, if Halberstam indulges b(l)oggy overkill, Traub does let fly! Sling she does! And she slings mud in ways that suggest, as do the slingings of Bruster, Kastan, Garrard, Fraiman, Halberstam, and Menon, that when it comes to ensuring purity or building turf, what works best is a little impurity, a little mud, going so far as to make one's adversary feel a bit like Hamlet, "a dull and muddy-mettled rascal ... [who] can say nothing."[18] But, remembering Polonius, and because we are professionals, not so far as to make that adversary feel like George in *Who's Afraid of Virginia Woolf?*, reduced to drunkenly imploring his drunk wife, Martha, to stop, stop, stop slinging mud. Without effect. "So anyway," says Martha, turning from her husband to address the young academic couple Nick and Honey,

> I married the S.O.B., and I had it all planned out.... He was the groom ... he was going to be groomed. He'd take over someday ... first, he'd take over the History Department, and then, when Daddy retired, he'd take over the

> college . . . you know? That's the way it was supposed to be. . . . [But] George didn't have much . . . push . . . he wasn't particularly . . . aggressive. . . . In fact he was sort of a . . . a FLOP! A great . . . big . . . fat . . . FLOP! . . . I mean, he'd be . . . no good . . . at trustees' dinners, fund-raising. He didn't have any . . . personality, you know what I mean? Which was disappointing to Daddy, as you can imagine. So, here I am, stuck with this flop . . . this BOG in the History Department . . . who's married to the President's daughter, who's expected to *be* somebody, not just some nobody, some bookworm, somebody who's so damn . . . contemplative, he can't make anything out of himself, somebody without the guts to make anybody proud of him.[19]

Here's mud in your eye, George!

Yorick in the Bog

George's emergence as the bog in the history department may have disappointed Daddy, and Martha too, as well as, of course, George himself, but disappointment bogs (down) the academy in 2013 just as it did in 1962, though usually with less shouting. To what extent disappointment does bog us (down), and whether it bogs us more or less fiercely and tightly now than then, is beyond the scope of this chapter and my own muddled research skills to address; on this, all I have are anecdotes. Or hypotheses. Which to answer would require a questionnaire. Or interviews. For now, I wish merely to point to the confluence in *Who's Afraid of Virginia Woolf?* of disappointment, mudslinging, and being bogged down professionally, or being a bog of a professor, in the academy. And to suggest that the (mostly) polite, highly edited mudslinging I have identified in professional disputation finds monumental expression in that of Martha and George. Martha slings because she is disappointed that George is a failure, a bog of a professor, the bog of the history department. We sling—again, politely—to shore up turf, or mostly, hopefully, to build it up, with the fate of George always on our minds: entangled, snared, mired, unable to move, drowned even. Or we sling with an even worse thought on our minds, the thought that, like George, if you believe Martha, we might not just be bogged down but *become* a bog, the bog of the English department, that into which the dead, or possibly the alive, are thrown, some of them sacrifices, others criminals, still others the demonized, like the Danish native in Williams's poem "A Smiling Dane," found "intact / with a rope / also intact / round the neck." Writes Williams,

> The cast of his features
> shows him
> to be
> a man of intelligence.
> It did him no good.[20]

What if the turf I build is a bog? What if I fall into it? Or become it? I am a man of intelligence. What if it does me no good? What if I am . . . *disappointed?* Obviously, how someone deals with professional disappointment varies: One can drink, like Martha and George. Here's mud in your eye, "cruel . . . times"![21] One can take up running. Or running, biking, *and* swimming! Triathlons! Worse—or better: Ironmans! One can keep working, and complete the second or third book, the one, perhaps, that will end disappointment, allow one to escape the bog, to stop being the bog. One can shift gears, write a romance novel, or any novel, or a memoir. Or begin to write criticism, as Jeffrey Williams once said, that is "relatively disinterested and detached from the exigencies of employment."[22] One might, for instance, propose that *Hamlet* is a bog. Which in Danish, literally the play is, because the Danish for *book* is *bog.*[23] And from this creepy, uncanny bog Claudius, the smiling Dane, emerges, leaving us frightened, wondering "what his eyes saw," whether "his ghost might walk."[24] From this creepy, uncanny bog emerges the smiling Dane, whose tragedy this might be, a body that reveals to us his last meal, "local grains / swallowed whole," and, in his smile, his grimacing executioners: "Do we not know / their features / as if / it had occurred / today?"[25] Hamlet's features? Horatio's? Laertes's? Maybe Gertrude's?

Or maybe Hamlet himself emerges from the bog. Seamus Heaney arguably thinks so, allowing his speaker in "Viking Dublin: Trial Pieces," to follow "a worm of thought / . . . into the mud," and becoming, then,

Hamlet the Dane,
skull-handler, parablist,
smeller of rot

in the state, infused
with its poisons,
pinioned by ghosts
and affections,

murders and pieties,
coming to consciousness
by jumping in graves,
dithering, blathering.[26]

In the mud, a worm of thought becomes Hamlet, dithering, blathering, handling skulls. And if, like Polonius, Hamlet becomes the diet of worms, they who, in Heaney's "Kinship," help constitute "the slime kingdoms . . . [the] Ruminant ground," then one might well ask: is the skull that Heaney's Hamlet holds his own?[27]

Maybe in Heaney, but not in Shakespeare, because I know, we know, that the skull Shakespeare's Hamlet handles is Yorick's. The play tells us so:

GRAVE: Here's a skull now hath lien you i' th' earth three and twenty years.
HAMLET: Whose was it?
GRAVE: A whoreson mad fellow's it was. Whose do you think it was?
HAMLET: Nay, I know not.
GRAVE: A pestilence on him for a mad rogue! A poured a flagon of Rhenish on my head once. This same skull, sir, was Yorick's skull, the King's jester.
HAMLET: This? (Takes the skull.)
GRAVE: E'en that. (5.1.166–177)

Alas, poor audience! I knew you, knew you were certain that in the play, the skull Hamlet handles isn't his own, but can you with equal certainty accept that "this same skull . . . was Yorick's?" Recall that as Hamlet and Horatio observe the gravedigger, while Hamlet meditates on questions large and small, the gravedigger twice "throws up a skull" (5.1.73). Yorick's is the third the gravedigger uncovers. How does he know which is Yorick's? How does he know it is *that* one, and not another? He does not, we do not, and neither does criticism. Critics skirt the problem, and sometimes offer explanations—the graves in the cemetery are ordered and the gravedigger orderly in his business; next to the bones lies archaeological evidence—a coxcomb or bells; or, as Ann Thompson and Neil Taylor suggest in the Arden 3 edition of the play, "the gravedigger is . . . guessing."[28] Frustrated or pedantic, Harold Jenkins slings some mud at audiences and readers who, in this instance as in others, "have looked for a kind of consistency Shakespeare does not always bother to supply."[29]

But does not Jenkins also sling some mud at Shakespeare, accusing him of muddy thinking? Or muddy play construction? Of being, in the Australian idiom, "up to mud," good for nothing? A bit of a slacker? Probably not, because the sentence preceding argues that Yorick is one of many inconsistencies in *Hamlet* that "have to be accepted—sometimes even gratefully—for the clues they give to Shakespeare's mind." Perhaps. But perhaps Jenkins genuflects, and then tosses up a bit of skullduggery, pointing out the inconsistencies in the world's most famous play. Here, *consistency* suggests the sort of coherency associated with modernist criticism of the twentieth century, but happily for me, the word also, and principally, means viscosity or density; *consistency* points to how firm or thick a substance or thing is, whether it is able, as the *Oxford English Dictionary* (n.2a) notes, "to 'stand together' or retain its form." The gravedigger's identification of Yorick's skull doesn't hold water, and the water falls to the ground, making it . . . muddy. According to Gaston Bachelard, "the desire to dig in the earth immediately takes on a new aspect, a new duality of meaning, if the ground is muddy."[30] But how muddy? How muddy before the ground attracts and repels, like feces to a child, or mud pies? How muddy is the graveyard in Elsinore? How soft? In Gaelic, *bog* means soft. In Scottish, *fen* means bog. "Consistency is all I ask," says Rosencrantz in *"an anguished cry,"* almost four hundred years later, on a different stage in London.[31]

What distinguishes bogs from fens for most of us is that fens receive water from sources other than precipitation, from runoff, groundwater, or streams, and thus are less acidic. But that's not much of a difference; Heaney, in "The Tollund Man," locates "the flat country . . . / Where they dug him out" as fen *and* bog.[32] For the archaeologist, what distinguishes them, in addition, is burial practice; in northern Europe, so far as science knew in 2012, societies did not practice "burial in watery contexts," whether in bog or fen. But, as the archaeologist Francesco Menotti is quick to point out, "'real' wetland cemeteries" did exist in North America, in Florida, where, in the most striking sites, over half of 168 individuals identified include crania with preserved brain. Further, "the absence of archaeological evidence" for watery burial practice in northern Europe "cannot be used as an *argumentum ex silencio*," perhaps especially when evidence does exist, and strikingly so, for the watery disposal of miscreants.[33] Those miscreants, according to Menotti, constitute one sort of bog body, those buried in the more acidic peat bogs; these are the bodies that, in the 1950s and 1960s, surprised and fascinated Williams and Heaney and the whole world; bodies buried in peat bogs reveal "perfectly preserved skin and internal body organs (but not bones)." The other sort of bog body, buried in more alkaline fen, reveals bones (and sometimes brain) but not the rest."[34] Could it be, then, that the gravedigger's cemetery in *Hamlet* exists in a fenny shore—it is Denmark, after all—where the water's chemical composition and pH are such that Yorick's skull might contain the jester's preserved brain? In which might be found, someday, with technology we cannot imagine, his "gibes . . . gambols . . . songs . . . flashes of merriment"? Could it be that Yorick is a bog body, fenned? That, like Ophelia, Yorick found a "muddy death" (4.7.182), and then, unlike the poor girl, was preserved?

Deficits of Power . . . and Peat

Or could it be that Yorick is a bog body, peated? Uncannily well preserved? Such would be a skull the gravedigger could identify as Yorick's: peated. The Elsinore Man! But as I hope you recall, I do not intend here to solve the problem of identification in the graveyard scene, and besides, as each of you doubtless is aching to protest, Hamlet holds a skull, not a preserved head: "Here hung those lips that I have kissed I know not how oft," says the prince (5.1.181–2), and those lips are gone, vanished. But even so, a bog body Yorick, very well preserved, would underscore the play's gloomy, uncanny ambience and many of its themes, including temporality, epistemology, criminality, authority, hierarchy, and the boundary between the physical and spiritual worlds. A bog body Yorick could lead one to the sort of analysis Todd Borlik accomplishes;[35] one could link *Hamlet* to early seventeenth-century controversies over draining the fenlands of East Anglia, which were, according to the environmental historian John F. Richards, "the most heavily capitalized early modern English effort[s] to increase arable land." And possibly were among the most fiercely resisted, especially by those, the dwellers of the fen, "who feared, rightly, irretrievable loss to their way of life,"[36] a way of life Michael Drayton aestheticizes in Song 25 of his vast chorographic poem, *Poly-Olbion:*

> The toyling *Fisher* here is tewing of his Net:
> The Fowler is imployd his lymed twigs to set.
> One underneath his Horse, to get a shoot doth stalke;
> Another over Dykes upon his Stilts doth walke:
> There other with their Spades, the Peats are squaring out,
> To draw out Sedge and Reed, for Thatch and Stover fit,
> That whosoever would a Landskip right hit,
> Beholding but my Fennes shall with more shapes be stor'd
> Then *Germany,* or *France,* or *Thuscan* can afford:
> And for that part of me, which men high *Holland* call,
> Where *Boston* seated is, by plenteous *Wythams* fall,
> I preemptory am, large Neptunes liquid field,
> Doth to no other tract the like aboundance yeeld.[37]

Given all this, the tenuous and aestheticized but real historical links, the inconsistency in the muddy grave as it stands, and the rich theatrical possibilities of Yorick's skull as the Elsinore Man, one may wonder if such a reading could be staged, without committing too much violence to the text? Might such a staging not shock an audience into a view of the new? Perhaps; but remember, this reading of Yorick's skull is a mud bath at the spa, a peat body wrap, like a mask of Irish peat, finely textured for ladies of the Isle. Like the peat mask, this reading of Yorick's skull draws away inflammation even as it warms and soothes; it demonstrates one remedy for professional disappointment. An attractive remedy it is, too, particularly if the spa resides in the Napa Valley or the south of France, and offers a fine glass of chardonnay. But I fear solutions to problems like professional disappointment that burden only the individual. And disappointment, I would suggest, is not unique to any given critic; disappointment—being bogged (down) in the academy, being a bog—is today constitutive, structurally, of professional identity. So the question is not how you, disappointed professional, deal with this condition; the question is not what's your peat wrap? The question is this: how should one read professional disappointment in the context of the profession and of the profession in society? And can such a reading illuminate the meanings of mudslinging, of professional disputation, particularly regarding ecocriticism?

To provide an answer, I turn hopefully to the captivating work of Sianne Ngai, who has brilliantly, and without lamentation, come to terms with "art's diminishing role as the privileged locus for modern aesthetic experience."[38] This she does by acknowledging art's interpenetration with mass culture and, thus, with the judgments, however equivocal, of the demos. Those judgments, Ngai believes, "are 'objectifications' of feeling," feeling generated by life in bureaucratic, administered, yet fully market-driven societies, feeling that "index[es] situations of suspended agency," of "weakness."[39] To ignore the feelings Ngai examines—anxiety, irritation, envy, and paranoia among them—is to ignore the aesthetic categories they generate, categories ubiquitously present but nonetheless inconsequential, like the zany, the cute, and the interesting. And to ignore those ubiquitous but inconsequential categories is to ignore the status of art in bureaucratic and hypercommodified societies, art's "problematically limited agency," its "social inefficaciousness."[40] Art's interpenetration with commerce undermines not only the avant-garde and the production of the new but also art's status as a marker of "of nonalienated labor," a status it has held for at least two hundred years, "since the inception of aesthetic discourse in the eighteenth century."[41] Art, Ngai implies, is problematically inconsequential or, at least, no more consequential than anything else one can buy in the market. And so, too, are artists. Or critics.

Far more than aesthetic theory, art—or aesthetic practice—has responded to the conditions in which it finds itself. For this reason, Ngai's target in *Our Aesthetic Categories* really is aesthetic theory; it is aesthetic theory that needs resuscitation, not aesthetics, not art. And resuscitation is possible: philosophers just need to think differently, she argues, to recognize that their focus on beauty and the sublime—or "distance, play, and disinterested pleasure"—impairs their ability to recognize both "the theoretical significance of 'aesthetic categories' as a finite and intensively variegated class" and the "decades of aesthetic practice that have put increasingly direct pressure on [their] defining concepts and terms."[42] We do not need to jettison the defining concepts and terms; we just need to recognize that they are not privileged categories of aesthetic response. Even within the cute, the interesting, and the zany, Ngai insists, reside possibilities for play and distance.

But, if I can indulge here in a bit of what is becoming or is, indeed, now the old-fashioned hermeneutics of suspicion, I wonder if this is not a distinction without a difference. Which may be to ask: in late capitalist society, can "distance, play, and disinterested pleasure—essentially images of freedom" actually reside within the cute, the interesting, and the zany, essentially images of "compulsion or determination"?[43] Or it may be to ask: just how tied up with locations of privilege are distance, play, and disinterested pleasure? And in late capitalist society, will the social locations where distance, play, and disinterested pleasure thrive, thrive themselves? Some have argued, and Ngai implies, regarding the penultimate question, that they are bound tightly: "distance, play, and disinterested pleasure" were thought up to demonstrate the philosopher's, the artist's, and the art consumer's "distance from necessity," the necessity, principally, of working, of being useful, of being subject to markets and industrial rationalization, but also, as Ngai adds, of being powerless, or weak.[44] Let me grant that such thinking, such demonstration, may have been wishful, even two hundred years ago. But if Pierre Bourdieu and others are right, then jettisoning the privileged categories of aesthetic response would require recognition that one is no longer distanced from necessity, from work, from powerlessness. One's thinking or writing is not disinterested or playful, not even in one's imagination. Or in the public imaginary. This recognition is difficult for many of us to accept, but should it be? Perhaps this is Ngai's point, that it should not be. If Ngai is right that aesthetic categories are generated from feeling associated with particular social and economic conditions, then these privileged categories should feel as phony to us—we who are ranked and rated on numerical scales and speak of "our research productivity this week" or of "feeling pressure to increase FTEs in our courses next year"—as they do to the woman on the street, enjoying a noon-time sighting of cute puppies before returning to a cubicle to receive, for hours, complaints about credit card fees. As Ngai insists, "all art in the late capitalist society of high-powered media spectacles is, in a certain manner of speaking, 'cute.'" And almost all of us, in a certain manner of speaking, are powerless, suffer from "a deficit of power," a state we have, seemingly, small voice to protest.[45]

Admired Antony!

In 2005, in *The Future of Environmental Criticism,* Lawrence Buell surveyed the field of ecocriticism, noting two significant and related movements in it. First was ecocriticism's increasing tendency to ignore its foundational call to connect "academic work and public citizenship and advocacy." And second was ecocriticism's increasing cosmopolitanization, its move away from its origins "as an offshoot of an association of second-level prestige [the Western Literature Association] whose principal support base lay mostly outside the most prominent American university literature departments."[46] Buell then ventriloquized the concerns of those who dreamed up this field not so many years prior:

> Might this process of cosmopolitanization wind up amounting to a forfeiture of the original mission? To a taming down of first-wave ecocriticism's original schismatic disaffection with business-as-usual literary studies? To the consolidation of environmental criticism as just another niche within the culture of academic professionalism, now that it is on the way to becoming more "critically sophisticated," increasingly more engaged with the other critical games in town?[47]

Buell's answer to these questions was this: "Probably so, to some extent." But his hope was that "the promise is well worth the risk, both on the intrinsics and the pragmatics—especially if the alternatives are a too narrow conception of environmentalism and environmentality."[48]

At the time, some people—like me—thought this at least partially self-interested: of course the professor employed by Harvard would espouse the benefits of ecocriticism's becoming legitimate within "the most prominent American university literature departments"! But seven years later, in an article published in 2012, to which I have referred above, Garrard is not so sure the risk was worth taking, even though, like a lot of us, me included, he has profited from it. "Ecocriticism," he writes,

> may be at something of a crisis point, if that is not too melodramatic a way to put it. Not because of institutionalization and professionalization, nor because of the intrusion of Theory, but because the growing nature-skepticism of the field, which in some respects represents increased scientific and philosophical sophistication, risks subverting its ethical and pedagogical *raison d'etre.*[49]

This seems a bit muddy to me, since "increased scientific and philosophical sophistication" seems very much like "institutionalization and professionalization [and] the intrusion of Theory," but I am willing here to let Garrard avow and disavow. For it is difficult even to suggest, muddily, that "increased scientific and philosophical sophistication" in the field results not in solving the problems of the environment but in solving the problem of the field's and one's own institutional and professional status. It is difficult to suggest, even muddily, that "increased scientific and philosophical sophistication" might, and seemingly paradoxically, register as "cute" in Ngai's sense, as a sign of our powerlessness. For, in contrast to Cheryll Glotfelty, who, in her interview in *PMLA,* also published in 2012, nervously insists on, clings to, the trickle-down practical effects of pedagogy—if you train graduate students and they teach undergraduates, perhaps one of them "will later have jobs in national policy making"[50]—Garrard bravely considers that trickle-down may not occur at all and that maybe his ecocritical pedagogy, though theoretically and scientifically sophisticated, has a problematically negative effect. "I'm reminded," he writes, "of the student who finished my course . . . and said, 'I used to be an environmentalist, but now I'm just confused.'"[51] Or as an early modern student might put it, "now I'm just muddied." Have our efforts at sophistication left "the people muddied / Thick and unwholesome in their thoughts" (*Hamlet,* 4.5.80–81), uncertain what actions, if any, to take to, um, save the planet? Or worse, are they left "thick and unwholesome in their thoughts," certain no actions can do so?

As Garrard concludes his article, he puts forward a number of questions about the objects of our analyses and arguments, the ways ecocriticism has developed, questions that, given the muddy thinking I have followed and put forward in this chapter, should be easy to answer:

> Why does Sandilands level her critique not, for the most part, at the defiantly unsustainable discourses of modern consumerism, but instead, like [Timothy] Morton, at environmental rhetoric? Why have so many postcolonial critics attacked the conservationist policies of environmental NGOs? Why are ecofeminists seemingly more concerned about the rhetoric of "population control" than the effects of burgeoning human populations on biodiversity and global climate? Why do I question the analogy of personal and ecological health in environmentalist texts rather than, say, the cheerful accumulation of Air Miles by the international haute bourgeoisie—among them academics?[52]

And then Garrard asks the question I quoted above, "When, in short, did ecocriticism come to focus so much on criticizing environmentalism?"[53] Offering a number of reasons—the habits of critique developed in the academy over the past forty years, the tendency to "debate . . . with those whose work confronts and intrigues us," and the fact that "taking on the greenwashing of BP (even pre-Gulf oil spill) might seem at once impossibly quixotic and too laughably easy"[54]—Garrard ignores another obvious answer: when we decided to elevate the field's and our own professional status. Advocacy, much less activism, much less acting differently in one's professional life, screams "second-tier"; it screams "feminized"; it screams bogged down, stuck in the mud. And in a professional environment itself in crisis, in which departments or colleges—or, more tellingly for us, the separate fields of medieval and Renaissance British literature—may begin to disappear as rapidly as muddy wetlands, that fate, being second-tier, being bogged down, is to be avoided perhaps above all others, by colluding, by slinging mud, by embracing the late capitalist demand for productivity, and hence consumption. Productivity and consumption *growth*. Thus when Garrard questions himself—why don't I interrogate "the cheerful accumulation of Air Miles by the international haute bourgeoisie—among them academics?"—implying thereby, like Timothy Morton a few years ago, that we are part of the problem, guilty of destroying the environment, the answer must be that doing so, acknowledging this truth, is not just inconvenient but impossible. The answer must also be that he did not read my chapter "Slow Shakespeare," published in 2008, where I did interrogate, and forcefully, "the cheerful accumulation of Air Miles."[55] Here's mud in your eye, Greg.

Over the past forty years or so, criticism has tried, with much success, to recuperate the low, the despised, the forgotten, to turn the mired into the admired. In this chapter, I have tried not to do so, not to recuperate mud. I have not offered a move one might have expected: a reading, perhaps, of *Beasts of the Southern Wild* or the benefits of restoring the fens of East Anglia. Rather than suggest we admire the mired, I have tried to show that the mire sticks even to those we admire, those who are not low, despised, or forgotten. Is it presumptuous of me to suggest that *admire*'s roots in the verb "to look" can't quite shake off the slime of the unrelated but identical verbs "to defile, to pollute" or "to swallow up," to bog down? When Antony handles the drunken Lepidus in the scene whose consideration begins this essay, in an exchange that inspires laughter or mockery, we, like the onlookers onstage, relish Antony's handling of, his deflection of, the drunken triumvir. Ad mire, we admire Antony; we look upon him and up to him. It is difficult not to do so. But we know, in another time and place, Antony was mired differently, his soldiers swallowed up and bogged down in the muddy marshes at Philippi. And we know, in another time and place, Antony was mired again, in strong Egyptian fetters, in dotage both sexual and intellectual, looking foolish, inactive, muddied.

Antony wants to melt Rome, to bring its kingdoms to clay, knowing that "our dungy earth alike / Feeds beast as man" (1.1.36–37). Antony wants to read his life as Giorgio Agamben reads Titian's *Nymph and Shepherd,* as a reworking of "the enigma of the sexual relationship" from "a new and more mature formulation." For the aged painter, as, perhaps, for the aged general, "sensual pleasure and love . . . do not prefigure only death and sin. . . . [But] a new and more blessed life, one that is neither animal nor human." Perhaps like Antony and Cleopatra, perhaps like some of us, perhaps like me and my lover, Titian's nymph and shepherd share a "most intimate secret," having "initiated each other into their own lack of mystery"; "they mutually forgive each other and expose their *vanitas.*" Tumbling from love-making, ardent, wet, breathless, looking into each other's eyes, admiring each other's slightly stunned visage, "the lovers who have lost their mystery contemplate a human nature rendered perfectly inoperative—the inactivity *[inoperosità]* and *desoeuvrement* of the human and of the animal as the supreme and unsavable figure of life." Crucially, crucially for me and the lovers, their spent and intimate "condition is *otium,* it is workless *[senz'opera].*"[56] But it is not worthless. It is, indeed, the hope present in this chapter, this bit of muddy thinking, that we may become, at least on occasion, "perfectly inoperative" or "workless," that we will, perhaps, stop slinging mud to build turf, or empires. That we will, perhaps, reconsider productivity and growth as models for intellectual work, and then perhaps we will conclude to collude, to gather 'round, on behalf of a model of education and scholarship different from that offered by the purveyors of technology and the managed university, where we celebrate mud's and muddy thinking's miraculous fecundity, its spontaneous generativity, which allows intellectuality to ooze, to spread outward in community, in *otium,* resisting the demand, at least on occasion, to sling upward and to sling upward again, for personal glory or fame. Work less: I am confident this prescription would satisfy Antony, if not disapproving Caesar.

Notes

This chapter was first delivered as a lecture at "Elemental Ecocriticism," the 30th Alabama Symposium on English and American Literature, held in Tuscaloosa, Alabama, in April 2013, which was organized by Sharon O'Dair and supported by the Department of English and the Hudson Strode Program in Renaissance Studies at the University of Alabama. Many thanks to Jeffrey Jerome Cohen and Lowell Duckert for editing this volume and for their helpful comments on this chapter in particular.

1. William Shakespeare, *Antony and Cleopatra,* ed. John Wilders (London: Routledge, 1995), 2.7.113–14, 117–18. Further citations appear parenthetically in the text.
2. Edward J. Geisweidt, "'The Nobleness of Life': Spontaneous Generation and Excremental Life in *Antony and Cleopatra,*" in *Ecocritical Shakespeare,* ed. Lynne Bruckner and Dan Brayton (Burlington, VT: Ashgate, 2011), 90, 94.
3. William Shakespeare, *Macbeth,* ed. Kenneth Muir (London: Arden Shakespeare, 1997), 1.5.70.

4. Susan Sontag, *Against Interpretation and Other Essays* (New York: Farrar, Straus and Giroux, 1967), 136. See my chapter "Tragedy's Honor, and Ours," in *Renaissance Shakespeare/Shakespeare Renaissances: Proceedings of the Ninth World Shakespeare Congress,* ed. Martin Procházka, Michael Dobson, Andreas Hōfele, and Hanna Scolnicov (Newark: University of Delaware Press, 2014), 306–13.

5. Terry Eagleton, *Sweet Violence: The Idea of the Tragic* (Malden, Mass.: Blackwell, 2003), 93.

6. Catherine Gallagher and Stephen Greenblatt, *Practicing New Historicism* (Chicago: University of Chicago Press, 2000), 1.

7. For the former, see Douglas Bruster, *Shakespeare and the Question of Culture: Early Modern Literature and the Cultural Turn* (New York: Palgrave Macmillan, 2003), 51–52. For the latter, see David Scott Kastan, *Shakespeare after Theory* (New York: Routledge, 1999), 18. See also Kastan's faculty page at Yale University.

8. Gallagher and Greenblatt, *Practicing New Historicism,* 19.

9. Bruster, *Shakespeare and the Question of Culture,* 51–52.

10. Greg Garrard, "Nature Cures? Or How to Police Analogies of Personal and Ecological Health," *ISLE* 19, no. 3 (Summer 2012): 510. To contrast Garrard's take on "citizen science," see Stacy Alaimo, *Bodily Natures: Science, Environment, and the Material Self* (Bloomington: Indiana University Press, 2010), 22–59.

11. Susan Fraiman, "Pussy Panic versus Liking Animals: Tracking Gender in Animal Studies," *Critical Inquiry* 39 (Autumn 2012): 91–93.

12. William Shakespeare, *The Taming of the Shrew,* ed. Brian Morris (London: Methuen, 1981), 5.2.143–46.

13. Jonathan Goldberg and Madhavi Menon, "Queering History," *PMLA* 120, no. 5 (2005): 1609.

14. Valerie Traub, "The New Unhistoricism in Queer Studies," *PMLA* 128, no. 1 (2013): 21, 29, 23, 35.

15. Ibid., 21. Traub quotes Vin Nardizzi, Stephen Guy-Bray, and Will Stockton, "Queer Renaissance Historiography: Backward Gaze," in *Queer Renaissance Historiography: Backward Gaze,* ed. Vin Nardizzi, Stephen Guy-Bray, and Will Stockton (Burlington, Vt.: Ashgate, 2009), 1.

16. Traub, "The New Unhistoricism in Queer Studies," 31.

17. Jack Halberstam, "Game of Thrones: The Queer Season," *Bully Bloggers* (April 8, 2013), http://bullybloggers.wordpress.com/2013/04/08/game-of-thrones-the-queer-season-by-jack-halberstam-house-of-nemo/. Menon alludes to these misspellings as well, in her mudslinging contribution to *PMLA*'s forum about Traub's essay: "Indeed, Traub's essay repeatedly misnames the queer theorists of those insights. On one occasion, I am referred to as 'Madhavi' rather than 'Menon'; 'Jasbir Puar' is rendered 'Jasbir Paur'; and 'Gayatri Gopinath' becomes 'Gayatri Gopinah.' The seemingly polite surface of the Russian novel, as Freud pointed out, always has an other scene—the unconscious—whose political incorrectness cannot be controlled. I want to insist that I don't mind being misnamed; in fact I find such oddities of

language delightful. But it is fascinating that at the moment of trying to fix both historicism and unhistoricism into separate camps, the essay finds itself at the limit of fixity. Something disrupts and interrupts the boundary at which historicism—despite its multiple uses—finds itself" (Madhavi Menon, "To the Editor," *PMLA* 128, no. 3 [2013]: 783).

That Halberstam and Menon make a mountain of a (no doubt muddy) molehill seems not to matter to this intellectual discourse, part of it, at least, conducted in the profession's most prestigious journal. One wonders why not? The editors of *N+1* recently offered an answer: "all contemporary publications tend toward the condition of blogs, and soon, if not yet already, it will seem pretentious, elitist, and old-fashioned to write anything, anywhere, with patience and care" ("Please RT," *N+1* 14 (June 3, 2012), https://nplusonemag.com/?s=%22Please+RT%22.

18. William Shakespeare, *Hamlet*, ed. Harold Jenkins (London: Methuen, 1982), 2.2.561, 564. Further citations appear parenthetically in the text.

19. Edward Albee, *Who's Afraid of Virginia Woolf?* (1962; rpr. New York: New American Library, 2005), 93–94.

20. William Carlos Williams, *The Collected Poems of William Carlos Williams*, vol. 2, *1939–1962*, edited by Christopher MacGowan (New York: New Directions, 1986), 306.

21. Shakespeare, *Macbeth*, 4.2.18.

22. Jeffrey Williams, "The Posttheory Generation," *symploke* 3, no. 1 (1995): 60.

23. Karin Sanders, *Bodies in the Bog and the Archaeological Imagination* (Chicago: University of Chicago Press, 2009), 17.

24. Williams, *Collected Poems*, 306.

25. Ibid., 307.

26. Seamus Heaney, *Opened Ground: Selected Poems, 1966–1996* (New York: Farrar, Straus and Giroux, 1998), 178.

27. Ibid., 196.

28. Ann Thompson and Neil Taylor, "Introduction," in William Shakespeare, *Hamlet*, ed. Ann Thompson and Neil Taylor (London: Arden Shakespeare, 2006), 5.1.163–64n.

29. Jenkins, "Introduction," in Shakespeare, *Hamlet*, 10.

30. Gaston Bachelard, *Earth and Reveries of Will*, trans. Kenneth Haltman (Dallas, Tex.: Dallas Institute of Humanities and Culture, 2002), 98.

31. Tom Stoppard, *Rosencrantz and Guildenstern Are Dead* (New York: Grove Press, 1967), 39. Appropriately, Guildenstern repeats the line a minute or two later: "Consistency is all I ask!" (45).

32. Heaney, *Opened Ground*, 125.

33. Francesco Menotti, *Wetland Archaeology and Beyond: Theory and Practice* (Oxford: Oxford University Press, 2012), 195.

34. Ibid., 199.

35. See Todd Borlik, "Caliban and the Fen Demons of Lincolnshire: The Englishness of Shakespeare's *Tempest,*" *Shakespeare* 9, no. 1 (2013): 21–51.

36. John F. Richards, *The Unending Frontier: An Environmental History of the Early Modern World* (Berkeley: University of California Press, 2003), 214–16.

37. Michael Drayton, *Poly-Olbion,* in *The Works of Michael Drayton,* corr. ed., vol. 4, ed. J. William Hebel (Oxford: Basil Blackwell & Mott, 1961), 514–15, ll. 139–52.

38. Sianne Ngai, "Our Aesthetic Categories," *PMLA* 125, no. 4 (2010): 951.

39. Adam Jasper, "Our Aesthetic Categories: An Interview with Sianne Ngai," *Cabinet* 43 (Fall 2011): 45.

40. Sianne Ngai, *Ugly Feelings* (Cambridge, Mass.: Harvard University Press, 2005), 36.

41. Sianne Ngai, *Our Aesthetic Categories* (Cambridge, Mass.: Harvard University Press, 2012), 21.

42. Ibid., 242.

43. Ibid., 241.

44. See, for example, Pierre Bourdieu, *Distinction: A Social Critique of the Judgement of Taste,* trans. Richard Nice (Cambridge, Mass.: Harvard University Press, 1984), 34–44, 53–63.

45. Ngai, *Our Aesthetic Categories,* 22, 18.

46. Lawrence Buell, *The Future of Environmental Criticism: Environmental Crisis and Literary Imagination* (Malden, Mass.: Blackwell, 2005), 7.

47. Ibid., 27–28.

48. Ibid., 28.

49. Garrard, "Nature Cures?," 497.

50. Cheryll Glotfelty, "The Formation of a Field: Ecocriticism in America," interview by Michelle Balaev, *PMLA* 127, no. 3 (2012): 613.

51. Garrard, "Nature Cures?," 510.

52. Ibid., 509–10.

53. Ibid., 510.

54. Ibid.

55. See Sharon O'Dair, "Slow Shakespeare: An Eco-Critique of 'Method' in Early Modern Literary Studies," in *Early Modern Ecostudies: From the Florentine Codex to Shakespeare,* ed. Karen Raber, Thomas Hallock, and Ivo Kamps (New York: Palgrave Macmillan, 2008), 15–57. See also Sharon O'Dair, "The State of the Green: A Review Essay on Shakespearean Ecocriticism," *Shakespeare* 4, no. 4 (2008): 475–93.

56. Giorgio Agamben, *The Open: Man and Animal,* trans. Kevin Attell (Stanford: Stanford University Press, 2004), 87.

six

The Quintessence of Wit

CHRIS BARRETT

In the northwest corner of the Boston Public Gardens, there stands a monument to ether. The ether monument was the first statue moved into the gardens, preceding the stone-straight statesmen and rigid generals who stare unblinkingly over the precisely cultivated flowerbeds and meticulously tended walking paths of this green patch at the center of the city. Tree branches shade the monument, dappling light over the small pool fed by fountains in the shape of water-spouting lion heads at the memorial's base. Upon the base sits a pedestal topped by a statue of two figures: a Samaritan doctor tending to a young man splayed over the doctor's knees. The latter's body arcs with the kind of desperate geometry that suggests the granite itself is overcome by pain. One of the four panels along the squared base explains the monument commemorates a discovery at nearby Massachusetts General Hospital in October 1846. On what has since become known as Ether Day, it was demonstrated that "the inhaling of ether causes insensibility to pain."

In many ways, a granite memorial is the least likely way to begin a history of the fifth element, which—like other elements taxonomized in classical antiquity—strongly militates against fixity. Anaximenes had defined "aither" as the originary material of the cosmos; Heraclitus had associated ether with the fiery work of change, the destruction that produces creation.[1] The most powerful exponent of ether, however, was Empedocles, who in the fifth century BCE proposed the "roots" of the universe, the "only immortal and indestructible things" (Aristotle would later rename these "roots" as "elements").[2] In extant fragments of his poem, Empedocles introduces the essential components of the cosmos and their protocols of separation and containment by way of analogy to the primordial *agon* encoded in the human body that is always poised—as the ether monument's boy attests—on the knife edge of suffering, the human body over which ether and laughter fight. "This is very clear in the bulk of mortal limbs," Empedocles writes,

> at one time all coming together into one by love,
> all the limbs, [that is], which have found a body, in the peak of flourishing life;
> at another time again, being divided by evil quarrels,
> they [the limbs] wander, all of them separately, about the breakers of life.[3]

The power of ether rests somewhere in the motion that governs this transition from love to the violent dismemberment into elementary components: the body ether stakes as its conceptual ground is itself positioned between a recuperative unity and a divisive articulation—love and strife. The Empedoclean love into which "at one time all [were] coming together into one" suggests both bodily integrity and the desire for enmeshment in a community: that is, the love that floats between the embodied parameters of individual existence and the porous exchanges among ecologically interrelated agents. This love is countered by agony, the corruption of the individual agent in this system, or the corruption of the system itself: the avulsion of a limb, or the division of the body into extremities that will not collaborate, cooperate, mutually engage.

Long before Hamlet ruminated on the human body as a quintessence of dust, and long before T. S. Eliot's Prufrock—who is not Prince Hamlet, nor was he meant to be—invited readers to

> Let us go then, you and I,
> When the evening is spread out against the sky
> Like a patient etherized upon a table;[4]

the fifth element had been defined by the way damaged bodies writhed in this world. The suffering body that struggles between unity and separation offers the essential map of this Empedoclean elementary world—a vision that oddly anticipates the twenty-first century's (often affirmative) understanding that every atom in human bodies has been forged in the cores of stars.

Empedocles offers this vision of the distressed body that is half joined in love and half wandering in strife, and the vision haunts this chapter, which takes civil war as the background against which the workings of ether are most vibrantly defined. As the pageant of love and strife, the division of the body politic into agonized members, civil war—American, English, environmental, all of which follow in the coming pages—threatens the destruction of agents (human and nonhuman) longing for ecological union. Where the complex of interrelation might produce a supple environment of love, proliferation, and exchange, civil war instantiates a tragic ending against which Joseph Meeker's "comedy of survival" (discussed below) is starkly outlined. In my exploration of ether's witty intimacy, war allows for the articulation of a cosmic alternative: the ethereal dream of life that endures its agony long enough to laugh again.

"Come then!" says Empedocles, anticipating and echoing the invitation to let us go, then, you and

> I shall tell you first the source from which the sun in the beginning
> and all other things which we now see became clear:
> earth and billowy sea and fluid air
> and the Titan aither squeezing all of them around in a circle.[5]

This aither "separated and flew off from air and fire," though as usual for ether and its otherworldly ways, this passage leaves open the question of ether's status:[6] it might be, for Empedocles, a distinct root itself, or it may be simply "a mixture of air and fire sufficiently stable to separate off from them,"[7] or, as for Plato in the *Timaeus*, "the most translucent kind" of the species of air.[8] In any case, this already elusively natured ether "evolved into a heaven revolving in a very wide orbit" while the earth resolved itself into one location, and the ether "moves all around it without diversion."[9] Superlunary and undeterred, ether's essential nature is circular, simultaneously constituting the outer cosmos while mirroring itself in human bodies hovering between an Empedoclean love and agony. Between this love and this agony, ether cycles. And that cycle, that ethernal return, circles the leitmotif of the suffering body waiting for a return to its initial love, its originary, ecological desire.

That body returns me to the ether monument in Boston, where the dying young man stonily incarnates one aspect of quintessence's history: ether is the element that accompanies laughter—of the bleakest, darkest sort. Herman Melville, whose *Moby-Dick* is only slightly older than the ether monument itself, wonders in the novel, "In what rapt ether sails the world," and at one point suggests the work of a cosmos built of ether: "There are certain queer times and occasions . . . when a man takes this whole universe for a vast practical joke, though the wit thereof he but dimly discerns, and more than suspects that the joke is at nobody's expense but his own."[10]

Because humor is so often a communal celebration of brokenness, waste, and cruelty, it should not be surprising that the history of ether and laughter is an often dark one, full of brutal, bleeding jests written on agonized bodies: oscillating between an Empedoclean unifying conspiracy of parts, and the susceptibility to severance and injury, ether follows humor as it convenes participants and isolates victims. Since the early modern period, literature has chronicled the secret intimacy of ether and laughter, which for centuries have twinned and twined themselves like caduceus snakes, hissing bleakly of violence and irony. With every interroping curve around the staff, ether and laughter transform themselves into a new version of an old joke, one that returns again and again.

It is worth spending a moment here to consider the paradigmatic motion of ether, which in its Empedoclean instantiation is characterized by circularity and cyclicity, and which I have here associated with the motion of intertwining—with laughter, with agony. Each of these rhythms (circularity, intertwining) comprises repetition, torqued or tweaked. The "laughether" I trace—the product of ether's and laughter's intertwining—belongs to the realm of the repetitive, like humor itself. In his famous treatment of laughter, Henri Bergson presupposes the specifically elemental nature of the comic, and he begins by wondering how to get at comedy's essence. "What does laughter mean?" he asks. "What is the basal element in the laughable?" To find this elemental essence, Bergson suggests the chemist distilling and titrating the way to a comic truth only accessible in the language of the maddeningly variable, vaguely perceptible: "What method of distillation will yield us invariably the same essence from which so many different products borrow either their obtrusive odour or their delicate perfume?"[11] It is difficult to think of Bergson's elemental laughter without thinking of anesthetic ether, wafting in the coppery air, or with the permeating intimacy with which the ethereal creeps into the body. Indeed, the ethereal essence of humor creeps into Bergson's treatise itself, which is divided within its chapters into five principal subchapters: the quintessential shape of a text that has inhaled the sly ethereality of its subject. For Bergson, laughter is, at its barest minimum, ethereal, elusive, pervasive; its basal element is as common and fleeting and certain as scent.

Yet for all its immanent insubstantiality, the workings of laughter can be attributed, in large part, Bergson argues, to repetition: "living life should never repeat itself," he explains. "Wherever there is repetition or complete similarity, we always suspect some mechanism at work behind the living." This "is here the real cause of laughter."[12] Perhaps ether, perennially repetitive in its tireless self-reinvention and relentless reappearance, manufactures this laughter born of repetition. Perhaps the fifth element is stalked by laughter because it continues to resurface, each time looking a little different—just as the humanity elementally engaging this laughter itself looks a little different in each historical moment. Perhaps ether returns, in each instance, as a quotation or allusion, an always already uncanny concept, familiar in its desire, unfamiliar in its punchline. If this is so, can we learn to laugh at this intermingling of ether and laughter, learn to laugh at its ethernal return, like the farce that follows tragedy?

If we could get access to that repetitive joke, what would it sound like? And would it train us to tell different stories—stories in which the intermingling of ether and laughter produces not discord but attraction, not agony but love? How might critics as modern alchemists reimagine the ethereal cosmos as a realm suffused by an elemental laughter? And what might it mean for a group of scholars seeking a vocabulary of vibrancy and agency to inhabit a universe quintessentially defined by laughter? Might ether's involvement in the affective ecology of laughter, humor, jest, and wit somehow sharpen the contemporary moment's confrontation with an existential crisis that is literally ecological? And might there be a joke we can tell, after the catastrophe?

That looming catastrophe for which the anaesthetized patient waits is one that advances the motion of intertwining as the privileged motion of ether; that intertwining suggests the dark labor of a cosmic comedy that seeks to turn strife into love. Threading ether and laughter together into the ropy substrate of a universe indifferent to human exceptionalism but susceptible nonetheless to destructive forces, intertwining allows for the fifth element's work as a principle of interconnectedness. Ether returns the wandering limbs to the integrated body. This interconnectedness, however, is not anodyne or untroubled: there is agony and loss and suffering in the comic ropes that rebind the wandering limbs. As Timothy Morton's theory of "dark ecology" suggests, a principle of interconnectedness produces a desire "to stay with a dying world."[13]

This sinewy tale of ether and laughter begins with bodies in pain.

On the morning of Ether Day, dentist William Morton, in front of surgeon John C. Warren and an operating theater full of first skeptical and then astounded witnesses, put a tube of a glass retort—the first modern anesthetic contraption—to the lips of the housepainter Gilbert Abbott, who was about to undergo surgery to remove a tumor from his neck. Within minutes of inhaling Morton's preparation of oil of orange mixed with sulfuric ether (ether being in chemistry an organic compound including an ether group, or an oxygen atom connected to two alkyl or aryl groups), Abbott became insensible, and Dr. Warren removed the growth from his neck without the patient reacting to pain at the time, or later remembering any pain. Abbott became proof of the possibility of painless surgery.[14]

Prior to Ether Day, patients had only alcohol, mesmerism, and gritted teeth to push back the shattering, world-obliterating pain of incision, amputation, cauterization.[15] But on October 16, 1846, ether changed all this. The fumes of a compound that shares its name with the fifth element, the quintessence whence comes the other elements—these fumes, on Ether Day, pushed back the edges of a world contracted by pain.

In this modern-era instantiation of ether, its quintessential power was the palliation of the suffering body, the ability to make the body withstand ever greater damage and intrusion, avulsion and contusion, incision and laceration, without rushing to death in a blaze of torment. Ether made the waiting for death newly possible. As the body of the young man eased by the column-top Samaritan in the northwest corner of Boston's Public Gardens suggests, while his statue waits stonily through ticking seasons (summers, and winters, and summers again): the ether makes the waiting possible, even if the end is assured.

But in this slant history of ether and laughter, the waited-for end turns out to be a punchline. By the time it was transformed into anesthesia, ether had itself been waiting decades for a cruel historical joke to unfurl.[16] The use of ether "discovered" in 1846 had, in fact, been widely known at least fifty years earlier. The fumes of sulfuric ether, or its closely associated fellow gas nitrous oxide, had been established as having the power to induce insensibility to the world so as to deaden reaction to corporeal stimulus, or to heighten sensitivity to the world so as to produce laughter, raucous behavior, and intensified moods. These properties were well known, for example, to the participants in any number of "ether parties" held around the United States, at which young people would revel in the brief euphoria of ether intoxication.[17] These properties of the gas had a side-show quality, though. They were often demonstrated not by scientists or doctors—who for half a century ignored the anesthetic possibilities of ether and nitrous oxide—but by exhibitors and entrepreneurs, who would take their mountebank charm and their traveling wagons from town to town, charging the curious for small whiffs of laughing gas. Among these quintessential capitalists was a young Samuel Colt, who wound his way around the country, giving demonstrations of the intoxicating power of laughing gas in order to raise sufficient funds for the manufacture of his revolver.[18]

It would likely have been of no anesthetic comfort to the Civil War soldiers writhing on their field hospitals to know that the guns burying bullets in their bones were wrought by the gas that alone could quiet the pain of limb or life limping away. Walt Whitman in *Drum-Taps* describes the field hospital's scene of "surgeons operating, attendants holding lights, the smell of ether, the odor of blood."[19] The twinned history of the comic and the ethereal is not always amusing; this history encompasses the savage irony of laughing gas turning into steel turning into pain.

The memory of such horrors was not lost to the anonymous individual who commissioned the Ether Monument. A second panel on the monument's base adds the origins of its construction: "In gratitude for the relief of human suffering by the inhaling of ether a citizen of Boston has erected this monument" in 1867, when the nation had just seen several years of suffering and death on an unprecedented scale.[20]

Even before the dire joke of its artillery afterlife, anesthetic ether was already embedded in a deep kind of laughter. In the decades before Ether Day, ether was not just making people laugh in mind-altered hilarity; it was being laughed at. Though Coleridge, Southey, and other poets loved the inebriating effect of the gas, humorists saw it as rich material for parody and satire.[21] Rather than positing ether as the blazing force between fire and air in the upper reaches of the sky, or as the macrocosmic mirror of the soul, the scribblers of the 1800s saw a fallen kind of ether, debased and confined to the realm of the parlor trick, the peripatetic exhibition, and the frivolous excess of idle youth. Poets weighed in with scurrilous bits of skeptical mockery. In 1808, a chemist writing in defense of laughing gas observed that "poetry indeed was enlisted to expose the delusion, as it was termed, and to laugh it into contempt."[22] This witty, lampooning literature generated a laughter that kept laughing gas on the sidelines of medical practical knowledge. That attendees of a laughing gas exhibition in 1845 would report a volunteer under the influence of the gas spontaneously performing a scene from *Richard III* only underlines the complicity of literature in the wretched punchline.[23] These writers manufactured laughter that was directed at a gas; that gas in turn manufactured laughter; and all the while surgeons kept cutting into the livid flesh of all-too-sober patients. This cycle of literary hilarity kept ether from its anesthetic work for decades, in which plenty of young broken men and women without a monument suffered the kind of pain that made waiting unimaginable.

This, then, is the traffic of ether in the world of wit: the transactions of the fifth element with the material of laughter play out on damaged, desperate bodies. The joke ether tells, over and again in the pages of literature and history, begins with the emphatically mortal, intensely vulnerable body. Consider, for example, that the fifth element's most famous appearance in Renaissance literature spills from the mouth of a Danish prince who is known for his capacity for waiting. Hamlet greets his one-time friends and newly charged monitors Rosencrantz and Guildenstern with an account of the quintessence, as it intersects the prince's own musings on his recent unhappiness.

> I have of late—but wherefore I know not—lost all my mirth, forgone all custom of exercise; and indeed it goes so heavily with my disposition that this goodly frame, the earth, seems to me a sterile promontory. This most excellent canopy of the air, look you, this brave o'erhanging, this majestical roof fretted with golden fire—why, it appears no other thing to me than a foul and pestilent congregation of vapours. What a piece of work is man! How noble in reason, how infinite in faculty, in form and moving how express and admirable, in action how like an angel, in apprehension how like a god—the beauty of the world, the paragon of animals! And yet to me what is this quintessence of dust? (*Hamlet*, 2.2.287–98)[24]

Hamlet's yoking of mirthlessness and quintessence is itself only somewhat mirthless and only somewhat elemental. His "wherefore I know not" seems—nay, is—unlikely, considering the litany of woes he rehearses in the preceding act. The gesture at the elusive cause of his lost mirth becomes a quiet, dark jibe: the emptying out of laughter becomes itself a joke that ripens in his speech into the fallen, unimpressive quiddity of dust. The subsequent invocation (probably with a metatheatrical wink at the stage's roof, the "heavens") of the elements of air and fire, the nearest analogues of ether, set apart the fifth element's debased human instantiation. The fiction of mirth leads the prince to ponder the purity of dust that is the human body: laughter and ether entwine, even in their alleged absence, and at the intersection of ether and laughter sits solid, sullied, sullen flesh.

As Joseph Meeker observes, though, that flesh is initially protected by this sullen humor. Addressing the same passage, Meeker reads Hamlet's indulgence in mirthless laughter about the ethereal as the substitution of symbolic, verbal violence for the physical violence demanded by tragedy. This swap of word for sword delays the tragic end of the play, suggesting that Hamlet's is a program of game-playing and sublimation of aggression, designed to avoid death and prolong life. Hamlet's laughter is a comedy of survival.[25]

Since Hamlet's quintessential, half-jesting meditation on the fifth element, ether has kept resurfacing, each time with a different kind of wry, dust-dry mirth attached to it, each time with a different body on which to write its laughter—and sometimes literally writing that laughter, as I'll suggest later in this chapter. Not all bodies belong to humans, though, and ether attends to celestial bodies, too—those superlunary subjects classically associated with elemental ether, and, for Newton, driven through the cosmos in a mysterious substrate that would conduct forces between these whirling planets and stars. The modern legend of ether bifurcates into the anesthetic fume and the cosmic field; before ether parties and Ether Day, there was ether, the substrate of space.

These two iterations of ether as fume and field share, too, a quintessential attachment to humor. Sulfuric ether's battle to attract the serious attention of the medical establishment in some ways resembles the ups and downs of another theory of ether—that of the luminiferous ether as the universe's stable and pervasive medium, through which energy moves and according to which relative motion is set. By 1922, when Einsteinian relativity had upended nineteenth-century models, H. Bateman, writing in *The Publications of the Astronomical Society of the Pacific,* found it necessary to explain the different concepts of long-flexible ether in order to defend it from laughter. Having once been the breath of the gods and now more and more associated with what might just as ably be called "radiation," the conceptual plasticity of ether has become a "success [that] has led men to expect more and more from the ether and occasionally, when men have been disappointed in their expectations, the idea of an ether has lost its popularity and has even been ridiculed."[26] That ridicule produced a singularly creative destruction: from the (partial) dismantling of ether theory emerged the theory of special relativity.

Since Newton, variations on the ether had been modulating, so as to account for what troubled Newton about the universe sketched by his calculations: the power of bodies to act at a distance.[27] Surely the sun would not be able to draw the earth in orbit, for example, unless the gravitational force was conveyed by some interstellar substrate. Subsequent scientific theories elaborated on Newton's ether, and by the late nineteenth century, the ether was imagined to be the medium by which electromagnetism and light were propagated; that is, until the Michelson-Morley experiment of 1887 sought to isolate the effects of the ether and, in one of the more dramatic reversals in the history of science, accidentally disproved the existence of the ether as widely understood in the moment. The effort here to squeeze ether into a metric, rather than let ether intertwine itself with any and every part of the universe, simulated an excision of ether itself. Forty years after a different kind of ether had started to soothe lacerated bodies opened on operating tables and waiting to be twined back together, the Michelson-Morley experiment sliced open the body of physics' ether theory to pluck out the heart of its quintessential mystery.[28]

The destruction of ether was overstated, though; other theories popped up to conserve the theory of the luminiferous ether, while another theoretical paradigm was being assembled by Albert Einstein. In 1905, Einstein began a long and vexed relationship with the ether, a phenomenon he would often hail as the "diseased man of physics" (language resonant of ether's modern twin, the anesthetic sulfuric ether that stretched a patient upon a table). Einstein shunted aside conventional ether theory in outlining relativity, but he later reconciled himself not just to the possibility of some kind of cosmic substrate but perhaps its necessity. "More careful reflection teaches us, however," he told auditors of an address delivered in 1920 at the University of Leyden, "that the special theory of relativity does not compel us to deny ether. . . . According to the general theory of relativity space without ether is unthinkable."[29] In so doing, he reproduced the familiar pattern of ether's modern existence: when one instantiation fades, another appears.[30] Indeed, one new sense of ether appeared in the 1980s, when Lawrence Krauss coined the term "fifth essence" to name the dark matter that seems to make up the bulk of the universe.

At a dinner party in April 2013, I sat across from two physicists who had been drafted by the other guests to explain the significance of the recently discovered Higgs boson. Describing the Higgs field, which makes mass possible, they outlined a theory that seemed to—nay, did—resemble the ether banished by the twentieth century and relativity. The Higgs field, the indulgent physicists patiently explained, does not pervade the universe like the luminiferous ether but rather constitutes space itself; it makes possible the conditions under which materials interact. "This still sounds an awful lot like the nineteenth century's ether?" I said, preparing for them to explain to me all the esoteric ways in which this was not so. "It's not really much different," said the one physicist. Added the other, grinning, "It's kind of funny, isn't it?"

"You have no idea," I said.

This conversation, between a specialist in the humanities and two specialists in the sciences, highlights ether's tendency not just to return but to conjoin. Like the Empedoclean primordial body seeking originary love through its divisive strife, ether seeks a continuum of multidisciplinary understanding in its effusive promulgation of its many possible meanings. To speak of ether as a singular concept—in physics or in any discourse—disavows the chief insight of ether's modern physics sojourn. Having been the hinge for dispelling absolute space and time, ether caught up to its own lifelong eschewal of absolute definition—and the opportunity for humanists and scientists to lay hands on its body and remember its conceptual integrity. As Joe Milutis observes in his account of ether's history,

> The idea of the ether as both a powerful and vague term is not merely a recent historical shift. The ether has always existed relatively free of gravity, even as it also had a tendency to buttress political and spiritual structures. . . . Just as nature abhors the void, power adores the protean, cryptic ubiquity of the ether. . . . The writer who takes on the task of historicizing the ether, however, is constantly faced with impossibilities, lacunae, and loss of words. The irrational is behind every cloud.[31]

Alluringly elusive, seductively fluid, ether promulgates itself in a dizzying plurality verging on the incoherent. The history of ether overlaps itself: it is difficult, for example, to pry apart the luminiferous ether and the industrialized ether of commercial radio technology, or even the ether "netted" by cables weaving communication among computer terminals in the digital network age.[32] Ether as fume and ether as field run alongside each other in time. The Heraclitean element of persistent change and creation relentlessly persists, changes, creates.

Each time ether reinvents itself, it reasserts its dark humor, its promulgation of a joke written in agony but seeking a recuperative punchline. This work is often subtle enough, though, that its secret intimacy with wit goes unremarked. It is worth considering the moment in its history when that work was explicitly associated with the element as its quintessential labor. Having begun with the American Civil War, I turn to England's, to examine the early modern moment when ether formally fused itself to laughter under the sign of the broken body.

At some point in the English Renaissance, when ether was transforming itself from the grail of alchemy into a necessity of astronomy, the busy element also attached itself to the witty compendium. In the sixteenth century, ether became the sign under which was organized the book of mirth. Titles ranging from Francesco Sansovino's 1578 *The Quintessence of Wit, being a Corrant Comfort of Conceits, Maximes, and Poleticke Devises* (trans. Robert Hitchcock, 1590) to John Taylor's *The Essence, Quintessence, Insence, Innocence, Lye-sence, & Magnifisence of Nonsence upon Sence: Or, Sence upon Nonsence* (1654)—discussed below—and the 1657 translation of *Boccace's Tales, or, The Quintessence of Wit, Mirth, Eloquence, and Conversation* all attracted readers by promising wit (variously defined) as signaled by the fifth element. For these texts, ether is imagined as the constitutive essence of the grin: mirth as ethereal, concretized in the codex.

Subsequent titles followed this literary lead: *Rochester's Jests: Or, the Quintessence of Wit: Containing a New Collection of Merry Stories, Repartees, Jokes, Puns, the Most Admired Songs . . .* (1647–80); Christopher Smart's 1757 *The Nonpareil: Or, the Quintessence of Wit and Humor; Being a Choice Selection of Those Pieces That Were Most Admired in the Ever-to-be-Remember'd Midwife . . .*, the full title of which trumpets it as soon to "stand the Test of all ages, and live and be read 'till Time is no more," thus acquiring for the book something of the eternality of the ether governing its contents; *The Book of Fun, or, the Quintessence of Wit and Mirth* (London, 1759); *The Banquet of Momus, Or, The Quintessence of Wit and Humour: Containing the Most Complete, Rational, Merry, Diverting, and Humourous Collection of Agreeable Entertainment for Winter Evenings, and a Leisure Hour, Ever Before Published in the English Language . . .* (1801); and so on. These texts invited the intertwining of ether with narrative, and they reflect ether's tendency to appear—as I mentioned earlier—as quotation, as uncanny reappearance. Each of these texts compiles anterior events and jests, collecting conversations and jokes preceding the text itself: the quintessence of wit is itself an echo, a reformulation of what comes before.

While this quintessence of wit first appeared in English during the Renaissance, "quintessence" as a strictly alchemical term had, indeed, come before: it had been in circulation since the fifteenth century, and its figurative uses had arrived alongside the adjective "quintessential" in the sixteenth century. The *Oxford English Dictionary* reports the arrival of the "quintessential" meaning "Of, relating to, or of the nature of a quintessence; that is the purest, most typical, or most refined of its kind" in 1551. A translator of Vesalius (best known for his images of bodies spread out like patients) Englished the anatomist's treatise on a "lately invented oil" used for the treatment of all sorts of maladies; self-deprecatingly, he acknowledges that inquiring into the "quintessental properte" of the medicine "wolde breede a long prossess to discuss"—appropriately enough, for an element of such long and sinewy history.[33]

Even before its arrival in the mid-sixteenth century as quintessential, the ethereal had already been permeating English, hiding in everyday words, fading in and out of familiar speech: binding people "together" and "altogether" (like the dream of the pre-agon Empedoclean body, united in love); intensifying our connection by "tether"; flickering in a contingent "whether"; punning on the possibilities of "either," a homophone happily spelled in the sixteenth and seventeenth centuries with or without its essential "i." Shakespeare's Sonnet 44 plays with the half-present ether in its last line:

> But ah, thought kills me that I am not thought,
> To leap large lengths of miles when thou art gone,
> But that so much of earth and water wrought,
> I must attend time's leisure with my moan,
> Receiving naught by elements so slow
> But heavy tears, badges of either's woe. (lines 9–14)

Though the subsequent, linked sonnet describes the poetic persona as possessing "life, being made of four" elements, ether flickers in the last line of Sonnet 44 every bit as "present-absent" as the "slight air and purging fire" of Sonnet 45's first line. As quintessential to the poem as is the lover's melancholy, this fifth element creates, by way of its aural half-appearance at the end of Sonnet 44, the continuation of the lover's elemental anatomy in Sonnet 45. The encounter with ether produces reflection on "the dull substance of . . . flesh." Hamlet would not be surprised: what is the lover's suffering body, after all, if not the quintessence of dust?

By 1621, Robert Burton brought the woe of the punny, witty quintessence to his *Anatomy of Melancholy*, itself a text spread out like an expansive patient etherized upon a sky-broad table. Hailing Aristotle and Longinus as the "quintessence of wit,"[34] Burton consolidates the reception of the elements with the various, ethereal substrate that is the sly, wry, dry turn of the perfect phrase. Where better to encounter the fifth element than in the precision of written expression? Where better to find the quintessence than in the mirthful volume?

In some ways, the codex—especially in its relentlessly innovative, unruly, and experimental early modern instantiation—offers the perfect medium for detecting ether, and the assimilation of the element's laughing work into a literature unafraid to represent bodies in pain came quickly. Indeed, ether's relationship to the vulnerable literary body, and the appropriateness of the book as receptacle for the quintessence, were evident to those most actively engaged with the business of books. John Milton's most rhetorically striking reason in *Areopagitica* for opposing prepublication censorship turns on the quintessential nature of the codex:

> For Books are not absolutely dead things, but doe contain a potencie of life in them to be as active as that soule was whose progeny they are; nay they do preserve as in a violl the purest efficacie and extraction of that living intellect that bred them. . . . Many a man lives a burden to the Earth; but a good Booke is the pretious life-blood of a master spirit, imbalm'd and treasur'd up on purpose to a life beyond life. 'Tis true, no age can restore a life, whereof perhaps there is no great losse; and revolutions of ages do not oft recover the losse of a rejected truth, for the want of which whole Nations fare the worse. We should be wary therefore what persecution we raise against the living labours of publick men, how we spill that season'd life of man preserv'd and stor'd up in Books; since we see a kinde of homicide may be thus committed, sometimes a martyrdome, and if it extend to the whole impression, a kinde of massacre, whereof the execution ends not in the slaying of an elementall life, but strikes at that ethereall and fifth essence, the breath of reason it selfe, slaies an immortality rather then a life.[35]

Milton's famous vision of the book as a vial containing the purified substance of its writer depends upon the elemental distinction between the friable body and the potentially perdurant quintessence. Ether within the codex asserts itself by its analogy to the broken body—which is emphatically subject to being slain, murdered, massacred, or martyred—and the book that outlives the hands of its writer. To be visibly quintessential, the book requires the elemental mortality of its author. The fifth element reveals itself as immortality most sharply visible against the bleeding imagery of homicide and death. The material enmeshment of the human and the ethereal produces a delicate ecology of living and nonliving agents balanced on the edge of disappearance.

The preoccupation of ether with the body—whether the Empedoclean body that hovers between love and strife, or the damaged body calmed by the inhalation of sulfuric ether, or the body martyred in an allegory of literary quintessence—can conceal the humor of the fifth element's appearances. The joke that ether tells in the language of fragile bodies makes its mirth unpleasant; it violates the rules of decorum, the expectation that laughter will not come at the cost of the victim. Yet the indecorous laughter occasioned by destroyed bodies is too powerful to be denied. In *A Midsummer Night's Dream,* Theseus refuses to be dissuaded by an exercised Egeus from hearing the Rude Mechanicals' play. It might be, as Egeus points out, "extremely stretched, and conned with cruel pain" (5.1.80) but Theseus insists on seeing its "very tragical mirth" (5.1.57). Even when Egeus describes the rehearsal of "Pyramus and Thisbe" as staging the death of Pyramus so unsuccessfully that it "made mine eyes water; but more merry tears / The passion of loud laughter never shed" (5.1.69–70), Theseus will not be deterred from the show. It might be that the promise of a redemptive tragedy allures Theseus, who having returned from war (the preferred metaphor of tragedy) might seek comedy, the problem of which, according to Meeker, "is always how to resolve conflict without destroying the participants."[36] This "tragical mirth" cannot resolve the deep problem of laughing at the mimetic representation of death, but it names the phenomenon of ether's unsettling work in the books of Renaissance diversion, merriment, and wit. Ethereal humor belongs to the category of tragical mirth, the anthologized laughter that only partially conceals its dead seriousness. Comedy devotes itself to staving off an end—of making the waiting possible.

That partial concealment might account for the relative dearth of scholarship centered on the humorous writings of the English Civil War, as though "tragical mirth" were in short supply. In fact, the Interregnum years of the 1650s saw the arrival of numerous humorous pamphlets and broadsheets, beyond the political satire by major figures. These texts wittily and subversively treated the country's contentions and conflagrations in the 1640s and 1650s, but scholars have not tended to invest seriously in considering these jesting texts.

The work of these brief texts could not be more serious, though: while obliquely or directly challenging the political situation of the Commonwealth and Protectorate, they probe the sharp edges of literature's limited ability, as complicit witness, to represent the vulnerability of citizen bodies to state violence. Perhaps the best exemplar of these texts is the flight of edgy ludicrousness that is John Taylor's 1654 pamphlet *The Essence, Quintessence, Insence, Innocence, Lye-sence, & Magnifisence of Nonsence upon Sence: Or, Sence upon Nonsence . . .*

Taylor's loopy *Sence* intertwines copious literary allusions to Chaucer, Jonson, continental romance, and other texts in order to create a preposterous papery landscape over which the pamphlet's lilting rhyme carries its ecumenical critique of contemporary events chronicled in "the booke of Weekly Newes." Those diverse events—again, the uncanny returns of earlier happenings, intertwined now with the fifth element's tendency to return—range from the leveling efforts of "Rowndhead[s]" planting turnips and carrots, to the death of a Scottish horse who was exhausted by the relentless sectarian debates among the equine faithful. Declaring an intention to "speak silent and write aloud," the pamphlet skewers current events with a biting silliness: though treated with satiric amusement, the subjects of *Sence*'s mockery reflect the moment's deeply unsettled politics. This quintessence of wit entertains only by virtue of having so many imperiled parties to mock.

After much loudly written scatology, word play, and parody, *Sence* concludes with a surprisingly harrowing meditation on what "Wealth, Wit, Sword, & furious Gun [have] done" to London. The text ends its formerly relentless wordplay in a devastating blaze of puns, promising that "Ordinance of Parliament shall scatter ye / Our Ordinance is Ordnance, that can batter ye," in a city "undone" by the recent years' upset. In a bitter conclusion to a raucously mirthful text, the pamphlet states that

> Thrice happy had it been for our tranquility,
> If th' Authours of this civility [the Civil War]
> Had been a little check'd by Gregory Brandon,
> With each of them a hempen twisted band on.
> FINIS.

Invoking the executioner of Charles I, Richard Brandon, who had acquired his axeman post from his father, Gregory, and who was routinely called "Young Gregory," the text yearns for a history in which Brandon's initial refusal to execute the king had been internalized enough by the forces of war to "check" their ebullient belligerence. The rhyme resuscitates the London/done/undone rhyme of the preceding lines, concluding the pamphlet with the sonic coherence of death by hanging, death by cannon, death by beheading, death by sword. The quintessence of wit, here, literally writes itself on bodies in agony. Yet this aural orgy of mortality cannot absorb the emphatically unrhymed "Finis." On the facing page this signal of an ending had successfully been tucked into the concluding couplet of the previous section: "Who sets his wits my Sence to undermine, is / A cunning man at Nonsence, farewell. Finis." Distorting its already haphazardly, perhaps perversely reordered bibliographic markers, the text excises even its end from its body. By cutting out the tumorous conclusion, the pamphlet evinces a longing for a populace that would have been better prepared to wait for a salve to a city's violently wrenched bodies.

By meditating on its own incoherence and urgency, *Sence* suggests the uses of humor to be circumscribed by their participation in the conventions of literary expression: only by deforming the bibliographic shape of literature—and by thus coming to resemble the "undone" victims of revolution—can the pamphlet speak of nonsense in an age of war, or find the laughter in slaughter. Indeed, the pamphlet seeks to undo itself, reordering its constituent elements improbably: its dedication appears in the middle, its second part comes only after the interpolation of the horse's death, and there are at least three stated endings to the text.

The ethereal humor of *Sence* might help account for the flourishing of new genres and new innovations in English literature (e.g., the newspaper, the reformed epic) at this moment: the search for a kind of savagely humane mode of humor writing might be a more significant driver of literary experiment than previously understood. Heretofore, however, the secret history of laughter's quintessential necessity has hidden in its subtle ubiquity, seething quietly as the cosmic substrate of our literary history. In the words of Peter Quince (or is it Quintess-?) in *A Midsummer Night's Dream,* this tragical mirth is a "most lamentable comedy" (1.2.9)—which is, of course, also a comedic lament.[37]

But ether is fond of such lamentable comedies. The definition of "quintessential," after all, refers to the "most typical, or most refined" of a kind. This dual, seemingly incompatible quality of the ethereal—to be lamentable and comic, tragic and common, cosmic and laughable—surfaces in the twentieth century's own counterpart to *Midsummer*'s ludicrous, supernatural adventures: the 1997 film *The Fifth Element.* The film provides the quintessence with its highest-profile cameo in modern popular culture. The plot arc turns on the status of the fifth element as alone capable of saving the planet from the imminent and catastrophic Great Evil. (It is worth noting that the fifth element, incarnated in the person of Milla Jovovich's Leeloo, manages to save the earth by sacrificing her own body in the last seconds before tragedy strikes; though she recovers after the pyrotechnic event, ether asserts itself in her momentarily, climactically contorted frame as the element of bodily deformation and peril.) Though the film's excesses are themselves the stuff of laughter, Luc Besson's sci-fi fantasia does return the viewer to comic ether's dual work: to be the common substrate of the mirthful universe and to be the most refined instance of that mirthful universe's dark laughter. At the core of ether's bleak jokes and disastrous punchlines is the dream of recuperation—even perhaps the recuperation of a world on the brink of the kind of existential annihilation gleefully awaited in *Fifth Element.*

A version of that existential annihilation is eerily anticipated amid the hilarity of *Midsummer,* which offers its own uncannily familiar vision of a lamentable comedy that far outstrips the humor and horror of Pyramus's end. When Titania and Oberon's strife upends the natural rhythms of the climate, their fighting floods crops, drowns livestock in the fields, spreads contagions, and leaves the mortals to "want their winter here" (2.1.88–114). Confused, the seasons

> . . . change
> Their wonted liveries, and the mazed world,
> By their increase, now knows not which is which:
> And this same progeny of evils comes
> From our debate, from our dissension;
> We are their parents and original. (2.1.112–17)

The ecological nightmare roots itself squarely in the actions of the land's chief agents, the regnant fairies whose interventions in the landscape define both their own nature and the demise for which the world is waiting. Their creation of perverse summers—with all the attendant meteorological freaks and agricultural damage of such action—anticipates the twenty-first century's experiments in altering the planet's features.

We might know both our own nature and our own era's demise by a different name, anachronistic to Shakespeare's comedy: Anthropocene. And we know, too, that the strife of Titania and Oberon is nothing compared to the strife that could potentially be generated by a rise in global temperatures: as a group of researchers suggest in a recent précis of their statistical meta-analysis findings, "higher temperatures and extreme rainfall led to large increases in conflict: for each one standard deviation change in climate toward warmer temperatures or more extreme rainfall, the median effect was a 14 percent increase in conflict between groups, and a 4 percent increase in conflict between individuals." The logic of scarcity and aggression promises that if, as is widely projected, the global temperature increases at least 3.6 degrees Fahrenheit, "our results imply that if nothing changes, this rise in temperature could amplify the rate of group conflicts like civil wars by an astonishing 50 percent in many parts of the world."[38] The environmental prodigies of Oberon and Titania pale beside the death toll of a new kind of ecological strife.

This end, being our own creation, bears the distinct mark of humanity.[39] Although contemporary scientists dispute Aristotle's assertion, the classical theorist of the elements elsewhere suggests that humans are the only animal to laugh;[40] unsurprisingly then, our era's end comes with its own brand of dire humor. Offering one jest among many in the new comedic subgenre of the climate change joke, Jay Leno remarked that "according to a new U.N. report, the global warming outlook is much worse than originally predicted. Which is pretty bad when they originally predicted it would destroy the planet."[41]

Perhaps the availability of this crisis as a site of bitter satire and lamentable comedy should have predicted its ethereal quality. In November 2011, United Nations Secretary-General Ban Ki-moon described climate change as "the quintessential global challenge."[42] Among the dangers posed by global warming, he says, is "the risk that a warming world will facilitate the spread of deadly disease." The ethereal endangerment of the world's population remembers the distressed body, fragile and flailing in unanaesthetized throes, the body torn between Empedoclean love and strife. Or is the love and strife more Titanian and Oberonic, killing flocks and suffocating harvests off-handedly, casually even, the mere backstory to a comedy playing out on late-night television monologues and in wedding halls emptied after the festivities have ended and the guests gone to dream?

If we think of this quintessential challenge in terms of Shakespeare's regnant faeries, battling in a catastrophic corner of the comic, then ether here might offer us both a joke we cannot withstand and the vocabulary for confronting this mortal hilarity. This chapter began with the Ether Monument poised in a quiet corner of the Boston Public Gardens, and it is to the base of that monument I would like to return in these last pages. William James was intrigued by the uses of ether and nitrous oxide to induce various altered states, and he sought to describe the effects these gases had on him. Groping for words, he reported that ether conveyed for him an "immense emotional sense of reconciliation," a feeling he suggested might be termed an "anesthetic revelation."[43]

Is it possible, ether asks, for the agents of ecological disaster to be reconciled with an environment? Is an anesthetic revelation possible? Can there be a discovery of what was known before, under so many names, but was never known with such piercing urgency: that in this portion of the laughing cosmos there bleeds a vicious wound against which we have so long been anaesthetized? To repeat Milton's ethereal meditation on the book, "'Tis true, no age can restore a life, whereof perhaps there is no great losse; and revolutions of ages do not oft recover the losse of a rejected truth, for the want of which whole Nations fare the worse." Bodies split themselves apart on national scales when the quintessential joke is lost. The comedy of survival requires actors willing to put on an antic disposition.

If ether's intimacy with dire laughter is recovered, though, what can this fifth element do for the twenty-first century's earthly environment? What can this secretly hilarious quintessence manage to recuperate? Though it became the fifth element for Aristotle, the philosopher would typically refer to it as the "first body."[44] Can a consciousness of its witty entwining with the suffering body that began this chapter—the "first body" perched in stone atop a pillar in the northwest corner of the Boston Public Gardens—change the fate of the latter? Can the fifth element intervene in the ecological crisis of a world dying as patiently and inevitably as the etherized?

Describing the inability to attach to Shakespeare the author a fixed identity encompassing the diversity of his creations, Bergson extrapolates in *Laughter* that "our character is the result of a choice that is continually being renewed. There are points—at all events there seem to be—all along the way, where we may branch off, and we perceive many possible directions though we are unable to take more than one. To retrace one's steps, and follow to the end the faintly distinguishable directions, appears to be the essential element in poetic imagination."[45]

It is tempting to indulge a deep pedantry and extrapolate some concluding moral about the importance of taking a step in a better direction, but Bergson observes, too, that life is funnier than art will ever be. To think otherwise, he notes, "is the quintessence of pedantry."[46] So let me suggest instead the perverse moral of hilarity, the succor of laughether, the eternal centrality of the first body and fifth element that reaches through millennia, patiently waiting for us to get the joke, to hear the relentless mirth of the cosmos, and say: this is a humor we cannot survive. This is a lamentable comedy. We know the truth of ether and are waiting to the evening of this world to apply that quintessential knowledge to a suffering body stretched like a patient unetherized upon an ecological table. Maybe if we see how dire and funny this is, we will retrace our steps to the essential element in poetic imagination: the quintessence of dust that longs for love even as it writhes in agony; the quintessence of dust that wills itself to laugh, even having—we know wherefore—lost all its mirth.

Notes

I owe thanks to several people for their help with this chapter. First, thanks to Max Sender for his research assistance. I express my deep gratitude to Benjy Kahan and Elsie Michie for their quintessentially helpful thoughts on an earlier version. Finally, many thanks for their insights and suggestions to the participants at the 30th Alabama Symposium on English and American Literature: Elemental Ecocriticism, April 2013, where a lecture version of this chapter was first delivered.

1. G. N. Cantor and M. J. S. Hodge, "Introduction: Major Themes in the Development of Ether Theories from the Ancients to 1900," in *Conceptions of Ether: Studies in the History of Ether Theories,* ed. G. N. Cantor and M. J. S. Hodge (Cambridge: Cambridge University Press, 1981), 3. Cantor and Hodge offer a concise overview of early ether theories (2–11).

2. Helle Lambridis, *Empedocles: A Philosophical Investigation* (University: University of Alabama Press, 1976), 43.

3. Brad Inwood, *The Poem of Empedocles: A Text and Translation with an Introduction* (Toronto: University of Toronto Press, 1992), 225, fragment 38/20.

4. T. S. Eliot, "The Love Song of J. Alfred Prufrock," lines 1–3, poem reproduced in Helen Vendler, *Poems, Poets, Poetry,* 2nd ed. (Boston: Bedford/St. Martin's, 2002), 200–203.

5. Inwood, *Empedocles,* 97, CTXT-26, as quoted by Clement of Alexandria in the *Stromateis.*

6. Lambridis notes the controversy over whether there were four elements or five elements, with ether being the fifth (*Empedocles,* 43) within the context of describing the Milesian philosophers in whose tradition Empedocles inserted his theory of the elements, and Empedocles's reception by Aristotle (40–52).

7. Inwood, *Empedocles,* 98n35 to CTXT-27.

8. Plato, *Timaeus,* in *Plato in Twelve Volumes,* vol. 9, trans. R. G. Bury (Cambridge, Mass.: Harvard University Press, 1975), 145.

9. Inwood, *Empedocles,* 227, fragment 40/A49a.

10. Herman Melville, *Moby-Dick or, The Whale* (New York: Modern Library, 2000), 704–5, 329.

11. Henri Bergson, *Laughter,* reprinted in George Meredith and Henri Bergson, *Comedy: An Essay on Comedy; Laughter* (Garden City, N.Y.: Doubleday, 1956), 61.

12. Ibid, 82.

13. See Timothy Morton, *Ecology without Nature: Rethinking Environmental Aesthetics* (Cambridge, Mass.: Harvard University Press, 2007), 184–85.

14. I am indebted to Julie M. Fenster's account in *Ether Day: The Strange Tale of America's Greatest Medical Discovery and the Haunted Men Who Made It* (New York: HarperCollins, 2001).

15. Ether had perhaps helped in the development of this first option. John of Rupescissa's fourteenth-century treatise *On the Consideration of the Fifth Essence of All Things* describes his practice of what came to be a primary principle of early modern alchemy: the preparation of medicines. Half a millennium before a different ether would quiet pain, John "sought a substance that could prevent corruption and decay and thus preserve the body from illness and premature aging." His efforts to refine and distill this substance produced alcohol. See Lawrence Principle, *Secrets of Alchemy* (Chicago: University of Chicago Press, 2013), 69–70. For the quality of pain that makes it obliterate the world, language, and meaning, see Elaine Scarry, *The Body in Pain: The Making and Unmaking of the World* (New York: Oxford University Press, 1985).

16. Fenster, *Ether Day,* describes "the laughing gas joke" (3).

17. René Fülöp-Miller, *Triumph over Pain* (New York: Literary Guild of America, 1938), 94–110; Fenster, *Ether Day,* 39–46.

18. Fenster, *Ether Day,* 33–35.

19. Walt Whitman, "A March in the Ranks Hard-Prest, and the Road Unknown," in Walt Whitman, *Drum-Taps (1865) and Sequel to Drum-Taps (1865–6),* ed. F. DeWolfe Miller (Gainesville, Fla.: Scholars' Facsimiles & Reprints, 1959), 44.

20. Drew Gilpin Faust, *This Republic of Suffering: Death and the American Civil War* (New York: Alfred A. Knopf, 2008), describes the unexpected scale of the calamity and its far-reaching effects in U. S. history and culture. See, for example, xi–xiv.

21. Fenster, *Ether Day,* 37.

22. Quoted in ibid., 39.

23. Fenster (ibid., 2) quotes a newspaper critic who observed the Richard III impression.

24. All citations of Shakespeare are from *The Norton Shakespeare,* 2nd ed., gen. ed. Stephen Greenblatt (New York: W. W. Norton, 2008), and give act, scene, and line numbers.

25. Joseph Meeker, *The Comedy of Survival: Studies in Literary Ecology* (New York: Charles Scribner's Sons, 1972), 60–78, esp. 61–62, 68, and 74–75.

26. H. Bateman, "The Form of the Ether," *The Publications of the Astronomical Society of the Pacific* 34, no. 198 (April 1922): 94.

27. Frank Wilczek, *The Lightness of Being: Mass, Ether, and the Unification of Forces* (New York: Basic Books, 2008), 77, describes Newton's vexed frustration on this point.

28. Loyd S. Swenson Jr., *The Ethereal Aether: A History of the Michelson-Morley-Miller Aether-Drift Experiments, 1880–1930* (Austin: University of Texas Press, 1972), 171–89, describes the experiments and the fallout for concepts of ether. See Valerie Allen's chapter in this volume for more on the intimate and discomforting work of

"groping" bodies (whereas here I think in terms of dissection) for purposes of satisfying doubt or seeking truth.

29. Quoted in Cantor and Hodge, *Conceptions of Ether,* 53–54. An alternate translation is quoted in Wilczek, *The Lightness of Being,* 97.

30. Lawrence Krauss, *Quintessence: The Mystery of Missing Mass in the Universe* (New York: Basic Books, 2000), 3–22, describes his interest in Aristotle's quintessence and Krauss's own reasons for adopting the term in this new sense.

31. Joe Milutis, *Ether: The Nothing That Connects Everything* (Minneapolis: University of Minnesota Press, 2006), xii.

32. For more on the ether of the radio and digital age, see ibid., chapter 3 and conclusion.

33. *Oxford English Dictionary,* s.v. "quintessential" (a.2 and first attestation).

34. Robert Burton, *The Anatomy of Melancholy,* ed. Holbrook Jackson (New York: New York Review of Books, 2001), 43.

35. John Milton, *Areopagitica: A Speech of Mr. John Milton for the Liberty of Vnlicenc'd Printing to the Parliament of England* (London, 1644), 4.

36. Meeker, *The Comedy of Survival,* 38.

37. My thanks to Jeffrey Jerome Cohen for this latter reformulation of "lamentable comedy" as being simultaneously "comedic lament."

38. Marshall Burke, Solomon Hsiang, and Edward Miguel, "Weather and Violence," *New York Times,* September 1, 2013, SR12. Their findings are published in *Science* 341, no. 6151 (September 13, 2013), http://www.sciencemag.org/content/341/6151/1235367 (the article was first published online on August 1). Other researchers have expressed some skepticism about these findings in "Study Links Climate Change and Violence, Battle Ensues," *Science* 341 (August 2, 2013): 444–45.

39. See Steve Mentz's chapter in this volume for reflection on the "hubristic *anthropos* in the Anthropocene."

40. Aristotle, *On the Parts of Animals,* trans. A. L. Peck, Loeb Classical Library (Cambridge, Mass.: Harvard University Press, 1937), 3.10.

41. The joke is well attested on various websites, including the site maintained by the Texas A&M Student Chapter of the National Association of Environmental Professionals, http://naep.tamu.edu/funstuff.

42. Ban Ki-moon, "Secretary-General Calls Climate Change 'Quintessential Global Challenge,' Citing also Crime, Pandemics, in Security Council Meeting on New Challenges to Peace," remarks to the Security Council meeting, November 23, 2011, available through the United Nations' Department of Public Information, News and Media Division, New York, at http://www.un.org/News/Press/docs/2011/sgsm13964.doc.htm.

43. Quoted in Daniel J. Cook, "James's 'Ether Mysticism' and Hegel," *Journal of the History of Philosophy* 15, no. 3 (July 1977): 310, 311.

44. Cantor and Hodge, *Conceptions of Ether,* 5.

45. Bergson, *Laughter,* 168–69.

46. Ibid., 91.

seven

Wet?

JULIAN YATES

> I would like to listen to . . . things freed of . . . [their] packages, the way they presented themselves before finding themselves named. Betelgeuse disappeared into the bag of its star naming; I only eat asparagus or carrots folded in bunches in the daily newspaper of their appellation; I see winds and rains below their satellite image map; your first name and your words hide your body from me and even, almost, your voice which, in turn names me. . . . How to estimate at their exact thickness the layers of media under which all things lie, thus multiply wrapped under writings, folded under sounds, choked under languages, lost under a hundred screens? A screen, quite a confession: obstructing as much as revealing.
>
> —MICHEL SERRES, *Biogea*

> It remains for us to define the attitude we called naïve, which rests on the belief that poetry is capable of effecting reconciliation because it provides an immediate contact with substance through its own sensible form. In a famous letter, Keats had already cried out: "O for a life of sensation not of thought," but he had sense enough to speak of sensation as something one desires but cannot have.
>
> —PAUL DE MAN, *"The Dead-End of Formalist Criticism"*

It is hard to imagine two more different statements than appear in these two epigraphs. Tired of mediation, fed up with the exhausting "layers of media under which all things lie," Michel Serres longs, so he says, to listen to things freed from their "packages," shorn of their "screens," prior to the confessions extracted from them that tell only a partial truth. He wants to turn back a figural clock and encounter things prior to their presentation within the infrastructure of a built world. He wants to do away with purgatorial screens. Throughout *Biogea,* he argues that the mounting ecological crises of our collective present already indicate that the world has been speaking to us or "opening" *(mundus patet)* and that the multiplication of screens or delivery systems makes it impossibly difficult to attend to this "opening."[1]

Set against Serres's expression of desire, Paul de Man cautions us against giving into what he names a "naïve attitude" that might falsely synch things up, plugging them in to effect an order of poetic reconciliation that will deliver the goods (substance) as well as the *good* (the well, the true). He worries that this orientation will turn all too quickly into what elsewhere he calls a "salvational criticism" that unpacks things so completely that it produces a false holism if not an actual holiness. He cites John Keats, approvingly, as he who knows of and speaks to this desire for what cannot quite be had or managed. Keats, as it were, knows all about packages (media specificity, rhetoric, and substance). He knows how to package things in a manner that observes and inhabits the tension.

I begin with these two epigraphs because they capture quite precisely a hinge or point of contact between two differing critical households or projects (pre or post) on the subject of translation. Ostensibly, Serres disavows mediation or the complexity of the translational mechanisms that render things mobile in our built world. He opts instead not for things quite in themselves, as the phrase goes, but for things at some logically if not chronologically prior moment, in and as matter and language combine and so phenomenalize—things without their human-given names in all their density. It's not that there are no names, but that there exists a more fundamental level of coding than human language. Elsewhere in *Biogea,* Serres writes "the coding of my DNA says my true proper name."[2] De Man, by contrast, stands as the avatar of a correlationist absolutism that insists that what matters is quite precisely the shape "packaged" things take, the work these packages do or are made to do for us as we create worlds.[3] It is easy, I think, to cultivate an attitude that maximizes the difference or dissonance between these two positions. My aim in this chapter is instead to inhabit the productive, indeed complementary, tension I see between them, to think the two positions together as two differently calibrated or oriented responses to the pull of *things* upon us: Serres tuned to an unreduced multiplicity or monism that manifests in *Biogea* as an ongoing metaphorics of fire, flood, and earthquake; de Man captivated by the likes of Serres, but disavowing metaphor and remaining trained on the tropic packages in which *things* come. I do so because it is this tension, so I now understand, that has scripted my response to the element I was assigned by the editors of this book. My chapter is an amphibian, a creature of two houses, at home in both and neither.[4]

So the story goes, our editors assigned these elements by chance. The names of the elements were written on small pieces of paper and then plucked at random from a plastic burrito bowl and given to each contributor. I was not able to be present at this event and received the news via e-mail. I learned that said "burrito bowl," if there ever was such a "bowl," had disgorged some papery water into my figurative lap. This water left me feeling wet, that is to say, almost entirely adjectival. I knew what I should write about immediately. Two watery haunts occurred to me automatically, without any appearance of conscious thought. Words simply formed in my head. And this automaticity or quasi-automaticity constituted a symptom, a reaction, but also, given that it is so hard these days to keep the difference between a supposedly organic (living) response and a machinic (deathly) reaction straight, a response.[5]

The first is John Keats's stated desire that the epitaph on his gravestone should read as follows: "Here lies one whose name was writ in water." The second is Prospero's stated desire or intention near the end of *The Tempest*, "I'll drown my book."[6] In this chapter I aim to make sense of the immediacy of my reaction, an immediacy that generated two examples of mixed or, even, hypermedia. In the first instance, stone, water, writing, and speech combine in order to project a desire beyond or beside the grave in the form of some posthumous or posthumographic writing machine, Keats's name living or dying on, in, and by its defacement. In the second, Prospero's desire takes the form of a metaphorical transcoding or transduction: for how do you drown a book exactly? Can a book be said to drown? And if so, what, then, does it mean for you and me to drown? In what follows I respond first to the orienting brief that accompanied the e-mail I received; offer a reading (in small) of my two watery or water-logged haunts; and end by returning to the problem of "packages," screens, and translation.

Of Briefs and Burrows

The brief was fairly straightforward and quite inviting. We were to think through and with Jane Bennett's generous responses to an earlier set of articles on ecomaterialism published as a special issue of the journal *postmedieval.*[7] More particularly, it was hoped that we should imagine modes of writing that do not reduce the elements to metaphors merely but actively dig or sink into them. "The topic of material agency, me thinks, is like quicksand," writes Bennett in her response, "a sinkhole that threatens to suck even the boldest ecomaterialist back into a human-centered burrow." Like "quicksand, 'the elements' readily become metaphors for something beside themselves: the elements as the Big Other or Nature or What Lies beyond Human Knowing." "Yeah," she concludes, "the Elements are metaphorical. But they can also kill you, or inspire you, or help to organize you—with or without the help of quicksand."[8] Yes. They can kill and they do. And, yes, certain burrows or configurations of the *oikos* or collective are more and less hospitable to the project of a common becoming and to different polities who thrive or die by their action. Some do not allow themselves to be organized by or with the elements but against them, the elements already, for Bennett, keyed to a question concerning hospitality and modes of collectivity. The word *burrow* comes from the Old English term for a refuge or fortress (*burg,* from the verb *beorgan,* "to protect"). It condenses those processes by which our orientation to matter, to the elements, assumes the contours of a metaphor, of matter pressed to use for and as a shelter from the brute facticity and exposure of existence.[9] How then to write, to build a burrow, *with* the elements, inviting them in, that allows them to help organize us or poses the limits of that organization as an ongoing question?

Wet? Yes. The adjective registers a small measure of resistance to Bennett's formulation. I am not sure that I mind the elements acting as "metaphor magnets." Metaphors have a magnetic force (they can kill). Like de Man (and like Serres), then, I remain cautious of invitations to outrun metaphor or to regard metaphor as in conflict with questions of matter or materiality. Packaging matters. It cannot (and should not) be disposed of without due care and attention. Otherwise, it has the habit of popping back up in the most unlikely and sometimes catastrophic of ways. This seems as true now of tropes as it is of the wrapper that Serres's asparagus comes in.

Wet registers several orders of meaning or constraint. It introduces a "cut" into the proceedings, confessing that, for me, water comes as packaged as asparagus and as bunched as carrots. Wet names a time-bound condition or sensation keyed to the perceptual limits of my sensorium: water on my skin. It registers the clammy clinging of my clothes to what I take to be my body, and so the inundation of one particular habit world, set of routines, the negentropic eddy on which we construct our shelters, our burrows, by the elements, in this case, by water. Does this mean that I have "been sucked back into a human-centered burrow?" Well. Yes and no. "The human need for shelter," we know, "is lasting," but that need is so readily extended across the increasingly confused lines of species and kind to other beings or forms of life, and so obviously exceeds the "asininity" or "bêtise" of human exceptionalism, that the word *burrow* ceases to figure in quite the way Bennett intends.[10] All sorts of creatures above and below the surface build, live, rent, and reuse "burrows." My corpse, also, depending on its fate, will become a burrow to still other forms of life—alive with the wet death that Donna Haraway describes as a "symphony of biota" or that, a while ago, John Donne named "vermiculation" (being eaten by worms).[11] When I say that I am left feeling "wet," then, the word comes freighted with a provincializing of the words *burrow* and *metaphor* as human constructs, and so with an open question concerning shelter.

Do I feel wet on the inside? No, given the accidents of my birth, sex, and age, I do not, or do not any more or do not yet, even as, of course, I shall, I will, I am, and I do. Once upon a time, it was common to find descriptions of the human body "as 70 percent salty water," each of us a little ocean or sea, variously titrated hydraulic systems. Wet through and through, then. But, as the cultural anthropologist Stefan Helmreich reminds, such pronouncements have been "edged out" by statements such as "we have ten times more bacterial cells in our bodies than human cells, so we're 90 percent bacteria."[12] "Once upon a time," he continues, "the *human,* plunged into the sea (as blood, sweat, tears, milk), was baptized into communion with the planet. But plunged into the sea as a swirl of microbial genes something more unsettling happens." As Helmreich's work with oceanographers and marine biologists has taught him, such storying of the sea that posits a synecdochal sympathy or equivalence between human bodies and bodies of water plays differently when the sea is modeled already as a network of deterritorialized particles of life effects in the form of microbes and genetic fragments. The putative universalism that functions by cutting us off from archaic, ancestral precursors who remain at sea finds itself orphaned. We "must go down to the sea again, to the lonely sea and sky," but when we do so, we find not an origin story but a rival set of beginnings. "Microbes," writes Helmreich, "are not simple echoes of a left-behind origin for humans, orphaned from all evolutionary association. Microbes are historical and contemporary partners, part of our bodies' 'microbiomes.' We do not get to turn our backs on *this* ocean as one story of human development posits. Our stories remain conjoined with microbial stories. "Human nature," by which Helmreich means merely one "form of life," does not "reflect . . . ocean nature. It is an entanglement of natures, an intimacy with the alien."[13] We are soaked in the lives of others.[14]

Do I feel "wet" when talking to you at a conference or when representing my university at this or that meeting, or when sitting here at my computer, or signing up for something online, or getting an injection at the doctor's office, or verifying that I am who my passport says I am and having my biometrics reaffirmed? No, not really, even though my arm or fingers ache a bit, and I am, in all these instances, in the phrasing of Richard Doyle, along with all manner of other plant and animal actors, a form of "wetware," the biological component to a media platform or system that deterritorializes "life" from the individual organism or form of life, my body, in essence, played and crisscrossed by successive orders of information (physiological, chemical, rhetorical, metaphorical, forensic).[15]

Both more and less than a metaphor, "wet" keys the elements to questions of media or packaging in ways that I do not wish to reduce. Not "water," then, even as the ocean and shipwreck beckon, but "wet," registering the element's pull on one form of life and also one of the media that condition its engagements: in my case, language. So, even as I am "wet," even as I know that my burrow is predicated and already inundated by still other forms of being, "water" seems too much. I cannot breathe under water (unenhanced). I am, if you like, medium specific, one particular order of burrower. My rendering of water remains medium specific. And embracing our particular order of finitude renders us precisely, in Serres's terms, a screen or medium for the elements as they presence in and through our sensorium, our way of being. Of course, there exist multiple orders of finitude, "trillions of finitudes, as many as there are things," as Timothy Morton observes, but this broadening of finitude as property of multiple types of beings does not grant any principle of equivalence that might generate anything on the order of a universal category or commonality. Instead, it requires of us a renewed commitment to thinking various orders of finitude in media-specific terms.[16]

And this burden of thinking medium specifically about what we name "human" as a language-bearing order of finitude is, in part, what I find laid out for me in the introduction to Cary Wolfe's *What Is Posthumanism?* Wolfe offers that

> the question of posthumanism . . . far from surpassing or rejecting the human—[posthumanism] actually enables us to describe the human and its characteristic modes of communication, interaction, meaning, social significance, and affective investments with *greater* specificity once we have removed meaning from the ontologically closed domain of consciousness, reason, reflection, and so on. It forces us to rethink our taken-for-granted modes of human experience, including the normal perceptual modes and affective states of *Homo sapiens* itself, by recontextualizing them in terms of the entire *sensorium* of other living beings and their own autopoietic ways of "bringing forth a world"—ways that are, since we ourselves are human animals, part of the evolutionary history and behavioral and psychological repertoire of the human itself.[17]

Such a provincializing of the human, our exposure and reduction to being merely one among the myriad forms of other ways of being, knowing, and "bringing forth a world," means attending very carefully to "the specificity of the human," Wolfe elaborates, and "acknowledging that it is fundamentally a prosthetic creature that has coevolved with various forms of technicity and materiality, forms that are radically 'not-human' and yet have nevertheless made the human what it is. . . . For Derrida, of course, this includes the most fundamental prostheticity of all: language in the broadest sense."[18] How then to read, to write, to live in a world in which we exist as merely one set of medium-specific beings among a host who share in a general relation to writing or coding?

As I hope to show in the readings of two wet or watery haunts that follow, this desire for a different order of burrowing, for a more capacious mode of hospitality, for me, cannot be thought or attempted other than by owning our own particular order of "wetness," the vulnerabilities and viabilities that come with medium specificity—a symbio-politics of wetness whose putative universalism remains essentially untranslatable, ruptured, and knowable only by and through that rupture.

"Writ in Water"

February 23, 1821. Rome. John Keats drowned on dry land, in his bed. He had survived the voyage to Rome—no shipwreck—but still over an agonizing course of weeks his tuberculosis constituted a death by drowning, drowning in his own blood, in the mucus that overwhelmed his lungs. "When I am stronger," wrote his friend the painter Joseph Severn in a letter to John Taylor some few weeks later, "I will send you every word—the remembrance of this scene of horror will be fresh upon my mind to the end of days."[19] The descriptions in Severn's earlier letters as he attended Keats are indeed harrowing.[20] His voice failing, treatment, such as it was, entailed what amounts to a continual resuscitation. Severn has to right him, help him up in order to void the matter from his lungs. He stayed on hand also waiting for it to become clear when things would end, in which case, there was enough money (though things were tight) for opium. The day before Keats dies, Severn writes to William Haslam saying that "last night I thought he was going—I could hear the Phlegm in his throat. . . . I watchd him all night."[21]

The day after Keats died, Severn and Charles Armitage Brown arranged for Keats to be buried in the Protestant churchyard in Rome. Famously, the gravestone bears the following inscription:

> This Grave
> contains all that was Mortal,
> of a
> YOUNG ENGLISH POET,
> Who,
> on his Death Bed,
> in the Bitterness of his Heart,
> in the Malicious Power of his Enemies,
> Desired
> these words to be engraven on his tomb stone:
> Here lies One
> Whose Name was writ in Water.
> Feb. 24th 1821

The delay of one day was, apparently, so that Severn and Brown could add their own enframing devices: the anonymous text that bears witness to the anonymous voice, rendering Keats an abused poet, and the figure of the lyre that frames the inscription. These devices sought to put blame, it is argued, on the poor reception and negative review *Endymion* received in the *Quarterly Review.*[22] Severn and Armitage's paratextual framing of Keats's last wishes, if not his last words, supplement them, already, in spite of their manifest content, with evidence that there were and had been other poems, words that have gone missing. There remains a whole *corpus,* out there, that has been severed from the corpse. Their additions supply, already, a reading of the grave's claim to anonymity, to the gravestone as marker, as minimal guarantee that the grave is occupied. They gesture also toward the force of the name that is not marked but to which the grave alludes, bearing witness to an absence that they reinvest with the vitality of a last wish, a desire, and the promise of restitution.

This grave generates an odd series of effects. Keats's words, now framed as a quotation, as words that, had things been different, he might have taken back, perform a partial or self-ruining but concrete *ekphrasis.* They prescribe a very deliberate set of effects that we do and do not see as we read or hear them. Even as it is possible to write your name in water, to perform an act of writing coterminous with itself, your name disappearing as and by your writing, the image, by definition, fails to disclose the name being written. The script slides into the medium. The water takes the name, inundates or drowns it, refusing to act as a stable substrate or backing (even as it still does). The past-tense image so generated, in effect, disappears the name before it can be named but also, thereby, preserves its facticity, encrypts it, ensuring that it lives on even as the body does not, the poetic force or vitality (what Serres might call his "true name," his DNA) translated into words in stone. Keats's voice stands already, before the fact, then, as an uncertainly objectal prosthesis, a *prosopopoeia,* that turns back on itself—volubly mute.

As various readers from Percy Shelley to the present have mused, the effect has a *pathos* that demands repackaging. The shaping agency of the voice slides into the motive force of the water such that the lines seem to enact the disappearance itself. Disinterested spectators on the shore, we watch as a name drowns. What else may we do than desire to intervene and, in doing so, stand recruited?[23] The words aim to arrest the hearer or the passersby on whom they make a lasting impression, recruiting them as wetware, the fact of the name if not the name itself, whatever it was, living on, in, and by a translation that captures it by losing it. It is left to us to think through and with that order of sensation that Keats's words effect in our bodily and mental packages.

For Keats, then, the grave transforms anonymity into an archiving procedure or archive. Anonymity, by this gesture, registers adjectivally as a condition into which a name may fall; it constitutes a betweenness or loss of media, a failure of reference that the architecture or burrow of Keats's barrow seeks to render.[24] It does so by asking the reader to become a perfect medium. You need not know the name in order to imagine the act of its disappearance, and yet, your response, your responsiveness or hospitability to the image, which your imaginary faculty generates, serves to write the name, in transducted form. "Keats" designates the historical being who lies defunct in the grave. The image, the affective relay it forms as it takes me as its backing, designates or *names* what matters or causes things to matter: the ability to produce a certain order of concrete word-images that issue forth from an uncertain place. Drowning in his own wetness, which entails a loss of voice, Keats drowns his name and by that drowning creates a signature, not of a human person but of one order of *poiesis.* Of course, this is all entirely moot, as Severn and Armitage stood already recruited, and so we cannot help but know the name and reconnect it to the historical *bios* that was Keats and so the textual *corpus* to the corpse. His gravestone, properly speaking, is already an edition, a bio/bibliographical artifact. Thus it is that I, at the mere mention of water and writing, summon up a name that, properly speaking, was never there. My recruitment has been so total as to constitute a reaction to which this chapter attempts to respond.

The Message from the Mud

The architecture of perception to Keats's gravestone remains predicated on a human sensorium, which it enlists by its oscillation of media. The resulting correlation between the effect of immediacy and mixed or hypermedia has an enduring legacy, however, as it migrates to other registers. Such an attention to transductive technologies, to media-specific renderings of phenomena, for example, might be said to drive the projective analyses of science studies and actor-network theory accounts of scientific practices: Bruno Latour's ever more complicated models of translational practices; Hans Jörg Rheinberger's analyses of radio labeling in molecular biology that render the invisible knowable by way of a chain of reference in which "there is nothing to see at any stage, and yet, there is no other way of seeing genes."[25]

In a more thoroughly watery context, Helmreich finds a similar multiplication of screens or packaging devices on board the Monterey Bay Aquatic Research Institute's (MBARI) research vessel, *Lobos.* He joins the crew as they set out for a day exploring "muddy methane-rich zones of the sea floor known as 'cold seeps'" on the lookout for "deep-sea microbes that eat methane, a potent greenhouse gas."[26] They shall "dredge up the sediment . . . so that . . . [they] can decode 'the message from the mud' . . . [a] message, stowed in the cells and genes of methanotrophic (methane-eating) microbes." The boat, so we learn, is "studded with surveillance" and boasts a remotely operated submersible named *Ventana* that will "collect cross sections of methane-infused ooze" from the seabed.[27] What interests Helmreich is the way in which "the scientific sea manifest[s] as a media ecology," best captured in his description of the "array of computer and video screens" in the Lobos's forecastle where the control room is located.[28] The room, he continues, "is a sensory scramble, a layering of ocular, auditory, and corporeal disorientations: a multimedia experience, a dip into the *media sublime*" that is necessary to "'provide not just a window into the sea, but the resources required to move other inscription devices within it.'"[29] Immediacy, both the effect and the ability to operate the submersible in real time and space, derives from "a grappling dynamic between surfaces and flesh that [Donna] Haraway, following phenomenologist Maurice Merleau Ponty, calls 'infolding.'"[30] All this—the relays, the imaging technologies, as the crew, the MBRAI, and its grantors hope—exists in order to decipher the message, the name, the "true name" or DNA of these microbes.

Keats's epitaph works, perhaps a little differently. The gravestone speaks declaratively of the past. The referential certainty of the impersonal statement "Here lies" is hollowed out by the ephemeral cast to the act of writing on water. If the expression functions as a self-predicating archive to a name then its viability in successive presents—now, and then, and still to come—is predicated also on the forgetting, the anarchivability or unarchivability of the voice or name as it was hosted by a time-bound living poet. The gravestone functions as a site of passage between differently "wet" bio/media as the "name" migrates to its new host: a stone that speaks of water. Keats's epitaph, along with its paratexts and edition, register that there is resistance and there is loss even as there is also (thereby) gain and even progress. We may be seized, as is Shelley, by a desire to supplement and augment the statement, but that recruitment registers also the force of the poetic mode of the defunct poet—the shape the name takes by and in its transmission to a different media ecology. Keats's body, accordingly, all used up or "drowned," gets left behind.

Helmreich discovers a similar tension on board the *Lobos*. It occurs when it comes time to "archive [the] mud," to "read" but also therefore to "write" the sea.[31] Such acts of inscription begin at sea in the protocol developed for gathering the "mud" and they operate continuously through to the laboratory ashore where the "gene library" or "DNA library" that captures "fragments of this sea" is produced and stored. "If *Ventana* promises oceanic transparency, genetic libraries promise legibility" and decipherment that may lead to still-to-be-imagined acts of inscription. But these "wet databases of fragmented life, of life as media technique," entail also the forgetting and perhaps trashing of other archives that will become, in effect, untended graves, discarded life forms whose packaging makes them irrelevant to our new forms of life. "In an air-conditioned room downstairs, a place humorously known as the Necropiscatorium," the institute stores "jars of dead fish," a collection of "squids, jellyfish, and other creatures," that may soon be discarded as a leftover of times and archives past. As "life" becomes an effect that moves through or is deterritorialized by successive orders of media, the life form, like the poet, comes unmoored—it gets left behind, forgotten, anonymous. "'We are losing sight of the organism,'" observes one of the marine biologists Helmreich interviews, but it is hard to say what and how that sense of loss means or how it registers on board the ship, in the lab, at the granting session that makes up this extended platform for writing the message from the mud.[32]

Here, and elsewhere in *Alien Ocean*, Helmreich worries about the deterritorializing of fragments of life become *zoe* from their organisms or life forms. He poses an open question concerning the "bareness," in Giorgio Agamben's terms, of what gets forgotten or falls into disuse in the process.[33] For even bare life requires a medium—it has to be successively backed or remediated for the message from the mud to become legible as a mode of microbial writing that might disclose a name—a name that might be said quite literally to have been "writ in water." Biopolitics turns out always also to be a question of bibliography and archive management, of the backing that life (and death) requires.[34] Likewise, the abyssal indistinction between reaction and response shall be reckoned always also in media-specific terms as a question of compatible and incompatible involutions. Life comes in packets. It is only by tracing the contours of those packets, by understanding, in my case, the adjectival "wetness" that water takes as it takes me, that I can tune into the translational density of the media ecologies by and through which we seek to know (and write) the world, to listen to things, in Serres's sense, opening ourselves to the world's opening.

What is the message from the mud? Let us sink into what I call the zoo/bio/bibliographical ooze from which messages are deciphered and find out.

"I'll Drown My Book"

So, we are on an island, courtesy of Prospero and Ariel, and the plot is essentially on cruise control. Welcome to the world of romance! Media effects abound: "Be not afeard. The isle is full of noises, / Sounds and sweet airs that give delight and hurt not" (*The Tempest*, 3.2.135–44), but there are also pinches and pain effects. The noise won't hurt, says Caliban, who is habituated. Relax. May as well allow the noise, the acoustic effects the island's full of, recalibrate your bodily rhythms, the way you take your sleep, live on, in, and through dreams. They will do so anyway. So, give in; give over. Good advice from he who enters the play as what Prospero and Miranda describe as a being "which any print of goodness wilt not take" (1.2.354)—Caliban, if you like, proving resistant to Prospero's inscriptive regime. If the entire project upon which Prospero embarked, showing "kindness" or "humane care" to Caliban, figures a misapplication or misrecognition of Caliban, who by his resistance reveals himself, from Prospero and Miranda's point of view, to be some order of self-predicating "filth"—"Filth that thou art" (1. 2. 346)—then, *The Tempest*'s bibliographical metaphors are primed, from their inception, by the biopolitical capture of "life" that marks and makes distinctions between persons by the articulation not simply of races but species. Indeed, Prospero's sovereign command of the island, by this gesture, comes to look very straightforwardly like the accumulation of various technical and administrative advantages backed by the media that underwrites his attempts at "printing." The mode of sovereignty he enjoys derives from the comparative advantages of technology and resources that allow him to broadcast his effects.

No wonder that Caliban wants to burn Prospero's book and kill him. Take his books away, says Caliban, and Prospero will become but "a sot" (silly person, drunk) "as I am." He will have "not / One spirit to command" for they "all do hate him / As rootedly as I" (3.2.90–95). Burn the book and all of the "spirits" at Prospero's command will fail to show up. Burn the book and we all shall be revealed as "sots," prosaically "wet," bodily forms, rendered variously high or variously traumatized by our uptaking of different orders of information (the script or spell in a book, the "sack" or "celestial spirit" in the butt or bottle that Trinculo and Stephano give to Caliban).

But no book burning, even as it is plotted, occurs. Instead, Prospero offers that he shall drown it:

> . . . But this rough magic
> I here abjure; and when I have required

> Some heavenly music (which even now I do)
> To work mine end upon their senses that
> This airy charm is for, I'll break my staff,
> Bury it certain fathoms in the earth,
> And deeper than did ever plummet sound
> I'll drown my book. (5.1.50–57)

Projecting forward into a future that no longer requires such sonic effects as "heavenly music" to "work" his "end upon" his subjects' "senses," that "end," at an end, Prospero's language gestures forward but fails properly to close on an image. The lineaments of an image take shape but then dissolve. The staff shall be broken but its burial "certain fathoms in the earth," sea terms ("fathom" designates a unit of six feet and was and is used most usually of sea depths) momentarily coding the land, loses focus.[35] How deep shall the staff go? The act of decision, the strongly agentive act of breaking, falls prey to an uncertain inhumation, a burial that even as it locates the staff's fragments specifically in a certain spot remains uncertainly deep, the word *fathom* rendering the land watery.

Likewise, the book shall drown "deeper than did ever plummet sound," the sonic returning now as the technical term for measuring depth or finding bottom with a lead weight.[36] The agentively strong specificity of the act of drowning (go on, throw a stone, feel the projective force of your arm, picture the stone entering the water) loses itself in the impossible cast to the depth. To drown a book comes to constitute a permanent condition of the book, a continuous drowning that vanquishes forever the tactile specificity of the hand holding the line attached to the lead weight that never hits bottom, that never therefore feels the line slacken, the friction on the hands (as opposed to the ears) cease. Before it even happens, the decision to drown the book finds itself transformed into a permanent condition of waiting, a gerundive conditionality of living on, dying on, as the book keeps on drowning. No more noises then; no more sonic effects that we can person with the wetware that is Ariel, elves, demi-puppets, and so on such that Prospero calls upon at other occasions—they have vanished, which is not to say that they have departed.

Here, it seems worth recalling that Prospero's distinction between inhumation and drowning remains muddied by the way the phrase "deeper than did ever plummet sound" echoes three words Alonso uses when speaking of the drowning of his son, Ferdinand: "Therefore my son i' th' ooze is bedded, and / I'll seek him deeper than ever plummet sounded, / And with him lie there mudded" (3.3.100–102). Alonso's first, soul-destroying voicing of this intention follows hard on the "winds" or "billows" or "organpipe" that he says sung the name "Prosper" in his ears (3.3.95–102). Prospero's repetition of three words Alonso used to describe the burial of Ferdinand's corpse ("deeper," "plummet," and "sounded") create something like static interference in the distinction between burying his staff and drowning his book. The biological metaphor that derives from Ferdinand, even if all humans resort to clay or earth, does not quite translate to either staff or book. Instead the image and the repetitions create the aura of a sinking or gradual enfolding in an oozy medium.

If in Prospero's lines the future seems marked by a set of uncertainties that prevent the generation of complete images, the word *sound* compensates; it takes on a vibratory heft that resonates across them and their levels of sense, condensing the auditory and the tactile. The vibratory effects of the "heavenly" noise named "music" by human, or more properly, Prospero's ears, cohabits, then, with the silent sounding of a depth—drowning figuring here as a passing beyond the range of hearing and seeing, accessible only by a kind of blind hearing or deaf seeing. This splicing of the tactile and the auditory, the musicality of certain orders of noise taking on an efficacy in the pursuit of "ends," enters into a strange relation with the vanishing of the book, whose fate lies beyond the reach of Prospero's language, other than his inability to render the image. It begins to feel that we might mistake the whole tenor of the lines—there is no loss here, no regret—and so "I'll drown my book" offers a gleeful solution, a casting off that will recuperate Prospero in successive futures.

In the epilogue to the play, in which it is unclear whether Prospero speaks as a character or as an actor from the media platform that hosts him, he proclaims his own "sottishness," pronouncing on his own "wetness," as he asks to be sent off, to disembark with the "gentle breath" of the audience to fill his sails, as if he were a boat, set free, like Ariel, whom he set free only a few lines earlier. Lacking "spirits" now to help, we assume, perhaps, that his book has been drowned for it has not been burned, and so it is up to us, the wetware of the theater, to fill his sails with the "breath" of our applause. Caliban's word, which posits a universalizing, drunken equivalence, finds itself reclaimed and reanimated. But what do we witness by this ending exactly, except, perhaps, the blackboxing of a media ecology that renders this "sot" sovereign? The play ends by systematically denying drowning to the living, whom Prospero now "makes live," his sovereignty premised on the disappearance and broadcasting of the book as a series of techniques. The book drowns and a brave new world of creaturely life forms issue forth, but the putative universalism that might attach to their collective "sottishness" seems compromised.[37]

Drowning the book, then, augurs an infinite storage with and as disposal or loss and a transductive migration to other, creaturely media. It figures the drowning of one code become input for still other acts of making that might figure as "new" but replay old routines. The site of this exchange in the play remains closed to view, alluded to in the figure of the book that is taken by the water and of the supposedly drowned Ferdinand, who sinks into the ooze. This "ooze" or slime or scene of slow decay but also of coming into life is the play's name for this pre-phenomenological scene of bio/biblioprocessing, the parceling out or packaging of bio/bibliographical forms such as *The Tempest* imagines as it first de- and then rezones the distinctions between persons, animals, spirits, the living, and the dead. The book Prospero drowns, that he consigns to drowning, enters into a forever coming back, a salvaging that occurs as much by chance and error as by earnest labor and design. Strange aftereffects or leftovers do and did wash ashore.

Some fifteen or so years after *The Tempest* was written and performed, on June 23, 1626, it so happened that "a Codfish being brought to the Fish-Market of Cambridge and cut up as usually others are for sale" yielded something wondrous and perhaps, depending on how you were oriented to such things, miraculous.[38] "In the depth of the mawe of the fish was found wrapped in a piece of canvase, a book in *decimo sexto,* containing three treatises bound up in one," which are reprinted soon thereafter, prefaced by images of the fish, a short foray into the emerging field of ichthyology, and a thorough working through and over of the possible veracity of what the book names the "Book-Fish." The treatises that the fish carried in its mouth, and that had returned from their uncertain fate in the sea, were attributed to English reformer John Frith, who was martyred in 1533.[39]

Figure 7.1 depicts the fish and its contents—though it has been cut open so that the book may be properly revealed, having migrated from its mouth to its belly. Inquiring further into the circumstances that might have led to such a strange reappearance of these books, the author of the treatise writes that

> it seemeth most probable that vpon some wrack this booke lying (perhaps manie years) in the pocket of some man, that was cast away, was swallowed

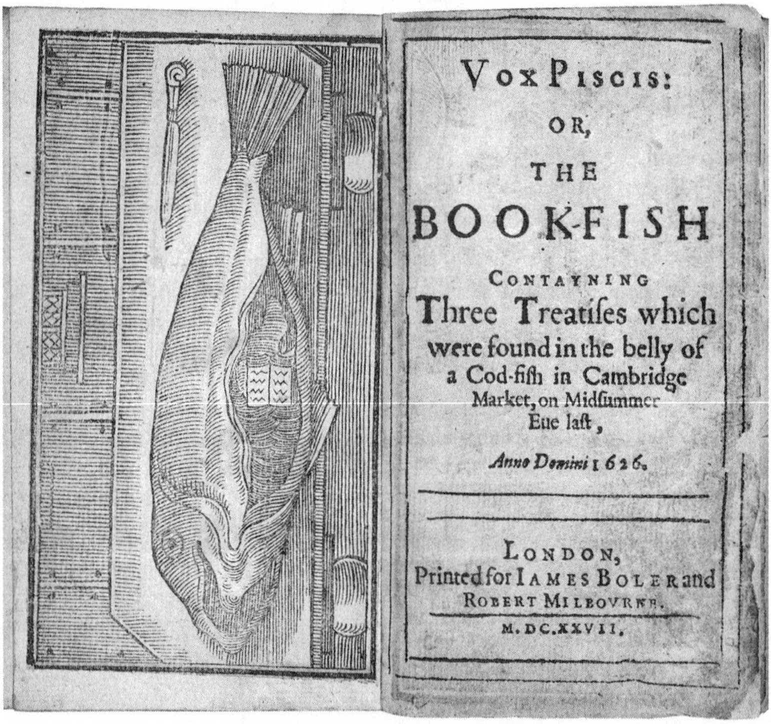

FIGURE 7.1. Title page to *Vox Piscis: Or, The Book Fish: Contayning Three Treatises Which Were Found in the Belly of a Cod-fish in Cambridge Market on Midsummer Eve last, Anno Domini 1626* (London, 1627), STC 11395, copy 3. Reprinted by permission of the Folger Shakespeare Library under a Creative Commons Attribution-ShareAlike 4.0 International License.

> by the Cod, and that it lay for a good space of time in the fishes belly. For the booke was much consumed by lying there, the leather couer being melted and dissolued and much of the edges of the leaues abated and consumed, and the rest very thin and brittle hauing beene deepe parboiled by the heat of the fishes mawe. (13–14)

This scenario narrativizes the condition of the "book," whose condition might best be described as "cooked." Not drowned so much as "parboiled" in the oven that is a fish's belly. But no virtue has been gleaned from this nondigestion.

The cod in question has not fared too well either, being very underweight from having its mouth blocked and so unlikely to fetch a good price at market. The fish itself seems to have "been cast into a surfeit or consumption" (14). It takes no profit from the encounter. Instead it becomes a mode of conveyance, a condition by which the book that was lost goes mobile once more.

As the text announces the identity of the treatises, prefacing them with a prayer to preserve its readers from storms and shipwreck, it begs the following rhetorical question, hoping that by reading them, by decoupling the fish from the contents of its mouth, severing bibliography from ichthyology, we can "fish out the reason why these treatises should bee so strangely preserued in a living dumbe speaking library in the sea" (17). But what order of entity or wetware is this book-fish, upon whose death the revelation of the treatises it stores depends? What strange paratextual creature has it become? Did this cod feed on human flesh, taking the canvass package from a man's pocket? If it did, it found that it could not eat this new food, let alone digest it. Instead, the book, by its newfound mobility, by the fact of its storage in a mouth that cannot speak its lines nor eat their backing, consumes the fish.

The library of the sea yields up its secrets only in a divided and dividing manner. Such books as "fish" keep in their mouths (be they radical Protestant tracts, DNA libraries, "messages from the mud") remain strictly unreadable, becoming so only when translated to still other media, pried or invited forth, and the fish (or the specimens) tossed in the garbage or back to sea, or rendered as illustrations, citational reminders to the biomedia archaeology that places these messages in your hands. The pages of the book represented in the mouth of the cod have been unwrapped, but such writing that appears there remains unreadable—the wavy lines, or fact of symbolic representation that we have seen before, awaiting a linearization that will both reveal and reduce their sense. The *Vox Piscis* serves, if you like, as an occasion for depicting an oozy, underwater archive come topside. Here, the retrieval is premised on a trans-species, bio/zoo-media specificity that trades on the things fish can and cannot say, rendering this historical cod, if there was indeed such a cod, "a living dumbe speaking library in the sea" (17).

Such book-fish or fish books disclose the translational mechanisms upon which we rely to know the world. But they offer little by way of surety, for biopolitics is as value neutral as a bibliography, even as there may be better and worse biopolitical fixes (and bibliographies). Bio/bibliographical apparatuses have within them no automatic ratio that renders "good" or "bad" worlds. Questions of hospitality, of a general question concerning shelter, such as Bennett requires of us, have to be judged retrospectively by and in and through the worlds that result.[40] Having attempted to think through and with my two watery haunts or symptoms, then, I find myself delivered directly back to where I began, to the dual (if not dueling) declarations by Serres and de Man concerning packages, screens, sensation, and thought.

Dead Ends

In "The Dead-End of Formalist Criticism," de Man was doing his best to untidy what he takes to be the overly neat ("dead end" or cul-de-sac) formalism that derived from the work of I. A. Richards and that he sees shaping Anglo-American criticism. He proceeds by interfering in this formalism's archives, offering a rendering of the work of Richards's student William Empson, which he reads as deconstructing the project of a practical criticism that attempted to orchestrate "a convergence between logical positivism and literary criticism" predicated "on a perfect unity between the sign and the signified."[41] As Empson's *Seven Types of Ambiguity* demonstrates, such a convergence, in de Man's rather bleak summary, "fails to materialize." Empson turns out, perhaps in spite of himself, to be almost as astute a thinker (and poet) as Keats. In *Some Versions of Pastoral,* he is said to take up where *Seven Types* left off and, masquerading the project as a genre study, he deals with the fundamental "ontology of the poetic," of Being itself, "but wrapped . . . as is his wont, in some extraneous matter that may well conceal the essential."[42] In every historically specific instance (Shakespeare's *Sonnets* through *Alice in Wonderland*), Empson's framing of pastoral reenacts the same core problematic that severs acts of making or thinking from what precedes them. This movement, or to and fro, describes for de Man "the movement of consciousness as it contemplates the natural entity and finds itself integrally reflected down to the most peculiar aspects of *phusis*." "But," he continues, "a reflection is not an identification, and the simple correspondence of the mind with the natural, far from being appeasing, turns troublesome." "Balance" is recovered only through "domination over that which is its complete other." Empson's readings stand, then, as an inventory or catalogue of variously historical expressions of the melancholy aftereffects of this structure of Being. They attempt to recover and name the pause or hiatus he hears in Keats's broken statement of desire "for a life of sensation" rather than a broken series of "thoughts." And such a statement (of blindness with and by and through insight) characterizes the fundamental "dead end" or emptied telos of still another formalism, the deconstruction that de Man performs and wrests from an Empson who, in a footnote, he imagines as unable to "endorse" and so resisting his reading.[43]

Such is the care de Man takes to undo the salvational criticism he abhors. But if the other option is the melancholy in which he wryly seems to take such pleasure, there remains still the naïve orientation that simply owns the problem and moves forward. Obviously, de Man does not refer to Serres in this essay. But there is a moment at the end of de Man's lecture on the untranslatability of Walter Benjamin's essay "The Task of the Translator" where he names Serres on the matter of translation and fragments. Following de Man's parsing of translation as a further fragmentation of what was already a set of fragments that will never "constitute a totality," he writes that

> I'm reminded of an example I heard given by the French philosopher Michel Serres—that you find out about fragments by doing the dishes: if you break a dish it breaks into fragments, but you can't break the fragments any more. That's an optimistic, a positive synecdochal view of the problem, because there the fragments can make up a whole, and you cannot break up the fragments.[44]

If de Man consistently chooses the melancholy but not unhappy option of proroguing a metaphor, of delaying such transports it might effect and so the translations it produces, all in the name of one form of deconstructive reading that would seek to open out against an inevitable telos, then his difference from Serres comes down almost precisely to a question of orientation—the difference between melancholy and optimism. For de Man, an assemblage or multiplicity is never more than a further fragmentation of a set of fragments, but it is precisely this media-specific rendering of the world, by and through such fragments that we have and that we are, that Serres takes as his point of departure.

De Man's mode of reading remains useful in parsing out the success and failure of those protocols that make (and unmake) worlds on land and sea by whose involutions of media the world is made readable and is re/written. But, likewise, how may I not share in and long for, and so join Serres in his optimism as he seeks after an optative series of translation tools? Far from eschewing packaging, mediation, or screens for substance, from the very beginning of *Biogea,* Serres, whose life's work might be described as a poetics of translation, performs a mode of archival politics hardly alien to de Man's own essay. He retells the story of several floods, sifting them for their efficacy in listening to what it is water says to us now. He recalls and praises Roman rituals for rendering the fact of "tectonic groaning." He recalls the particularized vocabulary of bargemen who work dredging the river Garonne, writing words that you might read almost nowhere else: "The *longueil* and the *traversier,* these are the names of the two cables that, wound on four winches called the *papillonnage,* tied our dredger."[45] Sensation and thought are everywhere, keyed to specific associations that form between persons and elements. Serres himself, his being, his language, just as much as Keats, whose voice names himself by drowning his name, figures here as a screen that registers the aesthetic heft of the elements—the metaphors they yield, tropes and transports that we play out, turning and tuning them in the hope they may generate still other futures than we can imagine. Threatened by extinction, by a loss that might not be archived, Serres owns this desire as an impetus to develop ways of attending to the media ecologies that enable things to speak and us to listen.

What emerges? Nothing like consolation. No exit to these problems. We never get to be "done" with the elements or with the ongoing translations and magnetic transfers between matter and metaphor. But, instead, perhaps, following de Man and Serres, we may tune into the possibilities to be had in understanding media-specific renderings of phenomena as momentary hostings of other orders of finitude than our own, the medial loops or packages in which things (and we) come always, by and in their use and abuse of others, expressions of the metaphysics of other ways of being in and by the localized particularities of the forms things take "now." A dark thought, in Morton's sense of "dark ecology"?[46] Perhaps. For still there comes the "cut," the break or breaks that eventuate the continuum. Keats dies; the book-fish is opened; the specimens of the Necropiscatorium find themselves remaindered. Hence, as I have thematized throughout this chapter, the amphibious nature of my response, of my time-bound, drying, dessicating wetness.

As it happens (of course), de Man misquotes Keats when he praises him for owning that he may not have his desire. In Keats's letter of November 22, 1817, to Benjamin Bailey, the words *sensation* and *thought* are actually plural—"O, for a Life of Sensations rather than Thoughts"—serial sensations, a series of thoughts.[47] It is tempting to splice the two and admit to another desire—something we might parse as a desire for a cascade of succeeding acts or instants of sensing, the body as the transcorporeal site of an emerging and morphing media ecology, a succession of screens, but syntactically "cut" by "thoughts," time-bound admissions of finitude that task our acts of translation with an accounting of losses and gains. Such a position constitutes, perhaps, a mode of melancholy optimism with regard to the packages in which things come.

The prospect leaves me feeling oozy. It leaves me, as I began, "wet"?

Notes

1. On the Roman ritual for responding to the sounds the earth makes as the world "opens," see Michel Serres, *Biogea,* trans. Randolph Burks (Minneapolis: Univocal, 2012), 34–37.

2. Ibid., 40.

3. For a characterization of what he calls the impasse of modern philosophy's post-Kantian "correlationist two-step" that ensures that we may inquire only into how we know things, see Quentin Meillasoux, *After Finitude: An Essay on the Necessity of Contingency,* trans. Ray Brassier (London: Continuum, 2008), 5–11.

4. For an elaboration of de Man's critique as it might identify salvational strains in the new materialism and neo-vitalist approaches to ecology, see Tom Cohen,

Claire Colebrook, and J. Hillis Miller, *Theory and the Disappearing Future: On de Man, On Benjamin* (New York: Routledge, 2012), esp. 8–10. I am grateful to Timothy Morton for suggesting this book to me.

5. On the abyssal "indistinction" between reaction and response and the difficulty of parsing the essence of either as the preserve or condition of the human, other animals, plants, and so on, see Jacques Derrida, *The Animal Therefore I Am,* trans. David Wills (New York: Fordham University Press, 2008). On the quasi-automaticity of the symptom, see J. Hillis Miller, "Paul de Man as Allergen," in *Material Events: Paul de Man and the Afterlife of Theory,* ed. Tom Cohen, Barbara Cohen, J. Hillis Miller, and Andrzej Warminski (Minneapolis: University of Minnesota Press, 2001), 183–204.

6. William Shakespeare, *The Tempest,* Arden Series 3, rev., ed. Virginia Mason Vaughan and Arden T. Vaughan (London: Bloomsbury, 2011), 5.1.54. Further citations appear parenthetically in the text.

7. See the articles edited by Jeffrey Jerome Cohen in *postmedieval* 4, no. 1 (Spring 2013).

8. Jane Bennett, response essay, "The Elements," *postmedieval* 4, no. 1 (Spring 2013): 111.

9. *Oxford English Dictionary,* s.v. "burrow" (n.3).

10. For this articulation of shelter, see Walter Benjamin, "The Work of Art in an Age of Mechanical Reproduction," in *Illuminations,* trans. Harry Zohn (New York: Schocken Books, 1969), 140. On the stupidity of human exceptionalism as he troubles the word *bête* (beast), see Jacques Derrida, *The Beast and the Sovereign,* vol. 1, trans. Geoffrey Bennington (Chicago: University of Chicago Press, 2009).

11. Donna J. Haraway, *When Species Meet* (Minneapolis: University of Minnesota Press, 2008), 4; John Donne, *The Sermons of John Donne,* vol. 2, ed. Evelyn Simpson and George R. Potter (Berkeley: University of California Press, 1962), 235–36, 238.

12. Stefan Helmreich, *Alien Ocean: Anthropological Voyages in Microbrial Seas* (Berkeley: University of California Press, 2009), 283.

13. Ibid., 284.

14. For a striking formulation of Helmreich's position and the coinage "transcorporeality," see Stacy Alaimo, *Bodily Natures: Science, Environment, and the Material Self* (Bloomington: Indiana University Press, 2010). For subsequent applications to questions arising from ways of modeling oceans, see, among others, Stacy Alaimo, "States of Suspension: Trans-Corporeality at Sea," *ISLE: Interdisciplinary Studies in Literature and Environment* 19, no. 3 (Summer 2012): 476–93, "Violet—Black," in *Prismatic Ecologies: Eco-Theory beyond Green,* ed. Jeffrey Jerome Cohen (Minneapolis: University of Minnesota Press, 2013), 233–51. On evolutionary narratives that plot a relation to technology with our backs to the sea, see David Wills, *Dorsality: Thinking Back through Technology* (Minneapolis: University of Minnesota Press, 2008).

15. Richard Doyle, *Wetware: Experiments in Post-vital Living* (Minneapolis: University of Minnesota Press, 2004).

16. Timothy Morton, *Hyperobjects: Philosophy and Ecology after the End of the World* (Minneapolis: University of Minnesota Press, 2013), 18. For an allied modeling of the human and the discourse of aesthetics as very precisely a screening of other forms of finitude, see also Timothy Morton, "An Object-Oriented Defense of Poetry," *New Literary History* 43, no. 2 (Spring 2012): 205–24.

17. Cary Wolfe, *What Is Posthumanism?* (Minneapolis: University of Minnesota Press, 2010), xxv–xxvi.

18. Ibid., xxv.

19. Letter from Joseph Severn to John Taylor, March 6, 1821, in *The Letters of John Keats*, vol. 2, *1814–1821*, ed. Hyder Edward Rollins (Cambridge, Mass.: Harvard University Press, 1958), 377–78.

20. See, for example, Severn's letters to William Haslam, dated January 15, 1821, and to John Taylor, dated January 25 and 26, 1821, in ibid., 366–73.

21. Letter from Joseph Severn to William Haslam, dated February 22, 1821, in ibid., 376.

22. On Keats's orientation toward death as it factors into his poetics, see Brendan Corcoran, "Keats's Death: Towards a Posthumous Poetics," *Studies in Romanticism* 48, no. 2 (Summer 2009): 321–48.

23. On responses to this epitaph, see Samuel Baker, *Written on Water: British Romanticism and the Maritime Empire of Culture* (Charlottesville: University of Virginia Press, 2010), 79–80. On the trope of the disinterested spectator observing a shipwreck, see Hans Blumenberg, *Shipwreck with Spectator: Paradigm for a Metaphor of Existence*, trans. Steven Rendall (Cambridge, Mass.: MIT Press, 1997). For the key passage in Lucretius designating the trope of gazing out to sea, see *De Rerum Natura*, trans. W. H. D. Rouse, rev. Martin F. Smith (Cambridge, Mass.: Harvard University Press, 1992), Book 2, 1–2.

24. On the literary history and etymology of "anonymous," see Anne Ferry, "*Anonymity*: The Literary History of a Word," *New Literary History* 33, no. 2 (Spring 2002): 193–94.

25. For these examples and others, see Bruno Latour, *On the Modern Cult of the Factish Gods*, trans. Catherine Porter and Heather MacLean (Durham N.C.: Duke University Press, 2010), 93.

26. Helmreich, *Alien Ocean*, 31–32.

27. Ibid., 36.

28. Ibid., 41.

29. Ibid., 42–43. Helmreich draws here on Charles Goodwin's "Seeing in Depth," *Social Studies of Science* 25, no. 2 (1995): 254–57.

30. Helmreich, *Alien Ocean*, 45; Haraway, *When Species Meet*, 249–51.

31. Helmreich, *Alien Ocean*, 51.

32. Ibid., 60.

33. Ibid., 279–84.

34. On the correlation between bibliography and biopolitics, see Jacques Derrida, "The Book to Come," in *Paper Machine,* trans. Rachel Bowlby (Stanford: Stanford University Press, 2005).

35. On fathoms and sea terms, see Steve Mentz, *At the Bottom of Shakespeare's Ocean* (London: Continuum, 2009), 8.

36. *Oxford English Dictionary,* s.v. "sound" (v.1, v.2). The word *sound* may mean both to emit a sound and to measure the depth of a body of water using a lead weight, which condenses the sonic and the aquatic.

37. On the figure of "blackboxing" as the closure of a complicated system to view such that all that may be detected or grasped are its inputs and outputs, see Bruno Latour, *Pandora's Hope: Essays on the Reality of Science Studies,* trans. Catherine Porter (Cambridge, Mass.: Harvard University Press, 1999), 304.

38. *Vox Piscis: Or, The Book Fish: Contayning Three Treatises Which Were Found in the Belly of a Cod-fish in Cambridge Market on Midsummer Eve Last, Anno Domini 1626* (London, 1627), 8. Further citations appear parenthetically in the text.

39. On the topical and political contexts of the book, see Alexandra Walsham, "*Vox Piscis: Or The Book-Fish:* Providence and the Uses of the Reformation Past in Caroline Cambridge," *The English Historical Review* 114, no. 457 (June 1999): 574–606. I am grateful to Steve Mentz both for his wonderful blog, "The Book-Fish," and for directing me to Walsham's essay.

40. On the neutrality of biopolitics and biopower, see Cary Wolfe, *Before the Law: Humans and Other Animals in a Biopolitical Frame* (Chicago: University of Chicago Press, 2013), 32–34.

41. Paul de Man, *Blindness and Insight* (New York: Oxford University Press, 1971), 232.

42. Ibid., 239.

43. "The French reader unfamiliar with Empson's work should be warned that this has been an interpretation and not an exposition, and that it is, therefore, subject to discussion. I suppose that the author especially, who has always proclaimed his agreement with Richards, would have some difficulty endorsing it." De Man, *Blindness and Insight,* 241n21.

44. Paul de Man, *The Resistance to Theory* (Minneapolis: University of Minnesota Press, 1986), 91.

45. Serres, *Biogea,* 11.

46. Timothy Morton, *The Ecological Thought* (Cambridge, Mass.: Harvard University Press, 2010), 16.

47. *The Letters of John Keats,* vol. 1, *1814–1818,* ed. Hyder Edward Rollins (Cambridge, Mass.: Harvard University Press, 1958), 185.

eight

Creeping Things

Spontaneous Generation and Material Creativity

KARL STEEL

Substance ↔ Earth ↔ Air

First option: at its heart, all is earthy.

Premodern theories of matter identify four elements, earth, air, water, and fire, as the constituent components of everything. Marius's twelfth-century *De elementis (On the Elements)*, for example, explains that milk is mostly liquid (water), but also thick (earth), greasy (air), and even fiery, since it is a warming drink.[1] To this point, only Marius's decision to talk about milk is unusual. But Marius's treatise—his sole surviving work, extant in a single, fragmentary manuscript, by an author unknown except for his name—breaks with tradition when it tries to determine what the elements actually are. According to Marius, the elements are just the materialized form of varying intensities of either rising or falling and heat, cold, dryness, and wetness. What seems to be earth is that which is temporarily cold, dry, and heavy, and so on with the remaining elements: water is cold, wet, and likewise heavy; air, hot and wet and light; and fire, finally, hot, dry, and the lightest of all. If these intensities change, so does their material form, and likewise the things they comprise: "earth may be changed into water, water into air, and air into fire, and the other way around,"[2] or milk may become ash.

According to Marius, underlying these shifting variations is a "substance," lacking any qualities of its own, which, however materializations change, "will always remain exactly the same."[3] His discovery of substance solves the problem of elemental identity by giving the elements a body, but not without raising still other problems. Despite substance's distinction from heat or motion, its stillness and mystery at least hint at earthiness, as if earth were in fact the fundamental quality of everything. Marius had to disprove this point. To guide readers through his science's more peculiar features, Marius structures his *De elementis* like many other medieval treatises, as a conversation between a master and a student who resists only long enough to be prodded toward the next correct answer. When the student accepts, as he must, that heat results from motion and cold from its absence, he fights back, temporarily, by suggesting that substance, this most stable of materials, must itself have a quality, coldness, since it preexists motion. The student may have something in mind like Bernard Silvestris's early twelfth-century *Cosmographia,* which calls earth "stable in tendency," the substance that more than any other "rest[s] firm."[4] Not so, insists the master, for coldness is motion too: while heat is motion away from the center, coldness is motion toward it. And earth, he adds, "always tend[s] towards the center from every direction." This answer in turn suggests that the cosmos' center may be nothing but a clod of cold earth, which Marius counters by arguing that the center is itself beyond all imagining or representation, "nothing but a certain indivisible geometrical point," perceivable only in thought.[5] The student accepts the answer, of course; but Marius can't seem to shut down the logical implications of his ideas. Later in the treatise, as if having forgotten his own lessons, the master explains how "the earthy will always drag the fiery downward after it and, if possible, even all the way to the center."[6] The center of all things may really comprise something so absolutely obscure, unthinkable, and still that it might be recognized as the very perfection of earth's primary qualities. At the same time, Marius has kept room in his natural science for the mobility of earth, whose very ceaseless motion away from us, or at least from our non-earthy elementary characteristics, keeps earth from ever being fully comprehended by us.

Marius's earth science closely resembles Martin Heidegger's, although happily without Heidegger's "old Protestant heritage of human nullity and . . .

gloom."[7] Per Bruce Foltz's classic summation, Heidegger's earth is "what bears and gives rise to what comes to light only by remaining intrinsically dark itself."[8] When Marius's student realizes the ungraspability of what he wants to know, he, like a sympathetic reader of Heidegger, also rescues things from his efforts to make things mere objects for academic manipulation. Marius's student also learns to "turn the transient and therefore preliminary character of object-things away from the inner and invisible region of the merely producing consciousness and toward the true interior of the heart's space, and there allow it to rise invisibly."[9] Heidegger famously insists that "ground" should no longer be understood as logos or rational basis but rather as something deeper, "what lies in the depths, for example, the bottom of the sea, the bottom of the valley, the bottom of the heart."[10] He argues that only by remembering the resistant otherness with which both being and thinking starts can we break with the "final delusion," that "man everywhere and always encounters only himself."[11] Certainly, that last, most important lesson may surpass anything Marius ever deliberately offered. Still, their similarities, at least on earthy inscrutability and foundation, are undeniable. With a host of other thinkers, Marius and Heidegger promote a sense of the earth as stable, as heavy, characteristics that support the common metaphors of "understanding," or the "ground," "foundation," or, for that matter, the "support" of the "matter" of an argument,[12] combined with a sense that, so long as we understand things correctly, the foundation is itself mysterious, dark and distant, always and ultimately extrinsic to our understanding or experience.

Second option: without air, there is nothing.

Air's levity floats free of all such ponderousness. In Luce Irigaray's riposte to Heidegger, air surrounds us, always on the move, neither a surface nor a depth, and also invisible, but in a way entirely different from earth's withdrawn chthonic mystery, that darkness so important, for example, to Graham Harman's speculative realism. Air enables thought, more vitally than Heidegger's earth, for without more air than earth, there could be no clearing that could make thought possible. "No other element," writes Irigaray, "is in this way space prior to all localization, and a substratum both immobile and mobile, permanent and flowing."[13] For Irigaray, *this* element, not earth, is the foundational substance, but one whose continual, necessary, invisible, unsolid, and acentric presence also requires abandoning any comfortingly terrestrial notions of either foundation or subterranean mystery.

Air is in us, and we in it, as it, not earth, fire, or water, is the only element in which we can live. With air, Irigaray observes, the "outside enters [us] limitlessly."[14] From similar observations, Emmanuel Levinas calls air a donation that preexists cognition, intention, or the distinction between spiritual and corporeal. We share our breathing with others through our incarnational being here; air reminds us that in being here together we also share an inescapable condition of shared vulnerability.[15] For, as Irigaray writes, were there a "gap, breach, spacing, or distancing" between us and air, were *dasein* to activate its "as such" relation to things,[16] we would die, a point Heidegger understands only too well. Barring the otherwise unconsidered needs of anaerobic bacteria, without air, there is no thought, no being, no life.

Earth - Air = Swarms

The imagination of air's relation to earth that drives Irigaray's response to Heidegger is not all that uncommon. Many thinkers, many folk stories, and foundational religious texts thought the earth needed air or something like it to get going. Lucretius, for instance, posited the necessity of a shifting void to keep matter from being "everywhere quiescent, packed into one solid mass."[17] Such ideas also appear in the stranger corners of folklore, like the "wind eggs" of the *Iliad* and other works, fragile and ephemeral, laid by hens impregnated by Zephyrus's fertility, or like the Cretan or Spanish wind that inspires mares to gallop for the shore, where they eventually birth foals as ephemeral as a breeze, living for a decade, or three years, or sometimes, as in one twelfth-century encyclopedia, only a few days.[18] Far more familiar is Genesis's second chapter, where God invests the earth, Adam, with *niš·mat,* in Hebrew, *pneuma,* in Greek, and in Latin, *spiritus,* all of which could be translated as breath, spirit, or soul (for the Hebrew, for example, see Proverbs 20:27). Even in the first creation story of Genesis 1:1–2:2a, God causes things to spring into being from his voice. Certainly this divine spirit-bestowing breath is not quite what Irigaray or Levinas intend. Neither antifoundational nor connecting us all in shared vulnerability and dependence, this breath is the masterful voice of Psalms 32:9, "For he spoke and they were made: he commanded and they were created."[19] All living things are tethered by this voice to the order inaugurated and controlled by the Divine Father. Still, whatever its differences from Irigaray's and Levinas's air, this divine voice also imagines the heavy earth as needing something extra to liven it up. This is an earth that, like Heidegger's, remains stolid and ponderous, a good ground precisely because it stays put. Earth needs a better advocate than any of these thinkers.

To do this, we need one more combination. So far, I have joined earth and air in various combinations: earth alone, air alone, earth and air together, and now one remains, earth without air, the subtractive conjunction that guides the rest of my chapter. Earth minus air is earth without spirit. For Irigaray and Levinas, as much as for Genesis, this equation equals isolation and death. For Lucretius, this means stasis. With a different archive, not taken from elemental binary fantasies of stable earth and mobile air, earth minus air equals *unspiritual* but still mobile and active matter. This is not the obscure earth of Marius and Heidegger, nor the weighty earth of Irigaray, nor the earth that needs some kind of transcendent "life" in order to be up to something. Because, at least in medieval Christian thought, earth was anything but stable.[20] Earth was not solid, dull stuff but "fertile, maternal, labile, percolating, forever tossing up grass, wood, horses, bees, sand, or metal."[21] What the earth does is life, if it can be called that, but, as I will argue, life without any of the spiritual, genealogical, or reproductive qualities normally associated with this concept. This is the "creeping" or "swarming" life of the fifth and sixth days of creation, variously identified by the Hexamera, medieval commentaries on the first six days of Creation, as fish, crustaceans, snakes, insects, reptiles, and even more fantastical critters, like dragons or the *reguli* (basilisks) of Isaiah 11:8. This is a life that challenges God's creative monopoly, divisions between agent and object, human mastery, and ultimately, as I will argue, the division between spirit and matter, and information and form, that enables the fantasy of some separable, immaterial quality called "life."

Some creeping things were generally thought to be generated like other animals: hatched from eggs or born live from parents like them, produced sexually by males and females of the same species, in a series of mundane repetitions of the same originating in the voice of God. Others, however, came not from sex but from rejected, disordered, and shapeless materials—dust, filth, putrefaction, and slime[22]—or just from the restlessness of earth in general. This process, "spontaneous generation," the medieval thinkers normally called *generatio equivoca,* generation from an ambiguous source, contrasting it with *generatio univoca,* generation from a single source, cause, or even voice (*voca* from *vox,* voice). Aristotle's natural science was their key resource, as when he spoke of some insects

> not derived from living parentage, but . . . generated spontaneously: some out of dew falling on leaves . . . others grow in decaying mud or dung; others in timber, green or dry; some in the hair of animals; some in the flesh of animals; some in excrements: and some from excrement after it has been voided, and some from excrement yet within the living animal.[23]

Albert the Great's thirteenth-century Aristotelian commentary makes exactly the same point: "One must respond that some animals are generated from propagation, and some from putrefaction. In those generated from putrefaction there are no members designated for generation, because they are not generated from semen."[24] Bartholomew the Englishman's fourteenth-century encyclopedia in turn explains that the louse is "yngendered of most, corrupt ayer and vapours þat sweten oute bitwen þe felleand the fleissch by pores" (18.48, 1239; birthed from moist, corrupt air and vapors that sweat out from between the skin and the flesh from pores); the snail in "lyme oþer of lyme and is þerfore alway foule and vnclene" (18.70, 1222; lime or of lime, and is therefore always foul and unclean); butterflies lay eggs in fruit and "bredeþ þerinne wormes þat comeþ of here stynkynge filþe" (18.47, 1198; breed therein worms that come of their stinking filth); fleas lay eggs without "medlyng [mixing] of male and female" (18.49, 1240); and, more generally:

> A worm is called "vermis" and is a beast that often is birthed from flesh and plants and often birthed from cabbage, and sometimes from putrefaction of humors, and sometimes from mixing of male and female [i.e., sexual reproduction], and sometimes from eggs, as it occurs with scorpions, tortoises, and newts. (18.115, 1264)[25]

No one seems to have found this science anything but common sense. As if everyone knew it, Basil the Great, fourth-century Bishop of Caesarea, remarks that on hot rainy days in Thebes, hordes of field mice swarm from the earth and the "mud alone produce[s] eels; they do not proceed from an egg, nor in any other manner; it is the earth alone which gives them birth."[26] Isidore of Seville's *Etymologies,* a massive early medieval encyclopedia, just as blandly observes that everyone knows that bees come "from the carcasses of oxen," hornets from horses, "drones from mules, and wasps from asses."[27] Without any expectation of disagreement, Saint Augustine explains that Noah did not need to gather spontaneously generated critters, because God specifically commanded him to gather only male and female animals, in other words, those generated through sexual reproduction, and anyway vermin would have infested the ark, as they do any house, "not in any determinate numbers."[28]

The science of worms was even key to a widespread medieval interpretation of Psalms 21 (22 in the Latin Vulgate),[29] which used worms to free Christ from the fluid conjunctions of bodies in sex, original sin, and the pollution of desire and bodies bucking our spiritual control. The main body of the Psalm begins, "O God, my God, look upon me: why hast thou forsaken me?," which Christ famously quoted while hanging from the cross. Some medieval Christian interpreters took this quoted verse as an *incipit* and thus as a shorthand indicating that the crucified Christ actually recited the whole chapter, including 22:7, "But I am a worm, and no man: the reproach of men, and the outcast of the people." Exegetes explained that Christ is a worm by rebuking humanity, as the so-called worm of conscience, or that by suffering humiliation, or, most importantly, by being born miraculously. Unsurprisingly, Saint Augustine's commentary establishes the main exegetical road: "'*But I am a worm, and no man*': But I, speaking now not in the person of Adam, but I in My own person, Jesus Christ, was born without seed in the flesh, so I might be as man beyond men."[30] As a worm, Christ could be the exception. Subject to no one, connected to no one, without lineage, as a worm he is freed from the dependencies of an ordinary life and ordinary death.

The problem was not the presumptive truth of the natural science but rather the way spontaneous generation challenged God's monopoly on creation. Medieval thinkers offered a range of solutions, more or less convincing, to this problem. For example, Robert Grosseteste, thirteenth-century Bishop of Lincoln, felt compelled to defend God's sole responsibility for the ongoing production of oysters, here presumably standing in as a paradigmatic "equivocal" critter. According to Grosseteste, since oysters evidently generate from the water itself, God's "increase and multiply" has to apply to oysters in some specific way particular to them, not "by the propagation of things brought forth one from other" but rather "through a multiplication of individuals that are begotten from water."[31] Other writers, using Aristotle, concocted better explanations by following a more logical, less haphazard system, in which the earth is cold, and life requires warmth. Thus for Duns Scotus, stars operated on a cow's corpse, inscribing the matter in such a way that it might produce bees.[32] Pseudo–Albert the Great meanwhile explains that when the sun heats rotting matter, trapped heat causes vibrations within the matter, which produce spirit, and thus life.[33] The actual Albert the Great insists that animals sprung from putrefaction require

> a superior power and an inferior power. The inferior power disposes the matter for putrefaction, into which, once it has been disposed, the celestial power is introduced, operating on the matter just as sperm operates on the menses. And this is why, just as the power of the sperm disposes the menses to the form of a perfect animal, so the celestial power operates through an elemental power on matter that is disposed to the form of an imperfect animal.[34]

This solution suggests an effort to keep God ultimately responsible, in this case through a deputized *virtus caelestis,* a heavenly patriarchal force, working, like God, on merely receptive, feminine sublunary matter.

In still other explanations, this engagement is not obviously one between spirit and matter but rather a fully material interaction that produces qualities like life and even reason, normally thought of as wholly immaterial. The meeting of heaven and earth might therefore be a meeting of different operations of matter rather than an encounter of matter and spirit. The key work here is the *Quaestiones de anima* (Questions on the Soul) of Blaise of

Parma (ca. 1347–1416), whose "materialistic concept of the soul" denied the soul's separability from matter and therefore its immortality;[35] using these ideas, he proposed that all animals, not just gnats, bees, mice, toads, and the like, emerged spontaneously from the mud after Noah's Flood, and argued, finally, that, at least theoretically, even humans and the rational soul could emerge from this process. Blaise allowed that things come to be from form imprinting itself on matter, but, in contradistinction to most thinkers, the imprinting form of his model was entirely immanent to materiality. Forced by the church to recant these views, he was shockingly allowed to die a natural death.[36]

If God was responsible for spontaneously generated critters, then thinkers had to determine just *when* they were created. In Genesis's first creation story, God creates creeping things on both the fifth and sixth days, while birds and fish get only the fifth day, and quadrupeds and humans only the sixth. Saint Augustine even idiosyncratically gives them another day, when he proposes that God might have implanted some vermin in the earth on the third day, which means vermin would have been the very first form of life, preceding even plants and the lights of heaven.[37] This idea, as interesting as it is, seems not to have been popular.

The very many medieval illustrated accounts of creation confuse more than help matters, underscoring how spontaneously generated critters are filth, "matter out of place," "excremental life,"[38] or just an embarrassment to otherwise neat systems of creation. These accounts tend to collapse Genesis's two creation stories into one coherent story: rather than having man and woman created simultaneously (as in the first creation story), or having Adam appear first, then the animals, and then Eve (as in the second), medieval art tends to show the creation of animals first, then Adam, and then the creation of Eve from Adam's rib.

Illustrations sometimes simplify things even further by crowding the creation of all nonhuman animals into one panel between that of plants and humans (Figure 8.1, Harley 616; Figure 8.2, Egerton 1895), or, if illustrations grant animals multiple panels, then fish and birds receive one and quadrupeds another. The rare pictured creeping things are generally those thought to hatch from eggs, like the basilisk, perhaps pictured among the land animals in the later fifteenth-century *Bible historiale* (Figure 8.3, Harley

4412).[39] The problem is partly technical. Creeping things are too small to illustrate easily, particularly on the sixth day, crowded as it is with the creation of quadrupeds and humans.

However, even when artists had ample space, as in carvings on cathedrals, they still tended to omit the creation of vermin.[40] A gargantuan thirteenth-century French translation of the Bible, whose manuscripts are very frequently illustrated, leaves them entirely out of its creation account except as a moral aside that explains that snakes are those *"qui sevent deviser le bien du mal"* (who know how to distinguish good from evil), and, somewhat self-referentially, also those who know how celestial things can be

FIGURE 8.1. Bible, French, last quarter thirteenth century, Creation, f. 1, British Library, Harley 616. Copyright the British Library Board.

FIGURE 8.2. Old Testament, German, 1465, Creation, f. 5v, British Library, Egerton 1895. Copyright the British Library Board.

FIGURE 8.3. *Bible historiale,* France, third quarter fifteenth century, Creation, f. 22, British Library, Harley 4412. Copyright the British Library Board.

understood through earthly things.[41] The rarity of vermin in medieval creation art indicates that the problem is less technical than it is doctrinal and scientific: if spontaneously generated critters come from putrefaction and disorder, then they could not have existed in the prelapsarian perfection. Such life seems to have no proper place in the order of creation, and they seem to come not from God but from the introduction of disorder into Creation by sinful humans.

The most widely recognized resolution to the problem appears in Saint Augustine's work, not in his Genesis commentary but rather in his commentary on the Trinity. In the course of examining the competing serpent-creating miracles between Moses and the magicians of Pharaoh's court (Exodus 7:10–12), Saint Augustine explains that demons have no power to create matter, and neither, in fact, does anything else but God. He then asserts that at Creation God had "interwoven" a "natural seminal power" in all life from which they produced particular kinds of seemingly new things.[42] Living things, Saint Augustine argues, come from some kind of seed: some are visible, but not all. And though putrefaction had not yet happened, the living results of putrefaction were already present *potentially* through God's foresight, and we know this simply because of the emergence of these creatures from putrefaction.

Saint Augustine's definitive answer, like the other, less popular solutions, is less interesting than the problem, which is that everyone knew the earth produced swarms, and that these swarms confounded a host of foundational binaries: that between agent and object, male and female, and even human and animal. For the products of spontaneous generation, many of them pests or otherwise annoying to humans, had no easy place in logics that comfortably opposed human to animal. In mainstream medieval Christian doctrine, on this point an outgrowth or ally of Stoicism, all other living things are subject to human dominion. Humans train other animals, ride them, eat them, and in some places subject them to criminal courts. By hunting some animals, and especially by restricting hunting rights, certain humans convince others and themselves of their own nobility. Humans cooperate with dogs to join an animal community and fancy themselves its beloved masters. Knights cooperate with horses to transform themselves into horsemen, human/animal/technological hybrids.[43] Humans might single out some of their fellow creatures for love, with all of love's cultivated or surprising vulnerabilities. Or they might deny any connections, to generate human difference. Through all these repeated, particular points of contact, some loving, most thoughtlessly violent, humans convince themselves of their worldly supremacy.[44]

Not so with swarming things, except perhaps for bees, admired as "model insects."[45] In several medieval stories, bees, the sole domesticated creeping thing, even surround consecrated hosts left in their hives in waxy Gothic chapels.[46] Other bugs could be cared about only in parody, as in the pseudo-Virgilian "Culex," in which a gnat lands on a shepherd's eye, waking him in time to avoid an approaching snake. The next night, the gnat reproves the shepherd for ingratitude and describes an underworld to him populated by all too human heroes.[47] No premodern people, however, trained bugs, and no one rode them, except possibly in the sillier late medieval marginalia and misericords. They routinely feed on us, not we on them, in life and death both. They were our enemies or our colleagues, meat-eaters who, like us, "were never eaten themselves."[48]

Confronted with this swarming, hungry mass, medieval champions of human superiority fought to assure themselves that vermin were still as much our servants as any other animal. In a typical argument, Gervase of Tilbury's twelfth-century wonder collection explains that God made "cattle, the creeping things, and the beasts—the cattle to help us, the creeping things and the beasts to challenge us—in the last place he fashioned man."[49] By humiliating and harassing us, the creeping things remind us to fix our concentration to eternal things. That, at least, is how it should work. Gervase's contemporary Gerald of Wales, in his *Journey through Wales,* tells a story that muddles even this stopgap explanation. There was once an ailing Welshman to whom "it seemed as if the entire local population of toads had made an agreement to go to visit." Though his friends kill "vast numbers," the swarm grows again "like the heads of the Hydra. . . . Toads came flocking from all directions, more and more of them, until no one could count them." Apparently lacking a better plan, his comrades stuff their sick companion into a bag, strip a tree of most of its branches, and hoist their toad-afflicted friend into its summit. Undaunted, the toads scale the tree and when they come back to ground, nothing of the Welshman remained "but his skeleton."[50] Gerald fumbles for an explanation, gesturing toward the inscrutable judgment of God, but what the story finally offers is one in which some kinds of life or matter, if this distinction works at all, elude the logic of dominion and the human particularity this dominion defends.

Furthermore, by not being victims, vermin just as messily confound the pieties of most common forms of critical animal thinking. Critical animal theory tends to focus on marketable, sympathetic, and above all vulnerable charismatic megafauna, which people might name, admire, love, pity, exploit, save, or eat, head to tail. The snake, on the other hand, is notably one of the animals Levinas finds himself most reluctant to recognize as having a face.[51] Critical animal theorists delight in Levinas's failure to recognize the dog Bobby's face; very few have thought to challenge him for failing snakes as well. Swarming life has no place in analyses focused on animal rights and struggles to reduce or eliminate the cruelties of, for example, factory farming,[52] nor, in a larger sense, in those focused on frustrating transcendent principles like soul, mutuality, recognizable suffering, or even the face. No one or nothing can be responsible for vermin, indifferent to care, present to us, if at all, only as an annoyance, or a parasite, or as our killer, there to make use of our body, and, by doing so, there to destroy our otherwise unidirectional and therefore parasitic exploitation of everything else.[53]

The final challenge presented by the vermin of medieval spontaneous generation, perhaps most relevant for a volume on ecology, is that between spirit and matter. This life could be produced in the same way as some minerals, also generated through the coordination of earth and sky, frustrating any neat divisions between organic and inorganic.[54] Like these minerals, vermin seem just to happen, without any obvious intervention from their fellow vermin, from us, or even from God. They happen instead through the inscrutable, acentric operations of matter, without any transcendent pretensions of a cause disentangled from an effect. There is nothing in this production of what Thomas Aquinas called an "aspect of generation and sonship,"[55] where paternal life transmits information, a word here freighted with all its etymological weight of *giving form*. At its root, this information is both a pattern and the echo of the first, distinct, and active decision to inform inert and receptive feminine matter—Isidore of Seville, for example, correctly derives the word *materia* from *mater*, mother[56]—and to reproduce that form across time, as in medieval conceptualizations like these:

> so nature, once put in motion by the Divine command, traverses creation with an equal step, through birth and death, and keeps up the succession of kinds through resemblance, to the last. Nature always makes a horse succeed to a horse, a lion to a lion, an eagle to an eagle, and preserving each animal

> by these uninterrupted successions she transmits it to the end of all things. Animals do not see their peculiarities destroyed or effaced by any length of time; their nature, as though it had been just constituted, follows the course of ages, for ever young.[57]

Feminine matter might horrify this informational, paternal order by being forever young in a wholly other sense. For example, one medieval scientific text explained that a menstruating woman should "hide her hair, because . . . when the moon is in Scorpio or Aries, or when Venus is in Virgo," the hair is sure to generate serpents, at least if it somehow finds itself buried under manure. This kind of life offers a model of material creativity beyond binary genders, information and matter, and agent and object. Lacking father or mother and children, barely distinct from the matter from which they temporarily emerge and to which they will return, creeping things refuse family orders. They can be gendered only insofar as the female is a sign of absolute otherness and formlessness, a gender beyond all gendering.

The information of supposedly normal paternal life is matter's informing spirit, potentially separable from any particular materialization so long as it can be transmitted and received properly by other matter, so long, that is, as it can continue to establish a lineage.[58] By these criteria, spontaneous generation fails. The signal meant to be transmitted by God's first creative command has been cut off or has reconstituted itself on its own terms. Vermin swarm from matter without any sexual intermediary, without parental transmission, without a singular cause or singular voice, without a quality separable from their temporary affiliations. Vermin then return to earth, possibly to arise again at some point if conditions are right, but possibly not. What returns has no informational line distinct from the matter that could possibly be traced from parent to child. If life in its pre-Darwinian conceptualizations is ahistorical because it transmits itself unalterably across time, spontaneous generation is ahistorical because it lacks any continuity or narrative or identifiable struggle. Its noise is its matter is its motion, all together.

If this stuff is life, it must be life completely immanent to its temporary ordering of stuff, without any of the informational, transcendent, and spiritual implications that "life" carries, and without any split between its particular manifestation of life and a transcendent "life principle."[59] If information is not distinguished from material structure, then we have the tools for a radically nonspiritual, nonpaternal, and nonvital conceptualization of objects in general, living things included. Individuation now need not be something that happens through the application of spirit, or vitality, or writing, or code to matter. It can be understood to happen with matter itself, through its organization within a roiling field of other matter, in which a perfect description of the information particularizing a particular piece of matter would be nothing less than an exact copy of that piece of matter, and possibly of the larger constantly shifting spatiotemporal order of matter that made that particularization possible.

"Vibrancy" is therefore a better term than, for example, "vitality," for the same reasons Jane Bennett gives in the opening to *Vibrant Matter,* where she sets out "to theorize a vitality intrinsic to materiality as such, and to detach materiality from the figures of passive, mechanistic, or divinely infused substance."[60] This recognition of the vibrancy of matter itself, through its own operations, without any transcendence, itself suggests Slavoj Žižek's recent engagement of Karen Barad's philosophical work on quantum mechanics. While Barad argues that phenomena are the fundamental ontological element, not determinate objects, Žižek observes that even to recognize particular phenomena as phenomena requires making a cut in the field of being. Something must therefore be more fundamental than the phenomenon; there must be an as-yet-unresolved thing preexisting any determination.[61] Žižek argues that this something is pure difference, a term that might be replaced without much distortion with undifferentiated "vibrancy," as yet unmapped into that chain of entangled and contingently arranged cause and effect that constitute a Baradian phenomenon. This fundamental mobile indeterminacy in turn suggests Ben Woodard's *Slime Dynamics,* where the underlying, preexisting, and still persisting oneness of all things is not some "ideal form" nor "a kind of perfect totality of the cosmos" but rather an "obscurity . . . the fundamentally unstable beginning of all processes and entities of the universe," "corrupted or degenerate instead of being transcendent" in that its existence at all "sets in motion the engine of spatiotemporality," which is itself a kind of tumbling outward into creative, ongoing collapse.[62]

Yet to emphasize vibrancy, pure difference, or corruption at the fundamental operations of things, before the imposition or recognition of life, and to see this vibrancy as vermin, crawling chaos, or some other repulsive non-thing, is to see things from the perspective of the presumptively living. It is to see things from the side of God or of masculine order. It is to place ourselves and our counterparts on the side of life with politics and a face, as if we, at least, are echoes of God's primordial commandment, preserving the proper paternal traditions of Creation through our well-ordered but threatened bodies, and to relegate everything else to the side of mere being. The old, self-regarding mistake of splitting *bios* (our life, worth preserving) from *zoe* (their life, hardly recognizable as life) can be avoided in ways that Žižek, Woodard, and, most easily, Bennett might each grant their peculiar endorsement. We must recognize the following: the fundamental disorder is not a problem particular to vermin but rather one general to all that is; to call it disorder rather than, for example, "endless generativity" is to continue to think too highly of ourselves; we ourselves and our worldly counterparts are also immanent to this material vibrancy or constantly erupting disorder; we are therefore not alive so long as "being alive" means having some escape from presumptively inert, "dead," or uncreative materiality; that the opposition of life/death, with fertility on the side of life and sterility on that of death, is insupportable;[63] our mistaken self-conception of being alive and wanting to stay alive is general to anything that seeks to persist; and vibrancy will always swarm forth from the putrefaction, exhaustion, failure, or, for that matter, the ineluctable instability of matter, to try to sustain its own new, temporary order, and it will continue to do so long past anything we can imagine is past the point of caring.

We are all swarms of the vibrant earth.

Present Swarms

My last section concerns the disappearance and return of spontaneous generation, not to free this chapter finally from the Middle Ages but to trouble our self-assured modernism, and to sketch out how generative matter has returned in some contemporary critical thought. We typically hear that the idea of spontaneous generation sprang up sometime before Aristotle, suffered its greatest assault in the seventeenth century, and finally surrendered in the nineteenth, when Louis Pasteur conclusively demonstrated that a sufficiently sterile environment would prevent even the smallest microbes from arising. We moderns have supposedly learned that things have no power in themselves to bring forth something new, though we might be reminded of James Halliwell-Phillipps's obscure mid-nineteenth-century pamphlet recording how Stratford-on-Avonians continue to believe in the eel-generating power of submerged horse hair.[64]

This usual triumphalist story has its typical set of counternarratives. Nearly thirty years ago, the story of the death of spontaneous generation became a hot zone in the social history of knowledge. Some scholars argued that the victory of Pasteur over Felix Archimede Pouchet should be understood not simply as the rise and triumph of experimental science over ancient superstition but instead, or at least also, as a victory of Pasteur's Catholicism and Imperial sympathies over Pouchet's Protestant Republicanism. This observation produces the now obvious critique: the history of science is also the history of whose voices can be heard and how.[65]

The campaign against spontaneous generation was motivated, allowing the distinction, not by reason but by piety. It was never just a matter of disinterested observation. Nor are the differences only political, but also about differences in the understanding of matter and what it can do.[66] In 1864, Louis Pasteur denounced spontaneous generation as an ally of atheism: "what a triumph, gentlemen, it would be for materialism if it could affirm that it rests on the established fact of matter organizing itself, taking on life of itself."[67] In the same year, Pasteur again argued:

> If we also granted matter this other force we call life, life in all its many manifestations, varying as it does according to the conditions under which it is encountered, what would remain but to deify it? What could then be gained from recourse to the notion of an original creation, to whose mystery we must defer? What use the idea of a divine Creator?[68]

Roughly 180 years earlier, Ralph Cudsworth's massive *True Intellectual System of the Universe* made exactly the same point without feeling compelled to don scientific costume: "to assert . . . that all the effects of nature come to pass by material and mechanical necessity, or the mere fortuitous motion of matter, without any guidance or direction, is a thing no less irrational than it is impious and atheistical."[69] To preserve reason, which, for both Pasteur and Cudsworth, is much the same thing as preserving God, matter must be dependent, ultimately, on some divine or quasi-divine monopoly on a final creative power.

Cudsworth's late seventeenth-century contemporaries Antoni van Leeuwenhoek and Jan Swammerdam examined insects and other tiny life microscopically and came to similar conclusions.[70] In this little world, they discovered a richness of detail, which, each argued, could never have arisen spontaneously from rotting, filthy, or coagulating matter. Insect wings were a particular surprise. They surely worked within the old traditions inherited from Aristotle and Albert the Great in which the more perfect an animal, the more differentiated its parts, while "the more imperfect the form is, the less variety there will be in its matter."[71] Leeuwenhoek and Swammerdam must have been astonished to find such complexity and beauty in what they expected would be imperfect and undifferentiated. The defense of old ideas needed new thought, for, as Swammerdam observed, if such creatures could arise from filth, then other complex creatures—humans, in particular—could arise ultimately in just the same way. Some three hundred years later, Swammerdam had arrived at the same conclusion as Blaise of Parma, and then rejected it, and spontaneous generation, to save human particularity.

The campaign against spontaneous generation and the various incongruent, profane materialisms must therefore be understood as something other than that of a modern split from medieval habits. Likewise, the recent intensification of interest in nonhuman materialisms are not a sign of the return of fecund medieval materiality, not least of all because there is no one medieval attitude about matter. Caroline Walker Bynum observes, for example, that later fifteenth-century scholars were more likely to think of magnets as alive than did their thirteenth-century peers.[72] At the least, knowing how the war on spontaneous generation allies with the defense of human and divine supremacy explains why various early modern scientists defended the doctrine of bodily resurrection even as they dismantled the received natural history.[73]

The line cannot be between medieval and modern or superstition and science but rather between acceptances of material immanence and a faith in immaterial transcendence, and, by extension, a belief in clear lines between decisive agents and mere objects. Saint Augustine, Swammerdam, Pasteur, and their many inheritors all insist on transcendence, their own especially, continuing to enable, for example, the belief that some humans are more agential and some base, bestial, instinctual, deserving only mastery. To repurpose Cary Wolfe, who himself draws on Gayatri Spivak's critique of humanism, "We all, human and nonhuman alike, have a stake in the discourse and institution of speciesism" *and* anti-materialism, "because the discourse of speciesism [anti-materialism] . . . can be used to mark any social other" for mere use, domination, or violent regimes of control.[74]

Even or especially when insisting that others should not be treated like objects, anti-materialists more or less wittingly continue to draw a line around themselves and their God to call themselves subjects while declaring whatever remains outside an object. The border must be understood as grammatical, per Nietzsche's famous critique in *Twilight of the Idols* of "the metaphysics of language," which, he argues, persists in differentiating between a "doer and doing" and asserting some "will as the cause," or, more simply, classifying things into clear subjects and predicates, between a matter that needs something or some*one* to make it happen, and matter whose operations cannot be neatly sorted into effect and external cause, object and external subject. The end of Nietzsche's critique is well known: "I am afraid that we are not rid of God because we still have faith in grammar."[75]

Spontaneous generation is godless. It is ungrammatical, like generation itself if tracked back far enough. Darwin himself admitted this in a letter written not long before Pasteur was celebrating his victory over Pouchet where he recognized that life must be at its origin abiogenetic.[76] To put all this another way: at the very moment spontaneous generation was giving way to modern science, abiogenesis returned. Life has to be at its root something other than life. Nonlife, that impersonal but inherent generative principle, remains with it, so that the so-called spirit of life is matter's own restlessness. Spontaneous generation has never really gone away.

The differences between spontaneous generation and origin of life research of course should not be obscured or dashed past. I insist on the ungrammatical quality of what we call life even while accepting, as I must, the general narrative of the defeat of spontaneous generation.[77] Origin of life research provides hypotheses about the development of a paired genetic continuity *and* openness to adaptation across generations; it provides irreversible historical narratives, with key transitional points, of the long rise of DNA out of an RNA world; and it tends to insist that the time of abiogensis is long over. Life requires at least a combination of both genetic continuity *and* an openness to the environment that allows for adaptation, which is to say, life requires cross-generational genetic continuity *and* discontinuity. Spontaneous generation by contrast is discontinuous, as much a closed loop in its own way as pre-Darwinian assertions that like always produces like: filth produces flies, the flies die and return to filth, and so on. And unlike origin of life research, spontaneous generation may be inscrutable but it does not relegate its processes to the great temporal distances of the hundred-million-year rise of DNA out of RNA or to the great speed of chemical reactions occurring in a millionth of a second. Spontaneous generation happens right before us, though, of course, it does not *actually* happen, as we now know. Yet matter still swarms, in mundane, perhaps inevitable ways that require no transcendent divine catalyst, or any supposedly atheological equivalent, to get going.[78]

In abiogenesis and spontaneous generation, and the continued operations of RNA and DNA, matter does operate on itself to bring something new and surprising into being in ways that meet Jane Bennett's call "to dissipate the onto-theological binaries of life/matter, human/animal, will/determination, and organic/inorganic." The continued, somewhat embarrassed response to spontaneous generation in some scholarship evidences a need to cling to subject/object binaries and a host of related oppositions. It evidences, in other words, that this work has not yet gotten rid of God the Father. Furthermore, the very resistance to spontaneous generation as embarrassing, something suitable for the past but not the present, and concerned only with the filthiest, least significant kinds of life all suggest that spontaneous generation offers a resource and challenge both to the still developing work of the new materialists and to critical animal thinkers who continue to concentrate on the so-called higher animals.

At minimum, we should know how matter's life swarms from the earth, without the help of immaterial air, without waiting mysteriously and concealed before us. We should know how the swarms of earth crawl out, with us among them, a hungry and uncountable hoard, here, like us, only for a while, needing to be loved, if possible, for something other than our spirits.

Notes

1. Marius, *On the Elements,* ed. and trans. Richard C. Dales (Berkeley: University of California Press, 1976), 128–30.

2. Ibid., 76.

3. Ibid.

4. Bernard Silvestris, *Cosmographia,* trans. Winthrop Wetherbee (New York: Columbia University Press, 1973), 72. For an introduction to the movement of the elements and the problems the heaviness of earth created for accounting for the existence of any dry land, see Robert Bartlett, *The Natural and the Supernatural in the Middle Ages* (New York: Cambridge University Press, 2008), 39–50.

5. Marius, *Elements,* 86.

6. Ibid., 134.

7. Quoted from the important early critique of the affinities of Heidegger's philosophy with fascism in Ernst Bloch, *Heritage of Our Times,* trans. Neville and Stephen Plaice (Berkeley: University of California Press, 1990), 282.

8. Bruce V. Foltz, "On Heidegger and the Interpretation of Environmental Crisis," *Environmental Ethics* 6, no. 4 (1984): 335. See also Kate Rigby, "Earth, World, Text: On the (Im)possibility of Ecopoiesis," *New Literary History* 35, no. 3 (2004): 427–42.

9. "What Are Poets For?," in Martin Heidegger, *Poetry, Language, Thought,* trans. Albert Hofstadter (New York: Perennial Classics, 2001), 127.

10. Martin Heidegger, "The Principle of Ground," trans. Keith Hoeller, *Man and World* 7, no. 3 (1974): 219.

11. Martin Heidegger, "Question Concerning Technology," in Martin Heidegger, *The Question Concerning Technology, and Other Essays,* trans. William Levin (New York: Harper & Row, 1977), 27.

12. Relatedly, see the excellent discussion of the problems of the word *materiality* in Tim Ingold, "Materials against Materiality," *Archaeological Dialogues* 14, no. 1 (2007): 3–4.

13. Luce Irigaray, *The Forgetting of Air in Martin Heidegger,* trans. Mary Beth Mader (Austin: University of Texas Press, 1999), 8.

14. Ibid., 41.

15. Silvia Benso, "Psychē, Pneuma, and Air: Levinas and Anaximenes in Proximity," *Athena* 2 (2006): 16–27; Silvia Benso, "The Breathing of Air: Presocratic Echoes in Levinas," in *Levinas and the Ancients,* ed. Brian Schroeder and Silvia Benso (Bloomington: Indiana University Press, 2008), 9–23.

16. Irigaray, *Forgetting of Air,* 84.

17. Lucretius, *De rerum natura,* 1.345, quoted in Steve Mentz, "A Poetics of Nothing: Air in the Early Modern Imagination," *postmedieval* 4, no. 1 (Spring 2013): 39,

whose championing of air as the paradigmatic mobile element has much in common with Irigaray.

18. Conway Zirkle, "Animals Impregnated by the Wind," *Isis* 25, no. 1 (1936): 95–130.

19. All biblical translations are from the Douay-Rheims. Latin citations are from the Vulgate.

20. Caroline Walker Bynum, *Christian Materiality: An Essay on Religion in Late Medieval Europe* (Cambridge, Mass.: Zone Books, 2011), 238.

21. Ibid., 233.

22. Maaike van der Lugt, *Le ver, le démon et la Vierge: Les théories médiévales de la génération extraordinaire; Une étude sur les rapports entre théologie, philosophie naturelle et médecine* (Paris: Les Belles Lettres, 2004), the best study on spontaneous generation, has guided my discussion.

23. Aristotle, *Historia Animalium,* trans. D'Arcy Wentworth Thompson, vol. 4 of *The Works of Aristotle* (Oxford: Clarendon Press, 1910), V.19, 550a.

24. Albert the Great, *Questions Concerning Aristotle's "On Animals,"* trans. Irven Michael Resnick and Kenneth F. Kitchell Jr. (Washington, D.C.: Catholic University of America Press, 2008).

25. John Trevisa, *On the Properties of Things: John Trevisa's Translation of Bartholomaeus Anglicus' "De Proprietatibus Rerum,"* vol. 2, ed. M. C. Seymour (Oxford: Clarendon Press, 1975), translation mine. Original text reads: "A worme hatte *vermis* and is a beste þat ofte gendreþ of fleisse and of herbes and gendreþ ofte of caule, and somtyme of corrupcioun of humours, and somtyme of medlynge of male and femele, and somtyme of eyren, as it fareþ of scorpiouns, tortuses, and euetes." Citations appear parenthetically in the text and give book, chapter, and page number.

26. Basil of Caesarea, *Letters and Select Works,* trans. Blomfield Jackson, Select Library of Nicene and Post-Nicene Fathers of the Christian Church, Second Series, 8 (New York: Christian Literature Company, 1895), IX.2, 102.

27. Isidore of Seville, *The Etymologies,* trans. Stephen A. Barney et al. (New York: Cambridge University Press, 2007).

28. Saint Augustine, *The City of God,* trans. Marcus Dods (New York: Modern Library, 1950), XV.27, 518–19. Genesis includes two distinct accounts of God's command to fill the ark; 7:2, unlike 6:19, omits the command to gather "omni reptili" (all creeping things).

29. Daniel A. Bertrand, "Le Christ comme ver: À propos du Psaume 22(21),7," in *Le Psautier chez les Pères* (Strasbourg: Centre d'Analyse et de Documentation Patristiques, 1994), 221–34; Enrica Ruaro, "God and the Worm: The Twofold Otherness in Pseudo-Dionysius's Theory of Dissimilar Images," *American Catholic Philosophical Quarterly* 82, no. 4 (2008): 581–92.

30. Jacques Paul Migne, ed., *Patrilogiae Cursus Completus: Series Latina* (Paris, 1844), 36:168, translation mine. Original text reads: "*ego autem sum vermis, et non*

homo: ego autem jam non ex persona Adam loquens, sed ego proprie Jesus Christus sine semine in carne natus sum, ut essem in homine ultra homines."

31. Robert Grosseteste, *On the Six Days of Creation,* trans. C. F. J. Martin (New York: Oxford University Press, 1996), 195.

32. van der Lugt, *Le ver, le démon et la Vierge,* 137.

33. Helen Rodnite Lemay, trans., *Women's Secrets: A Translation of Pseudo-Albertus Magnus's De Secretis Mulierum with Commentaries* (Albany: State University of New York Press, 1992), 98.

34. Albert the Great, *Questions Concerning Aristotle's "On Animals,"* 528–29.

35. Eckhard Kessler, "The Intellective Soul," in *The Cambridge History of Renaissance Philosophy,* ed. Charles B. Schmitt and Quentin Skinner (New York: Cambridge University Press, 1988), 487.

36. For more on Blaise of Parma, see van der Lugt, *Le ver, le démon et la Vierge,* 176–81.

37. Saint Augustine, *The Literal Meaning of Genesis,* vol. 1, Ancient Christian Writers 41, trans. John Hammond Taylor (New York: Newman Press, 1982), 90.

38. For one connection to Mary Douglas, see Mary Fissell, "Imagining Vermin in Early Modern England," *History Workshop Journal* 47 (Spring 1999): 22; for the latter term, see Edward J. Geisweidt, "'The Nobleness of Life': Spontaneous Generation and Excremental Life in Antony and Cleopatra," in *Ecocritical Shakespeare,* ed. Lynne Dickson Bruckner and Daniel Brayton (Surrey: Ashgate, 2011), 89–103.

39. For the *Bible historiale*'s general illustration patterns in its 150 extant copies, see Eléonore Fournié, *L'iconographie de la Bible historiale* (Turnhout: Brepols, 2012). For more on illustrations of creation, see Johannes Zahlten, *Creatio mundi: Darstellungen der sechs Schöpfungstage und naturwissenschaftliches Weltbild im Mittelalter* (Stuttgart: Klett-Cotta, 1979). I thank Aden Kumler and Ittai Weinryb for their expert art historical assistance.

40. See Zahlten, *Creatio mundi,* plates 15–20.

41. Michel Quereuil, ed., *La Bible française du XIIIe siècle: Éd. crit. de la Genèse* (Geneva: Droz, 1988), 98–100, translation mine.

42. Saint Augustine, "On the Holy Trinity," in *On the Holy Trinity, Doctrinal Treatises, Moral Treatises,* Select Library of the Nicene and Post-Nicene Fathers of the Christian Church, First Series, 3, trans. Arthur West Haddan and W. G. T. Shedd (Buffalo: Christian Literature Company, 1887), III.8.13, 60.

43. Susan Crane, *Animal Encounters: Contacts and Concepts in Medieval Britain* (Philadelphia: University of Pennsylvania Press, 2013); Jeffrey Jerome Cohen, *Medieval Identity Machines* (Minneapolis: University of Minnesota Press, 2003).

44. Karl Steel, *How to Make a Human: Animals and Violence in the Middle Ages* (Columbus: Ohio State University Press, 2011).

45. Lisa Jean Moore and Mary Kosut, *Buzz: Urban Beekeeping and the Power of the Bee* (New York: New York University Press, 2013).

46. For example, see Hilda M. Ransome, *The Sacred Bee in Ancient Times and Folklore* (Mineola, N.Y.: Dover, 2004), 215.

47. Jean Préaux, "De Culex de Virgile à son pastiche par Thierry de Saint-Trond," in *Présence de Virgile, actes du colloques des 9, 11 et 12 Décembre 1976,* ed. Raymond Chevalier (Paris: Les Belles Lettres, 1978), 195–208.

48. Fissell, "Imagining Vermin," 9.

49. Gervase of Tilbury, *Otia Imperialia: Recreation for an Emperor,* ed. and trans. S. E. Banks and J. W. Binns (Oxford: Clarendon Press, 2002).

50. Gerald of Wales, *The Journey through Wales; and, The Description of Wales,* trans. Lewis Thorpe (Harmondsworth, N.Y.: Penguin, 1978).

51. Emmanuel Levinas, "The Paradox of Morality," in *The Provocation of Levinas: Rethinking the Other,* ed. Robert Bernasconi and David Wood, trans. Andrew Benjamin and Tamra Wright (New York: Routledge, 1988), 171–72.

52. Kelsi Nagy and Phillip David Johnson II, eds., *Trash Animals: How We Live with Nature's Filthy, Feral, Invasive, and Unwanted Species* (Minneapolis: University of Minnesota Press, 2013), in a practical, unphilosophical way, begins to rectify this omission.

53. For this idea, see several points in Michel Serres, *The Parasite,* trans. Lawrence R. Schehr (Minneapolis: University of Minnesota Press, 2007), for example, "man is the universal parasite . . . plants and animals are always his hosts; man is always necessarily their guest. Always taking, never giving" (24).

54. See, for example, Valerie Allen, "Mineral Virtue," in *Animal, Vegetable, Mineral: Ethics and Objects,* ed. Jeffrey Jerome Cohen (Washington, D.C.: Oliphaunt Books, 2012), 130, and, in the same volume, Kellie Robertson, "Exemplary Rocks," 94–95 and 98; see also, at greater length, Jeffrey Jerome Cohen, *Stories of Stone: An Ecology of the Inhuman* (Minneapolis: University of Minnesota Press, 2015).

55. Thomas Aquinas, *Summa Theologica,* trans. Fathers of the English Dominican Province (New York: Benziger Bros., 1947), Ia.27.2.

56. Isidore of Seville, *Etymologies,* IX.5.4, 206.

57. Basil of Caesarea, *Letters and Select Works,* IX.2, 102.

58. For one discussion that inspired me, see Bill Benzon, "Culture Memes Information WTF!," *New Savanna,* June 14, 2013, http://new-savanna.blogspot.com.

59. For a monumental critique of the distinction between life itself and the living, see Eugene Thacker, *After Life* (Chicago: University of Chicago Press, 2010).

60. Jane Bennett, *Vibrant Matter: A Political Ecology of Things* (Durham, N.C.: Duke University Press, 2010), xiii.

61. Slavoj Žižek, *Less Than Nothing: Hegel and the Shadow of Dialectical Materialism* (London: Verso, 2012), 938.

62. Ben Woodard, *Slime Dynamics: Generation, Mutation, and the Creep of Life* (Winchester, UK: Zero Books, 2012), 59.

63. For one version of this point, see Ian MacInnes, "The Politic Worm: Invertebrate Life in the Early Modern English Body," in *The Indistinct Human in*

Renaissance Literature, ed. Jean E. Feerick and Vincent Joseph Nardizzi (New York: Palgrave Macmillan, 2012), 259.

64. Cited in Geisweidt, "'The Nobleness of Life,'" 98.

65. John Farley, *The Spontaneous Generation Controversy from Descartes to Oparin* (Baltimore: Johns Hopkins University Press, 1977); Nils Roll-Hansen, "The Death of Spontaneous Generation and the Birth of the Gene: Two Case Studies of Relativism," *Social Studies of Science* 13, no. 4 (1983): 481–519.

66. See especially Bruno Latour, *The Pasteurization of France,* trans. Alan Sheridan and John Law (Cambridge, Mass.: Harvard University Press, 1988).

67. Quoted in John Farley and Gerald L. Gieson, "Science, Politics and Spontaneous Generation in Nineteenth-Century France: The Pasteur-Pouchet Debate," *Bulletin of the History of Medicine* 48, no. 2 (1974): 197.

68. Louis Pasteur, "On Spontaneous Generation" (speech, April 7, 1864), trans. Alex Levine, rpr. in *Revue des cours scientifics* 1 (April 23, 1864): 257–64, http://www.rc.usf.edu/~levineat/pasteur.pdf.

69. Ralph Cudworth, *The Works of Ralph Cudworth, Containing The True Intellectual System of the Universe, Sermons, &c,* 4 vols., ed. Thomas Birch (Oxford: D. A. Talboys, 1829), 1:317–18.

70. Edward G. Ruestow, "Leeuwenhoek and the Campaign against Spontaneous Generation," *Journal of the History of Biology* 17, no. 2 (1984): 225–48. Henry Harris, *Things Come to Life: Spontaneous Generation Revisited* (Oxford: Oxford University Press, 2002), 22, quotes Leeuwenhoek, arguing that everything, "however small it may be," depends upon the first Creation.

71. Albert the Great, *Questions Concerning Aristotle's "On Animals,"* 110.

72. Bynum, *Christian Materiality,* 262. For more, see Kellie Robertson, "Medieval Materialism: A Manifesto," *Exemplaria* 22, no. 2 (2010): 99–118.

73. See, for example, the embarrassment in Harris, *Things Come to Life,* 22 and 25, over Francesco Redi's and Antonio Vallisnieri's Roman Catholicism.

74. Cary Wolfe, *Animal Rites: American Culture, the Discourse of Species, and Posthumanist Theory* (Chicago: University of Chicago Press, 2003), 7.

75. Friedrich Wilhelm Nietzsche, *The Anti-Christ, Ecce Homo, Twilight of the Idols, and Other Writings,* trans. Aaron Ridley and Judith Norman (New York: Cambridge University Press, 2005), 169–70.

76. Juli Pereto, Jeffrey L. Bada, and Antonio Lazcano, "Charles Darwin and the Origin of Life," *Origins of Life and Evolution of the Biosphere* 39, no. 5 (2009): 395–406.

77. The following account is indebted to Antonio Lazcano, "What Is Life? A Brief Historical Overview," *Chemistry & Biodiversity* 5, no. 1 (2008): 1–15; David Penny, "An Interpretive Review of the Origin of Life Research," *Biology and Philosophy* 20, no. 4 (2005): 633–71; Florence Raulin-Cerceau, "Historical Review of the Origin of Life and Astrobiology," in *Origins: Genesis, Evolution and Diversity of Life,* ed. Joseph Seckbach (Dordrecht: Kluwer Academic, 2004), 15–33; and Joachim Schummer,

"The Creation of Life in Cultural Context: From Spontaneous Generation to Synthetic Biology," in *The Ethics of Protocells: Moral and Social Implications of Creating Life in the Laboratory,* ed. Mark Bedau and Emily C. Parke (Cambridge, Mass.: MIT Press, 2009), 125–42.

78. For a recent treatment of life's inevitability, with an implicit challenge to the organic/inorganic division, see Natalie Wolchover, "A New Physics Theory of Life," *Quanta Magazine,* January 22, 2014.

nine

Earth's Prospects

LOWELL DUCKERT

Carbon and oxygen me, gold, silver and metal me, even rare earth. The value of someone, that is to say his health, is measured by the number and quality of his valences.

—MICHEL SERRES, *Biogea*

For the earth is "earthing."

—TIM INGOLD, *Being Alive*

Welcome to paradise. Gaze upon vast swamp forests, breathe in some of the highest levels of oxygen the earth has ever known, and observe evolution's first reptiles. Or should I say welcome to paradise *lost?* The prospect you now have in your mind is a view of a lost world: the earth at the peak of the Carboniferous Period 359 to 299 million years ago. This is a time when towering trees known as lepidodendrons dominated an entirely tropical world. Once they sank into the mud where they were deprived of oxygen, the plants hardened into the carbon seams we now call coal. *Carboniferous,* in fact, derives from the Latin meaning "coal bearing." Or should I say this is paradise *regained?* The swamp is not really lost because it continues to bear coal, the world's primary source of electricity, and one of the most debated pieces of earth on earth. For some, coal is unbearable: as the main contributor to climate disruption in the United States, burning it releases sulfur dioxide (SO_2), ozone (NO_x), and mercury—proven sources of acid rain, asthma, and a slew of other health hazards—that cause nearly thirteen thousand premature deaths a year.[1] Digging coal is not any better;

three different mining explosions occurred in West Virginia alone in the first decade of the twenty-first century, one of which killed twenty-nine in the Upper Big Branch Mine of Montcoal in 2010. For others, however, coal is more than bearable: supposedly inexhaustible, and getting "cleaner," coal in America represents economic independence; sourced locally, it powers national industry that outstrips the coal mines of India and China. As a result, coal becomes less of an environmental burden and more of a substance that humans burn to keep their energy going. Even the word *mine* signals both possession and a place. It is easy to find images of human domination over this fuel underfoot: Spike TV's program *Coal,* with its phallic spike-drill, is the epitome of uber- (or unter-) masculinity. All in all, if "thinking takes place in the relationship of territory and the earth,"[2] as Gilles Deleuze and Félix Guattari claim, then we need to think more about coal and our propensity to territorialize.[3] Seen as *either* a symbol of modernity's forward progress *or,* in the sociologist Rebecca R. Scott's words, "a . . . heart of darkness within the heart of modernity," coal *either* profits the blue collar *or* it plagues the green one.[4] Paradise is paved *or* it is preserved. Appalachia is an unfortunate case in point: depending on whom you ask, it is either a culturally valuable place *or* a commodified space.[5] How much more can the earth really bear, though—not just in terms of its coal supply but also of this debate that pits the human miner against the mined earth, Friends of Coal versus Friends of the Mountains?[6]

Earth/l/ings

I will not pretend to solve the energy crisis and get us off of coal by the end of this essay. Instead, I want us to think about *thinking* with the earth. Not merely to think about energy alternatives but of alternative *views* of energy, of coal, that undermine the antagonistic split between human and environment. "A view," according to the anthropologist Tim Ingold, "that grounds human beings within the continuum of life, and that situates the history of their embodied skills within the unfolding of that continuum."[7] For Ingold, participation within material mediums is the condition for our interactions. Thus coal, like the elements, never acts alone: in fact, its name comes from the Old English word *col* meaning "glowing ember" and "charred remnant."

Coal describes a relational process of shared energy and agency (a "glow") that leaves traces behind ("remnants") for us to follow. Coal is a reminder of our ongoing shaping of and being shaped by the earth, of living within the world rather than upon its outer surface. Ingold subverts the opposite viewpoint, "the groundlessness of modern society," by pointing out the historical (and thereby reversible) shift from the feet to the head as the center of reason and authority.[8] We have never been (solely) cerebral, it seems, but we have been good "exhabitants" by promoting "head over heels" as the right way to dwell.[9] While "exhabitants" agonize over how to understand an objectified earth, a proper inhabitant acknowledges that there is no separation of knowing from being, heads from heels, and that our coexistence with the earth may be felt through the grounded "continuum of life" at our feet. Such a reorientation actually disorients previous ways of meaning making. Look down as well as directly ahead, Ingold entreats: "the earth is 'earthing.'"[10] Earthing frees us to be better inhabitants, to be true earthlings.[11] The ways we narrate stories, and the stories themselves, can shape the earth/s to come.

So here is a deep *thought:* what is coal coaling? For one, I am able to write "Earth's Prospects" because of electricity generated by the Grant Town Power Plant located a little under twenty miles southwest of Morgantown. The plant, operated by Edison Mission Energy, purchases coal from companies that practice mountaintop removal strip mining (more on this devastating process below), and I purchase electricity from Monongahela Power, owned by Allegheny Energy Incorporated, which distributes Edison's product.[12] A coal-powered plant, Morgantown Energy Facility, is less than a mile away from my office. Farther away, West Virginia Senator Joe Manchin, who has felt increasing pressure from citizens to account for the catastrophic effects of mining in his state, postponed talks in September 2013 on "the future of coal" and traveled to Washington, D.C., to discuss possible American air strikes in the Syrian civil war. This local-global conflict of interest is significant, I think, since President Barack Obama's Climate Action Plan of June 2013—meant to "develop homegrown energy and steady, responsible steps to cut carbon pollution"[13]—has intensified another civil war, the so-called War on Coal. Both sides of this battle are embattled by his proposals: an expansion of natural gas drilling (hydraulic fracturing, or "hydrofracking"), for example, angers coal opponents for simply creating another dirty problem and at the same time aggravates coal supporters for taking away coal jobs.[14] Oftentimes these disputes uncomfortably unearth coal's racial connotations as well. Scott traces how specific privileges like land ownership police an idealized form of whiteness, ensuring that those who do not meet the society's overdetermined standards are labeled as "white trash." Noble suffering in the coalfields (is there ever such a thing?) is far from archetypal white citizenship; instead, (mistreated) miners represent "the specter of failed whiteness" haunting, but ultimately underpinning, "white" hegemony.[15] Yet poor whites are not the only subjects of racism: although West Virginia seceded from Virginia in the middle of the American Civil War in 1863, its historical "heart of darkness"—the spirit of its Confederate past—has not entirely vanished.[16] Whether "white" or "black" bodies, coal makes civil hands unclean. To be sure, this "War on Coal" has repercussions that not only ravage workers but also the earth itself. Here the earth is not just a site for *human* labor; it is a (suffering) third participant in the struggle. Non/human communities are divided by coal, hurled into (ineffective) political arenas that cannot bring nature into politics no matter how hard they try,[17] split between the earth's interests and their families'. Wars at home wait for wars abroad. Political ecology, to borrow a kingly phrase, is "dead as earth."[18]

I wish to extend my earthy thought process further through an unlikely alliance: John Milton's *Paradise Lost* (1667/74). In response to these coal wars, this seventeenth-century poet too familiar with civil war might have said: "And of thir vain contést appear'd no end" (9.1189).[19] Taking a cue from Alfred Kentigern Siewers, my elemental predecessor in the "Ecomaterialism" issue of *postmedieval,* I am going to "wander" within the hills of Hell and Paradise in the poem, hills "hinting of post-human futures interweaving categories of human and non-human on earth."[20] Combining the geophysical with the temporal qualities of earth under the keyword *prospect,* Milton's mountains bear visions of things to come over the terrestrial yonder: "ribs of Gold . . . the precious bane" of Hell or "fruits Joy and eternal Bliss" of Heaven (1.690, 692; 12.551). As coal industries literally remove the horizons of the Appalachian Mountains every day, destroying nearly five hundred mountains and 1.2 million acres of temperate deciduous forest to date, not to mention polluting or utterly burying two thousand miles of streams, and threatening one of the nation's richest levels of biodiversity in one of the oldest mountain ranges on earth,[21] this epic's earth helps us think about what we may gain as well as what we have lost.

The Argument: Many Prospects

Allow me a quick etymological lesson before we ascend these hills. In modern usage, the verb *prospect* almost exclusively conjures up images of mining and metals. The first reference to mining in any capacity did not occur until 1709: "An area considered likely to yield a mineral deposit that could be suitable for commercial exploitation."[22] Reading the *prospect* in *Paradise Lost* for its mining and visual implications might suggest, then, the sin of anachronism. The *prospect* in Milton's time was more multivalent than it is now, however. Etymologically combining both the root *pro-* ("forward") and *specere* ("to look"), *prospect* derives from the Latin *prospectare,* "to afford a view of, look out on, to look out for, to watch," and *prospicere,* "to look forward." Early modern writers like Milton had two basic meanings of the *prospect* available to them: (1) a phenomenological concept of facing forward, involving the physical senses, from 1475; and (2) a temporal term of futurity and anticipation from 1528, such as "looking forward" to something. As a noun, the *prospect* simply could be that which faces forward, the relative senses of such, or the view itself. Crucially, *prospect* also denotes an action beginning around 1555—*to* face forward, *to* situate. To sum up with an ecological example: the *prospect* could be a view that faces a mountain, a consideration of something in the future to be gained from viewing it, and the action of facing it. All aspects of *prospect* are highly visual; *a prospect* is *a* look and *to prospect* is *to* look forward across space and time—high and low, past and future—and sometimes all at once. I will not so much argue that Milton uses *prospect* in ways that anticipate its modern use—although he was almost certainly thinking about mining when thinking about prospects—nor will I simply trace the occurrences of the term in the poem to underscore its specific meanings in certain contexts. I believe that the broader idea of "prospecting" allowed Milton to see the environmental degradations of his time better, and, consequently, to envision better futures.[23]

But let us look forward to my argument about the prospects of bearing coal before I bury you with any more etymology. First, I will read *Paradise Lost*'s prospects alongside early modern attitudes to coal. John Rogers places Milton at the vanguard of the "Vitalist Movement," an exciting (and contentious) moment in mid-seventeenth-century England when "energy or spirit, no longer immaterial, [was] seen as immanent within bodily matter, and even nonorganic matter . . . [was] thought to contain within it the agents of motion and change."[24] Milton's vitalist environmentalism, while groundbreaking, is ultimately teleo-theological: the future always faces the Last Judgment, the end-time when the coal clouds finally disappear. Second, I will examine how this one-track mode of prospecting persists today. Coal companies rifle the earth, hoping to face future profits without end. Capitalistic surplus value replaces eschatology. To help illustrate this prospective continuity, I will turn to the coalfields of West Virginia, a state I have recently begun to call home. Third, I will depart from my Miltonic vistas. Picking up on the valences of the multivalent term *prospect* I just described, and digging Deleuze and Guattari's phrase "lines of flight,"[25] I will travel via "mines of flight." Mines of flight advance many futures over a future, immanence over transcendence, openings over terminations. In choosing earths over earth, futures over a future, I echo Bruno Latour's compositionist call: "What makes the times we are living in so interesting . . . is that we are progressively discovering that, just at the time when people are despairing at realizing that they might, in the end, have 'no future,' we suddenly have many prospects."[26] My project is avowedly presentist; but in "making the geologic now," this chapter imagines the geologic *to be* as well.[27] These are hard times and hard places as the war/s above make clear, moments when the end times truly seem near and no future (not even *a* future) is possible; it is for this reason that we must reconceive (or "recompose") the sides of the debate. The only "end" to mines of flight is the *end* of the human's entrenched position as autonomous earthling. Thus the excavation I undertake below is more than just literary:[28] my hope is that the *non/human* history of coal I tell here initiates open-ended becomings that pacify the "vain contést" with which I began. I will offer a prospect that imagines futures with coal rather than without it, futures that mutually enrich the lives of humans and nonhumans together.

"Darkness Visible": How Milton Mines

If you drive along the roads that wend through the Appalachian coalfields long enough—or if you happen to be near the town of Surveyor, West Virginia—you might see a billboard with plain white letters on a black background: "Stop destroying my mountains," it reads. "—God." Would Milton have agreed with this lost commandment? He could have easily cited Genesis 1:26's decree for man to "haue dominion . . . ouer all the earth,"[29] mountains included. Ecocritical Miltonists have argued that his works promote the restoration of Eden on earth through a georgic mode of stewardship; as Ken Hiltner notes, "Milton did not believe . . . that the world was in a state of irretrievable decay as a result of the Fall; rather, he held out hope for a regenerative era here on earth." The "hope that England could be fashioned into a new Eden," however, was a high one.[30] Such eco-consciousness did not come out of thin air, but out of thick kinds. Milton wrote his epic poem during various ecological crises of mid-seventeenth-century London, one of the worst being the city's pernicious air pollution. Coal burning became common in England centuries before; arguably the first coal scuffle in recorded history occurred between merchants and clergy at Newcastle-upon-Tyne in 1268. The air was already bad enough in London in 1285 that Edward I banned coal's use.[31] His attempts at regulation were not quite the Clean Air Act he had wished for, regrettably. By the early modern period the coal problem was only exacerbated by wood shortages across the country; coal burning surged in the 1570s, and by the death of Elizabeth I coal had become the nation's primary fuel. Despite its necessity, coal continued to be associated with disease, death, and the devil: because victims of the Black Death could be identified by dark swellings of the lymph nodes, these spots were known as *carbuncles,* a word that comes from the Latin *carbunculus,* "small coal" or "charcoal." (In fact, *anthrax,* a modern-day worry, is from the Greek word of the same spelling and means "coal.")

The harmful convergences of bodies and coal—whether in the shape of "sea coal" (retrieved underground) or charcoal—did not go unnoticed, though. In 1661, only six years before *Paradise Lost* was published, John Evelyn wrote *Fumifugium,* a deplorable report of London's air quality: "How easily the strong heavy charcoal fumes penetrate the brain," the title page proclaims.[32] "Black and smutty Atomes" invade everything so that "the City of London resembles . . . the Suburbs of Hell."[33] Evelyn cannily understands the infectious quality of coal and how it plagues bodily humors: "it visits and attaques, through . . . subtile and curious passages."[34] In a particularly gloomy passage, he describes the city of London as a grimy chimney:

> Let it be considered what a Fuliginous crust is yearly contracted, and adheres to the Sides of our ordinary Chymnies where this grosse Fuell is used; and then imagine, if there were a solid . . . Canopy over *London,* what a masse of *Soote* would then stick to it, which now (as was said) comes down every Night in the *Streets,* on our *Houses,* the *Waters,* and is taken into our *Bodies.*[35]

In a movement upward from the domestic ("Chymnies"), to the civic ("Canopy"), and even to the global ("Waters"), the human respiratory system follows suit: coal particles adhere to the "Sides" of the lungs, while the "masse of *Soote*" moves upward to the brain. Macro- and microcosm fall prey to the rain (or reign) of coal as it "comes down." Bottom-up becomes top-down in this "Fuliginous" feedback loop. Although it addresses the "inconveniencie of the aer and smoak of London,"[36] Evelyn's complaint concerns the larger embroilments of eco-cosmopolitanism—unprotected networks of "*Waters,*" "*Streets,*" "*Houses,*" and "*Bodies*"—that we know too well today, the "inconveniencie" of our coal-hardened truths.

Other writers were much more apologetic, and, in ways that are (unsettlingly) similar to contemporary practice, they cited economic reasons in order to quash any concerns for environmental health.[37] The go-to mining manual at the time, Georgius Agricola's *De Re Metallica* (1556), systematically refuted popular arguments against mining to argue that "of all ways whereby great wealth is acquired by good and honest means, none is more advantageous than mining."[38] Never mind that the land is literally peeled away in the process, for mining is morally productive as well: "who can fail to realize that mining is a calling of peculiar dignity?" he asks, adding that "the gain derived from mining is not sordid, for how can it be such, seeing that it is so great, so plentiful, and so innocent a nature?"[39] In response to complaints about injuring the landscape, Agricola answers that mining is done in unpopulated areas anyway, "exclusively in mountains otherwise unproductive, and in valleys invested in gloom."[40] Saying this would seem to support Marjorie Hope Nicolson's argument that, until the end of the seventeenth century, mountains were considered to be wild places in the European imagination, wastelands of "Mountain Gloom" devoid of aesthetic value, or, as she calls it, "Mountain Glory."[41] Freed from obligation, digging affords Agricola a "peculiar" dig-nity, a moral high ground sponsored by going underground. In reality, it is not so "innocent" a practice, of course; even he must be careful to keep the miner's body safe from venomous ants, cold water, stagnant air, corrosive dusts that eat away at miners' feet and implant "consumption" in the lungs, cave-ins, and even "demons of ferocious aspect."[42] All of these occurrences "rarely happen"; but when they do, they can be blamed on the careless worker. Safety, therefore, is first: "we should always devote more care to maintaining our health," Agricola mandates, "that we may freely perform our bodily functions, than to making profits."[43] And yet, then as now, the correlation between health and profit is skewed;[44] life expectancies are shortened by up to five years around mountaintop removal sites in Appalachia.[45] "Sometimes their lungs rot away."[46] The same could be said of victims of coal worker's pneumoconiosis: black lung disease, an affliction currently in resurgence.[47] With continued exposure to coal dust, lungs literally become coal.

Thus George Sandys could mention those "men [who] through the wounded Earth inforce their way; /And shew the under Shades an unknowne Day" in his *Paraphrase vpon Iob* (1638).[48] For a poet like Milton more invested in spiritual gains than fiscal ones, the mining debates usefully took on a theological tenor. Thomas Bushell (1659) claimed that coal mining could be "for the glory of the Nation" and God at once: "I conceive all Mines were created for Mans use, and Gods glory, but in what Age to be revealed, or by whom, is only known to the Searcher of all hearts, who can best judge of mine, and my designed ends."[49] But Bushell *does* have an ostensible "end": putting condemned men to work in his own country's mines rather than be "banish'd to Slavery in Foreign parts."[50] Spiritual and material redemption enfold: "The *Lost,* are drowned and desperately deserted Mineral Works; the *Dead,* convicted and attainted persons, who are indeed so in Law; and what is lost, is not in nature as to the use and proprietie of mankind."[51] Lost souls, lost mines: to bring them both back into "use," Bushell has some soul mining to do. He beckons those that are spiritually lost "to take [a] Mineral calling upon you, and to think, speak, and deport yourselves towards God in it."[52] Going down becomes a way of going up; not only does he include manners of draining "drowned" mines, but he also includes "The Miners contemplative Prayer" for workers who need to beat the gloomy feeling of being "desperately deserted" in life.[53] If Christ descended into Hell before ascending into Heaven, he argues, "who knows . . . but that this Mineral imployment is the best way found out for us Mortals"?[54] The "Prayer" was also meant to protect Christian miners from mischievous underground spirits, a widespread belief at the time (as cited by Agricola). For Bushell, however, these "multitudes of Evil Spirits in the Aery region, as also in the Waters, and the hollow Concaverns of the Earth" are more aggressive. Like the demons Christ cast out of the "Demoniack" into a herd of swine, "God hath permitted their temporal habitations therein, partly for mens trial . . . and partly for the punishment of the wicked."[55] By the eve of the Restoration, mining could put a miner's bodily, spiritual, and mineral prospects to the test.

Into this mineral madness—of fighting off "black . . . Atomes," of retrieving mines and men, and of reaping economic rewards—Milton found himself thrown. It seems only appropriate, then, that the poet draws upon Bushell's beliefs when he begins Book 1 of *Paradise Lost.* Where did the "Evil Spirits" of the caves come from? For Bushell, the answer is easy: "These were created in the beginning," and, along with Lucifer, fell "as Lightning fall from Heaven. What need I say more?"[56] Indeed. *Welcome to Hell:*

> . . . he [Satan] views
> The dismal Situation waste and wild,
> A Dungeon horrible, on all sides round

As one great Furnace flam'd, yet from those flames
No light, but rather darkness visible. (1.59–63)

When we first meet him, Satan has poor prospects; his "views" (what he sees) include his surroundings as well as his future (what he envisions). But Satan has a plan to brighten his "dismal" prospects; after he rouses his troops by assuring them that "space may produce new Worlds" (1.650), they dig for valuables. The hill of Hell, my first vantage point, falls victim to their mineral colonization:

There stood a Hill not far whose grisly top
Belch'd fire and rolling smoke; the rest entire
Shone with a glossy scurf, undoubted sign
That in his womb was hid metallic Ore,
The work of Sulphur. (1.670–74)

Milton might have known how to read the "undoubted sign" by reading mining texts like Gabriel Plattes's with its "plaine Directions and Rules for the finding of . . . *Gold* to the *Coale*."[57] The "grisly" nature of the hill gives it away. The paradox, Plattes explains, is that the most barren "Rocky and Craggy Mountaynes" actually prove the most bountiful: "For the more barren they are; the greater probability there is that they containe rich Mines and Minerals."[58] The venting ("belched") top and shiny ("glossy") surface indicate the balmy earthy exhalations that were believed to be responsible for mountains' (and their minerals') formation: "caused by the vapours of Bituminous and Sulphurious substances kindled in the bowells of the Earth . . . the veines of Mettalls are engendred in the crackes and crannies of the said Mountaines."[59] Egged on by these sure signs of success, the demons (or miners) work the "scurf":

. . . by [Mammon] first
Men also, and by his suggestion taught,
Ransack'd the Center, and with impious hands
Rifl'd the bowels of thir mother Earth
For Treasures better hid. Soon had his crew

Op'n'd into the Hill a spacious wound
And digg'd out ribs of Gold. Let none admire
That riches grow in Hell; that soil may best
Deserve the precious bane. (1.684–92)

Though Milton invokes Ovid's widespread myth of the Golden Age, in which the desire for gold sponsors the earth's first "spacious wound"—mining—and actually ends the age, he is also reacting to his own mineral moment.[60] The "grisly top" is typically seen as an allusion to New World gold mining, the "new worlds" that seventeenth-century space produced and that men exploited. Milton's tone is admonitory, and the lines about "impious hands" have come to represent his environmental ethics. According to Hiltner, "feeling the wound may offer the best chance at healing our shared loss with the Earth."[61] Only lacerations are left after the earth is "ransacked." Milton returns to the wound in Book 9. When Eve eats the forbidden fruit, he writes that "Earth felt the wound, and Nature from her seat / Sighing through all her Works gave signs of woe, / That all was lost" (9.782–84). The stolen ribs of gold foreshadow the later transgression of that other rib-taker, Eve, who guarantees that the prelapsarian "wound" becomes an irreparable tear separating nature from mankind for all eternity.[62]

But there is other earthy matter at "work" here besides gold. The "darkness visible" Satan senses is not just the lightless fires of hell but the coal fumes of London. "The work of Sulphur" is the work of a coal furnace, true fire and brimstone spouting from a "grisly top" ("Chymnies"), since coal vents a sulfurous smell when burned. Mammon, leader of the "impious" crew, is not necessarily the god of gold but of riches in general. Coal made (and still makes) money, and "precious bane" is exactly how many see coal today (as dirty, but necessary, energy). This black rock *makes things invisible.* Even Pandemonium, the gilded palace of sin, is immediately "*Soote*"-d. Though Belial believes that "our purer essence . . . will overcome / [the] noxious vapor" (2.215–16), Satan cannot stand the smoke: "Is this the Region, this the Soil, the Clime," he says, "That we must change for Heav'n, this mournful gloom / For that celestial light?" (1.241, 44–45). Early modern Londoners might have asked the same question as they huddled around their sooty home fires, forgotten—or coal camp "trash," thrust into tiny tarpaper shacks, forsaken. Paraphrasing Sandys: "But where above the Earth, or under ground, / Can Wisedome by the search of Man be found?"[63] *Seeing* sulfurous prospects on the horizon. Wondering whether the "mournful gloom" of environmental degradation would break. Thinking about how to move forward, through the coal clouds, toward their celestial sun-"light."

"In Clearest Ken": How Milton Ends

Or they might follow Milton a little further—ten books, to be exact—"and by *his* suggestion taught" make their way heavenward through the haze. *Welcome to Paradise,* my second vantage point, the hill in Eden upon which Satan alights in Book 4 and gains "a happy rural seat of various view" (4.247). The archangel Michael takes Adam up the hill in Book 11, introducing us to Milton's multivalent "prospect":

> So both ascend
> In the Visions of God: It was a Hill
> Of Paradise the highest, from whose top
> The Hemisphere of Earth in clearest Ken
> Stretcht out to the amplest reach of prospect lay.
> Not higher that Hill nor wider looking round,
> Whereon for different cause the Tempter set
> Our second *Adam* in the Wilderness,
> To show him all Earth's Kingdoms and thir Glory. (11.376–84)

The "prospect" here means "a view"—the mountaintop and everything one can see in "clearest Ken"—and it is also a view of the future. Michael has not brought Adam here to show him what he has lost but to show him what will be won by "our second Adam," Christ. The geo- and the temporal merge at this "prospect"; as the earth goes into flash forward, scenes from biblical history begin to "stretch out" before Adam in chronological order. He seems worried by Michael's View-Master effect at times. After witnessing Noah's Flood, for example, he asks his celestial guide "whether here the Race of man will end" (11.786). Michael sketches the Promised Land, a new heaven on earth, to assuage his fears: "each place behold," the archangel instructs, "in prospect, as I point them" (12.142–3). But we cannot stay here. Not surprisingly, Michael's narration ends with the Last Judgment. Christ will come, he says,

> . . . to dissolve
> *Satan* with his perverted World, then raise
> From the conflagrant mass, purg'd and refin'd,
> New Heav'ns, new Earth, Ages of endless date
> Founded in righteousness and peace and love,
> To bring forth fruits Joy and eternal Bliss. (12.546–51)

Christ will raise "new Earth" to replace the wounded earth Pandemonium had previously raised, not to mention the mountains that both demons *and* angels destroyed during the War in Heaven. Raphael had previously told him of how "Hills amid the Air encounter'd Hills / Hurl'd to and fro with jaculation dire" (6.664–65). Michael wants Adam to be cheered by this "meditation on the happy end" (12.605). But how "happy" is this eschatological "end"? While Adam has a panoramic prospect on the hill, he is nevertheless locked into visions of *a specific* future. Adam and Eve must go forth into a "perverted World" in the poem's last lines: "The World was all before them" (12.646), the world that will be "purg'd and refin'd" like ore. Some might welcome this refinement—*felix culpa*—believing in a "fortunate Fall." But the Fall is not fortunate for everyone; "our" adheres to a few, not all. Michael, or should I say Milton, assures us that all prospects lead to a single "conflagrant" end, and that the unborn will inherit "our" hardships until then.

Is this the "happy" end, Milton? On March 8, 1674, the same year that the poem's second edition was published, "sad and lamentable news" came from a dyer's house on Old-Street in London. A maid and a nurse suffocated to death in their sleep after building a charcoal fire in the night. This nightmare on Old-Street left one maid barely alive: the fumes had "besieged the brain with black stupifactive vapours, and suffocated the spirits that they could not perform their offices."[64] Like the biblical couple exiting the garden after being surprised by sin, the maid and the nurse depart this world after being surprised by smoke: "their souls had taken leave of their bodys till the

Resurrection, nor could all the art or means that could possibly be used, recal them to the forsaken clay."[65] While these two are liberated from the "forsaken" clay of their first parents, those they left behind were not so fortunate. In 1700, nearly twenty-five years after Milton's death, Timothy Nourse wrote "An Essay upon the Fuel of London." The consumption of coal in its variety of forms was only getting worse: "All the innocent Contents which the Mind can take from fair Prospects, whether of Buildings, or of the Country, are lost in these Clouds."[66] The fumes are so corrosive that even the hardiest buildings crumble: "all which are eaten away, peel'd and fley'd as I may say to the very Bones by this hellish and subterraneous Flume."[67] It is not hard to imagine that bodies were literally turning to dust as well: "The great Heaps, or Mountains rather, of Cole-Dust, upon the least puff of Wind (like the Sands in *Arabia*) invade and cover all Places."[68] Coal ashes to coal ashes, "Cole-Dust" to "Cole-Dust": if coal apologists like Bushell had concluded that the way up to heaven is really down to earth, they literally had their heads in the coal clouds. And those who pointed to "fairer" prospects through this mournful gloom could only "stand and wait,"[69] indefinitely, to leave the old world behind for the fiery prospects of Revelation.

West Virginia: "A Happy Rural Seat of Various View"

Is this the hill of Hell or Paradise? This is a prospect closer to home for me: Kayford Mountain, about fifty miles south of the West Virginia capital of Charleston. Here a cataclysmic form of coal extraction, Mountain Top Removal Mining (MTR), takes place on an almost daily basis. Predominant in the Appalachian region, MTR detonates anywhere from five hundred to eight hundred feet of rock off the surface of a mountain to expose coal seams below (the amount of explosives used in a single week is equal to the force of the Hiroshima bomb). As the coal is removed, the polluted land is dumped back into the landscape as "valley fills"; once the coal is depleted, the area is regraded and revegetated in what is dubbed "reclamation." MTR has been proven irrefutably responsible for ecological, economic, and social afflictions: from deforestation (the biodiversity of "reclamation" is practically nonexistent), to loss of jobs (mechanization replaces workers because surface work is much less dependent on human labor than underground

FIGURE 9.1. Kayford Mountain. Photograph by author.

mining), to cancer and birth defects (extremely rare forms of brain tumors proliferate in small populations), to flooding (including from toxic sludge compounds).[70] Though Milton predates this practice by hundreds of years, his method of prospecting works like a modern-day mining company's. Within a capitalistic system, the "end" terms shift from eschatology to economics. Here, MTR's geo-temporal prospects face financial benefits for family and country. When Scott defines Appalachia as a "sacrifice zone," she means "a place that is written off for environmental destruction in the name of a higher purpose."[71] Profit, energy independence, and nationhood: these are the "higher purposes" seen from Paradise hill. But not all support such visions of the future, fortunately. Environmental activists like the Keeper of the Mountains Foundation point out that "the happy end" of the American myth of progress does not pan out; in fact, my state's prospects are some of the nation's grimmest: in terms of economics alone, which proponents often use to justify MTR, the coal industry actually *cost* the West Virginia state government almost one hundred million dollars more than it brought in according to a 2010 report; one in three children in the Southern West Virginia Congressional District live below the federal poverty line; and the lack of economic diversity (nine counties have more than 20 percent employment in the industry) means that many jobs will disappear as coal dependency continues to decline.[72]

There are other views of Hell hill. Right now a battle is raging for Blair Mountain, a historic site endangered by Alpha Natural Resources and Arch Coal.[73] It was here in 1921 that thousands of miners rebelled against coal operators in what became known as the Battle of Blair Mountain, the largest labor uprising and insurrection in the United States since the Civil War, during the West Virginia Coal Wars of 1920–21. The U.S. Army and Air Corps put an end to the weeklong fighting that left approximately one hundred dead and the United Mine Workers of America (UMWA) crippled.[74] Blair Mountain shows us how, in Scott's words, the "past (and the past-to-be) haunts the present."[75] When the present exorcises its demonic past in the name of "sacrifice" and prospective gain, it is hard to see different futures. What is worse, when our prospects become an irrevocable *loss* of the present, nostalgia sinks in; it is difficult to look anywhere *but* backward. Milton might have known this kind of land battle well himself. In 1649, Gerrard Winstanley, leader of the radical English sect known as the Diggers, or True Levellers, attempted to convert unused land and "let the common people have their Commons and waste lands set free to them, from all *Norman* enslaving Lords of Mannors."[76] Planting on St. George's Hill in April 1649 in Weybridge, Surrey, they were later violently ousted in August by the lord of the manor, Francis Drake. For the Diggers, pre-Norman times symbolize a communal paradise before aristocratic oppression and privatization of property. The happy rural seat is always already lost or is soon to be; similarly, the coal wars invoke hardier, unionized days. One thing is certain: the wasteland is not just unused land but is physically laid waste. *Hardly happy.* As coal continues to accumulate struggles around it, new battles will inevitably rise on and around Blair Mountain and other mountains. *Welcome to battlefield earth.* And these battles will continue, I argue, so long as we decide *between* the views from Milton's hills—Hell or Paradise—and the *determined* "ends" they afford, whenever we ask if digging carboniferous earth ushers in a dirtier world of wounds *or* a newer one of riches. Yet we can come down from Hell or Paradise hill and cohabit "Commons" ground, composing with the coal beds. Let us look elsewhere, for all is not lost.

Coal: A Non/human History

Is it possible to imagine a world without coal? I contemplated this question during the November 2012 election season, passing under a billboard on my way to teach a class I called "Ecological Shakespeare," a course that on one day in particular put *King Lear* and MTR into conversation. Four dour profiles were depicted under the headline "Gang of Four: End of Coal": (then) Administrator of the United States Environmental Protection Agency, Lisa P. Jackson; Senator Joe Manchin, up for reelection that year; President Obama, also up for reelection; and Cecil Roberts, president of the UMWA. Ending coal would literally improve our prospects, for one: sulfate particles scatter sunlight and restrict visibility to about fourteen miles; otherwise we could see for forty-five to ninety miles on a clear day.[77] (Nourse would approve.) Ending coal would additionally end human labor. (Supposedly: John Raese, who lost the senate race, would agree.) Thus it seems that the arguments we make for or against coal only make us worse cohabitants with it. Both positions require privileging the human to a certain extent: our sight, our jobs. Raese's pro-coal stance is perhaps the most obvious. But take Barbara Freese's book *Coal: A Human History,* for example, a work that sets out to "recogniz[e] coal as a crucial part of humanity's destiny."[78] Her conclusion is that we can create futures without it, "a world that no longer need[s] coal."[79] Her prospect is too anthropocentric for me, as if the human timeline takes priority and delegates what is and what is not important to its trajectory. *As if we had that power.* To be clear: I am not advocating that humans do not have substantial agency and should not be held accountable for their actions. Rather, my point is that we should not privilege the human's prospects *as if* the future of the world for us depends on our regulation of coal. To Freese's human history I propose a non/human history of coal instead. But what would this history look like? The truth is, *we are already in it.*

"I am Earth."[80] When Henry Vaughan, Milton's contemporary, wrote that line he was composing a poem called "Misery." "Carbon . . . me."[81] When Michel Serres wrote that line he was within the joyful valences of *Biogea.*

When Stacy Alaimo developed her concept of "trans-corporeality" in *Bodily Natures,* "in which the human is always intermeshed with the more-than-human world," she considered the health of these valences.[82] Transcorporeality recognizes human rights and environmental justice as shared endeavors because of their shared materiality; though it "is a site not for affirmation," it is crucially one of potential.[83] Alaimo adds, "physiological responses to work environments spark lines of inquiry."[84] Like the miners, X-ray machines, and silica dust that come together in her work, I wish to trace a non/human history of coaly assemblages. We are coal, we are earth, and we are in "darkness visible." Admittedly, Miltonists familiar with the work of Diane Kelsey McColley will know that she has already shed much ecocritical light on this poem's "darkness," noting how, for example, London's worsening air pollution, one of the "results of transforming the idea of earth from a nurturing mother to a body of extractable minerals," finds its way into the epic's air.[85] Before I transform my Argument into an Apology, however, let me say where I am breaking new ground ecotheoretically at least: rather than transpose environmental history onto literature in a (new) historical interpretation of Hell hill, I am additionally arguing for a Miltonic "material turn":[86] how the *matter* of coal works upon the poet's body (of work). Consider coal authorship: we have seen how coal co-constitutes being in *Fumifugium:* "we, who are compos'd of the Elements, should participate of their qualities."[87] More than just a proto-environmentalist pamphlet, or an early toxicology narrative, Evelyn asserts that we *are* what we breathe in transcorporeal, "compos'd"-itional ways. Milton might leave coal in a "perverted" past but he proved to be an elemental, interactive participant with every breath he took. A non/human history would spark posthuman lines of inquiry that address the miseries of what Rob Nixon terms "slow violence,"[88] while hopefully leading to healthier futures, "some remedies humbly proposed," for all members involved—and with alacrity, even if the tracings themselves must be done slowly.[89] Flight lines like these would move away from the "our" of "our second Adam" toward a cavernous *we,* a non/human inclusivity that truly goes in-depth, farther than the "vain contést[s]" between the "mine" of possession and place, beyond the illusion of ever-begrimed bodies that can be, or should be, scrubbed clean and "white."

Mines of Flight

I call these temporal as well as material lines "mines of flight." In *A Thousand Plateaus*—there is a terrestrial title!—Deleuze and Guattari famously describe "lines of flight" as rhizomatic "becomings" that resist origins and endpoints. Earthy assemblages spark off their geo-philosophy: "*Every mine is a line of flight* that is in communication with smooth spaces."[90] "Mines of flight" engage our becoming-process with coal. The end of coal is ultimately an unbearable thought because coal permeates our bodies in un/foreseeable ways. How we narrate this coaly embeddedness, however, needs to be rethought. Latour speaks of "compositionism" as a facing-forward into multiple futures.[91] Timothy Morton's dark ecology—there is a cavernous title!—requires "forward thinking": "The future is one of those things like Nature, set up as a thing 'over yonder.' . . . We have barely become conscious that we have been terraforming Earth all along. Now we have the chance to face up to this fact and to our coexistence with all beings."[92] We may go forward into dark places, to be sure, but we may also, and strangely, go downward into brighter ones of being as well. Mines of flight are not returns to a swampy Eden, routes back in time along narrow chronological corridors, but a way of perceiving truly *deep* time, of the "untimely matter" that is coal:[93] early miners would find ferns underground, for instance, and these artifacts would disorient their sense of time just enough for them to (flimsily) attribute their presence to the Great Flood of biblical history.[94] The earth is in ongoing formation; the earth is earthing futures. Due to global warming, Freese believes that the Carboniferous swamplands are returning to the carbon dioxide–rich atmosphere: "It's almost as if the *lepidodendron* of old had found a way to use humanity to re-create the planetary conditions they once thrived in."[95] But coal does not usher in a return to something that *once* was: coal promotes a forward-down thinking that sees the earthing world differently, beyond the limits of ecocatastrophe. What prospects will come? We are still in the Carboniferous period, even if it is "passed." Realizing this coal hard fact sets us off along different futures that do not terminate in the Anthropocene—that do not attempt to transform a negative space into an affirmative site—but show us to be "interconnected in potent potential" deep down.[96]

I now want to take you down four (and counting) mines of flight. Imagine prospects that trail out of sight; new vistas that ceaselessly arrive; a horizontal ontology always at work on the horizon. Call it a prospect in the making, a meditation on happy open-ends.

(1) *Switch agency.* What if we thought of *live* coal prospecting us? It is a question meant not to switch energy policies but to switch off the idea of causality altogether[97]—the flicking human finger deciding whether thing-power is "off" or "on." Though modern science defines coal as organic plant matter, it is still dead material. Coal is energy *once* it is burned. By believing that spirits or demons infused not-quite-living mines, early modern writers (like Bushell) viewed the earth in vitalist (animist) ways. But some also thought along the lines of Jane Bennett's "vital materialism" in which "matter itself is lively."[98] A seventeenth-century mining engineer, Johannes Bünting, proposed two origins for coal: either God made it, or, more heretically, it was created by "the power of nature and the force of the earth." Though Bünting could argue that God planted it that way, coal had veggie power nevertheless; due to "special seeds for its reproduction and growth under the ground," its supply was endlessly regenerative.[99] Others noticed mines' "breath"—vaporous exhalations known as "choke," "white," and "fire" damps—that almost always resulted in their deaths.[100] To these secular suggestions, we may also ask: *was* coal living material or *is* it? Being primarily carbon, coal is particularly suited for challenging non/living demarcations (carbon is usually the determinant for "living" matter). Coal can articulate Cary Wolfe's "biopolitical point" about obsolete human and animal distinctions: the point is now "a newly expanded community of the living and the concern we should all have with where violence and immunitary protection fall within it."[101] If the law "installs its frame for who's in and who's out" and furthermore "disavows its own contingency through violence,"[102] living coal pushes against such biopolitical frameworks to question our legal grounds for judgment. At a time when the il/legality of MTR is constantly questioned, here is where "poetry of a living earth" takes a stand before the law.[103]

(2) *Argue autochthonally.* "Immanence . . . frees an Autochthon," Deleuze and Guattari set down.[104] Milton's vitalism, however, is slightly different, since, for him, coal does not create mountains; God creates mountains: "let

dry Land appear. / Immediately the Mountains huge appear / Emergent" (7.284–86). When Raphael describes Creation to Adam in Book 7, even the primordial waters are infused with spirit, changed from the common translation "moved upon the face of the deep" to "on the wat'ry calm / His brooding wings the Spirit of God outspread, / And vital virtue infus'd, and vital warmth / Throughout the fluid Mass" (7.235–37). At the heart of Milton's poem, Rogers believes, is "a philosophy of self-creation" appropriate to the "ontological speculation" of the Vitalist Movement. Creation is "nearly autonomous" because God *allows* self-creating substance to proceed through his vital spirit.[105] How much hinges on *nearly;* one clause away from Bennett's creed,[106] Milton's prayer is one of "material monism" in which all matter leads to God: a mantra that reads "one first matter all" (5.472).[107] His "speculation" (if not an ontological "prospect") should still be recognized. For McColley, Milton's anti-dualism has ethical implications: "An earth capable of union with heaven—a union dependent on human choice—is more like heaven already, and heaven more like earth."[108] But I wonder if suturing the heaven and earth divide (like matter and spirit) forges a union that *necessitates* said divide, and, moreover, implies that only human perceptions ("choice") matter. Like Milton did before each book of his poem, we should pose clear arguments, especially against injustice. We should ask why certain prospects come into view and why others do not. Yet we should also ask what we are arguing *with.* Autochthon literally means "sprung from the earth." What if we imagined ourselves as autochthons without the *auto-* of autonomy but with the *auto-* of a shared self sprung from the earth and yet tied to it? What if we argued for ever-emergence, without waiting for the voice of God for beings to "appear / Emergent"? What if we stopped trying to liberate the earth but delved deeper within it? *Freedom:* "As to emancipation, it does not mean 'freed from bonds' but *well-*attached."[109] (That was Latour.) "For inferior who is free?" (That was Milton, 9.825.) Carbon both bears and is borne. (That is the carbon *we.*)

(3) *Create coalitions.* In the sense that "coalesce" means "bring together, unite," such arguments would "coal-esce" new unions with coal. What coalitions may come? Milton assures us that "the Earth / Shall all be Paradise" in the end (12.463–64). I do not wish to trade one Paradise lost of perfect

harmony for a Paradise regained of heavenly sustainability, however. Be a stranger to "paradise"; it is a bounded place.[110] Coalitions follow a rubric of "postsustainability" that disturbs the vision—the illusion—of the eventually achievable "happy seat." "The era of sustainability is over," Steve Mentz pronounces. "Making political and personal choices to reduce the human ecofootprint can be thought of not as a route back to Eden but as a form of practical self-defense in a chaotic environment. . . . We need options, not sustainability."[111] I would rather lose the nostalgia for stabilization itself; I would rather coalesce creatively, make anew, unionize with the earth now for all of its earthing. Carolyn Dinshaw and Marget Long have used "romance" to describe our desire for an un/earthly paradise, one that is not accessible and yet is still part of the world. We roam through "scenes of promise and breakdown."[112] Let us go on strike against the prospects of a teleological human destiny or industry. Bringing down "King Coal" (human-engineered corporations) only reinstates ontological hierarchies and chronic tensions between bottom-up and top-down. If coal is king, then sovereignty should be abolished altogether.[113] (I think Milton would agree.) Employ a strategic anthropomorphization to recognize the interface between human faces and mountain faces instead.[114] Strike up conversations with fellow autochthons about how to go "hand in hand with wand'ring steps and slow" (12.648) toward new and healthier prospects, *collaboratively.*

(4) *Energize ethics.* "You have to love life before you can care about anything," declares Bennett.[115] A popular, though controversial, bumper sticker from the West Virginia Highlands Conservancy reads: "I ♥ Mountains." Despite its "dirty" name, coal has an allure; its materiality, to quote Bennett, is "enchanted." For most, however, coal is "utterly lacking in glamour."[116] Yet Stone Age Chinese were attracted to jet, the gemstone variant of coal, six thousand years ago; by the third century BCE, jet carving was a vibrant industry. The Roman writer Solinus called jet the "best stone in Britain" because it was easily carved and polished into beautiful jewelry.[117] I know this allure personally: two shiny pieces of anthracite lie next to my coal-powered computer screen. But how might coal fuel an "energetics of ethics" instead of our furnaces?[118] *This* is to love coal: not to do so because it is economically prudent, or to delight in the dig and burn, but to love its

life, to fight the enchantment of explosion and flame with the magic of our co-implication. The earth does not ask us to *tend* it better, for all that would do is revitalize the georgic mode of rightful stewardship or incite yet another radical form of pastoral that anticipates bowers of "eternal Bliss." *This* love is truly radical, from the Latin *radix, radic-* ("root"): a love that better *at-tends* earth's rhizomatic liveliness.

One of my "Ecological Shakespeare" students once showed me a photograph she took of a hill outside Oceana, West Virginia, a town within one of our counties hit hardest by MTR. *Welcome to earth's prospects.* I peered through branches both bare and blossoming, wondering if they announced the onset of spring or of fall; I tried to distinguish between bevels made by engines and by earth, mesmerized by lines that bedeviled my mind. I wished I could share her irreproducible view with others—and now I have, with *you,* in imagination—for it reveals the multiplicity of life that all prospects contain: from fossil fuels to flowers, miners to machines; it points to the precarious futures that all prospects afford; it reminds us that both creation and destruction are always on the horizon; and it asks us to never stop facing this fact, to never stop loving the earth, *to love,* or else everything will truly be *lost.*

Notes

For grounding this project, my thanks go to: Sharon O'Dair and the University of Alabama staff who organized the "Elemental Ecocriticism" symposium in April 2013; the audience members in attendance there (including the contributors in this volume); Will Stockton for his rich feedback; Jeffrey Jerome Cohen for his suggestions and our coediting coalition; my students at West Virginia University, especially Jordan Lovejoy, who introduced me to the desolation of mountaintop removal strip mining; my colleagues, who kept me digging as part of the Faculty Colloquium Research series; and, finally, to the environmental organizations, local and elsewhere, who will not "stand and wait" to see earthlings destroyed.

1. See the Sierra Club's "Beyond Coal" campaign and supplementary fact sheets, available at http://content.sierraclub.org/coal/.
2. Gilles Deleuze and Félix Guattari, *What Is Philosophy?,* trans. Hugh Tomlinson and Graham Burchell (New York: Columbia University Press, 1994), 85.
3. For more on territorialization, see Gilles Deleuze and Félix Guattari, *A Thousand Plateaus: Capitalism and Schizophrenia,* trans. Brian Massumi (Minneapolis: University of Minnesota Press, 1987), esp. "1837: Of the Refrain."

4. Rebecca R. Scott, *Removing Mountains: Extracting Nature and Identity in the Appalachian Coalfields* (Minneapolis: University of Minnesota Press, 2010), 222.

5. As Scott puts it, "How can two groups of people see the same landscape in entirely different ways, as a wasteland or an Eden, as an abomination or a site of technological improvement?" (ibid., 27).

6. Friends of Coal is a volunteer organization "dedicated to inform and educate West Virginia citizens about the coal industry and its vital role in the state's future." Though based in West Virginia, the website's opening question, "What Does Coal Mean To You?," could be asked in any coalscape. See http://www.friendsofcoal.org/. Friends of the Mountains is a network of regional environmental groups "working to stop [surface mining] madness." See http://www.friendsofthemountains.org/.

7. Tim Ingold, *Being Alive: Essays on Movement, Knowledge and Description* (New York: Routledge, 2011), 49–50.

8. Ibid., 44.

9. Ibid., 111, 33–35.

10. Ibid., 144.

11. Jane Bennett writes, "We are Earthlings both in the sense that we need a host of other bodies ('the planet') to live and in the sense that 'we' are made of the same elements as is the planet." Jane Bennett, "Earthling, Now and Forever?," in *Making the Geologic Now: Responses to Material Conditions of Contemporary Life,* ed. Elizabeth Ellsworth and Jamie Kruse (New York: Punctum Books, 2013), 244.

12. I learned this information from http://ilovemountains.org/, an anti-mountaintop removal website that allows you to locate where your energy comes from (via Google Earth).

13. See the White House fact sheet, available at http://www.whitehouse.gov/the-press-office/2013/06/25/fact-sheet-president-obama-s-climate-action-plan. A more user-friendly version is available at http://www.whitehouse.gov/share/climate-action-plan.

14. A quick search for "coal debates" will yield infinite results; for example, Fox News spread rumors about new EPA regulations that could "kill" coal. See "Rules That Could 'Kill'? Safety, Cost Concerns over EPA's New Coal Regs," *Fox News,* September 20, 2013, http://www.foxnews.com/politics/2013/09/19/rules-that-could-kill-safety-cost-concerns-over-epa-new-coal-regs/.

15. Scott, *Removing Mountains,* 174. See in particular chapter 6, "Traces of History: 'White' People, Black Coal."

16. The conflation of black non/human bodies became (disturbingly) apparent to me during the presidential election of 2012. Roadside signs along the West Virginia–Pennsylvania border read, "Stop the War on Coal: Fire Obama," transforming him into a combustible, like coal, fit for the flames.

17. Bruno Latour has argued that as long as the two houses of nature and politics are split according to the modern constitution, politics will be rendered impotent; political ecology "has to let go of nature." This same predicament applies to green

movements: "the ecological movements have sought to position themselves on the political chessboard without redrawing the squares, without redefining the rules of the game, without redesigning the pawns." Bruno Latour, *Politics of Nature: How to Bring the Sciences into Democracy,* trans. Catherine Porter (Cambridge, Mass.: Harvard University Press, 2004), 5. I emphasize the reconception of earth in this chapter.

18. William Shakespeare, *King Lear,* in *The Norton Shakespeare,* 2nd ed., ed. Stephen Greenblatt et al. (New York: W. W. Norton, 2008), 5.3.260.

19. All quotations of Milton's work are taken from John Milton, *Complete Poems and Major Prose,* ed. Merritt Y. Hughes (New York: Odyssey Press, 1957).

20. Alfred Kentigern Siewers, "Earth: A Wandering," *postmedieval* 4, no. 1 (Spring 2013): 16.

21. See the Appalachian Voices website for more info: http://appvoices.org/. The Sierra Club predicts that by 2020 1.4 million acres will have been destroyed. See http://content.sierraclub.org/coal/mining-destroying-mountains.

22. *Oxford English Dictionary,* s.v. "prospect" (n.1, v.1).

23. *Paradise Regain'd* and *Samson Agonistes* tend to dominate Milton's "visionary mode." See Peter E. Medine, John T. Shawcross, and David V. Urban, eds., *Visionary Milton: Essays on Prophecy and Violence* (Pittsburgh: Duquesne University Press, 2010). I hope that the "prospect" in *Paradise Lost* opens up prospective readings elsewhere.

24. John Rogers, *The Matter of Revolution: Science, Poetry, and Politics in the Age of Milton* (Ithaca, N.Y.: Cornell University Press, 1996), 1–2. See especially chapter 4, "Chaos, Creation, and the Political Science of *Paradise Lost,*" to which I will turn at the conclusion of this chapter.

25. See Deleuze and Guattari, *A Thousand Plateaus,* esp. "Introduction: Rhizome."

26. Bruno Latour, "An Attempt at a 'Compositionist Manifesto,'" *New Literary History* 41, no. 3 (2010): 485.

27. Ellsworth and Kruse, *Making the Geologic Now.* Sharon O'Dair has argued for a presentist approach in Shakespeare studies. See Sharon O'Dair, "Is It Shakespearean Ecocriticism If It Isn't Presentist?," in *Ecocritical Shakespeare,* ed. Lynne Bruckner and Dan Brayton (Surrey: Ashgate, 2011), 71–85. She has also argued for this approach through the issue of surface mining. See Sharon O'Dair, "A Way of Life Worth Preserving? Identity, Place, and Commerce in *Big Business* and the American South," *Borrowers and Lenders: The Journal of Shakespeare and Appropriation* 1, no. 1 (Spring 2005), http://www.borrowers.uga.edu/781421/show. To her original question, I would respond: is it Miltonic?

28. To riff on Virginia Zimmerman's use of the word: "'excavation' . . . demands the simultaneous interpretation of an object and of its situation, and it focuses on the recovery of the past while insisting on the primary act of interpretation in the present." See Virginia Zimmerman, *Excavating Victorians* (Albany: State University of New York Press, 2008), 22–23.

29. "And God said, Let vs make man in our Image, after our likenesse: and let them haue dominion ouer the fish of the sea, and ouer the foule of the aire, and oure the cattell, and ouer all the earth, and ouer euery creeping thing that creepeth vpon the earth." From the King James (1611) version, available at http://www.kingjamesbibleonline.org/1611_Genesis-Chapter-1/.

30. Ken Hiltner, "Introduction," in *Renaissance Ecology: Imagining Eden in Milton's England,* ed. Ken Hiltner (Pittsburgh: Duquesne University Press, 2008), 3.

31. Barbara Freese, *Coal: A Human History* (New York: Penguin, 2003), 285.

32. John Evelyn, *Fumifugium, or, The Inconveniencie of the Aer and Smoak of London Dissipated; Together with Some Remedies Humble Proposed* (London: W. Godbid, 1661). The quote, provided in Latin, is Lucretius's: "Carbonúmque gravis vis, atque odor insinuatur / Quam facile in cerebrum?"

33. Ibid., 6.

34. Ibid., 11.

35. Ibid., 14–15.

36. Ibid., 1.

37. Simon Sturtevant took what we might now call a "conservationist" approach, arguing that in order to preserve the forests, "Sea-coale, Pit-coale, Earth-coale" are to be used instead, "the principall end of which inuention is, that the Woods and Timber of our country might be saued." See Simon Sturtevant, *Metallica* (London: George Eld, 1612), "To the Reader."

38. Georgius Agricola, *De Re Metallica,* trans. Herbert Clark Hoover and Lou Henry Hoover (New York: Dover, 1950), xxv.

39. Ibid., 24, 22.

40. Ibid., 14.

41. Marjorie Hope Nicolson, *Mountain Gloom and Mountain Glory: The Development of the Aesthetics of the Infinite* (Ithaca, N.Y.: Cornell University Press, 1959).

42. Agricola, *De Re Metallica,* 217.

43. Ibid., 214.

44. Massey Energy (who operated the Upper Big Branch Mine at the time of the explosion) recklessly disregarded an incredible number of safety violations. See Howard Berkes and Robert Benincasa, "Other Massey Mines Showed a Pattern of Violations," NPR, April 13, 2010, http://www.npr.org/templates/story/story.php?storyId=125864847.

45. According to "The Human Cost of Coal," an online map, "people living near the destruction are 50% more likely to die of cancer and 42% more likely to be born with birth defects compared to other people in Appalachia." View the "cost" at http://ilovemountains.org/the-human-cost.

46. Agricola, *De Re Metallica,* 6.

47. See Howard Berkes, "As Mine Protections Fail, Black Lung Cases Surge," NPR, July 9, 2012, http://www.npr.org/2012/07/09/155978300/as-mine-protections-fail-black-lung-cases-surge.

48. George Sandys, *A Paraphrase upon the Divine Poems* (London: n.p., 1638), 34.

49. Thomas Bushell, *Mr. Bushell's Abridgment of the Lord Chancellor Bacon's Philosophical Theory in Mineral Prosecutions* (London: n.p., 1659), 3, 4.

50. Ibid., 1.

51. Ibid., 2.

52. Ibid., 5.

53. Ibid., 11.

54. Ibid., 14.

55. Ibid., 10.

56. Ibid., 10–11.

57. Gabriel Plattes, *A Discovery of Subterraneall Treasure, viz. Of All Manner of* Mines *and* Mineralls, *from the* Gold *to the* Coale (London: I. Okes, 1639).

58. Ibid., 9. Bushell repeats this logic in his prayer: "to discover those hidden Treasures, which thy inscrutable wisdom hath lodged in the Bowels of the most barren mountaines." Bushell, *Mr. Bushell's Abridgement,* 12.

59. Plattes, *A Discovery of Subterraneall Treasure,* 7.

60. Karl Steel, my elemental partner in this volume, has written about the legacy of the Golden Age in "A Fourteenth-Century Ecology: 'The Former Age' with Dindimus," in *Rethinking Chaucerian Beasts,* ed. Carolynn van Dyke (New York: Palgrave Macmillan, 2012), 185–202. He writes eloquently of "what it may mean to be open to moral consideration to all, to attempt to love without harm, without the certainty of any distinctions between subject and object, human and animal, nature and culture, flesh and the earth" (194).

61. Ken Hiltner, *Milton and Ecology* (Cambridge: Cambridge University Press, 2003), 134.

62. Ecofeminism usefully critiques the ways in which landscape is rendered female, wounded, and in need of (male) recuperation. Two excellent studies centered around coal are Joyce M. Barry, *Standing Our Ground: Women, Environmental Justice, and the Fight to End Mountaintop Removal* (Athens: Ohio University Press, 2012); and Shannon Elizabeth Bell, *Our Roots Run Deep as Ironweed: Appalachian Women and the Fight for Environmental Justice* (Urbana: University of Illinois Press, 2013).

63. Sandys, *A Paraphrase,* 35.

64. *Sad and Lamentable News from Old-Street* (London: John Newton, 1674), 3.

65. Ibid., 4.

66. Timothy Nourse, *Campania Foelix. Or, A Discourse of the Benefits and Improvements of Husbandry* (London: T. Bennet, 1700), 364.

67. Ibid., 350.

68. Ibid., 349–50.

69. John Milton, Sonnet XIX, line 15.

70. See http://ilovemountains.org for more on the (irreversible) damages of MTR.

71. Scott, *Removing Mountains,* 31.

72. See the "The Problems" at http://www.mountainkeeper.org/the-problems/. Also recommended: Shirley Stewart Burns, *Bringing Down the Mountains: The Impact of Mountaintop Removal on Southern West Virginia Communities* (Morgantown: West Virginia University Press, 2007).

73. The West Virginia Department of Environmental Protection prohibited surface mining within one thousand feet in May 2014, but the battle is still going. Visit the Friends of Blair Mountain website, http://friendsofblairmountain.org/.

74. For an accessible overview, see Robert Shogan, *The Battle of Blair Mountain: The Story of America's Largest Labor Uprising* (Boulder, Colo.: Westview Press, 2004).

75. Scott, *Removing Mountains,* 27.

76. Quoted in Karen L. Edwards, "Eden Raised: Waste in Milton's Garden," in Hiltner, *Renaissance Ecology,* 267.

77. Freese, *Coal,* 471.

78. Ibid., 10.

79. Ibid., 248.

80. Henry Vaughan, *The Complete Poems,* ed. Alan Rudrum (New Haven, Conn.: Yale University Press, 1981).

81. Michel Serres, *Biogea,* trans. Randolph Burks (Minneapolis: Univocal, 2012), 30.

82. Stacy Alaimo, *Bodily Natures: Science, Environment, and the Material Self* (Bloomington: Indiana University Press, 2010), 2.

83. Ibid., 144.

84. Ibid., 31.

85. I am indebted to Diane Kelsey McColley's work; see chapter 2, "Earth, Mining, Monotheism, and Mountain Theology," and chapter 3, "Air, Water, Woods," in *Poetry and Ecology in the Age of Milton and Marvell* (Surrey: Ashgate, 2007). Here, I quote from "Air, Water, Woods," 79.

86. For more on this critical turn, see Serenella Iovino and Serpil Oppermann, "Theorizing Material Ecocriticism: A Diptych," *Interdisciplinary Studies in Literature and Environment* 19, no. 3 (Summer 2012): 448–75.

87. Evelyn, *Fumifugium,* 22.

88. "By slow violence I mean a violence that occurs gradually and out of sight, a violence of delayed destruction that is dispersed across time and space, an attritional violence that is typically not viewed as violence at all." Rob Nixon, *Slow Violence and the Environmentalism of the Poor* (Cambridge, Mass.: Harvard University Press, 2011), 2.

89. Latour exclaims: "This is not a sociology any more but a *slow*ciology!" See Bruno Latour, *Reassembling the Social: An Introduction to Actor-Network-Theory* (Oxford: Oxford University Press, 2005), 122.

90. Deleuze and Guattari, *A Thousand Plateaus,* 412.

91. Latour's critique of Benjamin's Angel of History extends to Milton's face-forward yet end-driven angels: "What the Moderns called 'their future' has never

been contemplated face to face, since it has always been the future of someone fleeing their past looking backward, not forward. . . . It's no use speaking of 'epistemological breaks' any more. Fleeing from the past while continuing to look at it will not do." See Latour, "An Attempt at a 'Compositionist Manifesto,'" 486–87.

92. Timothy Morton, *The Ecological Thought* (Cambridge, Mass.: Harvard University Press, 2010), 119, 133. See in particular chapter 3, "Forward Thinking," 98–135.

93. One of five "directives" outlined by Jonathan Gil Harris "recast[s] matter as an actor-network, consider[ing] the traces of the past and the future within it, not just as that which is worked upon, but also as agents that work upon the present." Jonathan Gil Harris, *Untimely Matter in the Time of Shakespeare* (Philadelphia: University of Pennsylvania Press, 2009), 25. "Explosion" is one kind of temporal relation, and I suggest that coal is not just *exploded* but may actually *explode* previous ways of understanding our epistemological, ontological, and temporal relationships.

94. For more on the Deluge theory, see Martin J. S. Rudwick, *The Meaning of Fossils: Episodes in the History of Palaeontology*, 2nd ed. (Chicago: University of Chicago Press, 1976); *Bursting the Limits of Time: The Reconstruction of Geohistory in the Age of Revolution* (Chicago: University of Chicago Press, 2005); and *Worlds before Adam: The Reconstruction of Geohistory in the Age of Reform* (Chicago: University of Chicago Press, 2008).

95. Freese, *Coal*, 184.

96. Alaimo, *Bodily Natures*, 44.

97. Take, for instance, the documentary film *Switch* (2012), which has little to do with questions of environmental justice and more to do with economic analysis.

98. Jane Bennett, *Vibrant Matter: A Political Ecology of Things* (Durham, N.C.: Duke University Press, 2010), 13.

99. Quoted in Herbert Wendt, *Before the Deluge* (Garden City, N.Y.: Doubleday, 1968), 346. Johann Jakob Scheuchzer was the first to propose (1706) that coal was petrified vegetation.

100. Freese, *Coal*, 47–50.

101. Cary Wolfe, *Before the Law: Humans and Other Animals in a Biopolitical Frame* (Chicago: University of Chicago Press, 2013), 105.

102. Ibid., 9.

103. McColley, *Poetry and Ecology*, 62.

104. Deleuze and Guattari, *What Is Philosophy?*, 86.

105. Rogers, *The Matter of Revolution*, 122, 2, 144.

106. Bennett, *Vibrant Matter*, 81, warns us of "the temptation in vitalism to *spiritualize* the vital agent." See also her "kind of Nicene Creed for would-be vital materialists" (122).

107. A longer discussion of Milton's monism may be found in McColley, *Poetry and Ecology*, 69–78.

108. Ibid., 62.

109. Latour, *Reassembling the Social*, 218.

110. *Oxford English Dictionary,* s.v. "paradise" (n.1): "ancient Greek παράδεισος a (Persian) enclosed park, orchard, or pleasure ground."

111. Steve Mentz, "After Sustainability," *PMLA* 127, no. 3 (2012): 586, 591. Mentz's essay is one of seven in the journal's "Sustainability" cluster. In "Sustainable This, Sustainable That: New Materialisms, Posthumanism, and Unknown Futures," Stacy Alaimo asks an important question that I have attempted to address through Milton's earth: "Can sustainability be transformed in such a way as to cultivate post-humanist epistemologies, ethics, politics, and aesthetics?" (563).

112. Carolyn Dinshaw and Marget Long, "(Un)earthly Paradise," presentation at the BABEL Working Group's biennial meeting, Cruising in the Ruins: The Question of Disciplinarity in the Post/medieval University, Boston, September 2012.

113. As Mick Smith says, "sustaining a place for ecological politics and saving the natural world both depend on rejecting the antipolitical and antiecological principle of sovereignty." Mick Smith, *Against Ecological Sovereignty: Ethics, Biopolitics, and Saving the Natural World* (Minneapolis: University of Minnesota Press, 2011), xx.

114. Thanks to Julian Yates for bringing "interface" to my attention.

115. Jane Bennett, *The Enchantment of Modern Life: Attachments, Crossings, and Ethics* (Princeton, N.J.: Princeton University Press, 2001), 4.

116. Freese, *Coal,* 2.

117. Ibid., 204, 15.

118. Bennett, *The Enchantment of Modern Life,* 132.

Love and Strife

Response Essays

Response essays are typically tasked with synthesizing the materials contained in the works they follow, offering an aerial perspective on what from within might seem "shadowy parts" or "endless forms most beautiful and most wonderful," a bustle in search of a totality. Yet this volume testifies to the elements' ability to resist stilling into a view from on high: no sooner have earth, air, fire, and water conjoined in some powerful form than their restless labor begins again. Empedocles's twin and twined forces of *love* and *strife* therefore seemed appropriate to us as a rubric under which to gather responses composed by ecocritics who were vital to imagining the project of *Elemental Ecocriticism.* We asked each of these three writers to allow the contributors' chapters and the elements that flourish within them to spur a meditation on the invitation to ecological thinking that the elements in their activity extend: how they might be graspable and withdrawn at once, an "elementality" akin to magic (Timothy Morton); how the elements might be both discrete and conjoined, existing at the "edge" of relations (Cary Wolfe); how water, earth, air, and fire might disabuse us of anthropocentric arrogance while "igniting a love," queerly, for uncertainty itself (Stacy Alaimo). These response essays suggest that the elusive reality of the elements will continue to spark epistemological, ontological, and ethical debates—and that attending to the erratic work of love and strife urge us likewise to accept their invitation to a deeper contemplation of ecomateriality, and to respond humanely to that more-than-human world.

Elementality

TIMOTHY MORTON

It is so near that it is oppressive and takes away one's breath—and yet it is nowhere.

—MARTIN HEIDEGGER

One way to think elements, after Immanuel Kant, is to think them as fusions of subject and object. Fire is fiery; water is wet; earth is earthiness; space is spacious; and so on. An element is a -ness, a quality. It envelops. One finds oneself within it, always already. It is intimate yet strange at the same time. There manifests, as Jeffrey Jerome Cohen puts it in this volume, "a vortex of shared precariousness and unchosen proximities." Even though it does not have a here or a there, a subject or an object, an element has a specific vibrancy. It is a specific mode of how a thing appears: a specific style of pretense, a specific fog.

What is the -ness of this -ness, so to speak? What is, in the term invented here, *elementality?* We will find that elementality is a very strange thing, because elements are strange. A strange and wonderful thing, like the elements as such.

An element is a correlationist thing, insofar as it cannot exist without a subject-object fusion, like a rainbow, or the light in the refrigerator—I have to open the fridge to see whether it is on or not. Yet this fact, on further investigation, discloses a more peculiar—even downright weirder—reality, in which there is a fusion and fission between being and appearing in a thing itself, whether or not I "open" it or otherwise relate to it. This response essay pursues that investigation, to show that the elemental is not just a fanciful term with which humanists can while away their sense of alienation from things scientific but rather a profound "unthought known" within modernity as such.[1]

Contemplative Psychology is a form of psychology modulated with contemplative spiritual practices such as Tibetan Buddhism. Chögyam Trungpa developed the Contemplative Psychology program at the Naropa Institute (as it was then called) in 1974 in Boulder, Colorado. In this program, one of the courses concerns the elemental: the fact that space itself is not a blank, neutral container but is colorful and energetic. Maitri Space Awareness is named because *maitri* is the Sanskrit term for friendliness or loving-kindness.[2] The point of Maitri Space Awareness is to become familiar with the various types of energy, beyond distinctions between subject and object. Students are expected to practice Maitri Space Awareness several times during their training in Contemplative Psychology.

In Maitri Space Awareness students occupy five different rooms, all painted different colors and having different shapes. In each of these rooms the students hold one of five specific postures. The posture is held for about an hour, after which one practices "aimless wandering" in the external environment, seeing what comes up. There are five "families" of Buddhas in the esoteric Buddhism still practiced in Tibet and Bhutan. These families are different styles or qualities of spaciousness. They have specific colors, specific forms of neurosis—and correspondingly specific forms of enlightened cognition.

Maitri Space Awareness is remarkably similar to the art of James Turrell, the minimalist sculptor of photons, whose work such as *The Light Inside* and *Twilight Epiphany* employ subtle, gorgeous electronic light. Turrell is exquisitely attuned to the elemental. He exploits the *Ganzfeld effect,* which comes upon one during a blizzard. This effect renders here and there, up and down, foreground and background quite meaningless. One is immersed in vibrant color, color that seems to come all the way to the tip of one's nose, like rain or cold, or tropical humidity. Art as climate. I mean precisely art not as reified or distanced thing over yonder but as infectious, viscous givenness from which one finds oneself incapable of peeling oneself, like Luce Irigaray's air. As discussed in Karl Steel's chapter in this volume, as an aerobic being I find air inside and outside me at the same time.[3] There is a necessary feeling of abjection when I acknowledge how this element, this pervasive thing, determines my status as a being who so blithely distinguishes between me (subject) and others (objects). For every subject–object correlation, there is an excluded–included abject.[4] What is skillful about Turrell is his ability to allow us to soothe ourselves into this abjection, as if his Ganzfeld environment were hypoallergenic versions of the things that subtend us.

It appears that Turell's art is about environments, spaces, and notions of place. But when we think this environmentality, what we discover is a strange, overlooked feature of objects themselves. A double invagination: First the reified art object is opened and its givenness allowed to permeate everywhere. Then this opening is itself opened and we find ourselves, weirdly, on the inside of an entity, an uncanny entity that we cannot grasp yet which is palpable, luminous, exactly this shade of pink.[5] Defying Democritean atomism, such an entity is neither love nor strife, nor yet a blank nothing, but a weird superposition of love and strife.

What can we learn about the elemental by considering the art of Turrell? When I stand in a Turrell exhibit, the environment at its purest seems to press on me from all sides, without objects—or rather, the environment itself has become one gigantic object, not simply a background or blank slate or empty stage set or envelope.[6] Not even what in some phenomenological research is called *the surround.*[7] What precisely is it surrounding? That is the whole question. I find myself thrown out of my habitual sense of where I stop and start just as much as the curving walls and soft yet luminous colors melt the difference between *over here* and *over there.*

What am I experiencing? Not nothing, if by nothing is meant what Paul Tillich calls *oukontic* nothing: a sort of "not even nothing" that Spinoza believes in; there is substance, and absolutely nothing else. No: what I am experiencing is a *meontic* nothingness, a quality of nihilation as palpable as it is disturbing.[8] There is nothing to hold onto, yet space has become strangely solid—yet solidity has become strangely diaphanous and ductile. It is etheric, in Chris Barrett's sense.

There is a sharp difference between *nothing* and *nothingness.* Paul Tillich distinguishes eloquently between *oukontic* nothing and *meontic* nothingness. The *ouk* in oukontic means "not" and the *ontic* means "existing"—

this is a nothing that is purely the absence of existence. Absolutely nothing—or as I prefer to say, "not even nothing." I claim that this sort of nothing is complicit with plastic substance—it is just like it, insofar as it is the flip side of something that is constantly there, remaining the same all the time. Just a bland blank. This kind of nothing or void is plagued with the same paradoxes and inconsistencies as its cousin, the Easy Think Substance.[9] For instance, since it is absolutely nothing at all, movement across it would not be possible. It cannot be demarcated. So the most consistent way to think it is like Spinoza, for whom there is substance, and absolutely nothing else, not even nothing.

Meontic nothingness, however, is quite different. The *me* in the term is not privative in the same way—it does not mean "non-being" but instead it means something like "un-being," "a-being." A phrase from Valerie Allen's chapter in this volume elegantly describes meontic nothing: it is "undecidedly situated between being airy somethings and airy nothings." And here there are resonances (as often) in sync with Cary Wolfe's response in this volume. Nothingness in this sense is a way to think elementality.

One way of thinking the logical structure of nothingness is to think of set theory. If we allow nothingness to exist we allow sets to be members of themselves. Consider a set of things. When you remove those things, you have absolutely nothing—oukontic nothing; that is, unless the set itself can remain empty, without contents. Then you have nothingness. There is a subtle difference, on the second theory, between a set and its contents, which is absurd from the point of view of the first theory. Take the things out of the set, and you should have absolutely nothing at all, not even nothing. Yet if there is a slight difference between sets and things that sets contain, you can have empty sets that are members of themselves. Elementality is a set such as this—fuzzy sets with fuzzy contents. If we want elements to be real (and I think we do), we had better adhere to the idea that Bertrand Russell could not stand: the set of things that are not members of that set. We had better get used to violating the "law" of noncontradiction, which is, it turns out, far from sacrosanct.

Another feature of a set that is a member of itself is that it has a loop form—in other words, it is recursive. This loop form, or self-reference as Russell would have called it, is, for Russell, sinister and slippery, and should be abolished. Another thing Russell could not stand, this loop form corresponds to what Jeffrey Jerome Cohen and Lowell Duckert call the vorticular structure of elements. A tight, strange example is the Möbius strip (see below).

Nothingness comes in very handy, to say the least, when ecological thought is concerned. Consider a set of things called *meadow*. There are grasses, small mammals, birds flitting about, some trees and some water. I remove a blade of grass from the meadow. I ask myself a question—is there still a meadow? Why yes. So I remove another blade of grass. Is there still a meadow? Yes. I keep on removing blades of grass and asking the question. At every step I am able to ask the same question and obtain the same answer. I end up with a bald patch of ground. Do I still have a meadow, after removing the last blade of grass? Weirdly, yes! So I conclude, wrongly, that there never was a meadow in the first place. I might as well turn the bald patch into a car park. Since there never was a meadow as such in the first place, I might as well do this with the meadow long before I have started my experiment.

Covering up nothingness like this means covering it up with oukontic nothing. In gleefully turning a meadow into a car park I am a happy nihilist, otherwise known as a modern human. I want to distinguish happy nihilism from what I call dark nihilism, which is not necessarily unhappy nihilism but rather nihilism with a twist, even laughter. This laughter is as much a political affect as it is one of suddenly understanding something, such as a joke, or an ecosystem—which is perhaps a sort of joke. Yet we find this laughter inside the sadness and anger of ecological awareness. I am interested in how to get there. The path is, I claim, through the concept of elements.

The name of the paradox that arises from my experiment is the Sorites paradox. It is the paradox of the heap—what constitutes a heap? I can add or remove grains of sand from a heap (element: earth), and end up with one grain and there is still a heap, or I can go the other way and add tens of thousands of grains and there still is no heap. Things such as heaps and meadows are fuzzy sets whose members don't entirely sum to them. There is a weird gap between a heap of sand or a meadow and the things that are in heaps and meadows. Likewise there are an awful lot of ecological heaps—biosphere, climate, frog, eukaryotic cell, DNA strand.

What have we discovered? There is some kind of gap between a set of things and its contents. In other words, it is theoretically possible to have an empty set, because otherwise you get involved in Sorites paradoxes. It seems as if the kind of set that Russell did not like is here to stay whether we like it or not. The gap between a set and its contents is what we have been calling nothingness. This kind of nothingness is deeply related to the philosophical opening of the Anthropocene in the West, namely the advent of David Hume and Immanuel Kant.

Consider what Kant says about raindrops (element: water). There are these raindrops; I can feel them on my head; they are wet, round, small, cold. They are raindroppy. Sadly they are not gumdroppy, but never mind—I know they are raindrops, not gumdrops. But I do not have the actual raindrops. What I have are raindrop data.[10] This is, or should be, a bit of a shocking thought. Hume had made it clear that what you take to be causes and effects are impositions by your conceptual mind on associated phenomena that are only likely to conform to your concept. Science, since Hume, just has been statistical, because what science studies is data, not things in themselves. Thus the Intergovernmental Panel on Climate Change (IPCC) makes it more and more clear that humans have caused global warming, but they need to express this as a statistic—as this essay is being written, 97 percent of climate scientists now hold us responsible.[11] This of course leaves an out for those conservatives who like to deny global warming by saying, "Well, it snowed in Boise, Idaho, last week, so there's no global warming at all!"

In addition to denying global warming, statements such as this are denying modern causality theories. What they are denying is a gap between data, phenomena, on the one hand, and things on the other. To reiterate: nothingness does not mean that there is no thing really. It means that the thing eludes us, and eludes everything else. It loves and strives all at once. It is withdrawn. But withdrawal in turn does not mean that a thing disappears or recedes. A thing appears. What we are talking about here is a kind of specificity. Things are ungraspable not because they are vague clouds of blah. They are ungraspable because they are not. This essay attempts to flesh out that paradox.

It is not surprising then that modernity, capitalism, and individualism would have had some trouble with the elemental, seeking to banish it from its easy wipe surfaces. Elementality is givenness.[12] And in a society where you are supposed to make yourself, this givenness can get in the way. To have spent a lifetime molding oneself, only to find that one's environment was itself a kind of mold, might be disconcerting. The other word for this elemental givenness is *magic*. Elements belong with fairies, selkies, mermaids, and their ilk—it is no wonder that the Celtic lands, brutalized and colonized by centuries of imperia, should be regarded as sparkling corners in which magical beings still exist. There is something magical about James Turrell's work, because there is something elemental about it.

What is magic? Paradoxically, magic is a good way of thinking about that most modern and mechanical seeming of things, causality.[13] In a world after Hume and Kant, it is precisely impossible to specify a cause and effect in a metaphysical way—namely, in advance of data. This means that causality in our contemporary age is always statistical, which is why global warming deniers and tobacco companies are able to say, with something like a straight face, that no one has ever proved that humans cause global warming or that smoking causes cancer. In the same way, a post-Humean person is unable to claim that this bullet she is going to fire into my head at point-blank range is going to kill me. What she can say instead is that it is 99.9 percent likely, which is actually *better*—since it relies only on data, not on metaphysical factoids culled from Aristotelian arguments about final causes.

Modern causality is a shifting, slippery thing, which is to say that strangely modern causality approaches the status of the old indigenous Trickster, the magical realms in which swords can turn into puffballs and maidens from the sea can snatch your eldest son. "We are fire's doing" (see Anne Harris in this volume). What such a causality lacks precisely is a concept of Nature, which is also what James Turrell's art lacks. Nature is a highly normative thing: it tells you what is "in" and what is "out" as surely as the new-year pages of a jaded fashion magazine. Nature is a concept that simply cannot cover absolutely everything, because Nature depends for its existence on being able to specify the unnatural. But this is just what we moderns are incapable of doing in advance of the data, which is to say that the concept of Nature was a brief Romantic-period flicker of resistance to the oncoming metal army of industrialization, like a fake medieval sword made of rubber.

Natural and unnatural, just like *here* and *there* or *foreground* and *background,* are taking an ecological beating these days. When you flush the toilet, it is now painfully obvious that *away* is just an idea in your head: whatever you flushed does not go *away*—it goes into the wastewater treatment plant to be recycled, or it might go into the local ocean. Turrell's art also lacks *away,* in a gorgeous, scintillating magenta sense that appears far removed from the exigencies of the toilet—but still.

When there is no *away* and no Nature—I always capitalize the term now to show how artificial it is—you just cannot tell what is real from what is unreal, which is the basic job of metaphysics. One is compelled to acknowledge that Jacques Lacan had a point when he said, "What constitutes pretense is that, in the end, you do not know whether it is pretense or not."[14] You have left the illusion of Nature and have now arrived in the Highland realms of the Trickster. The air is strangely refreshing. Grasses are growing, bristled with gorse and its disconcerting spines, and thistled with strange violets and blues like a Turrell work. A rainbow appears in the gray sky shivered with lights and shadows. Things sparkle. Or as Tim Ingold, quoted by Lowell Duckert here, puts it, "the earth is 'earthing.'"[15]

The realm of ecology, which I shall now call the elemental realm, is not some boring substrate underneath artificial flavors and colors, precisely because we cannot peel flavors and colors away from substances without a prepackaged metaphysics, without Nature. The elemental realm is *weird,* which is to say precisely that it is in a loop, like a serpent biting itself, which is to say that it is a strange self-contradictory zone of nothingness that consumes itself to go on existing. *Weird* comes from Old Norse *urth,* which means twist (or vortex): the Norns, guardians of destiny, entwining the web of fate on their spinning wheels. *Weird* can mean *causal:* the spool of fate is winding. And yet *weird* can also mean a certain strangeness of appearance—or indeed the way in which appearance as such is strange.[16] Weirdness thus uncannily sutures together the aesthetic and the causal, categories that modernity strives to keep apart at all costs, precisely as I argue here to repress its innermost thought. Kant's raindrops, for instance, just are weird, insofar as their appearance is not them, yet this appearance is to be found nowhere else. Appearance is thus irreducibly weird. Things can look weird because things *are* weird.

There is a strange looping of appearance and being, or as Serpil Oppermann and Serenella Iovino put it in this volume, "story" and "matter." The modern mathematical term for a loop with a twist is *Möbius strip.* A Möbius strip is a very beautiful image for a weird thing whose appearance cannot be peeled easily and metaphysically from its essence. This is because a Möbius strip is a *non-orientable surface,* which is to say that at no point on the surface of the strip will you be able to discern where the twist begins: it is as it were everywhere and nowhere at the same time.

A thing—a thistle, a Turrell work, a blizzard—is like a Möbius strip insofar as it does not come with a ready-made dotted line and a little picture of scissors on it saying *Cut Here.* Western philosophy since Plato has been in the dotted line business, policing the difference between essence and appearance such that appearance has often come out as the evil, or degenerate, or ineffectual (or all three) twin of essence. In an ecological age philosophy must decisively get out of the dotted line business and into some other line of work. To think this way is to join the two epigraphs that begin Julian Yates's chapter in this volume. The palpability of the thing, which Serres asserts, and the necessity of the hermeneutical and medial loops in which they are caught, as de Man asserts—the deconstructive term for these loops might be arche-writing or the trace structure: it is strangely possible to think these together.[17] This thinking together is precisely the task of an investigation of the elemental and ecological.

I would like to suggest the manufacture of philosophical allergy medicines as a good alternative to the now defunct metaphysical dotted line business. Elements come in all shapes and sizes, since they are appearance and essence in an inseparable, non-orientable weird loop. It would be best for us to make friends with them rather than trying to police them or push them away—remember, there is no *away,* so trying to peel the elemental out of reality would be like trying to peel your mind from your thoughts. What we urgently need in an ecological era is like Maitri Space Awareness, a greater tolerance to the vibrancy and color of things—their wateriness, fieriness, airiness, spaciousness, earthiness. This is a kind of essence in the way that perfumes are called *essences:* not some boring odorless surface underneath, but precisely the opposite—a multidimensional sparkling that I cannot decisively locate inside or outside of myself. Some strange kind of magic. A realm of faerie. The etymology of *faerie* finds its root in the Latin *fatum,* whose Old Norse term is the one we already encountered, *urth.*[18] Whichever end of the Indo-European derivatives one seems to be grasping, language itself tells us that causality is aesthetic.

Magic—that is, action at a distance, or some kind of occasionalism in which a third thing (such as a god) mediates between one thing and another thing— is what the agency of the elemental can mean in our contemporary age, beyond the atavistic reductionism that is a curious reaction *against* the modernity that opens up the Pandora's box of nothingness. The "secular" age of modernity is evidently a religion in which two things are believed (unsupported by the Kantian strain in modern philosophy itself): (1) that a thing is precisely not magical insofar as it does not contradict itself, and (2) that (1) is not a belief. We are in a curious situation. The secret passageway between the elemental and the causal is precisely what modernity excludes. Yet it is also the innermost core of the thought that inaugurates modernity, as a logical consequence of the separation of phenomenon and thing (Hume, Kant) is that causality is on the hither side of things, rather than being a mechanism of balls and springs somewhere underneath. Far from being an outmoded, snigger-worthy concept, the elemental is the encrypted secret of modernity. What modernity marginalizes as indigenous superstition returns as a weird Celtic twilight around the edges, a spectral glow.

Brenda Hillman has recently been exploring ecological poetics. Her latest book, *Seasonal Works with Letters on Fire,* is an explicit delving into the elemental, its infinite yet palpable yet shimmering queerness. One prose poem is called "The Elements Are Mixed in Childhood":

> Our mother was baptized on a kerosene box, our father was baptized in a creek, & we were baptized in a plaster pool while turquoise ripples played around our feet & desert air poofed up to make the long black robe a nylon buffalo. *It makes your underpants wet,* said our brother. It's strange to be on fire with sins. This is how the part begins: it is the year of the missile crisis; it is the year of Barbie & Ken. Mama studies ridges in her gloves, the congregation sings a hymn while out in the desert, the worm grows tall & nature is a mixed-up miracle.

> We strain to see the cross behind our head: not only no penis on Jesus, no Jesus at all. That's how Baptists like it: the invisible is physical. That's the way it is, says Walter Concrete in the news. Talking flames get rid of hell. In college we'll read Emerson; in college we'll meet Robert Duncan dressed like a bat but we don't know that. Go ahead, says curlicue, the mind is what you need to make up & why should a child be dressed like a bat, wings flapping up to her sides like that? Bat-at-at-at.
>
> The congregation sings a hymn, they hold the stanzas up-up-up. Mama studies ridges in her gloves; she is our eternal love. Childhood certainly is odd: everything is everything, earth air beauty fire wood water love blood, time is what you need to mix up & what is anything not god. The choir circles the circles; they're singing to rehearse for glory, fiery stanzas fill our head. That's why words are round in every story; that's why we love music and talk the dead—[19]

So many elements, so little time. There are the "turquoise ripples," the Pentecostal "talking flames," the "everything is everything, earth air beauty fire wood water love blood." Then there is the "childhood." What isn't an element? It sounds facetious, but this is the key question. It is as if the category of the elemental absorbs everything—overwhelms it, gently, soaking into things like a telepath, "reading" things, bathing them in its aesthetic scan. A fuzzy set.

Elementality shares something with the way in which fiction, especially realist fiction, plays in a telepathic ocean of shared and distributed affects. Structuralist narratological concepts such as focalization—that moment in a novel where we appear to be reading a character's mind, precisely as a function of the dropping of the usual indirect speech tags—are like bulwarks against a more disturbing telepathic thought that leaks out everywhere.[20] The birth of photography was marked by an obsession with photographing the paranormal—in the same way, the birth of realist fiction was intimately bound up with accounting for specters in a way that refused to relegate them to irrelevancy or superstition. Don't we witness in those two phenomena a return of the repressed within modernity, a return of what the dominant, normative accounts of the Humean–Kantian shock wave, and their reductionist materialist defenses, strive to ward off?[21] A repressed that keeps leaking back in, like the phlogiston described by Steve Mentz, or the ether described in Chris Barrett's chapter, even, as she points out, as the Higgs Field, hysterical symptom of the correlationist Standard Model (of quantum theory)?

The gasoline of realism is supplied by the reader herself. It is anxiety, a flickering of uncertainty. "Is this for real or not?" is the realist question, par excellence. Consider the following sentences:

> Kermit the Frog woke up. He knew that it was going to be a nice day.

We can sense the tools of narrative in operation. An obvious tag marks the second sentence as belonging to Kermit. The tag is a tool. It juts out like a sore thumb, making the narrative world obvious and self-contained. Now consider these two:

> Kermit the Frog woke up. It was going to be a nice day.

At which level are we to read them? Who says, "It is going to be a nice day"? The narrator, or the Frog? It is as if there is a sudden, strange twist, a Möbius loop in which one level of the text flips over onto the other, such that they become indistinguishable, yet not reducible to a one.

Isn't there a literary equivalent of the Ganzfeld effect at work here? Something intangible is just functioning. And isn't there something a little sinister about Kermit, all of a sudden? Don't we suspect some hidden intention, some weird depth? Perhaps he nurses psychopathic tendencies. Martin Heidegger describes anxiety as a disturbing flatness:

> What anxiety is about is completely indefinite. . . . Nothing which is at hand and present within the world functions as that which anxiety is anxious about. The totality of relevance of things at hand and objectively present is completely without importance. . . . It collapses into itself. It has the character of complete insignificance.[22]

Is this not what we encounter when we think the elemental? Heidegger clinches it in the very next paragraph:

> Thus neither does anxiety "see" a definite "there" and "over here" from which what is threatening approaches. The fact that what is threatening is *nowhere* characterizes what anxiety is about. . . . But "nowhere" does not mean nothing. . . . What is threatening cannot come closer from a definite direction within nearness, it is already "there"—and yet nowhere. It is so near that it is oppressive and takes away one's breath—and yet it is nowhere.[23]

The basic anxiety Heidegger describes here is the characteristic attunement of an ecological age in which we know full well that there is no "away"—waste goes somewhere, but not ontologically "away." Nor is there Nature as opposed to the human world. Ecological awareness is necessarily elemental. Fear of a coming eco-apocalypse (or eschatology of any kind) covers over the elemental, by distorting this threat of nothing(ness) into a fear of something more palpable and "over yonder." Elemental anxiety is an existential Ganzfeld effect.

Perhaps anxiety is an element—perhaps indeed it points to some kind of thing, such as Irigaray's air. In anxiety, don't I experience myself in an elemental way—isn't this experience both an appreciation of "myself" as abject thing prior to subjectivity or objectivity, as a billowing cloud of unknowing? And isn't this good information about what constitutes a thing as such?

The elemental effect, whether in Turrell or in narrative or in ecological awareness, is the inverse of what is now called *thing theory.*[24] Thing theory relies on Heidegger's tool analysis. When a tool breaks or malfunctions, we notice it. This theory of malfunctioning points out that when things smoothly function, when they just happen, they withdraw from access. When I am involved in a task, the things I involve myself with disappear.

Yet the element in which I am involved does not disappear. Indeed, this is a precise definition of the element: the appearance of involvement. It is just that I only experience this appearance obliquely, as goosebumps for instance, or a sense of horror or of bliss. The elemental is precisely the set without contents that we investigated in this essay's exploration of meontic nothing.

Paradoxically the inverse of thing theory is not nothing at all, but what I call *object theory.* I here use the term *object* in the sense described by object-oriented ontology (OOO). It turns out that malfunctioning tools that we notice all of a sudden depend not only on smoothly functioning, without our attention, but also on a far deeper being that is strictly inaccessible no matter how deeply we probe, or how deeply anything probes—including the "tool" in question. But perhaps "deeper" is not quite the right term. Let us try this on for size: objects are so incredibly . . . themselves. Yet in this selfsameness they are weird, self-transcending. The contrary motion of what things are and how they appear jets out of a thing. Things emit uniqueness. They *bristle* with specificity. Purple, pale violet, light blue, their soft and sharp spines and flower-spines bristle forth. Bristle forth despite me, despite my subject–object scissions. This bristling is the magical causality that is neither absolutely love nor absolutely strife.

Imagine the colored space, the radiance of the bristling. This bristling of pure appearance, inseparable from the weird, *nihilesque* undulation of essence, is the being whereby I can think the elemental.[25]

Notes

1. I take this phrase from Christopher Bollas, *The Shadow of the Object: Psychoanalysis of the Unthought Known* (London: Free Association Press, 1996).

2. Chögyam Trungpa, "Maitri Space Awareness in a Buddhist Therapeutic Community," in *The Sanity We Are Born With: A Buddhist Approach to Psychology,* ed. Carolyn Rose Gimian (Boston: Shambhala, 2005), 165–75.

3. Luce Irigaray, *The Forgetting of Air in Martin Heidegger,* trans. Mary Beth Mader (Austin: University of Texas Press, 1999), 8, 41.

4. Julia Kristeva, *Powers of Horror: An Essay on Abjection,* trans. Leon S. Roudiez (New York: Columbia University Press, 1982).

5. I prefer this to the image of the flayed man in Michel Serres, *The Five Senses: A Philosophy of Mingled Bodies,* trans. Margaret Sankey and Peter Crowley (New York: Continuum, 2009), viii.

6. See Tim Ingold, "Footprints through the Weather-World: Walking, Breathing, Knowing," *Journal of the Royal Anthropological Institute* 16 (May 2010): 121–39.

7. See, for example, Glen Mazis, *Humans, Animals, Machines: Blurring Boundaries* (Albany: State University of New York Press, 2008).

8. Paul Tillich, *Systematic Theology,* vol. 1, *Reason and Revelation: Being and God* (Chicago: University of Chicago Press, 1951), 188.

9. There is an ethics and politics one can derive from this, as I explore in *Dark Ecology* (New York: Columbia University Press, forthcoming). For much further detail on this topic, see David Macauley, *Elemental Philosophy: Earth, Air, Fire, and Water as Environmental Ideas* (Albany: State University of New York Press, 2010).

10. Immanuel Kant, *Critique of Pure Reason,* trans. Norman Kemp Smith (New York: St. Martin's, 1965), 84–85.

11. Dana Nuccitelli, "Global Warming: Why Is IPCC Report So Certain about the Influence of Humans?," *The Guardian,* September 27, 2013.

12. See Jean-Luc Marion, *In Excess: Studies of Saturated Phenomena,* trans. Robyn Horner and Vincent Berraud (New York: Fordham University Press, 2010).

13. Timothy Morton, *Realist Magic: Objects, Ontology, Causality* (Ann Arbor: Open Humanities Press, 2013).

14. Jacques Lacan, *Le séminaire de Jacques Lacan,* vol. 3, *Les psychoses* (Paris: Editions de Seuil, 1981), 48, translation mine.

15. Tim Ingold, *Being Alive: Essays on Movement, Knowledge and Description* (New York: Routledge, 2011), 144.

16. *Oxford English Dictionary,* s.v. "weird" (adj. 1, 2.a, 3).

17. Michel Serres, *Biogea,* trans. Randolph Burks (Minneapolis: Univocal, 2012), 38–39; Paul de Man, *Blindness and Insight: Essays on the Rhetoric of Contemporary Criticism* (Minneapolis: University of Minnesota Press, 1983), 244.

18. *Oxford English Dictionary,* s.v. "faerie" (n.2).

19. Brenda Hillman, *Seasonal Works with Letters on Fire* (Middletown, Conn.: Wesleyan University Press, 2013), 55.

20. See Nicholas Royle, *Telepathy and Literature: Essays on the Reading Mind* (Oxford: Blackwell, 1991).

21. See Jeffrey Kripal, *Authors of the Impossible: The Paranormal and the Sacred* (Chicago: University of Chicago Press, 2010), 7–17, 26–35.

22. Martin Heidegger, *Being and Time,* trans. Joan Stambaugh (Albany: State University of New York Press, 2010), 180 (1.6).

23. Ibid.

24. Bill Brown, "Thing Theory," *Critical Inquiry* 28, no. 1 (Autumn 2001): 1–22.

25. I take the term *esque* from a manuscript by Brian Massumi. Thank you to Jane Bennett for talking about this with me.

Elemental Relations at the Edge

CARY WOLFE

The palm at the end of the mind,
Beyond the last thought, rises
In the bronze decor.

A gold-feathered bird
Sings in the palm, without human meaning,
Without human feeling, a foreign song.

You know then that it is not the reason
That makes us happy or unhappy.
The bird sings. Its feathers shine.

The palm stands on the edge of space.
The wind moves slowly in the branches.
The bird's fire-fangled feathers dangle down.

—WALLACE STEVENS, "*Of Mere Being,*"

"Of Mere Being"—one of the last things Wallace Stevens ever wrote, and the piece that concludes the collection *The Palm at the End of the Mind*—is drawn, like all of the chapters gathered in this collection, to the allure of the inhuman or ahuman, here figured as the song of a bird "without human meaning / Without human feeling."[1] To be sure, Stevens here takes his place in a very, very long line of poets, from a host of literary traditions, who are fascinated with the fundamentally ahuman character of birdsong. To wit, if the *bird* is traditionally twin to the *bard,* bringing in its song news from the above and beyond (or in the case of Edgar Allan Poe's raven, perhaps, the *below* and beyond), then Stevens in this poem attempts to detranscendentalize, detheologize, or naturalize the meaning of the bird and its message, now no longer taken to be a messenger of the gods or the heavens, along the lines of his assertion that another important bird poem, "Sunday Morning," presents "a naturalistic religion as a substitute for supernaturalism."[2]

As with all the authors collected in this volume—and perhaps with everyone at some point or another—Stevens desires contact with "things as they are" (as he writes in "The Man with the Blue Guitar") (*Palm,* 133), with "things freed . . . of their packages," as Michel Serres puts it in *Biogea* (a text invoked more than once in these pages).[3] Indeed, the epigraph at the opening of Julian Yates's chapter in this volume taken from Serres's text shares many of the desires, and even some of the specific imagery, found in Stevens's famous poem "The Man on the Dump," which complains that "The dump is full / Of images. Days pass like papers from a press," leading the poet to long for that moment when

> Everything is shed; and the moon comes up as the moon
> (All of its images are in the dump) and you see
> As a man (not like an image of a man).
> You see the moon rise in the empty sky. (*Palm,* 163–64)

Or as Serres puts it, almost as poetically: "How to estimate at their exact thickness the layers of media under which all things lie, thus multiply wrapped under writings, folded under sounds, choked under languages, lost under a hundred screens?" (*Biogea,* 39).

But the fine print of Stevens's poem makes it even more germane to this volume. It not only plumbs the question of the ahuman (or what has come to be called the "posthuman") in terms of the elemental (earth, fire, air, water, though those were not always the only elements, nor are they now); it also shares with the authors collected here an interest in how the elemental is as paradoxical and complex and it is seemingly, well, elemental. To fully describe the "love and strife" of the elements, in other words, the elements themselves have to both be, and not be, precisely what they are—a paradox I will attempt to articulate in some detail later through the machinery of second-order systems theory. As for Stevens's part, in "Of Mere Being" we find, right off the bat, the "bronze" of the setting, then later the "gold" of the bird's feathers, and between the lines the earth out of which the palm rises and the water that makes it grow. Near poem's end, we are confronted with the "fire" that "fangles" feathers and, more indirectly, the air that makes itself manifest in both the bird's song and the movement of the tree in the closing lines. But the elemental is immediately (and characteristically) complicated by Stevens in myriad ways. Take, for example, the word *mere* in the title. It may mean "only" or "just," of course (as it is usually taken), and as such is deflationary if not pejorative. But it may also mean "essential" or "very"—the very being of Being, as it were, its very elemental stuff—thus raising the question of being's essence turned inside out, subordinated to becoming, perhaps, in the transient nature of the bird's song, the movement of the breeze through feathers and leaves, "beyond the last thought," beyond reason.[4]

Or take the intertextual difference here between "decor" (used in the original typescript and restored in *The Palm at the End of the Mind*) and "distance" (used in the poem's publication in *Opus Posthumous* in 1957), which stages in miniature the co-implication of the given and the made, "reality" and technics, that is figured in the fusion of flesh and metal that suffuses the poem, most obviously in the "gold-feathered bird" singing as it sits in the palm tree, "on the edge of space." (Since when does space have an edge? On the other hand, as I have noted elsewhere, isn't it the case that *all* spaces have edges, and unavoidably so, precisely because the observation of space itself sets it off against *another* outside, another more spacey "space" you might say, which only maintains its character by virtue of being the outside *of* an inside, precisely in the manner of a "strange loop" or Möbius strip of the sort invoked in Valerie Allen's discussion of the torus?[5])

The thinly veiled allusion here to Yeats's bird in "Sailing to Byzantium," which every critic has noticed, shares that poem's rejection of naturalism, to be sure. But it also, and more importantly for our purposes, shares its paradoxical intrication of space and time, the strange loop of temporality of "what is past, or passing, or to come," the "artifice of eternity," in Yeats's memorable words, that obtains in the act of speaking and writing—here and now, from some location that is absolutely real and temporally located, radically contingent in the etymological sense of the word *radical* as "root"—about the elemental and the eternal, that whose time is radically *not* this time, untouched by the human. To put it another way, is "fire-fangled," as Stevens's neologism forces us to ask by way of adjacent association, paradoxically "*new*-fangled"? Maybe, but one thing we know for sure is that Stevens's bird does not just throw into question the distinction between the organic or biological and the mechanical or technical, it is also (as David Wills would remind us) *prosthetic,* its song as dependent on the *machinalité* of technics as ours is, whether a "program" produced by instinct or the artifice produced by "Grecian goldsmiths" (as Yeats writes)[6]—a point nailed down firmly by the poem's allusion to Yeats's bird of "hammered gold and gold enameling," doubled in Stevens's own gaudy alliteration and internal slant rhyme that we see flashing before our eyes only insofar as we can *hear* it: its "fire-fangled feathers dangle down." Or as Yates (Julian, not William Butler) succinctly puts it in these pages, "packaging matters"—and how.

We are thus now in a better position to appreciate an even finer point that etymology will help us put on Stevens's "foreign song": the fact that the etymology of *foreign* connects both the Old French and Latin for "external," "out of doors," and "outside" with a seventeenth-century change in the spelling linked to the "-reign" of "sovereign." "Foreign," then, as "sovereign"? That will indeed be the question we want to pursue, in league with the authors in this volume such as Steve Mentz, who finds in his reading of Coriolanus "the element's rage against plurality, its desire to transform many differences into one glowing thing": namely, how do we "reign" in (or reign *out*) the "sovereignty" of the "foreign"? If the logic of the sovereign thing is the logic, as Jacques Derrida reminds us, of the "self-same," of the "singular" and "ipseity," then might we not need another logic of the ahuman or inhuman to make it properly *post*human—or rather, posthuman*ist*[7]—or even better, "phlogisticated," if Mentz is indeed right that "a paradoxical entanglement of separation and combination . . . is itself characteristic of elemental relations"?

Here, then, we are squarely on the terrain of the "love and strife" among elements and their relations that results from the fact of nothing being separate even as everything is separate, those selfsame elements that, in their striving to be discrete, only trace all the more the arc by which we know them to be elements—know them to be anything at all—in the first place. One way to rephrase this problem is in terms of things and relations as taken up by what has come to be called object-oriented ontology (OOO) (an increasingly unsatisfactory label that homogenizes an increasingly diverse body of work).[8] Both object-oriented philosopher Graham Harman and actor-network theorist Bruno Latour are invoked regularly in this collection, and in his book on Latour, Harman argues against Latour's position that relations are primary—more specifically, that "a thing is defined entirely by its relations."[9] Or as Latour characterizes his position,

> The word "substance" does not designate "what remains beneath," impervious to history, but what gathers together a multiplicity of agents into a stable and coherent whole. A substance is more like the thread that holds the pearls of a necklace together than the rock bed that remains the same no matter what is built on it. . . . Substance is a name that designates the *stability* of an assemblage. (quoted in Harman, *Prince of Networks,* 81)

For Harman, however, the price that Latour's "relationism" pays is that "while the gaps between entities are rightly multiplied to infinity, he leaves no gap at all between a thing's inherent reality and its effects on other things" (ibid., 112). And what is this "inherent reality"? According to Harman,

> there will always be more to the hammer than any possible contact with its being. . . . We cannot assume that the hammer is made of molecules any more than of hammer-spirits. Any such theory is an attempt to format or formulate the hammer. This must not be confused with the hammer's own reality, to which no format ever does justice. And that is why Latour opposes materialism, though he rejects the withdrawn depths of the hammer in favor of its alliances with other things. (ibid., 142)

But if this "inherent reality" and "withdrawn depths" are neither "format" on the one hand nor unformatted "material" on the other, then what are they, if "not only *human* relations with a thing reduce it to presence-at-hand, but *any relations at all,*" including those between, say, fire and cotton? Harman's answer is that "in fact there is no such thing as matter, but only a descending chain of what used to be called substantial forms. These forms are not just real, but also purely non-relational. It is true that matter has no primary qualities, but only secondary ones, since it is always in relation with other things. Yet primary qualities do exist outside matter: in the heart of substance itself" (ibid., 145).

I cannot, in the confines of this essay, take up a full engagement of Harman's position here—suffice it to say for the moment that many of the objections I would raise have already been made by many others[10]—but it is worth noting that even within OOO the question of the "elemental" nature of things versus relations has been thought quite differently, as in the work of Levi Bryant, who attempts to adapt the theory of autopoiesis from second-order systems theory, with its emphasis on self-reference and operational closure, as a way to redescribe what Harman calls the "withdrawn" character of objects, the fact that "while substances can enter into exo-relations with other substances," as Bryant writes, "they only do so *on their own terms* and with respect to their own organization" or what he calls their "endo-consistency."[11] He observes that "like Harman's objects, Luhmann's systems are autonomous individuals that are closed and independent of other systems"—they confront environmental complexity from the "outside" or "environment" in terms of, and only in terms of, their own self-referential operational closure (*The Democracy of Objects,* 161). For Bryant this better enables us to make sense of Harman's claim that

> *all* objects, whether animate or inanimate, relate to other objects not as *real* objects, but as sensuous objects.... Sensuous objects are not the real object itself, but are, rather, what objects are for other objects. In this respect, sensuous objects are very similar to Luhmann's information events and system-states. Unlike real objects, Harman's sensuous objects exist only on the *interior* of a real object. These sensuous objects can arise both from the interior of the real object that encounters them or from other real objects. (ibid.)

Of course, the question that immediately arises—namely, if all objects only relate to other objects as sensuous objects, then how do we know that "real" objects exist "underneath" them, as it were, and even if they did, how could that fact be described in an accurate, nondistorting way?—is one to which systems theory has a ready answer: you *cannot* know that, since that statement, like all such distinctions and attributions about an environment, is made by a self-referential act of observation of an observing system embedded in overwhelming environmental complexity (and this need not mean, as Latour and Luhmann well realize, that the observer need be a "human" or a "person").

Such a response is usually summarily dismissed by object-oriented ontology and speculative realism as merely "epistemological" or "correlationist," but this misunderstands a couple of quite fundamental postulates of systems theory. First of all, for systems theory, the question is not epistemological but *pragmatic.* As Luhmann makes clear, the veracity of the systems theoretical analysis is not about epistemological adequation to some pregiven state of ontological affairs (whether realist *or* idealist) but is rather based on its *functional* specificity. Contrary to the understanding of autopoietic systems as closed in the same way that objects are thought to be "withdrawn," the operational closure of systems and the self-reference based upon it arise as a practical and adaptive necessity precisely because systems are *not* closed—that is, precisely because they find themselves in an environment of overwhelmingly and exponentially greater complexity than is possible for any single system. What this means, to use Jeffrey Jerome Cohen's term, is that systems are *vulnerable,* and they maintain themselves and achieve their autopoiesis, in a sense, against all odds. It is this dilemma (which can also, of course, be an opportunity) that gets thematized in Cohen's chapter when he asks, "What if the sea above is not a lesson in timeless theology so much as a demonstration of shared, elemental vulnerability? What if the closures offered by theological truth and sorting of ontological status matter less here than the invitation wonder offers to a more open world?"

To put it another way, systems have to operate "blindly" (as Luhmann puts it) not because they are closed but precisely because they *are not.* Commonsensically enough, no system can establish point for point correspondences between the dynamic internal states of its elements and all the myriad changes taking place in its environment at a given moment, and so, as Luhmann puts it, "the system's inferiority in complexity must be counter-balanced by strategies of selection. Complexity, in this sense, means being forced to select."[12] Systems are both open *and* closed, then, and the asymmetrical distribution of complexity across the system/environment difference is in fact what *forces* the strategy of self-referential closure. Indeed, the "second-order" turn, as I have argued elsewhere,[13] is to realize that the more systems build up their own internal complexity through recursive self-reference and closure, the *more* linked they are to changes in their environments to which they become more and more sensitive—which is why the stock market or academic specialties like cultural studies register with a higher degree of complexity the changes in their broader environment than an amoeba that responds only to either gradients of light or dark, higher or lower sugar concentrations, and so on—even though both are autopoietic systems. It ought to be obvious by now that this is not at all about "correlationism" as it us usually described—the idea that "being exists only as a correlate between mind and world"—and this is the case not least of all because "mind" is not a constitutive element of systems theory, for whom observers can be nonhuman and even, in Luhmann's work, inorganic communication systems.[14] Quite the contrary, it is about systems *not* being free to just think whatever they will at their whimsy about objects and things. Or as Luhmann puts it, it is "unproductive for meanings to circulate as mere self-referentiality or in short-circuited tautologies. . . . One can think, 'This rose is a rose is a rose is a rose.' But this use of a recursive path is productive only if it makes itself dependent on specific conditions and does not always ensue" (*Social Systems,* 61).

This limitation, again, is not epistemological but pragmatic, and the understanding of that fact seems to me hard-wired in both Anne Harris's emphasis on "fire's *doing*" (not Being) and in Lowell Duckert's methodological commitments about the kinds of stories he will and will not pursue about "the *matter* of coal" and our future with it (even though we could make up some nicer ones to make ourselves feel "greener"). Similarly, there is nothing to stop you on *epistemological* grounds from thinking that phlogiston exists, as Steve Mentz's chapter shows us, or from thinking, in the universe traced by Anne Harris's chapter, that you are made of glass, or from thinking—for that matter—that the primary qualities of objects exist outside of all matter in the heart of substance itself. Indeed, the history of philosophy and of science makes it abundantly clear that *epistemological* grounds will not stop you from thinking all sorts of things. But there is plenty to stop you on *pragmatic* grounds, even though (as Latour has brilliantly shown us time and again), "wrong" theories may work well enough, enough of the time, for extended periods under the right conditions. This is precisely where we can agree with Jane Bennett's assertion that the elements are not just metaphorical but they "can also kill you," but without seeing the practical force of that claim as deriving from the fact that it is grounded in some ontological purchase—realist, idealist, or otherwise. So if the first misunderstanding has to do with the nature of systems as closed or "withdrawn," the second has to do with the fact that, from a pragmatist, system theory point of view, claims of "epistemology" and "correlationism" are, strictly speaking, beside the point. As Richard Rorty quite elegantly puts it, "what shows us that life is not a dream, that our beliefs are in touch with reality, is the *causal,* non-intentional, non-representational, links between us and the rest of the universe."[15] The pragmatist, he continues, "believes, as strongly as does any realist, that there are objects which are *causally* independent of human beliefs and desires" (*Philosophical Papers,* 101). She "recognizes relations of *justification* holding between beliefs and desires, and relations of *causation* holding between those beliefs and desires and other items in the universe, but no relations of *representation*" (ibid., 97).

But this is an answer, however, of which OOO, at least in Harman's iteration of it, will not avail itself upon terror of the charge of "correlationism," and so we end up back in the all too familiar and untenable philosophical quandaries attendant upon line-in-the-sand distinctions between inside and outside, primary and secondary qualities, and so on, which (it is suggested) we have to believe if we believe that reality is real. Take, for example, the "Monster X" scenario that Harman spins out in his book on Latour. Monster X, unlike his friend's cat, is utterly a figment of Harman's imagination, and, as Bryant puts it, "is not withdrawn, and ceases to exist when he falls asleep at night or ceases thinking about it," whereas the cat is "an object out there in the world that is capable of being perturbed by other objects" (*The Democracy of Objects,* 162). But of course, "Monster X" does not exist solely in the "interior" of the object called Graham Harman's mind at all, and indeed is only possible as a psychic phenomenon on the basis of all sorts of cultural practices, languages, narratives, and the like that exist "outside" and are the very prosthetic condition of possibility for Harman (or anyone else) having any thoughts or imaginations (of this type or any other) in the first place—hence Luhmann's crucial distinction between "psychic" and "social" systems, the goings on in the neurophysiological wetware inside your skull, on the one hand, and the social modes of communication that are linked to them by means of "symbolically generalized media" such as language, on the other.[16] Is there a difference between Monster X and the cat? Sure. It is just not the *kind* of difference that Harman thinks it is.

In my view, the chapters collected here tend overwhelmingly toward the Latourian (if not Luhmannian) rather than the Harmanic end of the spectrum. Indeed we might say, with Karl Steel, that swarms, vermin, creeping things, and spontaneous generation are precisely about the untenability of maintaining the sharp divide between element and relation, the threatening and unpoliceable fact of "the inscrutable, acentric operations of matter" always already in relations of its own accord, always already doing its own thing, like Harris's fire. In short, "love and strife" are everywhere, ceaselessly, recombinantly so. Or as Steel puts it in this volume, "its noise is its matter is its motion, all together." This means that "the fundamental disorder is not a problem particular to vermin but rather one general to all that is; . . . we ourselves and our worldly counterparts are also immanent to this material vibrancy or constantly erupting disorder; we are therefore not alive so long as 'being alive' means having some escape from presumptively inert, 'dead,' or uncreative materiality."

True enough. The OOO people are certainly right when they assert that human beings are just another kind of object that exists "*among* the various types of objects that exist or populate the world, each with their own specific powers and capacities" (Bryant, *The Democracy of Objects*, 20). What must immediately be added, however, is that this concatenation of fecund and vibrant materiality may and does routinely give rise to particular ways of being in the world that cannot themselves be reduced to the facticity of their material substrate, precisely because they arise in temporally dynamic recursive relations in which, strictly speaking, there is no "there" there, no fixed location for the phenomenal domains located in opposite ways by Slavoj Žižek and Karen Barad in Steel's reading. To wit, it is true that all persons are things but not all things are persons (even though *person,* as we know, is not the word we want here). A long and slow and dramatic and obvious example of this fact is the concatenative crapshoot known as Darwinian evolution, in which multiple embodied temporalities exist in an organism chockablock with others to produce phenomenal domains that are, for that very reason, only partially accessible to being X (as both Barad and Žižek would agree for their different reasons)—including, of course, the being who is describing that very phenomenon by means of a knowledge map or schema or language that is both "dead" (that is, nonorganic) *machinalité* and radically exterior to any empirical form of life.[17]

Which brings us back to "packaging" and "prosthesis," and also explains, with Jeffrey Cohen, why one man's air is another man's water. To forget this fact is to drown by breathing. And it is also to forget the "mereness" of Stevens's "Of Mere Being," itself paradoxically rooted (as it were) in the palm that marks "the edge of space," "beyond the last thought," but only to also mark at the same time a "spacier" space, another thought, that lies beyond it. To paraphrase Luhmann, this makes no sense, but it makes meaning, and there, in "the bronze distance" (or is it "décor"?), "it is not the reason / That makes us happy or unhappy," but something more elemental.[18]

Notes

I would like to thank the editors for their remarkably insightful and suggestive comments on an earlier version of this essay.

1. Wallace Stevens, "Of Mere Being," in *The Palm at the End of the Mind: Selected Poems and a Play,* ed. Holly Stevens (New York: Alfred A. Knopf, 1971), 398. Further citations appear parenthetically in the text.

2. Wallace Stevens, quoted in Holly Stevens, ed., *Letters of Wallace Stevens* (Berkeley: University of California Press, 1996), 464n7.

3. Michel Serres, *Biogea,* trans. Randolph Burks (Minneapolis: Univocal, 2012), 38. Further citations appear parenthetically in the text.

4. See the notes on the poem in Eleanor Cook, *A Reader's Guide to Wallace Stevens* (Princeton, N.J.: Princeton University Press, 2007), 314.

5. For more on this, see my book *Critical Environments: Postmodern Theory and the Pragmatics of the "Outside"* (Minneapolis: University of Minnesota Press, 1998), 117–28 and esp. 123–24.

6. Regarding Jacques Derrida's late work on this topic, and in particular the relation of programmatic behavior to the difference between "reaction" and "response" that anchors the human/animal divide, see, for example, Jacques Derrida, *The Animal That Therefore I Am,* trans. David Wills, ed. Marie-Louise Mallet (New York: Fordham University Press, 2008). For David Wills's work in this area, see most of all *Prosthesis* (Stanford: Stanford University Press, 1995).

7. Jacques Derrida, *Rogues: Two Essays on Reason,* trans. Pascale-Anne Brault and Michael Naas (Stanford: Stanford University Press, 2005), 11. On the distinction between the "posthuman" and "posthuman*ism*," see my *What Is Posthumanism?* (Minneapolis: University of Minnesota Press, 2010).

8. Timothy Morton's work, for example, seems to me quite different from Levi Bryant's, which in turns seems quite different from Graham Harman's. See, for example, the important figure of "mesh" and meshwork in relation to ecological thinking in Morton's later work, as opposed to Harman's emphasis on "withdrawal."

9. Graham Harman, *Prince of Networks: Bruno Latour and Metaphysics* (Melbourne: re.press, 2009), 81. Further citations appear parenthetically in the text.

10. See, for example, Martin Hagglund's critique in "Radical Atheist Materialism: A Critique of Meillassoux," in *The Speculative Turn: Continental Materialism and Realism,* ed. Levi Bryant, Nick Srnicek, and Graham Harman (Melbourne: re.press, 2011), 114–29.

11. Levi Bryant, *The Democracy of Objects* (Ann Arbor: Open Humanities Press, 2011), 147, 141. Further citations appear parenthetically in the text.

12. Niklas Luhmann, *Social Systems,* trans. John Bednarz Jr. with Dirk Baecker (Stanford: Stanford University Press, 1995), 25–26. Further citations appear parenthetically in the text.

13. Namely, in *What Is Posthumanism?*

14. The characterization of "correlationism" is from Ian Bogost, *Alien Phenomenology, Or What It's Like to Be a Thing* (Minneapolis: University of Minnesota Press, 2013), 5, summarizing Quentin Meillassoux's definition of the term in his book *After Finitude* (London: Continuum, 2008).

15. Richard Rorty, *Philosophical Papers,* vol. 1, *Objectivity, Relativism, and Truth* (New York: Cambridge University Press, 1991), 159. Further citations appear parenthetically in the text.

16. On this point, see Luhmann's chapter "How Can the Mind Participate in Communication?," in *Materialities of Communication,* ed. Hans Ulrich Gumbrecht and Ludwig K. Pfeiffer, trans. William Whobrey (Stanford: Stanford University Press, 1994), 371–88.

17. I pursue this question in more detail in *Before the Law: Humans and Other Animals in a Biopolitical Frame* (Chicago: University of Chicago Press, 2013). See in particular 56–57, 67–86.

18. For a fuller exploration of these connections between Luhmann and Stevens, see chapter 10 of my *What Is Posthumanism?,* esp. 280–82.

Elemental Love in the Anthropocene

STACY ALAIMO

Thinking with elements is a strange practice. The attempt to extend the human mind to something in and of itself is reminiscent, perhaps, of William Carlos Williams's declaration "no ideas but in things," and yet elements are not things, not objects or artifacts, but that which is the substrate for things, as well as life, to emerge.[1] The desire to make sense of the elemental, that which is neither a being in the creaturely world nor a fabricated object already semiotically wrought, crashes into the obdurate nature of the world as substance. What can we make of these intrepid excursions toward what is only and utterly itself, these theoretical and cultural forays into the territory of scientific practice, the practice of disclosing something rudimentary about the physical world? The elemental is not bare life but something more denuded, perhaps, or more to the point, something not stripped at all but always only and ever itself, deep down. In modern science a chemical element was long defined as "a pure substance that cannot be decomposed chemically," until the discovery of isotopes altered the definition to "a substance composed of atoms with identical atomic number."[2] In either case, the definition is direct and simple. And the periodic table stands as an icon of orderly, transparent scientific knowledge, flat against the classroom wall. A commonsensical understanding of science as that which reveals timeless truths about the universe would understand elements as existing outside of history. As Jeffrey Jerome Cohen and Lowell Duckert state in the introduction to this volume, "the periodic table has no period." The fact that the periodic table now includes many artificially produced elements complicates the matter, however, since the elements brought into existence by human techne pull human knowledge practices, human history, and human productions into the ostensibly external and eternal wall chart of what is, what has been, and what will be. The new periodic table, with all these strange additions, many of which bear the names of people or places—curium, berkelium, californium, einsteinium, fermium, bohrium—parallels the geological concept of the Anthropocene, in that humans can now be considered an elemental as well as a geological force. But while the human impress on terrestrial foundations will endure, many of these humanly conjured elements vanish in an instant. Perhaps it makes us uneasy that elements, things we expect to remain within their designated square on that wall chart, may surprise us. Valerie Burn, in a chipper piece on "The World's Most Dangerous Elements," at Sparknotes.com, writes that Francium, "like a lot of those heavy elements, is highly radioactive and extremely unstable. There's basically no video or storage of it, because it becomes something else (... none of which are harmless) after about 20 minutes. Because of this, Fr is really hard to study and unpredictable and *we don't know what it will do next.* Fr is a total wildcard."[3] This colloquial rendition of the concept of material agency—of the building blocks of matter gone rogue—hints at the nuanced and sometimes bewildering lines of inquiry the authors in this volume pursue as they track the elements.

The recognition that some elements can be produced, often at great expense,[4] complicates but does not eviscerate the value of thinking about how, for the most part, the fundamental composition of the physical world is not a human achievement. The naturally occurring elements cannot, by definition, be at risk, in the sense of species extinction or ecosystem collapse. Elements may act as poisons or pollution when out of place or when combined with other elements and made to bear other, often xenobiotic chemicals, but they are not themselves threatened by inappropriate unions or monstrous transgressions. Moreover, most elements, except for a handful that are radioactive or otherwise harmful and persistent, do not ignite environmental ethics or politics; they are rarely matters of concern. (Even Francium, the "total wildcard," should not concern us, since, as Burn writes, "it's so rare and unstable, you probably won't run into it any time soon."[5])

The fact that elements are, for the most part, neither vulnerable nor threatening makes elemental ecocriticism a strange proposition, without obvious ethical or political trajectories. This very challenge, however, drives the chapters in this inventive collection.

Several of the chapters transport elemental engagements to ravaged bodies and regions, the sites of environmental crisis. Chris Barrett, for instance, brings ether, Aristotle's fifth element, to bear on our current, dire environmental condition, asking, "Can the fifth element intervene in the ecological crisis of a world dying as patiently and inevitably as the etherized?" The "perverse moral of hilarity," "the relentless mirth of the cosmos," seems a dark passenger, accompanying us on our doomed planetary trajectory, handing us a "humor we cannot survive." While Ursula Heise calls on ecocriticism to wage comic narratives against the overwhelming flood of tales of gloom and doom,[6] the black comedy of ether offers no escape from apocalyptic trajectories, and becomes even more disturbing when inhaled into posthumanist frames, as the human "patient etherized upon the table" may be anesthetized but the multitude of nonhuman species meeting their demise in the Sixth Great Extinction will receive no comfort, however dark or perverse.[7] The specter of the patiently dying world will haunt me, as it forever alters Eliot's Prufrock poem (aptly), and so perfectly conjures up the despair of those who passionately love this lavishly creatured world.

Yet the insubstantial ether occupies another atmosphere, distant from the elemental excursions that grapple with more tangible elements of earth, fire, and water. As a mode of material ecocriticism, elemental ecocriticism contends with the vexing sites where figures, narratives, concepts, and histories bear the marks of their worldly entanglements. The historical stretch of this collection, from the classical period to the modern, allows for the inclusion of a rich array of alternative ontologies, cosmologies, and elemental entanglements that make the dualisms of the moderns seem dull indeed. Witness instead the strange parade of elemental happenings—the spontaneous generation of vermin from mud, the men who became glass, or the sky above swimming with fish. In his chapter on earth, Duckert poses Milton as a vital materialist, explaining that Milton was one of several seventeenth-century poets who refused to posit dualities between God and nature, matter and spirit, body and soul: original matter is part of

God and animation is the spirit of God. By scrutinizing Milton's "vitalist environmentalism" and the "ultimately teleo-theological" limits of his monism, and by demonstrating that it is matter, including bodies, that spirit permeates, Duckert calls attention to the very elements that a transcendent theology or literary criticism would leave behind. Karl Steel, in his comparison of abiogenesis and spontaneous generation, notes that matter does not require spirit for liveliness: "spontaneous generation is godless." Steel insists that spontaneous generation cannot be dismissed by a ready recourse to the authority of modern science: "The line cannot be between medieval and modern or superstition and science but rather between acceptances of material immanence and a faith in immaterial transcendence."

Elemental ecocriticism, like other material ecocriticisms, must grapple with the elusive yet ever-present physical world.[8] Science studies scholarship, with its theories of capture, disclosure, and composition, is invaluable for these modes of inquiry, as it enables critical reflection on the embedded modes and processes that reveal, however partially, the makeup of the world.[9] But what makes new materialism essential for environmentalism, feminism, and other social movements is the insistence that matter is not something outside us that knowers capture or disclose but always the stuff that we ourselves are, the stuff that is lively and often unpredictable. Trans-corporeal subjects find themselves at the confluence of body, substance, and place, never distinct from the fluctuating world they seek to know.[10] Feminists, long cognizant of what it means to act as embodied minds, to occupy the often political sites where concepts and materiality mingle, have developed modes of art, activism, and theory that accentuate posthumanist, new materialist ontologies, avant la lettre.[11] One of the essential (nonessentialist) aspects of material feminisms and other new materialisms, in my mind, is that they underscore the agency and significance of matter, tracing how it interacts or, in Karen Barad's terms, intra-acts, with culture and discourse.[12] New materialisms, which both extend and depart from post-structuralisms, postmodernisms, and the linguistic turn in critical theory, assert the interconnections of what these theories, for the most part, kept separate—nature and culture, body and mind, world and word. Similarly, the elements running through the chapters in this collection are lively, active forces rather than passive, plastic matter. They are the stuff of the world that crosses into the domain of culture, moves from the inorganic to the organic, from the environment to bodies and back again. As Jeffrey Jerome Cohen puts it, "the elements are as restless as the human imagination, seldom content to remain in their allotted place. They ceaselessly embrace to compose new things and in that process disclose surprising worlds, challenging narratives, the tangling of nature's chain." Cohen's enticing formulation is not just a manner of speaking, but a manifestation of an ontology whereby what is typically in the background of the human—what is ostensibly inert—engenders and composes, disrupting cultural scripts and schemas. We encounter a restless world in Karl Steel's chapter as well; "matter's life swarms from the earth" in medieval theories of spontaneous generation and in recent theories of the origin of life. He writes that in "abiogenesis and spontaneous generation, and the continued operations of RNA and DNA, matter does operate on itself to bring something new and surprising into being." Steel cautions us not to conflate medieval conceptions of matter with contemporary new materialist theory: the "nonhuman materialisms are not a sign of the return of fecund medieval materiality, not least of all because there is no one medieval attitude about matter."

Notwithstanding the diversity of attitudes about matter in medieval and other time periods, it may still be useful, at times, to trace patterns with a broad brush, especially when conceptions of matter truly do matter, as some of these adamantine ideas underwrite harmful human exploits. An environmentally conscious new materialism that forwards conceptions of matter as generative and unruly counters both the tendency within the linguistic turn to minimize material agencies and the capitalist, consumerist attitude toward an external world, where substances are transformed into commodities for human use, consumption, and pleasure. The invisibility of these processes naturalizes the consumerist landscapes we inhabit, where a multitude of animal bodies, as Nicole Shukin has brilliantly demonstrated, silently surround us, as they have been "rendered" into ostensibly innocent products and the unseen material of media.[13] In such hypercultural, overproduced, insular landscapes that are all too human, where even the once lively animal bodies have been rendered into invisibility, thinking with elements becomes a formidable practice. Yet underscoring the material agency of the elemental is crucial for ecological thought. As Cohen puts it, "To acknowledge how the elements work, matter, and thrive, to realize our utter embroilment within a world of plants, animals, winds, seas, sky, stone, is to realize that environmental activism mandates ecological agentism."

The concept of transcorporeality, which I developed in *Bodily Natures: Science, Environment, and the Material Self,* was constructed to address the puzzling agencies of xenobiotic as well as radioactive substances, as they affect human and nonhuman creatures. Material agencies, especially those that are both dangerous and invisible, prompt individuals to live a kind of scientific practice that traces the movement of harmful substances through their own bodies, their own homes, their own communities. Such a practice is simultaneously a matter of epistemology, embodiment, ethics, and politics, as it demands new modes of being and knowing that can account for the bewildering and the unjust. A striking instance of the loss of sovereignty—a key term for indigenous peoples as well as for Ulrich Beck's theory of risk society—would be the struggle of the Diné people to learn how to live after uranium mining made their homelands hazardous. George Lapahe tells how refined uranium resembles corn pollen, a ceremonial, life-giving substance for the Diné, explaining what happened when Diné children played in the mining piles: "Whatever they brought home from the piles they used as toys. Corn pollen and uranium are the same color and they ate some uranium. This is true, they put them on their windowsills."[14] Treated as "experimental subjects,"[15] the Diné were not at liberty to take refuge in transcendent, Western notions of humans as distinct from their environs. Moreover, the traditional ecological knowledges of the Diné became inadequate, or even misleading, when their homelands were made radioactive, when what appeared to be corn pollen was uranium. Environmental justice movements, which address the brutally disproportionate distribution of hazards, caused in the United States, primarily by race and class stratification, hinge on the "scientific practices" of ordinary people who must discern how the agencies of invisible substances threaten intellectual and cultural sovereignty as well as bodily health.

Although the elements in medieval and early modern cultures are not the stuff of late twentieth-century risk society, several of the chapters in this collection depict other sorts of transcorporeal crossings that position the "human" as intertwined with elemental forces. Anne Harris interprets the fourteenth-century hermit Richard Rolle's *Incendium Amoris* as a material memoir that "gathers insistently around the materiality of fire: his fusing with fire, and fire's fusing with him."[16] The lived environment transforms the hermit, body and soul, in a dynamic interchange between self and world. The Glass Men that Harris analyzes, however, see themselves not just as subject to external forces but transformed in part, or entirely, into glass objects. Harris asks, "Was it their knowledge of their own madeness, of their easily destroyed manufacture, that terrified them? A pristine realization of self as object, flesh and bone fused into excruciating crystal clarity? Doing away with the illusion of an organic and emerging self and acknowledging that humans are fire's made things?" I am transfixed by these Glass Men, seized by the terrible sense of the self as object. The material memoirs that I have written about, especially those of Susanne Antonetta, dramatize the dreadful realization that both the body and the psyche have been manufactured by external forces.[17] But in late twentieth-century risk society, the ultimately unknowable chemical and radioactive forces do not yield a crystal clear sense of self, or a rigid, impermeable body, but a swampy self, emerging with toxic quagmires, uncanny homes, and compromised pharmaceuticals. The late twentieth-century human is rarely exposed to the elements but nearly always in contact with xenobiotic, manufactured substances. Such toxic substances move invisibly, silently, without the perceptible—and enchanting—image, aroma, or feeling of the flames. Late twentieth-century transcorporeal subjects navigate epistemological uncertainty and a negative aesthetic where nothing burns away. They must engage with scientific disclosures to even begin to clarify what they are and what made them. Their limbs, our limbs, are never as transparent as glass.

Another mode of transcorporeal manufacture appears in Duckert's chapter. Duckert argues for a "Miltonic 'material turn'" that results in an elemental, transcorporeal understanding of authorship, in which "the *matter* of coal works upon the poet's body (of work)." Starting with a supremely human achievement, that of authorship, leads us to the permeability of the breathing body, which happens, in this case, to be constituted, in part, by coal: "'we, who are compos'd of the Elements, should participate of their qualities.'" Disclosing the presence of coal within the pristine pages of the high canon opens the text to the world. As Cohen writes: "Even when our elemental stories are mired in anthropocentrism, their animating vectors are capable of inhuman transport, capable of provoking a vision of the world that does not simply reaffirm human primacy." Perhaps the most confounding of methodological challenges for new materialist humanities scholarship is how to approach the intermingling of world and text, substance and narrative, materiality and metaphor. Several forays into this terrain can be found here. Harris interprets the Glass Men as themselves traversing these gulfs, "moving between their reality and others' metaphors, the Glass Men of medieval and early modern Europe lived in impossible bodies fused by fire, perceived as decadence." Their physical rigidity belies the supple interchange between reality and metaphor. For Mentz, it is the critic who traverses these rifts: "Reading phlogiston requires repeated crossings of the divide between metaphor and materiality." Mentz argues that this type of reading epitomizes the value of humanities:

> I cherish this act of crossing. Sudden shifts of perspective, of subject matter, even of rhetorical mode, create intellectual combustion. What humanities scholars do best is perform that jump, the turn from the minutely textual to the wildly general, from tensions inside a single word ("phlogiston," in this case) to the endlessly flickering dance of the organic within and entangled with the inorganic.

While I embrace these leaps and turns and agree, to some extent, that humanities scholars are particularly adept at shifting perspectives and bridging divides, I think methodologies that are not corralled by dualisms between matter and metaphor, world and text, scientific capture and humanistic interrogation, are still very much in their infancy, even as scholars on many fronts are forging methodological alternatives to those that flourished within the linguistic turn. These alternatives, albeit in their infancy, will equip the humanities for the Anthropocene, an ominous moment when the seemingly innocuous filigree of culture, materialized in human practices, has infiltrated and transformed the planet.

I confess that I was not familiar with Empedocles, nor with the coupling of love and strife that propels this collection. But this framework (in my meager understanding) resonates with concepts put forth by feminist epistemology, feminist science studies, and environmental theories that I have long been pondering. Anne Harris explains, "Empedocles activated the four elements of water, air, earth, and fire to exist between the powerful pulls of coalescence (Love) and separation (Strife). Being (and reality) are not assured but in constant wondrous flux." I cannot help but recall Marian Engel's novella *Bear,* in which a woman comes to know a bear through both her epistemological ruminations and their sexual encounters.[18] I read this as a feminist/environmentalist cover of *Moby-Dick,* where love, not mastery, propels the epistemological quest.[19] But *Bear* also parodies the bad romance novel, in which the beastly paramour fails to be tamed.[20] A mashup of love and strife. Indeed, Empedocles's fundamental forces of love and strife express an epistemological dynamic for elemental inquiry, as the love of the world may propel us toward that which we seek to know, but we are bound to bump up against that which is unknowable. An oscillating epistemology of love and strife may be invaluable within the Anthropocene, as igniting a love for that which is elemental in this strangely altered and altering world seems queer indeed, yet the very improbability of such knowledge practices, the strife of being rebuffed, returns the human to a place within, as part of, the constantly churning world. A queer art of elemental failure, perhaps?[21] The inclusion of the imaginary phlogiston underscores an improvisational epistemological erotics and the perpetual strife of misapprehension. As Mentz writes, "phlogiston's scientific falsehood is a feature, not a bug. Its error makes it pure story, while its fiery heat recalls the physical process it was invented to explain." Even as Anthropocene turbulence necessitates reliable scientific knowledge, human errors and failures may offset the anthropocentric arrogance that undergirds the reduction of the lively world to inert capitalist resource. An epistemology pierced by love and strife, by wonder catalyzed by failure, also appears in some scientific accounts of the remarkable sexual diversity of nonhuman animals. When "queer animals" elude conceptual modes of capture, an epistemological-ethical sense of wonder is ignited. Suddenly, the world is not only more queer than one could have imagined but also, more surprisingly itself, confounding human categories and systems of understanding.[22] Desiring animals, agential matters, and unruly elements underscore the provisional status of human knowledges.

In the early twenty-first century, when countless species and interconnected ecosystems are perched at the tipping point, drenched in vulnerability, there is something bracing about engaging in a practice of contemplating that which because it is elemental has no need of human attention. The enormity of human impact evidenced in the category of the Anthropocene calls for a countervailing sense of that which is more impervious to human alteration—less fragile, less compromised by the events that strike or swirl through time. The anthropocentric arrogance of the very concept of the Anthropocene need be held in check by an elemental sense of the world as also, simultaneously, that which cannot be accessed, understood, and fundamentally altered by human practices. Elemental reckonings do not deliver us of our culpability but instead fracture the blithe obliviousness of humans toward the stuff of the world, opening up the possibility for attention and wonder that may feed a thoroughgoing ecological ethics attuned to catalysts and crossings as well as to a fearsome alienation from the world as fundamentally not human, a world as enduring as the elements and as fragile as glass.

Notes

Many thanks to Jeffrey J. Cohen and Lowell Duckert for inviting me to participate in this collection. Not only were their editorial comments immensely valuable, but it was such a pleasure to work with them. I am also grateful for Stephanie LeMenager's generous comments on this piece.

1. William Carlos Williams, *Paterson* (New York: New Directions, 1995), 6.

2. "General Chemical Glossary," *General Chemistry Online!*, http://antoine.frostburg.edu/chem/senese/101/glossary/e.shtml.

3. Valerie Burn, "The World's Most Dangerous Elements," The Mindhut, Spark Notes, September 6, 2013, http://www.sparknotes.com/mindhut/2013/09/06/the-worlds-most-dangerous-elements. (The idea that something that lasts twenty minutes could not be videotaped seems mistaken.)

4. Michael Lemonick discusses the short life of the newest element, ununpentium, which lasted only 173 milliseconds, concluding that in the face of such ephemerality a micromoment of witnessing such an element is an extravagance: "for scientists who study nuclei for a living, the prospect of keeping an element that heavy around for more than a handful of milliseconds is an almost unimaginable luxury." Michael Lemonick, "Ununpentium, the Newest Element," *New Yorker*, August 31, 2013. A lover's discourse haunts this scene, as the scientists are portrayed as wanting their object of desire to stay, just a bit longer. But it is also difficult not

to read a sort of anthropocenic melancholy into these contemplations of ephemeral elements, as multiple environmental crises provoke an awareness—on another scale entirely—of impending and monumental loss.

5. Burn, "The World's Most Dangerous Elements."

6. Ursula K. Heise, "Lost Dogs, Last Birds, and Listed Species: Cultures of Extinction," *Configurations* 18, nos. 1–2 (Winter 2010): 49–72.

7. Ironically, it turns out that ether is not very comforting for nonhuman creatures. Using ether to anesthetize or euthanize animals used for laboratory experiments has become controversial, with some universities banning it, partly because it is risky to store and partly because it induces anesthesia slowly, irritates mucous membranes, and produces stress. Boston University Research Compliance, Animal Care, "Ban on Use of Ether," n.d., http://www.bu.edu/animalcare/lasc-bumc/guidelines/ban-on-use-of-ether/.

8. See, for example, Serenella Iovino and Serpil Oppermann, eds., *Material Ecocriticism* (Bloomington: Indiana University Press, 2014).

9. See, for example, Andrew Pickering, *The Mangle of Practice: Time, Agency, Science* (Chicago: University of Chicago Press, 1995); Susan J. Hekman, *The Material of Knowledge: Feminist Disclosures* (Bloomington: Indiana University Press, 2010); Bruno Latour, "An Attempt at a 'Compositionist Manifesto,'" *New Literary History* 41, no. 3 (2010): 471–90; and Stacy Alaimo, *Bodily Natures: Science, Environment, and the Material Self* (Bloomington: Indiana University Press, 2010).

10. See Alaimo, *Bodily Natures.*

11. See Stacy Alaimo, "Thinking as the Stuff of the World," *O-Zone: A Journal of Object-Oriented Studies* 1, no. 1 (Autumn 2013): 13–21.

12. Karen Barad, *Meeting the Universe Halfway: Quantum Physics and the Entanglement of Matter and Meaning* (Durham, N.C.: Duke University Press, 2007).

13. Nicole Shukin, *Animal Capital: Rendering Life in Biopolitical Times* (Minneapolis: University of Minnesota Press, 2009).

14. George Lapahe, interviewed in Navajo Uranium Miner Oral History and Photography Project, *Memories Come to Us in the Rain and the Wind: Oral Histories and Photographs of Navajo Uranium Miners and Their Families* (Boston: Navajo Uranium Miner Oral History and Photography Project, 1997), 22.

15. Floyd Frank, interviewed in *Memories Come to Us,* 8.

16. Harris draws upon my book *Bodily Natures* for the term *material memoir.*

17. Alaimo, *Bodily Natures*; Susanne Antonetta, *Body Toxic: An Environmental Memoir* (Washington, D.C.: Counterpoint, 2002); Susanne Antonetta, *A Mind Apart: Travels in a Neurodiverse World* (New York: Tarcher, 2007).

18. Marian Engel, *Bear* (Boston: David R. Godine, 2002).

19. Feminist epistemology propels this reading. Evelyn Fox Keller's epigraph from June Goodfield suggests the possibility of love as an enmeshed mode of inquiry: "'the nearest an ordinary person gets to the essence of the scientific process is when they fall in love.'" Evelyn Fox Keller, *Reflections on Gender and Science* (New

Haven, Conn.: Yale University Press, 1985), 117, discussed in Stacy Alaimo, *Undomesticated Ground: Recasting Nature as Feminist Space* (Ithaca, N.Y.: Cornell University Press, 2000), 133–87. The graphic sex scenes in the novel, it should be noted, resist saccharine romance by relishing the corporeal particularities of human/ursine couplings, insisting on the actuality of both female desire and the bear as a bear.

20. See Alaimo, *Undomesticated Ground.*

21. The allusion is to Judith Halberstam, *Queer Art of Failure* (Durham, N.C.: Duke University Press, 2011). Halberstam writes, "Under certain circumstances failing, losing, forgetting, unmaking, undoing, unbecoming, not knowing may in fact offer more creative, more cooperative, more surprising ways of being in the world" (2). Within the Anthropocene, where human "mastery" of what we used to call "nature" has resulted in a failure of such immense proportions, environmentalists, as well as those most vulnerable to twenty-first-century risks, have no choice but to cultivate surprising arts of failure.

22. See Stacy Alaimo, "Eluding Capture: The Science, Culture and Pleasure of 'Queer' Animals," in *Queer Ecologies: Sex, Nature, Politics, Desire,* ed. Catriona Mortimer-Sandilands and Bruce Erickson (Bloomington: Indiana University Press, 2010), 15–36.

Coda

Wandering Elements and Natures to Come

SERPIL OPPERMANN
and SERENELLA IOVINO

Earth and sky, water and fire are the fundamental elements that bind the fate and presence of humans and other Earthlings in their interlocked journey of matter and imagination. Also the stuff of elemental passions, and the light of compositional *jouissance* sparkling into the world's bodymind, these four classical elements are the building blocks of whatever thinks and respires on this living planet. Our blood is saline water, our bones are calcified earth, our breath is volatile air, and our fever is fire—elements that have composed mountains, oceans, and the atmosphere, and have nourished all terrestrial creativities across time and space. Similar to the planet and its motley of residents, the *anthropos,* humans themselves, in diverse cultures and features, are multilayered and "*autochthones* (autochthonous), creatures born of the earth."[1] And so are plants, animals, and their abode, the earth itself as a cosmic body. "My tongue, every atom of my blood, form'd from this soil, this air," sings Walt Whitman, is born here.[2] "Just as the atmospheric air is multilayered," writes David Macauley, "so is earth more than monolithic."[3] For the earth is in unremitting formation; as Lowell Duckert notes in his chapter in this volume, "the earth is earthing futures." The same is true of all the elements. None is defined, even in an ephemeral way, as solitary. All are generative, always becoming, always in flux, going through inevitable stages of metamorphosis.

Unlike the earth encased in compact forms like rocks and clay with mass and weight, the sky is the stretching abode of enduring dreams, desires, mysteries, and gods. It is volatile air, "invisible and nearly intangible" (Cohen). Intangible though it may be, air connects the earth and the sky, bringing forth life, but always eluding the binary of surface and depth (Steel). It is also in every drop of moisture adding impetus to water that sculptures the planet as effectively as other elements. Every wind that blows makes a difference in earth, water, and fire. Each change in air matters in the fabric of existence. It has the gift of movement, heat and cold, and even sound and fury, like the hurricane. "Air is not empty," writes Morgan Llywelyn in her 1993 novel *The Elementals.* Indeed, the author is right in saying, "Air is alive." Because, she explains, "Every molecule of air on earth has its part to play in the whole. Myriad life forms dance in what appears, to human eyes, to be empty air."[4] In the face of the mystery evoked by the invisibility of the element of air, one can only "gaze into a sky of truths," as Luce Irigaray writes in *Elemental Passions;*[5] but this is the atmosphere where truths become "multiveiled" no matter how intensely we peruse the sky, and where "pollutants move or collect" alongside Llywelyn's dancing life forms.[6] Swirling and flowing in multifaceted forms, as sky, wind, and breath, air is the primordial abode of life and a shaping presence of aesthetic and environmental imagination.

Water figures prominently, too, in environmental imagination. From Gaston Bachelard's phenomenological insight water arises as "the most receptive of the elements."[7] It signifies reflections and images, and—embodied in rivers, lakes, and seas—it undeniably evokes "reverie." It is important to note that the "imagination" underlying this *reverie* in Bachelard as well as in other more ancient thinkers has a solid, material constitution. The solid mind of the earth thinks, and its dreams generate all beings natural. In the material fabric of emerging forms, water is the foremost component, the "essential, ontological metamorphosis," as Bachelard avers, "between fire and earth."[8] It is, he insists, "the maternal voice";[9] and just like the maternal, water is—literally, etymologically—matter itself. Water is primal milk, "the first substantive in the order of liquid realities," simply because "a material image of milk underlies the more conscious image of the waters."[10]

Echoing these ideas (or maybe simply re*imagining* them), the British postmodern author John Fowles refers to the sea as "our evolutionary amniotic fluid, the element in which we too were once enwombed, from which our own antediluvian line rose into the light and air."[11] Water and dreams, therefore, are elementally woven together. But Bachelard also makes a poignant point not to be missed in reveries: "The story of water is the human tale of a dying water."[12] Thus, although it evokes "a dream of limpidity" and "is the conqueror of fire,"[13] water is conquered by the human, made impure, nocturnal, and yes, utterly polluted, falling back as acidic rain in the domestication process (i.e., "engineering projects").[14] Once *aqua vitae,* water of life, but now almost turned *aqua mortis,* as Nâzım Hikmet, Turkey's revolutionary poet, put it in "The Dream": "Rain falls softly, / fearful / like secret whispers / of betrayal."[15] Water turns bad, though more metaphorically so when hyper-commodified as pure purity, and really bad, if not becoming absent, when engineered, diverted, dammed, and colonized. It simply becomes, as Julian Yates writes in his chapter, "a network of deterritorialized particles of life effects in the form of microbes and genetic fragments."

Domesticated like water, and signifying divine betrayal, fire has been central to human civilization. It brings the comforts of electricity, heat, and light but also death and destruction when used in weaponry. It is the element that transformed humanity when Prometheus stole it from the gods and offered it as a precious gift. Therefore, David Macauley claims, fire "opens up not only previously unthinkable possibilities but also a Pandora's box of problems."[16] Fire is creative passion. It is fiery and invigorating. Its culpability is more on the foreground than other elements. In *The Elementals,* Llywelyn calls it "inflaming, energizing, consuming," pointing to its "vigor, ardor, intensity, fervor, passion, fury, magic, inspiration, genius, brilliance."[17] Fire is the divine element that forged "post-Edenic" imagination. Elemental ecocriticism, as Anne Harris aptly puts it in her chapter, can claim it "as a living thing," a thing of hypnotic agency and unpredictability. With its pyrotechnic energy, "fire moves through metamorphosis" in the labyrinth of elements.

These fundamental elements are the primary inspiration behind the conception of the nine chapters in *Elemental Ecocriticism.* As they indicate, the book transcends, however, the primary elemental ground, subsuming them, adding "imaginary substance(s)," like "phlogiston"—"the fire-air combination" (Mentz), and reminding us of "the complexities of life beyond the organic" (Cohen). When elements "promiscuously combine," Jeffrey Jerome

Cohen writes, a "unique ecology" emerges, and in that process of composition new things "disclose surprising worlds, challenging narratives, the tangling of nature's chain." Even the fifth element, ether, here examined by Chris Barrett, is part of this entanglement. Is ether the essential component of cosmos as Aristotle has claimed? In Barrett's lyrical prose, the answer is yes; "the ethereal cosmos" is suffused, she contends, "by an elemental laughter." Ether is "elusively natured," writes Barrett. Its "essential nature is circular, simultaneously constituting the outer cosmos while mirroring itself in human bodies hovering between an Empedoclean love and agony." Ether, then, is about self-reflection, transformation, and an invitation to think the world anew. In other words, constituting baryonic matter ("everything we see, and everything that has form, plus all known energies"[18]), the elements comprise a tableau on which material imagination paints myriad literary images, sensual values, and ontological vicissitudes: fickleness, uncertainty, unpredictability, vacillation, evolution, and novelty. "Becoming other" is what happens in the cauldron of mixtures in element ecologies. Just like the sea becomes "the domain of what cannot be contained by wisdom and reason," as John Fowles says in his essay "Islands,"[19] elemental ecology is not only wisdom but is also affective involvement in fascinating labyrinths. One can call it "the site of intersection," quoting David Macauley, of counterbalancing elements and human visions, literary, scientific, philosophical, and technological.[20] It fosters "affective ecology" in confronting "an existential crisis that is literally ecological" (Barrett).

Thinking along this crisis, in fact, encourages "muddy thinking," as Sharon O'Dair exemplifies in her chapter. She claims that "literary criticism periodically seems to require the slinging of mud in the name of purity." And thus, ecocriticism turns elemental, but not in a perverse mood to celebrate the impure, though it certainly makes us think deeply about what it means to be impure. Rather, to curiously investigate "how matter's life swarms from the earth" (Steel), creating what Steve Mentz calls in his chapter "phlogisticated thinking." Underlining it as both "material and metaphor," Mentz proposes the imaginary element, "phlogiston," as a way to "advance the efforts of literary ecocriticism to reanimate stories about physical elements, to make them glow with renewed meaning." Another compelling image of ecocritical analysis is offered by Valerie Allen. Referring to doubting Thomas in her chapter on air, Allen philosophizes about his "doublemindedness." We can certainly imagine the doubling of human mind on crisis-laden ecosystems, or even existence in toto, "on this uncontrolledly sprouting planet . . . and its destiny," as Fowles puts it, that "waver and zigzag amid a triangle of opposing yet counterbalancing factors."[21] But even more significantly, this doubling is a way to "de-provincialize" the human both in its mind and materiality, to make it aware of the elemental porosity that determines its very being. The elements that constitute our being need therefore to be mutually permeable, as a form of "material sociability." Hence "wetness," as Julian Yates notes in his chapter, is both a condition and a medium for this "desire for a different order of burrowing, for a more capacious mode of hospitality"—something that makes us at once vulnerable and elementally open, enriching our elemental story with new, unrelenting becomings.

Putting together imagined and real elements, their stories and *logoi* as they appear in medieval and early modern authors and environments, *Elemental Ecocriticism* aims to reanimate elemental thinking, encouraging us to "think about *thinking* with" (Duckert) the elements. It aims not simply to explore how they have affected our stories but also to show that they *are* all the stories of the cosmic adventure—including our story, the story of how the two of us, like all the authors in this volume, came to "think about" these topics by way of "thinking with": with each other, with the elements, with the force of things. Acknowledging this fact implies radially extending the connective tissue of our relations as well as our relationships, of our materiality as well as our creativity. In "The Sea Above," Jeffrey Jerome Cohen expresses this objective eloquently:

> To acknowledge how the elements work, matter, and thrive, to realize our utter embroilment within a world of plants, animals, winds, seas, sky, stone, is to realize that environmental activism mandates ecological agentism. Not the anthropomorphic granting of rights, not the promulgation of dangerous myths of sustainability.

Elemental ecocriticism plunges us in the *ratio* of things, which is at the same time the mixture, the proportion, and the reason/mind of what is around and inside us, before and after us. An ecocritical gaze into this process of worldly "embroilments" is at once the claim that this process produces forms, and that the human subject deals with these forms physically and cognitively. In that it recognizes the agency of the elemental, such an ecocriticism wants to be involved in this telluric adventure of forces as a cognitive principle, even if this cognition culminates in a displacement of the human from its self-elevated maps of privileged lifeworlds. Containing such lifeworlds and their ruminations, elemental ecocriticism, like James Turrell's art as discussed in Timothy Morton's response essay in this volume, is a "double invagination" with "its givenness allowed to permeate everywhere," a "thinking together" of the elemental and the ecological with "distributed affects." To put it otherwise, elemental ecocriticism rides on the waves of elemental complexities that unfold from the threshold of their ecological, philosophical, and literary labyrinths. The elemental nature of things, their dynamism and complexity, and "all the myriad changes taking place" in a system's environment (Cary Wolfe, this volume) invite a strange practice of "thinking with elements," as Stacy Alaimo calls it in her own response essay, echoing Morton. This is at the core of elemental ecocriticism, even though, as Alaimo contends, elements "are rarely matters of concern," because they "do not ignite environmental ethics or politics." But, as the chapters in this volume attest to it, elemental ecocriticism has turned the elements into matters of concern, not only in terms of their ecological significance but also in terms of their profound effects on material imagination. The following step will be, as we can predict with confidence, that the elements will also figure in environmental ethics or politics in the near future.

Elemental ecocriticism wants to show that the elements *matter* and follow the forms qua stories that their mattering assumes. The narratives emerging from this process of mattering are stories of returns and encounters, and in fact they are the same that an ancient poet and philosopher, the Sicilian Empedocles of Acragas, *acknowledged* in the unremitting combinations of earth, water, air, and fire—all tied, mixed, and finally untied by the caprices of love and strife. In these stories, the "ego," the human self, is an accident of substance, an occasional emergence on a plot in which matters and forms slip into one another: "For there was a time when I was boy and girl, thicket and bird, and a scaly fish in the waves," the philosopher said.[22]

Creating ties with beings and voices from the past embedded within the past and present spaces, *Elemental Ecocriticism* wants to add new layers to these stories, reaffirming and perfecting the "disanthropocentric" shift of *Prismatic Ecology*. Here, like in that previous important volume, the "impure" is the cipher of life, knowledge, and love. Muddy, impure, and familial, the elemental gaze of the authors in this book recommends at once irony and hope. For they know that the human is an elemental episode, but they also know, as Lowell Duckert writes, "that the ways we narrate stories, and the stories themselves, can shape the earth(s) to come." In its being a disanthropocentric project of ongoing combinations, elemental ecocriticism wants to show that, in the earth(s) to come, our stories and the stories of the elements will be materially eloquent in their entwinements. They will enact nourishing and substantive resonances within the bodymind of the planet. As the German poet Friedrich Hölderlin, creatively echoing Empedocles's ideas and story, wrote in 1798–99:

> Let others speak on my behalf when I am far away,
> The flowers of the sky, the blossoms of the stars,
> And all those stars on earth, the myriad germinations;
> Divinely present nature
> Needs no speech; no, never she will leave you to
> Your own devices, if but once she has drawn near.
> For inextinguishable is the moment that is hers.[23]

If nature exists, elements are its (or her, or his, or their) words. Elemental ecocriticism wants to assemble these words into stories: not only stories to tell but also stories to come.

Notes

1. David Macauley, *Elemental Philosophy: Earth, Air, Fire, and Water as Environmental Ideas* (New York: State University of New York Press, 2010), 25.

2. Walt Whitman, "Song of Myself," in *The Norton Anthology of Modern Poetry*, 2nd. ed., ed. Richard Ellmann and Robert O'Clair (New York: W. W Norton, 1988), 22.

3. Macauley, *Elemental Philosophy*, 15.

4. Morgan Llywelyn, *The Elementals* (New York: TOR, 1993), 281.

5. Luce Irigaray, *Elemental Passions,* trans. Joanne Collie and Judith Smith (New York: Routledge, 1992), 37.

6. Macauley, *Elemental Philosophy,* 27.

7. Joanne H. Stroud, "Foreword," in *Water and Dreams: An Essay on the Imagination of Matter* by Gaston Bachelard, trans. Edith R. Farrell (Dallas: Dallas Institute of Humanities and Culture, 2006), ix.

8. Bachelard, *Water and Dreams,* 6.

9. Ibid., 116.

10. Ibid., 117.

11. John Fowles, "Islands," in *Wormholes: Essays and Occasional Writings* (New York: Henry Hall and Co., 1998), 282.

12. Bachelard, *Water and Dreams,* 47.

13. Ibid., 53, 105.

14. Macauley, *Elemental Philosophy,* 4.

15. Nâzım Hikmet, "The Dream," in *Beyond the Walls: Selected Poems,* trans. Ruth Christie, Richard McKane, and Talat Sait Halman (London: Anvil Press Poetry; Istanbul: Yapı Kredi Yayınları, 2002), 72.

16. Macauley, *Elemental Philosophy,* 36.

17. Llywelyn, *The Elementals,* 87.

18. Robert Lanza and Bob Berman, *Biocentrism: How Life and Consciousness Are the Keys to Understanding the True Nature of the Universe* (Dallas, Tex.: BenBella Books, 2009), Kindle edition, 6.

19. Fowles, "Islands," 297.

20. Macauley, *Elemental Philosophy,* 118.

21. Fowles, "The Nature of Nature," in *Wormholes,* 347.

22. Empedocles, Fr. 117: *ἤδη γάρ ποτ᾽ ἐγὼ γενόμην κοῦρός τε κόρη τε θάμνος τ᾽ οἰωνός τε καὶ ἔξαλος ἔλλοπος ἰχθύς.* Trans. Serenella Iovino.

23. Friedrich Hölderlin, *The Death of Empedocles: A Mourning-Play,* trans. with introduction, notes, and analysis by David Farell Krell (Albany: State University of New York Press, 2008), 93.

Acknowledgments

This book arises from a collaboration of long duration. Its two editors conceived the project of thinking with the elements in Barcelona, where Antoni Gaudí rendered stone difficult to distinguish from water. We brought together some scholars who share our elemental bent for a special issue of the journal *postmedieval* on "Ecomaterialism" (4, no. 1, 2013), and we thank Eileen Joy and Myra Seaman for making that initial combustion possible. Our contributors were inspirational: Valerie Allen, Steve Mentz, Sharon O'Dair, Alfred K. Siewers, Karl Steel, Stephanie Trigg, and Julian Yates. A muse for this endeavor, Jane Bennett, wrote a powerful afterword for the collection; Vin Nardizzi, an ecocritic we have both long admired, contributed an excellent review essay. We quickly came to realize, however, that the work of the elements is never finished. When Sharon O'Dair graciously proposed a symposium on the topic to be held at the University of Alabama, we were happy to accept her invitation to catalyze some new combinations. Although Alf Siewers and Stephanie Trigg unfortunately could not join us at the second gathering, we found new catalysts in Chris Barrett, Anne Harris, and Cary Wolfe. Jane Bennett pulled a series of paper slips with the four elements and their interstices inscribed upon them from a burrito bowl in Boston, thereby assigning each contributor a material force to befriend for this volume.

The April 2013 symposium "Elemental Ecocriticism" at the University of Alabama launched what has become the book you now hold. Besides Sharon O'Dair's unremitting good cheer, the creative presentations, the intense discussion, and the flow of water in the form of wine, we will always remember the clouds blazing yellow and orange at sunset, the swampy darkness of the woods surrounding the house at which we held our closing dinner, the exuberant sonority of mating frogs, and late night grooving to songs stored on cell phones. *The elements dance* is the principle we did not include in our introduction, because that dynamism is evident throughout. Stacy Alaimo and Timothy Morton joined Cary Wolfe as response essay writers, but we feel they have been present all along, influences and allies. So too our "coda" authors Serenella Iovino and Serpil Oppermann, whose profound scholarship and unremitting conviviality have been sustaining. *Elemental Ecocriticism* argues that the material world is rife with love and strife, but here at the end of a process that has brought all of us together in friendship, we observe that strife might be necessary, but love is more powerful.

Richard Morrison welcomed this book to the University of Minnesota Press. We cannot imagine a better editor with whom to have worked. His vision of what humanities scholarship should achieve is moving, and we are honored to have worked with him. Erin Warholm launched us, with good cheer, into production. We thank Laura Ogden, Kellie Robertson, and Vin Nardizzi for their engaged reading of our manuscript and their invaluable suggestions. The book was bolstered by their enthusiasm and is so much the stronger for their serious attention. Our thanks to Diana Witt, who created a superb index for the book. Finally, we acknowledge our debt to our colleagues, students, and fellow travelers of every sort, human and inhuman.

Jeffrey Jerome Cohen is grateful to his family, especially Wendy, Alexander, and Katherine. Their love of mountains, cityscapes, and oceans—and their companionship in some serious world wandering—have fostered his ecocritical explorations. Katherine and Alex are gifted with extraordinary imaginations, and if their father sometimes glimpses in distant clouds a ship-traversed sea it is only because they have taught him possibilities. Jeffrey thanks his collaborator Lowell for being an inspiration as well as a good friend. Working together has been a source of great pleasure, as well as a vast expansion of prospect. *Peace.*

Lowell Duckert offers his humble thanks to the Eberly College of Arts and Sciences for awarding him a book subvention stipend; the Keeper of the Mountains Foundation for inviting him to Kayford Mountain (may they continue to impact others); his nieces and nephew for their love of (extended) ecotrips; Jeffrey, his coeditor and friend, for the unswerving creativity and enthusiasm he brings, through stony mushroom forests and places yet unknown (he is a true earth-stepper); and, lastly, Erin, his partner on the long trail. *Love.*

Contributors

STACY ALAIMO is professor of English and Distinguished Teaching Professor at the University of Texas at Arlington. Her publications include *Undomesticated Ground: Recasting Nature as Feminist Space*; *Material Feminisms* (coedited with Susan Hekman); and *Bodily Natures: Science, Environment, and the Material Self*, which won the ASLE Award for Ecocriticism.

VALERIE ALLEN is professor of English literature at John Jay College of Criminal Justice, CUNY. Her main interests are medieval culture and literature and continental philosophy. She is author of *On Farting: Language and Laughter in the Middle Ages*.

CHRIS BARRETT is assistant professor of English at Louisiana State University. Her research interests include sixteenth- and seventeenth-century literature, especially Spenser, Shakespeare, and Milton; geocritical literary approaches; and animal studies, humor studies, and critical theory.

JEFFREY JEROME COHEN is professor of English and director of the Medieval and Early Modern Studies Institute at George Washington University. His books include *Monster Theory: Reading Culture* (Minnesota, 1996); *Of Giants* (Minnesota, 1999); *Medieval Identity Machines* (Minnesota, 2003); *Hybridity, Identity, and Monstrosity in Medieval Britain; Prismatic Ecology: Ecotheory beyond Green* (Minnesota, 2013); and *Stone: An Ecology of the Inhuman* (Minnesota, 2015).

LOWELL DUCKERT is assistant professor of English at West Virginia University, specializing in early modern literature, ecotheory, and environmental criticism. With Jeffrey Jerome Cohen, he edited "Ecomaterialism," a special issue of *postmedieval: a journal of medieval studies.* He has written on such topics as glaciers, polar bears, maroon, Walter Raleigh, and rain.

ANNE HARRIS is professor of art history at DePauw University. Her interests in the intersections of materiality, art, and audience have driven publications on manuscripts, ivory, wood, glass, and alabaster. Her research and teaching in medieval art history are shaped by feminist theory, postcolonialism, queer theory, object-oriented ontology, and ecocriticism. She is one of the cofounders of the Material Collective (http://thematerialcollective.org), which fosters alternative ways of thinking about objects.

SERENELLA IOVINO is professor of comparative literature at the University of Turin and a research fellow of the Alexander von Humboldt Foundation. She is creative writing and art section editor of the journal *Ecozon@* and cofounder and past president of the European Association for the Study of Literature, Culture, and Environment (www.easlce.edu). Among her recent works are *Material Ecocriticism* (coedited with Serpil Oppermann) and *Ecocriticism and Italy: Ecology, Resistance, and Liberation*.

STEVE MENTZ is professor of English at St. John's University in New York City. He is author of *Shipwreck Modernity: Ecologies of Globalization, 1550–1719* (Minnesota, 2015), *At the Bottom of Shakespeare's Ocean,* and *Romance for Sale in Early Modern England,* and coeditor (with Craig Dionne) of *Rogues and Early Modern English Culture*. He has written on ecocriticism, oceanic studies, Shakespeare, and early modern literature for journals such as *PMLA, Studies in English Literature,* and *Shakespeare*.

TIMOTHY MORTON is Rita Shea Guffey Chair in English at Rice University. He gave the Wellek Lectures in Theory in 2014. He is author of *Hyperobjects: Philosophy and Ecology after the End of the World* (Minnesota, 2013), *Realist Magic: Objects, Ontology, Causality*, *The Ecological Thought*, and *Ecology without Nature*, as well as other books and essays on philosophy, ecology, literature, music, art, design, and food. He blogs regularly at http://www.ecologywithoutnature.blogspot.com.

SHARON O'DAIR is Hudson Strode Professor of English and directs the Hudson Strode Program in Renaissance Studies at the University of Alabama. She is author of *Class, Critics, and Shakespeare: Bottom Lines on the Culture Wars*, coeditor (with David Lee Miller and Harold Weber) of *The Production of English Renaissance Culture*, and editor of "Shakespeareans in the Tempest: Lives and Afterlives of Katrina," a special issue of *Borrowers and Lenders*. She has published many essays on Shakespeare, literary theory, and the profession of English studies.

SERPIL OPPERMANN is professor of English at Hacettepe University, Ankara, and vice president of the European Association for the Study of Literature, Culture, and Environment (EASLCE). Her publications include essays on environmental humanities; ecophilosophy; ecocritical theory; material, postmodern, and feminist ecocriticism; postmodernism; and literary theory. Her publications include *International Perspectives in Feminist Ecocriticism* (edited with Greta Gaard and Simon Estok), *Material Ecocriticism* (edited with Serenella Iovino), and *New International Voices in Ecocriticism*. She is a founding member of the World Eco-Culture Organization (WEO) in Beijing.

KARL STEEL is associate professor of English at Brooklyn College and the Graduate Center, CUNY. He is author of *How to Make a Human: Animals and Violence in the Middle Ages* and articles on animals, materiality, and ecotheory. He is coeditor (with Peggy McCracken) of "The Animal Turn," a 2011 special issue of *postmedieval: a journal of medieval studies* and is a blogger at *In the Middle* (www.inthemedievalmiddle.com).

CARY WOLFE is the Bruce and Elizabeth Dunlevie Professor of English at Rice University, where he is also founding director of 3CT: The Center for Critical and Cultural Theory. His books include *Animal Rites: American Culture, the Discourse of Species, and Posthumanist Theory*, *What Is*

Posthumanism? (Minnesota, 2010), and *Before the Law: Humans and Other Animals in a Biopolitical Frame.* He has participated in multiauthor projects involving J. M. Coetzee, Cora Diamond, Stanley Cavell, Paola Cavalieri, and others. He is founding editor of the Posthumanities series at the University of Minnesota Press.

JULIAN YATES is professor of English and material culture studies at the University of Delaware. He is author of *Error, Misuse, Failure: Object Lessons from the English Renaissance* (Minnesota, 2003), which was a finalist for the MLA Best First Book Prize, and coauthor (with Richard Burt) of *What's the Worst Thing You Can Do to Shakespeare?* His work focuses on questions of ecology, genre, and the posthuman.

Index